The Sultan and the Queen

Also by Jerry Brotton

Great Maps
A History of the World in 12 Maps
The Renaissance: A Very Short Introduction
The Sale of the Late King's Goods: Charles I and His Art Collection
The Renaissance Bazaar: From the Silk Road to Michelangelo
Global Interests: Renaissance Art Between East and West (with Lisa Jardine)
Trading Territories: Mapping the Early Modern World

THE
SULTAN
AND THE
QUEEN

The Untold Story
of
Elizabeth and Islam

Jerry Brotton

Viking

VIKING

An imprint of Penguin Random House LLC

375 Hudson Street

New York, New York 10014

penguin.com

First published in Great Britain as
This Orient Isle: Elizabethan England and the Islamic World
by Allen Lane, an imprint of Penguin Random House UK

Library of Congress cataloging-in-Publication Data

Names: Brotton, Jerry.
Title: The Sultan and the queen: the untold story of Elizabeth and Islam/Jerry Brotton.
Description: New york: Viking, 2016. | Includes bibliographical references and index.
Identifiers: LCCN 2016029495 (print) | LCCN 2016031895 (ebook) |
ISBN 9780525428824 (hardcover) | ISBN 9780698191631 (ebook)
Subjects: LCSH: Great Britain—History—Elizabeth, 1558–1603. |
Turkey—History—Murad III, 1574–1595. | Great Britain—Foreign
relations—Turkey. | Turkey—Foreign relations—Great Britain.
Classification: LCC DA355 .B69 2016 (print) | LCC DA355 (ebook) |
DDC 327.4205609/031—dc23
LC record available at https://lccn.loc.gov/2016029495

Printed in the United States of America
1   3   5   7   9   10   8   6   4   2

Set in Sabon and Garamond Premier
Designed by Amy Hill

To my wife, Charlotte

Contents

Elizabethan England and the Islamic World, c. 1570–1603

N

ATLANTIC
OCEAN

NORWAY

SWEDEN

North Sea

DENMARK

ENGLAND
Hardwick
Great Yarmouth
Lübeck
Winchester London
Plymouth Southampton
Antwerp Wittenberg
Brussels
Paris
HOLY ROMAN
POLAND
LITHUANI
Prague
Lvov
Orléans
EMPIRE
Augsburg Vienna
FRANCE
Basel
Milan Venice
Ferrara
Belgrade
Florence
WA
O T
Lisbon
Madrid
PORTUGAL
Rome
SPAIN
Naples
Seville
Granada
Lepanto
Cadiz
M
e
d
Zante
Tangier Gibraltar
i
t
e
Arzila
Algiers
Sicily
El Ksar el-Kebir
r
r
Casablanca Fez
Tunis
a
n
Malta
e
a
Marrakesh
O
T
T
O
Agadir
M
MOROCCAN
SULTANATE
Tripoli
A
N
E

White
Sea
•Arkhangelsk

M U S C O V Y

•Moscow

0   100   200   300   400 miles
0   200   400   600 km

•Astrakhan

Bukhara•

Caspian Sea

CHIA

Black Sea

Tabriz•   •Qazvin

P E R S I A N   E M P I R E

Constantinople

O T T O M A N   E M P I R E

•Isfahan

hios

•Raqqa

Aleppo•

Fallujah• •Baghdad

Rhodes

Cyprus

•Babylon

Basra

Crete

•Damascus

S e a

Jerusalem•

Alexandria•

P I R E

•Cairo

The Sultan and the Queen

Introduction

Toward the end of September 1579, a letter arrived in London addressed to Queen Elizabeth I of England. Wrapped in a satin bag and fastened with a silver capsule, the letter was an object of exquisite beauty, unlike any other diplomatic correspondence the queen had ever received. It was written on a large parchment roll dusted with gold and dominated by an elaborate calligraphic monogram and emblazoned with a flourish across the top. The letter was composed in Ottoman Turkish, a stylized Arabic script that was used in all formal correspondence by its sender, the thirty-three-year-old Ottoman sultan Murad III. This was the very first communication between a Turkish sultan and an English ruler. It was written in response to the arrival in Constantinople that spring of an English merchant, William Harborne, who had requested commercial privileges for his country superior to those that had thus far been awarded to any other Christian nation by the Ottomans.

It had taken six months for the letter to make its way from Constantinople to London, where it was presented to the queen alongside a Latin translation prepared by an imperial scribe. The letter followed the standard conventions of an Ottoman *hukum*, a written order to a subject, and was addressed as a direct "Command to Elzābet, who is the queen of the domain of Anletār." Murad told Elizabeth that he had been informed of the arrival of her "traders and merchants of those parts coming to our divinely-protected dominions and carrying on trade." He issued an edict that if "her agents and merchants shall come from the domain of Anletār by sea with their barks and with their ships, let no one interfere." As long as this queen from a faraway country was prepared to accept Murad's superiority and to function as his subject, he would be happy to protect her merchants.

Elizabeth responded quickly. The opening of her letter, dated October 25, 1579, was as revealing as Murad's. The queen began by describing herself as:

> Elizabeth by the grace of the most mighty God, the only Creator of heaven and earth, of England, France and Ireland Queen, the most invincible and most mighty defender of the Christian faith against all kind of idolatries, of all that live among the Christians, and falsely profess the name of Christ, unto the most imperial and most invincible prince, Zuldan Murad Chan, the most mighty ruler of the kingdom of Turkey, sole and above all, the most sovereign monarch of the East Empire, greeting, and many happy and fortunate years.[1]

Elizabeth was eager to boast of her own imperial aspirations—although it was stretching credulity to suggest she was queen of France—and to assure Murad that she shared his antipathy toward Catholic "idolatry" and those "falsely" professing Christ. But her main interest was in establishing a commercial relationship with the Ottomans, even if it meant having to write from a position of subjection:

> Most Imperial and most invincible Emperor, we have received the letters of your mighty highness written to us from Constantinople the fifteenth day of March this present year, whereby we understand how graciously, and how favorably the humble petitions of one William Harborne a subject of ours, resident in the Imperial city of your highness presented unto your Majesty for the obtaining of access for him and two other merchants, more of his company our merchants also, to come with merchandizes both by sea & land, to the countries and territories subject to your government, and from thence again to return home with good leave and liberty, were accepted of your most invincible Imperial highness.[2]

This was the start of a cordial seventeen-year-long correspondence between the sultan and the queen that marked the beginning of one of history's more unlikely alliances. For the wily Protestant queen who had already held on to her crown for twenty-one years in the face of implacable Catholic opposition to her rule, it was yet another shrewd move designed to ensure her political survival.

Ever since Elizabeth's excommunication by Pope Pius V in 1570, Europe's Catholic powers had offered English merchants only limited commercial access to their ports and cities. In response to the growing economic crisis that ensued, a group of merchants came together and proposed to explore, with the queen's blessing, the possibility of direct trade with the fabled lands to the east. The Venetians and Spaniards had long acted as middlemen in the eastern trade, and most of the coveted spices and fine silks from Persia and the Indies came through their ports, but a handful of enterprising English traders came up with a new business model that would help them raise capital while minimizing their own personal risk.

Shortly before writing her first letter to Murad, Elizabeth had authorized the creation of England's first joint-stock company, known as the Muscovy Company, a model that would be replicated in Turkey and, much later, in the colonization of India and America. The idea was simple enough: given the expense and uncertainty of setting off on long expeditions to the east, the merchants contracted to share both the costs and the potential profits in relation to their investment of capital. It was the unwitting conception of a new model for conducting business, one that was to have revolutionary long-term consequences.

For the young and inexperienced Ottoman sultan, the alliance with the Sultana of Anletār was a small part of a much larger geopolitical world picture. Thirteen years younger than Elizabeth, Murad had ascended to the throne of the four-hundred-year-old Ottoman Empire at its height, when it still ruled vast swaths of North Africa, central Asia, the Middle East and the Balkans. He faced challenges on multiple fronts: protracted wars with the Safavid dynasty of Persia to the east, revolts against Ottoman rule in the Balkans, challenges from Spain and the Holy Roman Empire in Europe, as well as domestic factionalism within the ruling court in Constantinople. Pious, fragile, sedentary and prone to epilepsy, Murad was far more absorbed by his domestic situation within the walls of the Topkapi Palace than by the administration of his empire, which he largely delegated to his viziers and provincial governors.[3] He allowed his chief consort, the Albanian-born Safiye Sultan, to exercise unprecedented political power from within the protected space of his fabled harem and gave his mother, Nurbanu Sultan, free rein to dictate rival policies to those of his mistress, with disastrous consequences.[4] It was probably fortuitous for Elizabeth that the sultan was more interested in inviting Sufi mystics to interpret his dreams than in administering his extensive empire. Murad's court was complacent enough to claim that the alliance with England was so complete that all that was required for her merchants to become Muslim was to raise their forefinger and recite the confession of faith.[5]

England's fascination with the Islamic world went back even further than this first exchange of letters between the sultan and the queen. English merchants had begun doing business in Morocco and Syria as early as the 1550s. Henry VIII often appeared at festivities "appareled after Turkey fashion," dressed in silk and velvet and sporting a turban and a scimitar. His merchants imported rich silks, intricate textiles and exotic commodities such as rhubarb, currants and sweet wines from the east—as well as the Moroccan sugar that his daughter Elizabeth consumed in such copious quantities it blackened her teeth.[6] His daughter increased the tempo of exchange and embarked on a new policy of outreach to the Muslim world. The trade reached such a level that by the end of Elizabeth's reign thousands of her subjects were to be found in the Islamic world, some working in trade and diplomacy, others as pirates or adventurers, and many forced to convert and live as slaves. They traveled through and lived in places like Aleppo, Raqqa, Fallujah, Baghdad, Tripoli and Algiers.

The merchants and adventurers who left England to travel in the east returned with new commodities and new ideas that transformed culture and society at home. Few prosperous Elizabethan homes were without "Turkey carpets," elaborately knotted floor and wall coverings with Islamic motifs made by Anatolian, Egyptian, Syrian or Persian weavers, as well as silk quilts or embroidered tapestries. Even the language of sixteenth-century England was replete with terms drawn from commercial exchanges with Islamic countries. "Sugar," "candy," "crimson" (from the Turkish *kirmiz*), "turquoise" (or "Turkey stone"), "indigo," "tulip" (from the Turkish pronunciation of Persian *dulband,* or "turban") and "zero" all entered the language and took on their modern associations during this period, primarily thanks to Anglo-Islamic trade.[7]

Despite the extensive nature of such exchanges, Elizabeth and her subjects would not have recognized the term "Muslim," which was first used in English in 1615, defined as "one that is instructed in the belief of the Mohammetanes."[8] The first mention in English of "Islam" appears in 1625, when the travel writer Samuel Purchas quoted a Javanese prince as saying that the "religion of Islam doth not agree with the Christian Religion."[9] Various terms were used by the Elizabethans instead: "Mahometans," "Ottomites," "Saracens," "Persians," "Moors," "Pagans" and "Turks"—a catchall term for anyone who would be recognized today as a Muslim. These terms conjured a range of beliefs and assumptions, from horror and disgust to wonder and curiosity. Few people attempted to understand Islam on its own theological terms at the time. Instead, throughout the Tudor period a powerful set of misrepresentations, misconceptions and misunderstandings developed that defined relations between the two faiths. The amicable relationship that prospered under Elizabeth arose not from a principle of tolerance but as a result of political expediency. Nevertheless, the exchanges that ensued gave rise to a variety of encounters and transactions between Muslims and English Protestants, which have largely been ignored in most histories of the Elizabethan era.

England still likes to regard itself as a world power, but in the sixteenth century it was a country that lay on the fringes of the known world, and the Ottoman sultan, whose empire stretched from Egypt to central Europe, was widely recognized as a far more powerful and important player on the world stage. As exchanges with the Islamic world increased throughout Elizabeth's reign, English scholars made some attempt to try to understand the scale and power of the Ottoman Empire. In 1603 Richard Knolles, a grammar-school teacher from Kent, published a monumental twelve-hundred-page survey, *The General Historie of the Turkes, from the first beginning of that Nation to the rising of the Othoman Familie,* the first chronicle of the Ottoman Empire written in English. Drawing on continental European accounts describing the rise of the Turks in minute detail, Knolles's book became the standard authority on the Ottomans, whom he described as "the glorious empire of the Turks, the present terror of the world."[10]

Curiosity for all things from the Orient gripped Elizabethan England and inevitably reached its theaters. In early August 1601 the great theatrical impresario Philip Henslowe recorded in his diary that he had paid ten shillings and four pence for a new play about the Prophet Muhammad that included "apparel for Mahewmet," and "the making of crowns and other things for Mahewmet." Three weeks later he paid forty shillings to the actor Edward Alleyn for "the book of Mahemett," a reference on this occasion to a play, since lost. Famed for his grand declamatory style, Alleyn portrayed most of Christopher Marlowe's lead characters, including Tamburlaine, who, at the climax of Part II, curses Muhammad and burns the Qur'an onstage, an act notoriously censored when *Tamburlaine* was performed at London's Barbican theater in 2005 following the London bombings. Henslowe's diary contains numerous references to props, apparel and payments relating to plays that featured and named "Mohammed," including an item listed on March 1598 as "old Mahemetes head."

This fascination intensified in 1600, when the Moroccan sultan Ahmad al-Mansur sent a delegation led by his ambassador Muhammad al-Annuri to London to meet with Queen Elizabeth and propose a military alliance against Catholic Spain. The Muslims had only recently been expelled from southern Spain, and al-Mansur was eager to recapture these lands. Elizabeth was equally eager to deflect the Spanish navy from heading north (as it had tried on many occasions since the first failed armada, of 1588) to topple her government and bring

England into the Catholic fold. The embassy was the culmination of more than twenty years of cordial correspondence between Elizabeth and the Moroccans, and it succeeded in establishing an alliance similar to the one made between the queen and Sultan Murad III. It forged a broad anti-Spanish alliance between Protestant England and Muslim Morocco, and led to the creation of the Barbary Company in 1585. This enabled English merchants to sell wool and munitions to the Moroccans, and in return they imported saltpeter (to make gunpowder), silk, cotton, spices, gold and the ubiquitous sugar. Elizabeth's friendly relations with the Moors of Morocco were tempered only by her fear, not of Christian censure, but of the damaging effect they might have on her friendship with the Ottomans, who were at this time adversaries of al-Mansur's Moroccan kingdom vying for political control of North Africa.

Toward the end of 1601, some months after the arrival in London of the Moroccan ambassador, William Shakespeare began *The Tragedy of Othello, the Moor of Venice.* Produced at the height of his dramatic powers, *Othello* stands alongside Shakespeare's other great tragedies, *Hamlet, Macbeth* and *King Lear,* all written during a period of intense creativity stretching from 1599 (when he began *Hamlet*) to 1606 (generally agreed to be the year in which *Macbeth* and *King Lear* were written). In contrast to these other plays with their northern European settings, *Othello* is set in the Mediterranean and is a largely sympathetic portrayal of the tragic downfall of a soldier from North Africa destroyed by his adopted Christian community. Retracing his movements across London over the six months of his stay, it is possible to discern some of the topical raw material on which Shakespeare may have drawn for his portrayal of the "noble Moor."

Othello is simultaneously admired and feared by his Christian hosts. He is cultivated as a military asset, yet denigrated as an outsider. Al-Annuri and Othello, both Moors, one real, the other fictional, move into a Christian world that first embraces but eventually rejects and expels them. Othello is called "an extravagant and wheeling stranger / Of here and everywhere."[11] In Shakespeare's play the Moor's obscure origins and paradoxical identity are lost in his contradictory "traveler's history,"[12] as Othello seems to move among paganism, Islam and Christianity, "taken by the insolent foe"—presumably the Ottoman Turks—then "sold to slavery" before his eventual "redemption" by Christians.[13] It is a play in which the protagonist captures the hopes and fears that defined Elizabeth's relations with Islam that are the subject of this book.

Protestant England came closer to Islam under Queen Elizabeth than at any other time in its history up until today. Antagonism between Christianity and Islam stretched right back beyond the Crusades to the Muslim invasions of Europe in the early eighth century, but the more recent split between Catholics and Protestants had complicated the simple division between the two faiths. The pope's dramatic decision to excommunicate Elizabeth forced her to reconsider England's position in the world. She turned her back on conciliation with the Catholic powers of Europe and decided to ally herself with the more powerful Muslim courts of Morocco, Persia and the Ottoman Empire. For many English Catholics and Puritans, these alliances were an abomination, but to a number of statesmen and merchants they represented profit and possibility.

This book tells the remarkable story of the Elizabethans who traveled to the Muslim world, what they learned and how their discoveries, and the stories they told, affected life back home. It shows how, for some, there was real enthusiasm for a Protestant-Islamic alliance to oppose the papacy and the Catholic power of Spain, both determined to wipe out all forms of heresy, be it reformed Christianity or "Mahometan" Islam. It reveals how far Elizabethan England had to come in its willingness to perceive Islam as a faith with which it could do business and also shows how the fear, or allure, of converting to Islam, which became known at this time as "turning Turk," was taken seriously by many men and women who had already experienced one shift in state religion and were thus capable of imagining another. Catholic Europe reacted with horror at the rapprochement between Queen Elizabeth and the sultans of Ottoman Turkey and Morocco, and sought to conflate Protestantism with Islam as two sides of the same heretical coin. In an age when the Ottoman Empire was regarded as the world's most powerful and successful military machine, the possibility of an Anglo-Ottoman alliance was viewed with genuine alarm in Spain and Italy as a direct threat to Catholic hegemony in Europe.

The Protestant preacher Thomas Becon voiced many people's concerns when he wrote in 1542: "Consider how grievously and without all mercy the people of Christ in many places be most cruelly invaded, handled, led captive, miserably entreated, imprisoned, slain, murdered, and all their goods spoiled, brent, and taken away of that most spiteful and Nero-like tyrant the great Turk, that mortal enemy of Christ's religion, that destroyer of the Christian faith, that perverter of all good order, that adversary of all godliness and pure innocency."[14] For many Christians, Islam was the antithesis of Christianity and an implacable foe. But others took a very different view. These included the influential French political philosopher Jean Bodin, who wrote in 1576 praising Islam, and the Ottomans in particular, as a tolerant and meritocratic society whose success was based on a belief in civic welfare, social justice, military discipline and charity. Bodin ridiculed the suggestion that the Spanish Empire could maintain the imperial mantle of ancient Rome, arguing that "if there is anywhere in the world any majesty of empire and of true monarchy, it must radiate from the [Ottoman] sultan. He owns the richest parts of Asia, Africa and Europe, and he rules far and wide over the entire Mediterranean."[15] Bodin knew that history offered many examples of Christian states forging alliances with the Ottomans. After the fall of Constantinople in 1453, the Venetians agreed to mutually beneficial commercial treaties with Sultan Mehmed II, and in 1536 the French king Francis I forged a formal alliance with Sultan Süleyman I to confront their common enemy Charles V. Polemics like Becon's have tended to drown out more considered voices like Bodin's in most histories of Christianity's relations with Islam. One of the purposes of this book is to show how Elizabethan England performed a delicate balancing act between the two that was unique in Europe.

The English responded to the Muslim powers in a number of ways: as a force that might just save England from Catholicism, as a military empire that could overrun all of Christianity and as an international commercial power capable of enriching those who worked with it. The thousands of English merchants, diplomats, sailors, soldiers, preachers, artisans and servants who spent time in Muslim countries from North Africa to Persia each offered his own perspective. Among them were some remarkable characters like Anthony Jenkinson, a merchant who from the 1560s met the Ottoman sultan, the Russian tsar and the Persian shah, and almost single-handedly opened up England's trade with Asia; William Harborne, England's first official ambassador to the Ottoman Empire; the merchant Samson Rowlie, who was captured, castrated, converted and lived the rest of his life as chief eunuch and treasurer of Algiers under the name Hassan Aga; and Sir Anthony Sherley, a renegade, recusant and opportunist who traveled all the way to Persia, where he befriended Shah Abbas I and "went native," becoming the shah's personal envoy, touring Europe's capitals dressed as a Persian and extolling the virtues of a Euro-Persian military alliance against the Turks. Each one traveled with his own particular agenda and expectations, which all fed into the diverse and often contradictory body of experiences that collectively made up Elizabethan approaches to Islam.

The story of how Elizabethan men and women engaged with the Muslim world has never been part of the Tudor historians' view, which has always assumed that Shakespeare's England, "this sceptred isle," existed in splendid isolation from much of the rest of the world and encountered Turks, Saracens and Mahometans only at the furthest limits of its literary imagination. This was far from being the case. Queen Elizabeth was a minor player on the margins of a geopolitical world dominated by the empires of Persia, the Ottomans, the Habsburgs and Spain, who at various moments openly acknowledged the superiority of the Muslim powers with which she repeatedly put England on friendly terms. This does not mean that England under Elizabeth was a halcyon world where Christians and Muslims happily coexisted in an atmosphere of religious toleration and acceptance of each other's cultural differences. The relationship was often based on mutual suspicion, misunderstanding and ambivalence. Its consequences were various and sometimes contradictory. Those involved were mostly driven by self-interest and did not believe they were playing out some profound clash between civilizations. It is a subtle and complicated history that illuminates the Elizabethan period, and also our own.

1

Conquering Tunis

Unseasonably stormy weather greeted Prince Philip as he sailed up the English Channel in June 1554. Under the terms of his imminent marriage to Mary Tudor, the future King of Spain and Portugal and ruler of much of the New World was about to become King of England and Ireland *jure uxoris*—by right of marriage. This alliance would have a lasting effect upon the subsequent history of Tudor England. At the age of six, Mary, the eldest child of King Henry VIII, by his first wife, the Spanish Catherine of Aragon, had been betrothed to her mother's nephew, the Holy Roman Emperor Charles V, but Charles found better prospects closer to home and Mary would eventually be offered to his son. Before Henry VIII's decision to separate the Church of England from the Roman Catholic Church, an alliance between Spain and England would have been regarded as a convenient formality between royal cousins, but the Reformation changed everything. By the time Mary's sickly and childless younger brother, Edward, died in 1553, leaving his sister to inherit the throne, England and Spain were on opposite sides of a deep religious divide.

Just five days before the marriage, Philip landed at Southampton in a Spanish flotilla escorted into harbor by a fleet of twenty-eight English vessels. As he stepped onto English soil, the lord steward, Francis Talbot, Earl of Shrewsbury, ceremonially presented the twenty-seven-year-old Spanish prince with the Order of the Garter, the highest chivalric honor an English monarch can bestow. Philip's Spanish advisers were on their best behavior, but they remained suspicious of a country that for five years had broadly embraced Calvinism as the official religion of the state. The English, as one Spaniard privately noted, were "a barbarian and highly heretical people" who murdered monks and were contemptuous of God and his saints. Simon Renard, Spain's resident ambassador, fully anticipated the difficulty of selling the marriage to a deeply divided country. Many Englishmen and -women feared they were "going to be enslaved, for the queen is a Spanish woman at heart and thinks nothing of Englishmen, but only of Spaniards and bishops. Her idea, they say, is to have the King crowned by force and deprive the Lady Elizabeth of her right, making the operation of the law subject to her own will."[1]

Philip was told to avoid alienating his hosts and to tread carefully. He spent three days in Southampton recovering from his journey before riding to Winchester with a magnificent retinue of two thousand English and Spanish nobles on horseback. The lord chancellor and Bishop of Winchester, Stephen Gardiner, met him at Winchester Cathedral with an English audience of five other prominent English bishops, who lavished him with "as much love as one could say."[2]

That evening, Philip met his future wife for the first time. Mary was immediately taken with her young fiancé. He was, in the words of one observer, a "well-favored" youth with "a broad forehead, and gray eyes, straight-nosed and manly countenance."[3] Philip and his entourage were less flattering about Mary. Although she was described as "a perfect saint" ("who dresses badly"), the first meeting with the thirty-eight-year-old queen led one of his advisers to observe drily that she was "older than we were led to believe." Others were less diplomatic, finding her "small, and rather flabby." Publicly the encounter was reported as a great success, as the two "pleasantly talked and communed together under the cloth of estate."[4] Philip spoke Spanish, and Mary, who understood her mother's tongue but spoke it poorly, replied in French.

Whatever the public rhetoric, this was a marriage of expediency, undertaken on the orders of Philip's father, Charles V. Ruy Gómez, the prince's adviser and confidant, brusquely explained the reasons. "The king," he wrote, "understands that this marriage was effected not for the flesh but for the restoration of this realm and the conservation of those states [in Flanders]"[5]: that is, the marriage would bring England back under papal jurisdiction and would give Charles greater leverage over his troublesome Protestant dominions in the Low Countries, who bridled at the authority of their distant Catholic king. It would draw England into an alliance against his imperial rival, the French king Francis I, who had by this point allied himself with the Habsburgs' other great adversary, the Ottoman Empire and its sultan, Süleyman I.

For Mary, the marriage offered the personal and political stability that had eluded her for most of her life. When she was just seventeen, her father had married Anne Boleyn and nullified his marriage to her mother, pronouncing Mary illegitimate. Mary remained devoutly committed to her mother's Catholic faith and was thus barred from inheriting the crown by her brother, Edward. At his death, she led a successful rebellion to depose Edward's chosen successor, his first cousin the Protestant Lady Jane Grey. Once crowned queen, Mary faced further opposition when she announced her intentions to marry Philip. In January 1554 Sir Thomas Wyatt led a rebellion against the proposed alliance with Spain. Although it was quickly suppressed and Wyatt was executed, the rebellion captured the mood of a country polarized between those who supported the English Reformation and opposed the Spanish match, and those who remained loyal to papal authority and welcomed the marriage as signaling the end of a twenty-year religious aberration.

Mary and Philip were married by Bishop Gardiner in front of a packed congregation in Winchester Cathedral on Wednesday, July 25, 1554, the Feast Day of St. James, or "Matamoros," the patron saint of Spain. A raised scaffold was erected for the procession of the bride and groom, the walls were lined with rich tapestries and cloth of gold, and two wooden stages or "mounts" were built near the altar, "her Majesty standing on the right side of the said mount, and the king on the left side."[6] Mary and her advisers ensured that it was she, not Philip, who stood on the right, the dominant position usually reserved for kings. Philip assumed the supplicant position of a queen, to the left, a decision that was not lost on either Spanish or English observers. Before

the service began the Spanish presented Gardiner with a patent desig-
nating Philip King of Naples, a title relinquished by Charles V and given
to his son, ensuring that Mary was marrying a king and an equal. The
nuptials concluded, heralds pronounced the newlyweds' titles in Latin,
French and English (though not Spanish). They were now King and
Queen of England, France, Naples, Jerusalem and Ireland, Defenders
of the Faith; Princes of Spain and Sicily; Archdukes of Austria; Dukes
of Milan, Burgundy and Brabant; Counts of Habsburg, Flanders and
Tyrol.

To ease any potential qualms about the marriage, the English circulated celebratory verses reminding everyone that Philip was descended
from King Edward III and so was, as one writer put it, an *"English
Philip."* They "tell us that he is English and not Spanish," wrote one of
Philip's advisers, while noting with equal satisfaction that Mary was of
course Spanish through her maternal line. On July 31 the newlyweds
left for London on a tide of public goodwill. Philip stopped at Windsor
on August 3 to be installed officially as a Knight of the Garter, and on
the eighteenth they made their triumphant entry into London. The gal-
lows erected to execute supporters of the Wyatt Rebellion were taken
down and replaced with stages hastily erected to display pageants and
tableaux celebrating the union. Philip admired the elaborate displays
created in his honor, boasting that throughout the city he was greeted
"with universal signs of joy and love."[7]

The procession ended at Whitehall, where the couple entered the
privy apartments to find one of the most astonishing of all wedding
presents from Philip's father. Hanging from the walls were twelve enormous tapestries, woven from the finest gold, silver and silk thread. Each
one was over fifteen feet high, ranging in width from twenty-three to
forty feet, a physically overwhelming presence even in such grand
chambers. They were, in the words of one onlooker, a woven account
of Charles V's "proceedings and victories against the Turks."[8] Known
today as the *Conquest of Tunis* tapestries, the cycle, now hanging in
the Palacio Real in Madrid, provides a blow-by-blow account of one of
the sixteenth century's greatest clashes between Islam and Christianity:
Charles V's military expedition to Tunis in the summer of 1535 to crush

the Turkish pasha and grand admiral of the Ottoman fleet, Kheir ed-Din, known to westerners as Barbarossa.

"Barbarossa" means red beard in Italian, though by conflation with "barbarous" the name was also an acknowledgment of Kheir ed-Din's fearsome reputation for raiding Christian towns and destroying Christian ships across the Mediterranean. In 1534 Süleyman the Magnificent appointed Kheir ed-Din head of the Ottoman fleet, encouraging him to plunder the Italian and North African coasts, an assault that culminated in his capture of the strategically important city of Tunis in August. Kheir ed-Din had deposed the city's king, the tyrannical Mulay Hassan, a vassal of the Habsburg emperor. Worse still for Charles, Barbarossa was supplied with arms by Francis I, whose growing alliance with the Ottomans threatened Spanish influence in the Mediterranean basin.

Charles felt he needed to respond decisively. The prospect of a latter-day crusade against the infidel in North Africa appealed to him, as he saw himself as "Defender of the Faith." In 1269 the French king Louis IX had died of dysentery while unsuccessfully besieging Tunis—an unfortunate ending that led to his canonization. Charles had his eye not only on succeeding where Louis had failed, but also on achieving sainthood. In the autumn of 1534 he began assembling a huge armada. He financed the expedition in part with gold sent back to Spain by conquistadors to be used, as one put it, "in the holy enterprise of war against the Turk, Luther and other enemies of the faith."[9]

A combined fleet of more than four hundred ships carrying 30,000 Spanish, Italian, Portuguese, Flemish and German soldiers set sail on June 14, 1535, and reached Tunis later that month. After a punishing siege and ferocious battle on the city's outskirts that left an estimated 30,000 dead, Kheir ed-Din fled and Tunis fell to Charles's forces on July 21. Habsburg dispatches claimed that around 20,000 Christian slaves were freed, although many more Muslims were slaughtered in the three-day sack and pillage of the city, and some 10,000 more (it is estimated) were sold into slavery.[10]

Charles was so confident of victory that he took the Flemish artist Jan Vermeyen with him to record events in meticulous detail. He then commissioned William de Pannemaker, Brussels's finest tapestry maker, to weave twelve enormous tapestries based on Vermeyen's drawings. The series began with a panoramic map of the Mediterranean theater of operations and followed key moments in the campaign, culminating in the final graphic scenes of the fall and sack of Tunis. It took forty-two weavers many years to complete the set, at the enormous cost of fifteen thousand Flemish pounds. When the tapestries were finally completed in Brussels in the summer of 1554, they were packed up immediately and sent to London, where they were unveiled for the first time to celebrate the union of Mary and Philip.

Each tapestry emphasized the awesome military might and financial power of the Habsburg Empire. For the English and Spanish entourage admiring them that August, the message was clear: the Spanish king would go to any lengths to protect his religious and imperial interests. For many of the English gazing up at these beautiful but intimidating scenes, the tapestries provided the first eyewitness depictions of Muslims in such realistic detail. For generations of Englishmen and -women, Muslims were distant and exotic people, glimpsed on the edges of hazy world maps or in literary romances. Suddenly Mary's court was confronted with images of life-size turbaned Turkish and Berber soldiers bearing down on their victims, whose women and children were slaughtered and sold into slavery. This vivid image of the crushing of the "infidel" provided a stark warning to English Protestants that the heretical break with Rome would not be endured. Islam and Protestantism were both heresies, to be eradicated where possible by political unions, or, if necessary, by direct military assault.

For Catholics, this message seemed a blessed salvation from the twin specters of Lutheranism and Islam. But to English Protestants it confirmed their worst fears. As one Protestant commentator observed in July 1555, Mary and Philip's religious advisers were arguing that "the Turks are one and the same thing as we who embrace the pure doctrine of the Gospel."[11] Mary had already made the connection between Protestantism and the Muslim "heresy" as early as the autumn of 1535, when she took the dramatic step of imploring Charles V to lead a crusade against her father following his divorce from her mother and the split from Rome. "In so doing," she wrote, he "will perform a service most agreeable to Almighty God, nor will he acquire less fame and glory to himself than in the conquest of Tunis or the whole of Africa."[12]

Given Henry's appalling treatment of his elder daughter, her emotional plea was perhaps not as shocking as it might first appear. Like that of so many Christians in the sixteenth century battling with profound changes to their faith, Mary's understanding of Muslim Turks had been shaped by misconceptions of Islam that had endured for centuries, and went right back to the religion's origins in seventh-century Arabia. Following the death of the Prophet Muhammad in Medina in AD 632, Christians provided a variety of inconsistent and contradictory responses to Islam, ranging from indifference and bemusement to horror and disgust. The first problem for many Christians was the rapid success of Islam as a religious and political force in the seventh and eighth centuries.

In direct contrast to Islam's political strength and theological unity, Christianity had suffered centuries of persecution under the pagan Roman Empire, only to emerge after the fall of Rome divided between an eastern Orthodox church based in Constantinople and a western Latin church led by the pope in Rome.

Like Judaism and Christianity, Islam traced its origins as a monotheistic faith at least as far back as Abraham. Noah, Abraham, Moses and Jesus were all regarded as prophets who had imperfectly described the word of God. The Torah, the Psalms and the Gospel were thus acknowledged as holy texts prefiguring the ultimate divine revelation provided by the Prophet Muhammad in the recitation of the Qur'an. Christians claimed that Jesus' message supplanted that of Moses and the Jewish faith; Muslims now claimed that Muhammad's prophecies had superseded those of Jesus. Their austere simplicity was based on the five pillars of faith: *shahâda*, the recitation of the foundational belief; *salât*, daily prayers and ablutions; *zakat*, giving alms; *sawm*, fasting through the month of Ramadan; and *hajj*, the pilgrimage to Mecca.

Islam rejected sacramental rites and holy intercessors and dismissed the Christian belief in the Holy Trinity. Jesus was regarded as a holy prophet, but he was not crucified, nor was he the son of God. To worship him as God was, as far as Muslims were concerned, a blasphemous error. Nevertheless, as People of the Book, Jews and Christians retained the right to freedom of worship even within the *dâr al-Islam* ("House of Islam"), where they were known as *dhimmi,* or protected minorities.

Most of the theological detail of Islam was lost on early Christian commentators, and for understandable reasons. Access to the culture and language of the Islamic world was difficult: by the mid-sixteenth century the Qur'an had been translated into Latin only three times.[13] Then there was the partiality of early Christian responses to Islam. Faced with an expanding, seemingly irresistible Muslim empire, some early Christian communities decided to convert but remained understandably silent about the reasons behind their decision. Those who did not convert sought to offer a persuasive account of the superiority of Christian providential beliefs. The result from the eleventh century and onward was a stream of written apologetics—defenses of Christianity—that made little attempt to understand Islam as an independent faith. Instead, they presented it as a scourge sent by a Christian God to test his followers' faith. These writings produced a series of insults, caricatures and myths about Islam that laid the foundations for many of today's stereotypes. Muslims, they claimed, were barbaric, licentious and gluttonous, practicing a bellicose, tyrannical and murderous religion. Muhammad was condemned as a lecherous, drunken, epileptic trickster with deviant sexual tastes, and the Qur'an derided as a fraudulent amalgamation of Jewish and Christian beliefs.[14]

As the terms "Islam" and "Muslim" appeared in English only in the seventeenth century, ethnic terms like "Moor" and "Arab" were used instead, though such was the importance of the Ottoman Empire that "Turk" was commonly applied to Muslims of any and all ethnic origins. Where religion was mentioned, it was in relation to the "law of Muhammad." But the faith's prominence had to be explained through the Bible in some way, which gave rise to the medieval use of the terms "Saracen," "Ishmaelite" and "Hagarene," a cluster of names derived from Abraham's offspring. In the Old Testament, Ishmael was Abraham's son, born illegitimately of his wife Sarah's handmaid, Hagar. Ishmael lived to father twelve princes whom Christian and Jewish writers regarded as founders of the twelve Arab tribes (named in Genesis 25:12–16). For medieval writers these terms—particularly "Saracen"—became synonymous first with Arabs, then with all Muslims.

By the time of the Crusades, the "Saracens" were regarded primarily as a military threat. Christian misconceptions of the rival faith hardened in two ways. The first was that Islam was perceived as a pagan religion. Saracens were idolatrous *perfidi*—treacherous or unfaithful, from where we get "infidel"—who worshipped idols, including Apollo and Muhammad. Over time, as Christians began to realize that their adversaries were monotheists rather than pagans, the idea emerged that Islam was just another heresy of the true faith, a confused amalgamation of Christian and Jewish theology that accepted God but rejected the Trinity. Muhammad was ridiculed as the ultimate heresiarch, a fraudulent prophet who had tricked his followers with the promise of a debauched paradise using demonic magic and feigned miracles.

It was easier to understand Islam as part of Christianity's more familiar struggles with heretical communities than to provide a meaningful explanation of its beliefs. Describing Saracens as heretics enabled the faithful to accept them as part of God's plan, a terrifying but necessary prefiguration of the Book of Revelation's Apocalypse, the Day of Judgment and humanity's redemption. Even the rise of the Ottomans— thought to be descendants of the Trojans or Scythians—and their conquest of Constantinople in 1453 were regarded as divine punishment for Christianity's inability to unify its eastern Orthodox and western Latin churches.[15] What Christians saw when they looked at Islam was not a rival religion but a distorted image of themselves.

This perception endured for centuries. Medieval England may have seemed a long way from Arabia, but events involving "Saracens" had already impressed themselves on the medieval Christian imagination throughout Europe.[16] The Arabs had only been defeated in France at Tours in 732. They conquered the whole of Spain and by 1187 they had taken Jerusalem. In 1143 the Lincolnshire-born theologian and Arabic scholar Robert of Ketton completed the first-ever translation of the Qur'an into Latin while studying Arabic in Spain. As its title suggested, *Lex Mahumet pseudoprophete* ("The Religion of Muhammad the

Pseudo-prophet") was designed to show Islam as a Christian heresy—or what Robert calls a "death-dealing" religion—and to convert Muslims to Christianity. Despite drawing on Arabic Qur'anic *tafsīrs* (commentaries), Robert's translation was little more than a loose paraphrase of the original and had little or no success in converting Muslims. It survives in twenty-five medieval copies, and remained the standard version of the text in Europe until the mid-seventeenth century.

In William Langland's poem *Piers Plowman* (c. 1360–1387) the Prophet is described as a "Cristene man," a pseudo-Christian schismatic whose followers can find salvation only if they understand their heretical error in worshipping the "wrong" Messiah (Muhammad), and convert instead to Christ and "oure bileue, *Credo in deum patrem*" ("our belief, *I Believe in God the Father Almighty*").[17] In contrast to this learned and literary approach to Islam, more popular English traditions continued to draw on older traditions that regarded Muslims as pagans. The mystery-play cycles performed in York and Chester were full of Greek and Roman emperors, as well as Herod and Pontius Pilate, who were all shown worshipping Muhammad as a pagan idol. Heresy, paganism and millenarianism had all defined Christian responses to Islam for generations.

The religious controversies that followed Luther's demands in Wittenberg in 1517 had many far-reaching effects, but one of their unintended and often overlooked consequences is in Christianity's perception of Islam. In 1518 Luther criticized the sale of indulgences to raise money for a new crusade in the Holy Land by arguing provocatively that "to make war on the Turks is to rebel against God, who punishes our sins through them."[18] Like many medieval theologians, Luther saw the "Turk" as another word for ungodliness, a scourge sent by God to punish a wicked, divided Christianity, part of a mysterious but irresistible divine plan.

In 1542, the Swiss publisher Johann Herbst was thrown in jail in Basel for printing Robert of Ketton's translation of the Qur'an in a revised, updated (though still very sketchy) volume produced by Theodore Bibliander, a Protestant reformer, under the title *Machumetis Saracenorum principis vita ac doctrina omnis* ("Life and Teachings of Muhammad, Prince of the

Caricature of Luther with seven heads, including that of a turbaned Turk (1529).

Saracens").[19] Luther intervened, petitioning the Basel authorities to release Herbst and offering to write a preface to the new edition, arguing that it was necessary to understand Islamic theology to refute it. In making this argument in his subsequent preface, Luther described Catholics, Muslims and Jews as all heretical. "Therefore," he wrote, "as I have written against the idols of the Jews and the papists and will continue to do so to the extent that it is granted to me, so also have I begun to refute the pernicious beliefs of Muhammad." In his typically blunt manner he went on:

> Accordingly I have wanted to get a look at the complete text of the Qur'an. I do not doubt that the more of the pious and learned persons read these writings, the more the errors of the name of Muhammad will be refuted. For just as the folly, or rather the madness, of the Jews is more easily observed once their hidden secrets have been brought to the open, so once the book of Muhammad has been made public and thoroughly examined in all its parts, all pious persons will more easily comprehend the insanity and wiles of the devil and will more easily refute them.[20]

Trying to understand Islam through a twelfth-century paraphrase of the Qur'an was never going to get Luther very far. Besides, his Catholic opponents had pounced on his apparent unwillingness to support a crusade against the Turks as proof of the Lutheran "heresy" (Luther had argued that Christianity should fight its own internal demons before turning on the Turks). When Pope Leo X threatened Luther with excommunication in 1520, his position on the Turks was cited as just one of his many "heretical" teachings. In January 1521 Luther was formally excommunicated in the papal bull *Decet Romanum Pontificem* ("It Pleases the Roman Pontiff") and was himself named a "heretic" and "schismatic."[21]

Luther later changed his mind about waging war on the Turks, arguing that this was the prerogative of rulers, not of clergy. He continued to describe Catholicism, Islam and Judaism as conjoined enemies of the "true" Christian faith, reserving his bitterest polemic for Pope Clement VII and the Ottomans: "as the pope is Antichrist," he wrote in 1529, "so the Turk is the very devil."[22] Catholics responded by depicting Luther as a divided monster with seven heads, one sporting a Turkish turban. Francesco

Chieregato, one of the pope's advisers at the Diet of Nuremberg (convened to discuss church reform), wrote in January 1523 that he was "occupied with the negotiations for the general war against the Turk, and for that particular war against that nefarious Martin Luther, who is a greater evil to Christendom than the Turk."[23] When Thomas More, author of *Utopia* and privy councillor to Henry VIII, was asked to respond to the Lutheran challenge, his *Dialog Concerning Heresies* (1528) referred to "Luther's sect" as worse than "all the Turks, all the Saracens, all the heretics."[24]

More's close friend the great humanist scholar Erasmus of Rotterdam tried to find a middle way between Catholic and Protestant sectarian divisions in his *De bello turcico* ("On the War Against the Turks"). Erasmus's treatise was written in 1530 to coincide with the Diet of Augsburg, a general assembly called by Charles V to discuss what he regarded as the two greatest threats facing Christendom: Lutheranism and Islam. Charles's advisers encouraged him to use the assembly to pursue the policies adopted by his grandparents Ferdinand II of Aragon and Isabella I of Castile toward Muslims in Spain: forced conversion or expulsion. "Luther's diabolical and heretical opinions," wrote Cardinal Lorenzo Campeggio, "shall be castigated and punished according to the rule and practice observed in Spain with regard to the Moors."[25] But Luther was only one-half of Charles's problem: the other was the spectacular rise of the Ottoman Empire, which by 1530 was knocking on the door of Christendom. Having taken Constantinople in 1453, the Ottomans had conquered Egypt and Syria and were challenging the Portuguese in the Indian Ocean. During the 1520s a series of military campaigns across the Balkans led to the capture of Belgrade and the invasion of Hungary, creating an Islamic empire that spanned three continents and ruled an estimated 15 million people. Just months before Erasmus wrote his treatise, Ottoman imperial expansion into Europe reached its zenith, with an Ottoman army at the gates of Vienna. Süleyman the Magnificent taunted the besieged Christian forces by parading outside the gates wearing an extravagant, bejeweled helmet made for him by Venetian goldsmiths that consciously emulated the Habsburg and papal imperial crowns.[26] It had proved almost impossible to unite Christendom against the Ottomans: Venice remained on amicable commercial terms with them, while the French pursued repeated diplomatic and military alliances with Süleyman as a bulwark against the Habsburgs. Worse still, there were rumors that Süleyman, having learned of the threat posed by Luther to his great enemy Charles V, was encouraging his imams in the mosques of Constantinople to pray for Luther's success.[27]

With many of the German states in the grip of Lutheranism on one side and the Ottomans in control of much of eastern Europe on the other, this was a critical moment for Catholicism, and Erasmus knew it. How, he asked, had the Ottomans "reduced our religion from a broad empire to a narrow strip?" The answer reverted to medieval commonplaces about Islamic paganism and heresy. Referring to what he called "this race of barbarians, their very origin obscure," Erasmus argued that the Ottoman "sect" was "a mixture of Judaism, Christianity, paganism, and the Arian [non-Trinitarian] heresy. They acknowledge Christ—as just one of the prophets." As was true of his medieval theological predecessors, Erasmus's interest in Islam was secondary to the assumption that the faith was just a projection of a divided Christianity. "They rule because God is angered," Erasmus continued; "they fight us without God, they have Mahomet as their champion, and we have Christ—and yet it is obvious how far they have spread their tyranny, while we, stripped of so much power, ejected from much of Europe, are in danger of losing everything."[28]

Erasmus's solution to the Turkish problem took on far greater significance when set against sixteenth-century Christian divisions. "If we really want to heave the Turks from our neck," he concluded, "we must first expel from our hearts a more loathsome race of Turks, avarice, ambition, the craving for power, self-satisfaction, impiety, extravagance, the love of pleasure, deceitfulness, anger, hatred, envy." Writing as a Catholic, but sounding very much like a Lutheran, Erasmus implored his readers to "rediscover a truly Christian spirit and then, if required, march against the flesh-and-blood Turk."[29] Christianity needed reformation, but it also needed unification; otherwise, the Turk buried within the heart of all believers, be they Catholic or Lutheran, would triumph. Trying to please both sides of a divided Christendom, Erasmus enabled Catholics to castigate Protestants as akin to Turks for dividing the faith, while also enabling Protestants to condemn Catholics as the worst representatives of "Turkish" avarice and impiety.

Those assembled at Augsburg responded as they usually did to humanist advice and ignored Erasmus's treatise, which was, for all its theological eloquence, vague in its practical application. The Diet did little other than keep the Habsburgs on a collision course with both Luther and the Turk, although the pressure to confront the Ottoman threat enabled Lutheranism to survive and prosper in these crucial early years of its emergence. Throughout the 1540s Charles V fought the dual "heresy" on two fronts and with mixed success. In 1541 he tried to follow his conquest of Tunis with an attack on Algiers, but the campaign was a complete disaster. By 1545 he was at war with Lutheran forces in Germany, which this time culminated in victory at the Battle of Mühlberg in 1547.

The arrival of the *Conquest of Tunis* tapestries in London in 1554 not only reminded those who saw them of Charles's earlier victory over Islam but invited inevitable comparisons with the defeat of Lutheranism at Mühlberg. Within weeks of seeing the Tunis tapestries, Mary and Philip set about stamping out the Lutheran "heresy" that had taken hold of England during Edward VI's reign. Legislation was prepared to restore papal authority in ecclesiastical matters, and in November an act was passed for the "avoiding of heresies which have of late arisen, grown and much increased within this realm."[30] By February 1555 the first public burnings began of "heretical" Lutherans, which would secure the queen's enduring historical notoriety as "Bloody Mary."

History is rarely kind to the losers, and Mary is no exception. Her short-lived restoration of Catholicism would forever pale in comparison with her half sister Elizabeth's forty-five-year Protestant reign, which became a touchstone of English national identity. For centuries Mary was condemned as a religious zealot who had pursued a murderous crusade against Protestants and prepared to sacrifice her crown to the Spanish Catholics rather than see the Reformation triumph in England. Much of this was due to the Protestant theologian John Foxe's *Acts and Monuments* (1563), popularly known as *Foxe's Book of Martyrs,* a polemical account of the Catholic persecution of Protestants, under what he called "the horrible and bloody time of Queen Mary."[31] More recent evaluations reveal a more complex picture of her reign.[32] Although she passed legislation relinquishing her title as head of the church and giving the pope jurisdiction over English ecclesiastical matters, Mary maintained a clear distinction between her religious and secular power. She quietly retained her father's statutes defining England as an empire over which she, and not the papacy or Philip, exerted *plenum dominium* (complete ownership) and ensured in all official documentation and on public occasions that she took royal precedence over Philip in their controversial co-monarchy. In a country that remained in most areas predominantly Catholic despite the reformed experiments of Edward VI's reign, Mary's marriage to Philip was welcomed by at least as many as opposed it. Eager to guarantee the City's position at the center of a commercial network that looked to Spain and the Low Countries for much of its export market, London's merchants were so supportive of the marriage that they designed and paid for the couple's carefully choreographed entry into London in August 1554.[33]

Such elaborate spectacles were also used by the newly married couple in the courtly festivities that took place during their London residence in the winter of 1554–1555. On Shrovetide, February 26, 1555, pageants were staged with actors dressed as Turkish magistrates, Turkish archers and Turkish women. Exactly what they performed was not recorded, but they presumably represented vices of some kind, intended as foils to Christian virtues. The costumes survived and were used throughout the 1560s in performances under Elizabeth I.[34]

Upon her accession, Mary swiftly acted to encourage international trade by stressing a surprising degree of continuity with her father's and half brother's foreign and commercial policies. Henry VIII's merchants had advised him as early as the 1520s that the dominance over global trade of the Spanish, Portuguese and Ottoman empires gave them little room in which to pursue their own commercial interests. To the west, Spain dominated the newly discovered Americas and exploited their silver and gold. To the south Portugal monopolized Africa and the eastern trade routes, objecting when English merchants sought to establish trade with Morocco and Guinea. And to the east the overland route to Asia lay in the hands of the Ottomans. In 1527 Robert Thorne, an English merchant based in Seville, advised Henry that the only way to outmaneuver his imperial rivals and reach the Spice Islands in

Indonesia was to order his merchants to sail north. By "sailing north-wards and passing the Pole, descending to the Equinoctal line," Thorne explained, "we shall hit these islands, and it should be a much shorter way, than either the Spanish or the Portuguese have." He speculated that the northern polar region contained a navigable temperate belt beyond the freezing Norwegian seas. His hope was that English merchants could develop an export trade "profitable to our commodities of cloth" while importing spices.[35]

In the 1550s English cloth exports collapsed due to political instability in the Low Countries as the Spanish authorities came into increasing conflict with many of the Dutch Calvinist provinces. The crown and City were faced with an economic crisis and had to decide "how this mischief might be remedied." Although it seems mere folly today, many merchants began advocating Thorne's "new and strange navigation," a route that would become known as the Northwest Passage.[36] In May 1553 Edward VI's counselors concluded an agreement with London's merchants and the explorer Sebastian Cabot, issuing "ordinances, instructions and advertisements of and for the direction of the intended voyage to Cathay," led by Cabot, the governor of the "Mystery and Company of the Merchant Adventurers for the Discovery of Regions, Dominions, Islands and Places Unknown." It was a grand title for an amorphous organization with only a vague idea of where it wanted to go. The ultimate destination was Cathay—an Anglicization of the name given to China by Marco Polo—but the expedition was driven by a broader desire to discover "places unknown" en route.

The Merchant Adventurers' ordinances represented the first attempt to formalize the terms of an English joint-stock company, an association jointly owned by shareholders in proportion to the amount of money they invest. The capital is then deployed to a common purpose— such as a commercial voyage—with the profits (or losses) split proportionally among those shareholders. There were medieval examples of guilds coming together across Europe to form joint-stock companies, but never in England. Where the physical distances and financial expenditure were too great for individual merchants, the joint-stock company's collective capital mitigated the risks. It was also a sign of the growing power and unity of London's merchant community that it was able to initiate such a project free of royal influence (though with the crown's tacit assent). A total of 240 subscribers, including many merchants and some of Edward's closest political advisers, invested £25 each to raise the £6,000 required to outfit Cabot's Cathay voyage. It was a global initiative aiming to establish Tudor England as a significant player on the sixteenth-century world stage.

When the expedition set out on May 10, 1553, led by Sir Hugh Willoughby (rather than the aged Cabot) and his pilot, Richard Chancellor, it sailed past Greenwich Palace and fired off a salute to the king within. Many on board knew that Edward VI was mortally ill and suspected that, should they manage to successfully negotiate the frozen northern wastes, they would return to find a new monarch on the throne. Striking out for the Norwegian seas, the three ships faced treacherous weather, and Chancellor became separated from Willoughby, who found himself stranded on the Lapland coast. Willoughby was painfully ill equipped for such a climate, and as temperatures dropped down to minus 30 degrees Fahrenheit, he and his crew of seventy froze to death in the winter of 1553–1554. Their bodies were recovered the following summer, along with Willoughby's diary, which ends abruptly, describing search parties sent out to seek help who "returned without finding of people, or any similitude of habitation."[37] Chancellor was luckier, sailing on to the White Sea on Russia's northwest coast, then continuing to Moscow by sleigh, where he met the Tsar of All the Russias, Ivan IV Vasilyevich, better known as Ivan the Terrible.

Chancellor returned to London in triumph in the summer of 1554 to discover Mary and Philip installed as England's new monarchs. While Chancellor had gone north to Russia, other members of the Merchant Adventurers had gone south into west Africa, establishing a lucrative trade in gold, pepper, ivory and slaves. Philip had no wish for this enterprise, as it threatened the Spanish monopoly of the Atlantic slave trade and risked antagonizing Portuguese control of west African commerce, so he persuaded Mary to support her merchants' pursuit of the northern trade routes instead.

On February 26, 1555, the "Charter of the Merchants of Russia, granted upon the discovery of the said country," was granted "by King

Philip and Queen Mary." Effectively superseding King Edward's 1553 ordinances, this was the first formal charter for an English joint-stock company, described as "one body and perpetual fellowship and communality." It would come to be known simply as the Muscovy Company. Its merchants were given a monopoly on "sailing northwards, northeastwards, and northwestwards" to "traffic in and out" of Russia, for the "increase of the revenues of our crown, and general wealth of this and other of our realms." The monarchs made some gesture toward requiring the merchants to "subdue, possess and occupy all manner of cities, towns, isles and mainlands of infidelity," but this was primarily a document of trade and exchange, not of plunder and conquest.[38]

The company's original aspiration had been to reach Cathay and the Spice Islands by heading north, but it had settled instead on cultivating Ivan the Terrible's Russia as an intermediate trading partner. In the process, however, another destination had emerged. In 1557 Mary and Philip wrote to Ivan confirming their new commercial alliance and requesting safe passage for the Muscovy Company's representatives to the neighboring imperial power and commercial powerhouse, the Safavid dynasty of Persia.[39] Having begun their reign with the express intention of eradicating the heresy of Protestantism at home, economic and international imperatives pushed Mary and Philip into pursuing tentative relations with one of the great leaders of that other perceived heresy: Islam.

In August 1555, little more than a year after his wedding, Philip left England for Brussels. His father, weary after nearly four decades of rule, was preparing to abdicate and divide his increasingly unwieldy Habsburg dominions between Philip, who would become ruler of Spain and the Netherlands, and Charles's younger brother Ferdinand, who would become Holy Roman Emperor. Philip was pleased to escape his troublesome new kingdom, to which he would never return for any significant period of time. Mary was bereft. Knowing her husband's fondness for maps, she commissioned the Portuguese mapmaker Diogo Homem to create a lavishly decorated atlas for him as a reminder of their personal and political union. Known simply as the Queen Mary Atlas, its nine richly decorated, hand-drawn maps show the world in

Mary and Philip's image. The Habsburg imperial eagle flies over the Americas and northern Europe; French and Portuguese political ambitions are diminished and the threat of Lutheranism is not even acknowledged. One map shows the Mediterranean region in the aftermath of Charles V's Tunisian and Algerian campaigns. North Africa, adorned with Islamic banners, is labeled "Mahometania"; off the coast a Christian galley flying the flag of St. John engages a Turkish battleship; and to the north the crescent banner of the Ottoman Empire dominates the Balkans. The inference is that only Mary and Philip's Anglo-Spanish alliance could unify a fractured Christendom and rid it of Muhammad's heresy.

The map of northern Europe on the previous folio tells a somewhat different story. The largest escutcheon over England depicts the entwined heraldic devices of England and Spain, surmounted by an imperial crown in acknowledgment of Mary and Philip's union. But on closer inspection it is clear that the Spanish coat of arms has been scratched out from this escutcheon. Having begun work on the atlas in late 1555, Homem labored over its exquisite decoration for three years, completing it too late to present to Mary, who died on November 17, 1558. Philip never saw the atlas, which was presented instead to the new queen. Elizabeth was the only person with the authority to scratch out the Spanish escutcheon from a royally commissioned book.[40] Whether or not she herself was the originator of this stroke of political iconoclasm, it symbolized a decisive end to the brief Anglo-Spanish union, terminating Habsburg influence and with it the hopes of returning England to papal jurisdiction.

Mary bequeathed to her half sister a country divided both politically and religiously. Some of its elite had followed the European theological lead and decided that Protestantism was a heresy akin to Islam, an analogy that would come to dominate political discourse for the rest of Elizabeth's reign. Yet that same elite—for strictly pragmatic reasons—had allowed English merchants to reach out to the Muslim world. Elizabeth would exploit this divided legacy to the full as she tried to survive as a Protestant ruler in a predominantly Catholic Europe.

2

The Sultan, the Tsar and the Shah

Within days of her accession in November 1558, the new queen Elizabeth began plans for her coronation, which took place in Westminster Abbey on January 15, 1559. Superficially the event bore many similarities to Mary's coronation just five years earlier, but there were some striking theological differences, as Elizabeth began the delicate task of steering a course between the Protestant reforms of her half brother and the Catholic restitution of her half sister. Breaking with tradition, the coronation mass was read in both the traditional Latin and the English vernacular. Even more controversially, while conducting the mass, George Carew, dean of the Chapel Royal, stuck to the Catholic ritual of performing the elevation of the bread and wine, at which point Elizabeth seems to have followed her reformed principles by silently refusing communion and withdrawing. It was in fact a carefully rehearsed scene that tried to appease both sides of Elizabeth's divided theological inheritance. As her reign progressed, the religious and dynastic realignments that took place across Europe would conspire to prevent Elizabeth's attempt to find a godly "middle way" through the period's sectarian conflict.

With his wife dead less than two months, Philip, now King of Spain and Lord of the Netherlands but ever the political pragmatist, gallantly proposed to his sister-in-law as a noble but rather halfhearted "service to God" to keep England Catholic.[1] He was anxious to prevent the pro-French Scottish queen Mary Stuart from claiming the English throne and creating what for the Habsburgs would have been a disastrous

Anglo-French alliance. Elizabeth politely declined her brother-in-law's offer with the argument that he was, well, her brother-in-law. She wanted to end Philip's influence over English affairs, but she was keen to avoid alienating Spain, which she knew could easily interdict her merchants' trade with the Low Countries.

Just two months later, on March 3, 1559, Philip and the French king Henry II signed the Treaty of Cateau-Cambrésis, which after decades of conflict united the two kingdoms in peace and concerted opposition to Protestantism. Although the treaty formalized peaceful relations between France and England, no one was fooled. Elizabeth proceeded to reform the Book of Common Prayer and reinstate an oath of supremacy, established by her father, Henry, but repealed under Mary, acknowledging the sovereign as "Supreme Governor of the Church" in England. These initiatives only increased Elizabeth's isolation from the rest of Catholic Europe, which responded by starting to assemble a loose alliance against her new English brand of Protestantism.

This hostility made it more imperative than ever for the new queen to circumvent the continental powers by pursuing new markets via the Northeast Passage. But Elizabeth and the Muscovy Company, her newly inherited joint-stock company, were faced with a serious shortage of personnel. Hugh Willoughby had frozen to death in Lapland and his lieutenant, Richard Chancellor, who repeated the journey the following year, had again reached the White Sea only to drown in a storm off the Scottish coast on his return voyage in 1556. To make matters worse, Sebastian Cabot, the company's director and guiding light, died in 1557. Only one man had the experience and credentials to develop the fledgling Elizabethan trade with the east. Unfortunately, as Elizabeth was being crowned queen in January 1559, he was on Muscovy Company business nearly four thousand miles away in Bukhara, a guest of the Islamic khanate's Shaybanid ruler, Abdullah Khan II. His name was Anthony Jenkinson.

Although scarcely remembered today, during his lifetime Jenkinson was regarded as one of the great pioneers of Elizabethan travel. Born at Market Harborough in Leicestershire, he trained as a merchant and spent his apprenticeship working with English factors (commercial agents) in the Low Countries and the Levant, where he specialized in textile fabrics. In 1546 he left England and went to Flanders, Germany, Italy, Portugal and Spain, before traveling across North Africa and the Mediterranean islands and throughout what he called the "holy land."[2] By November 1553, at the ripe age of twenty-four, Jenkinson reached the Syrian city of Aleppo. Together with its neighbor Damascus, Aleppo was one of the oldest cities in the world. It stood at the western end of the Silk Road and, renowned for its trade in Iranian silk and Indian spices, had drawn merchants from east and west for centuries. The city came under the Ottomans' control following their victory in 1517 over the Mamluks (the ruling Egyptian military caste), and quickly attracted resident communities of Jewish, Armenian and Italian merchants who established permanent trading posts there. By the time Jenkinson arrived, drawn by the volume and quality of silk passing through the city's fifty-six markets and the colossal central *suq,* it was already displacing Damascus as the region's premier trading center and was widely regarded as the Islamic world's equivalent to Venice.

Then, on November 4, a visitor with very different aims came marching into the city. Jenkinson was there as Sultan Süleyman I entered Aleppo at the head of a vast Ottoman army, which was embarking on a campaign against the neighboring Persian Safavid Empire. Jenkinson watched in wonder as one of the sixteenth century's great armies swept past, led by "the Great Turke himself," Sultan Süleyman, "with great pomp and magnificence." Jenkinson's experience as a mercer ensured that his description of the scene reads more like a fashion show than a military campaign. Watching an estimated 88,000 men march past, he noted that the cavalry were "clothed all in scarlet," the infantry "all in yellow velvet, with hats of the same, of the Tartary fashion, two foot long, with a great robe of the same color about their foreheads." The sultan's elite fighting corps, the Janissaries, were wearing "silk, and apparelled upon their head with a strange form, called *Cuocullucia.*" This was the famed Turkish *bork* hat "in the manner of a French hood," topped with "a great bush which wavereth up and down most bravely when he marcheth." Finally, Süleyman himself appeared, "mounted upon a goodly white horse, adorned with a cloth of gold, embroidered most richly with the most precious stones."

It was the sultan's headgear that fascinated Jenkinson. With a mercer's eye for gauging cloth, he noted that Süleyman wore "upon his head a goodly white tuck [turban], containing in length by estimation fifteen yards, which was of silk and linen woven together, resembling something of Calicut [Indian] cloth, but is much more fine and rich, and in the top of his crown a little pinnach [plume] of white ostrich feathers."[3] Such dazzling displays of power and panache had earned Süleyman the sobriquet "the Magnificent." Jenkinson concluded his awed account by observing that Süleyman's army, "intending to march into Persia, to give battle to the Great Sophie," Shah Ismail I, would winter in Aleppo.

The title "Sophy" came from the Safavids' founder, Safi ad-din Ardabili, and his self-proclaimed designation *çafī-ud-dīn* or guardian of "purity of religion." But it was also combined in the Christian Renaissance imagination with the Greek word *sophia,* wisdom, which led many scholars to regard the Persian rulers mistakenly as venerable magi. Little did Jenkinson know that what he was witnessing was a chapter in a conflict between the Ottoman and Persian empires that would have a profound bearing on subsequent Anglo-Islamic relations. It was a conflict that bore an uncanny resemblance to the religious Reformation then convulsing Christendom. This was the Ottomans' third military campaign against the Persian Safavids, arising out of the centuries-old enmity between the Sunni (Ottoman) and Shi'a (Persian) branches of Islam, whose origins can be traced right back to the struggle for political control of the *umma,* the Muslim community, after Muhammad's death in 632.

The issue revolved around the title of "Khalifat Rasul Allah," or "the successor to the messenger of God"—that is, the caliph. The question that consumed Islam throughout this period was whether the caliph should be appointed by the community or follow Muhammad's direct line of descent. As tensions mounted and factions hardened, the *umma* descended into a period of civil wars, known as *fitna* ("strife"). In 656 'Ali ibn Abi Talib, Muhammad's cousin and the husband of his daughter Fatimah, claimed the caliphate as his hereditary right, but he was immediately challenged by Mu'awiyah, the governor of Damascus and part of the Umayya clan, who was not directly related to Muhammad. When 'Ali was assassinated by one of his own hard-line former followers in Al-Kufa, south of Baghdad, in 661, Mu'awiyah became the uncontested caliph, and the first of the Umayyad dynasty based in Damascus, shifting the center of Muslim imperial power away from the Arabian Peninsula for the first time in its short, turbulent history.

The majority of Muslims, those who accepted Mu'awiyah's leadership, became known as Sunnis, taking their name from "Sunnah"—the traditional teachings of Muhammad. However, a significant minority, the "Shī'atu 'Ali" or "the party of 'Ali," rejected the elective succession of the subsequent Umayyad, Abbasid, Mamluk and Ottoman caliphates. Their political objections over the succession gradually hardened into a theological schism dividing the followers of 'Ali from the Sunnis after 'Ali's son, Husayn, was killed by the Umayyads at the Battle of Karbala in present-day Iraq in 681. To the Shi'a, as these minority believers became known, Husayn was a Christlike figure who had martyred himself in anticipation of a final, divine revelation that would fulfill the prophecies of Abraham, Muhammad and 'Ali. In contrast to Sunnis, the Shi'a invested absolute authority in a line of imams descended from Muhammad through his daughter Fatimah and endowed with divine and infallible knowledge. When 'Ali's line disappeared in the ninth century, the largest branch of Shi'a, known as "Twelvers," developed a belief that God had hidden the twelfth, "lost" imam, who would one day reveal himself as the Mahdi ("divine guide"), or messiah, and unify Islam in its millenarial triumph over all other religions. Sunni theologians condemned these messianic beliefs as *bid'a,* or religious innovation, schismatic and heretical beliefs in salvation. Their condemnations were strikingly similar to the language with which sixteenth-century Catholics condemned Protestants.

Having rejected the authority of the caliphate, the Shi'a regarded with suspicion any form of political governance before the return of the hidden imam. The fragmentation of Persia under the Timurid dynasty in the late fifteenth century encouraged the rise of various Shi'ite rulers espousing Sufism (a mystical dimension of Islam), the most militant of whom were the Safavids from Ardabil in northwest Persia. In 1501 their fourteen-year-old spiritual and political leader, Sheik Ismail Safavi, completed a victorious campaign throughout Azerbaijan and Iran, proclaiming himself the first shah of Persia and founding the Safavid Empire in his newly conquered imperial capital, Tabriz. In a defining moment in Iran's history, Ismail proclaimed Shi'ism the empire's official religion, and announced himself as the long-lost Mahdi. His followers worshipped him as a god, and he immediately launched a jihad against his neighboring Sunni rivals, the Ottomans, marching into Anatolia and Syria, conquering Baghdad and destroying Sunni holy sites wherever he found them. Persian chroniclers described how, when Ismail conquered Tabriz, he commanded "that Abu Bakr, Umar and Usman [Sunni caliphs] should be cursed in the bazaars, on pain of death to him who refused. In those days men knew not . . . of the rules of the twelve Imams [but] . . . day by day the sun of the Shi'a faith rose higher."[4]

In response the alarmed Ottoman sultan, Selim I, declared war on the Safavids as the biggest political and religious threat to his commercial power and title of "Protector of the Holy Cities" of Mecca, Medina and Jerusalem. As Islam officially forbade war between Muslims, Selim was required to issue a fatwa against Ismail's Shi'a followers, condemning them as "infidels and heretics" and asserting that "to kill them and to destroy their communities is an implicit and essential obligation for all Muslims."[5]

As news of the Ottoman-Safavid conflict reached Europe's capitals in late 1501, Venice, France, Portugal and even the papacy began corresponding with Shah Ismail in an attempt to build an anti-Ottoman alliance. Venetian merchants in Damascus wrote to the city's senators following Ismail's accession, advising them that it was an "opportune moment to form an alliance among the Christian princes and Persia to engage in the most holy war to throw the Turk out of Europe."[6] A mixture of political expediency and a garbled understanding of Shi'a beliefs led others to justify such an alliance by mythologizing Ismail as a warrior saint who led his pious warriors into battle against "infidel" Sunni Muslims, not unlike crusading Christians.

In 1502 the Venetian spy Constantino Laschari returned from an encounter with Ismail and reported to the city's senate that the shah's "Sophi [Sufi] religion has always fought against the Ottoman royal house because the Ottomans are heretics and usurpers of the territories of many Muslims." Turning to the shah himself, he concluded, "Ismail is considered a prophet, rich, just, generous, and divinely inspired. He is much beloved of his sect which is a certain religion—Catholic in their way."[7] Venice saw the advantages of securing its eastern Mediterranean trade against Ottoman aggression by allying with Ismail, and the Portuguese sought his favor in their naval battles with the Ottomans in the Indian Ocean. None of Ismail's Christian suitors was concerned to inquire too deeply into the exact nature of his Shi'a faith. One Venetian thought him "more Christian than otherwise," an erroneous but expedient assumption: as one historian has argued, "a political alliance with a Sufi saint was easier to justify than one with a Muslim king."[8]

When a vastly superior Ottoman army equipped with artillery defeated Ismail at the Battle of Chaldiran (in modern-day eastern Turkey) in 1514, the shah's divine invincibility was shattered. His capital was soon overrun by the Ottomans, and Ismail retreated eastward, taking refuge in hunting and drinking (known in Persian poetry as *bazm u razm*), never to regain sufficient authority to challenge the Ottomans seriously. After his death in 1524 he was succeeded by his son, Shah Tahmasp I, who was faced with a series of attempted Ottoman invasions throughout the 1530s and 1540s. In the late 1550s Tahmasp responded with incursions into eastern Anatolia. Süleyman replied by mobilizing his army in 1558 and marching toward Aleppo. But the sultan was not free from his own domestic problems. In his early sixties, he was beset with illness and domestic squabbles among various wives and eight politically ambitious sons, and he was particularly suspicious of his youngest, Prince Mustafa. Just weeks before Jenkinson marveled at his forces marching into Aleppo, Süleyman camped in Konya, central Anatolia, and called Mustafa into his tent, where the sultan's eunuchs strangled the young prince with a bowstring as his father looked on.

There is no evidence to suggest that Jenkinson knew much about any of these theological and political machinations, which makes it all the more remarkable that within weeks of watching Süleyman entering

Aleppo he not only had engineered an audience with the sultan but had come away from it with the kind of formal trading privileges usually granted only to heads of state, signed by Süleyman himself. Without any diplomatic training or credentials and no history of English relations with the Ottomans, Jenkinson had secured virtually unprecedented rights to "lade and unlade his merchandise wheresoever it shall seem good unto him" throughout the Ottoman Empire, free from "any other custom or toll whatsoever." Even the sultan's long-standing commercial allies France and Venice (one of which probably provided Jenkinson with safe passage into Aleppo) were told not "to intermeddle or hinder his affairs."[9]

One wonders what Süleyman and his advisers made of this precocious (some might say foolhardy) young Christian mercer from a small, peripheral Christian island standing in front of them, with no diplomatic credentials and unable to speak Turkish, boldly negotiating exceptional commercial access to their vast dominions (presumably speaking in a mixture of Italian and French, the Levant's lingua franca). If the history of Anglo-Ottoman relations begins anywhere, it is with the twenty-four-year-old Jenkinson's extraordinary achievements in Aleppo in the winter of 1553–1554.

That spring Süleyman and Jenkinson both left Aleppo. The sultan headed east, marching into Persia, while Jenkinson went west, returning home to London, where the following year the Mercers' Company acknowledged his success in the Levant by making him a full member. Two years later, with Willoughby, Chancellor and Cabot all dead, Jenkinson's commercial and diplomatic experience made him the obvious person to lead the Muscovy Company's next Russian voyage. Jenkinson, still only twenty-seven but already described by the Muscovy Company directors as "a man well traveled, whom we mind to use in further traveling,"[10] was appointed captain general of a fleet of four ships heading back to Russia via the forbidding White Sea to take advantage of the trading rights granted to Chancellor by Ivan the Terrible. In May 1557 Jenkinson set sail, reaching the White Sea in the relatively clement month of July, before traveling overland to Moscow and the tsar's court, where he arrived in December.

Once again, Jenkinson found himself dealing with a powerful emperor ruling an eastern empire that was in transition; once again, he managed to charm his way into the ruler's affections and extract unprecedented access to him and his kingdoms. On Christmas Day 1557, Jenkinson was given an audience with Ivan. He kissed the tsar's hand, presented letters from Mary and Philip, and sat down for dinner with "diverse ambassadors and other strangers, as well as Christians and heathens." Ivan's advisers then told him almost immediately that "the emperor would give me that I desired": unfettered commercial access to the Caspian Sea and trade with Persia.[11] It was a perfect time for both men to do business. England needed to reach the east by avoiding both the overland routes through mainland Europe and the seaborne routes controlled by Spain and Portugal. Ivan had recently conquered Kazan and Astrakhan, Turkic Muslim khanates that had controlled the regions around the Volga delta and Caspian Sea. This enabled him to offer European traders unrestricted access to Persia and, by optimistic extension, China, in exchange for closer commercial and military ties. But ongoing hostilities with Poland, Lithuania and Livonia on his western borders made it difficult to establish an overland trade route to Low Country markets. Jenkinson and the English seemed to provide a solution by offering a sea route via the White Sea. Tortuous though it might seem, Jenkinson (now wearing Russian dress) and Ivan agreed to establish a trading route that involved a 1,700-mile sea voyage from London to the White Sea, followed by a 3,000-mile overland route to Persia.

Sailing to Russia and reaching Moscow was the easy part of Jenkinson's expedition when compared with the daunting Persian journey via the Caspian Sea that now faced him. On St. George's Day, April 23, 1558, he left Moscow with just two English companions and a Tatar (Turkic) translator provided by Ivan. He headed southeast to Kazan, where he picked up the Volga River and headed south toward Astrakhan. As he traveled by horse, boat and camel, he was appalled by the devastation, including "famine and plague," that had been wreaked on the local khanates by Ivan's brutal military campaigns. In July he reached the recently conquered city of Astrakhan, less than sixty miles from the Caspian, but was disappointed to find that "there is a certain

41

trade of merchandise there used, but as yet so small and beggarly, that it is not worth the making mention." The following month he became the first Englishman to reach the Caspian Sea, knowing that its southern shores marked the beginning of the Persian Empire.[12] The intrepid Englishman was now beyond Ivan's jurisdiction and faced repeated harassment, theft and extortion as he traveled in caravans, leading a train of camels with his meager merchandise, brokering deals as he went with local Tatar warlords who were at perpetual war with both Russia and Persia. Finally, in late December 1558, just weeks after Mary's death and Queen Elizabeth's accession (both of course unbeknownst to him), Jenkinson reached Bukhara and the relative security of its Muslim Shaybanid ruler, Abdullah Khan II.

Jenkinson was now within touching distance of Persia. But as he began to grasp the region's complex political, commercial and religious tensions, it became clear to him that, at least on this occasion, he could go no farther. The main impediment to his progress was the sectarian divisions between his Muslim hosts. In describing the history of Bukhara, Jenkinson wrote that it "was sometimes subject to the Persians, and [its people] do now speak the Persian tongue, but yet it is a kingdom of itself, and hath most cruel wars continually with the said Persians about their religion, although they be all Mahometists." The Shaybanids were Sunni, while their Persian rivals were Shi'a, a distinction grasped somewhat vaguely by Jenkinson through recourse to pogonology. "One occasion of their wars," he wrote, is "that the Persians will not cut the hair of their upper lips, as the Bogharians [Bukharans] and all other Tartars do, which they account a great sin, and call them *caphars* [from the Arabic *kafir*], that is, unbelievers, as they do the Christians."[13] To a mercer obsessed with sartorial appearance, it was the Sunni injunction to trim the mustache as opposed to the Shi'a practice of letting it grow that commanded Jenkinson's attention, rather than any deeper understanding of their theological difference. Nevertheless, it is the first surviving English eyewitness account of distinctions between the two branches of Islam.

Ultimately Jenkinson was far more concerned by Bukhara's disappointing commercial potential than by the varieties of its faiths (and beards). In peace there had been "great resort of merchants to this city of Boghar [Bukhara], which travel in great caravans from the countries thereabout adjoining, as India, Persia, Russia, with diverse others, and in times past from Cathay, when there was passage." But now in times of "incessant and continual wars," Jenkinson feared that "these merchants are so beggarly and poor . . . that there is no hope of any good trade there to be had worth the following." Even worse, the hot central Asian climate meant its merchants had little interest in the coarse, heavy woolen English cloth offered by Jenkinson. Instead, Indian and Jewish merchants traded in silk and cotton, "but of kerseys [coarse woolen textile] and other cloth, they make little account," and despite his best efforts, "they would not barter for such commodity as cloth."[14]

He considered pushing on to China but seemed to have grasped the unlikelihood of successfully realizing such an arduous and dangerous venture. He noted that the route was treacherous because of the "great wars that had dured three years before my coming hither" between Tatar and Persian warlords, making it "impossible for any caravan to pass unspoilt" to China. Besides, he concluded, "it is nine months' journey." This was a gross exaggeration, but a sign of just how far away Jenkinson certainly felt he was from the legendary "Middle Kingdom."

Even his attempt to reach Persia was beset with difficulties. His local sources told him that Abdullah Khan had left Bukhara to defend it from an imminent siege by the Prince of Samarkand; beyond the city "rovers and thieves" were robbing and murdering merchants en route to Persia; Jenkinson's safe-conduct letters had been confiscated by the Bukharan authorities, and as he had already concluded rather glumly, his heavy English cloth was (once again) "not vendible in Persia."[15] Perhaps the Bukharans had had enough of the tenacious Englishman and wanted to get rid of him; perhaps Jenkinson had little appetite for further danger after nearly two years of constant travel. Whatever the reasons, on March 8, 1559, he left Bukhara and headed home. When he reached the Caspian he "set up the red cross of St. George in our flags, for honor of the Christians which I suppose was never seen in the Caspian Sea before."[16] By September he was in Moscow, where he planned to spend the winter before heading for the White Sea and then on to England.

Upon his arrival in Moscow he wrote to his fellow Muscovy Company agent Henry Lane, who had traveled to Russia on Chancellor's second expedition and was now based in Volgograd in southern Russia. Jenkinson conceded that "although our journey hath been so miserable, dangerous and chargeable with losses, charges and expenses," there was still a profitable "trade of merchandise to be had in such lands." He signed off his letter to Lane, "giving you most hearty thanks for my wench Aura Soltana." When the Elizabethan geographer and travel writer Richard Hakluyt published Jenkinson's letter in the second edition of his *Principal Navigations, Voyages, Traffiques and Discoveries of the English Nation* (1598–1600), he added a marginal note that read, "This was a young Tartar girl which he gave the Queen afterward."[17]

In the midst of his loquacious accounts of heroic derring-do and profit and loss, Jenkinson's casual aside gives a sobering insight into the traffic in men and women as slaves that was also part of his commercial mission and that of most other merchants operating in central Asia at this time. He may have bought the unfortunate "Aura Soltana" in Astrakhan in July 1558, where he noted, "I could have bought many goodly Tartar children, if I would have had a thousand, of their own fathers and mothers, to say, a boy or a wench for a loaf of bread worth six pence in England, but we had more need of victuals at that time than of any such merchandise."[18] Having bought the girl and sent her as "merchandise" to his friend Lane, he seems to have reclaimed her while in Moscow in preparation for bringing her back with him to England as the first recorded Muslim woman to enter the Tudor kingdom and, if Hakluyt is right, presenting her as a gift to Queen Elizabeth.

By the late autumn of 1560, Jenkinson was back in London. He had spent three years away from home, negotiating with some of central Asia's most powerful rulers. The England he had left behind was a Catholic country ruled by Mary and her Spanish consort; what he found on his return was a Protestant nation with a new queen, trying to impose a new religious settlement on a country still deeply divided along religious lines. Whatever he thought of all this he kept to himself as he reported back to the Muscovy Company's directors on the possibility of further trade with Persia. If the English could somehow exploit the Sunni and Shi'a conflict in the region and access commercial traffic through the Persian Gulf, it could be of huge financial benefit to the new Protestant kingdom. Elizabeth came to the throne facing a national debt of nearly £300,000 incurred by her late father's wars with France, poor harvests and a slump in the cloth trade. Her creditors threatened to repossess English assets abroad.[19] Neither the company's directors nor the queen needed much convincing to support an immediate return voyage to Persia via Russia, and by the following spring preparations were advanced for a new expedition by Jenkinson. His aim, this time, was to reach Persia's ruler, Shah Tahmasp.

The Muscovy Company had extracted royal assent from Mary and Philip for its northern ventures but could not encroach upon Spanish imperial dominions in Africa and the Americas. Elizabeth had no such scruples. Supported by her counselors—many of whom had invested heavily in the Muscovy Company and had an interest in its success—Elizabeth wrote letters to both the "Emperor of Russia" and the "Great Sophy of Persia" requesting safe-conduct and trading privileges on Jenkinson's behalf.

Elizabeth's letters drew on a standard template used in such royal correspondence, praising the recipient and requesting safe passage and commercial preferment for Jenkinson through the realm. But the letter to the Persian emperor, the first she ever wrote to a Muslim ruler, required some significant amendments. The queen and her advisers knew little about the religion, politics or even identity of the Safavid Shi'a ruler, Shah Tahmasp. Whatever Jenkinson had conveyed about Safavid rule is scarcely reflected in Elizabeth's letter. It began: "Elizabeth, by the grace of God, Queen of England, &c. To the right mighty and right victorious Prince, the great Sophy, Emperor of the Persians, Medes, Parthians, Hyrcanes, Carmanarians, Margians, of the people on this side, and beyond the river of Tigris, and of all men, and nations, between the Caspian sea, and the gulf of Persia, greeting."[20]

With—unsurprisingly—almost no contemporary understanding of the Safavids and their ruler, Elizabeth's address fell back on classical and biblical assumptions about the region. What she describes is not Shah Tahmasp and his Safavid dominions, but the Achaemenid Empire of Cyrus the Great (reigned 558–529 BC), who was venerated by Christian theologians for conquering Babylon and freeing the Jews in what was regarded as part of the faith's providential history. Unlike the Ottoman Turks, who seemed to have sprung out of nowhere, the Persians could be put within a providential biblical history, which enabled Elizabeth to avoid any mention of the fact that she was seeking a commercial alliance with a Muslim empire.

Despite "the huge distance of lands" between the two countries, Elizabeth promised the shah that Jenkinson's "enterprise is only grounded upon an honest intent to establish trade with your subjects." Taking care to avoid references to explicitly Christian beliefs, she anticipated that if Jenkinson were granted "good passports and safe conducts" through Persia, "the almighty God will bring it to pass, that of these small beginnings, greater moments shall hereafter spring . . . that neither the earth, the seas, nor the heavens, have so much force to separate us, as the godly disposition of natural humanity, and mutual benevolence have to join us together."[21] Written in Hebrew, Latin and Italian, signed and sealed on April 25, 1561, "in our famous city of London," the letter was presented to Jenkinson as he boarded his ship, the *Swallow*, at Gravesend on May 14, laden with "80 fardles [parcels] containing 400 kerseys," as he prepared to sail for Russia.

Jenkinson's second voyage passed without great incident. On this expedition it was politics, not geography, that would present him with his biggest challenge. Upon his arrival in Moscow in August 1561 his attempts to see Ivan were frustrated by an obstructive imperial secretary and the tsar's imminent marriage to Maria Temryukovna, a Circassian princess who was, according to Jenkinson, "of the Mahometicall law." Ever resourceful, Jenkinson used his time in the city to sell most of his woolen cloth, waiting until the following April, when he finally obtained an audience with the tsar. A clearly relieved and delighted Jenkinson wrote that Ivan showed him special favor and "committed matter of importance & charge unto me, to be done when I should arrive in those countries whither I intended to go."[22] Jenkinson had been appointed the Muscovy Company's factor, Queen Elizabeth's de facto ambassador, and was now tasked with acting as Ivan's representative once he reached Persia. After yet more delay, he finally left Moscow on April 27 and headed for the Volga in the company of a Persian ambassador, with whom he "had great friendship and conference all the way."[23]

Over the next few months Jenkinson retraced the route of his first journey, traveling through Astrakhan to the Caspian Sea. As he moved on southeast and passed into Safavid territory, he seemed to travel back in time, describing regions through events and individuals from the classical past. In August 1562 he reached the Caspian town of Derbent at the foot of the Caucasus Mountains. His only point of reference was to identify it as part of the ancient Persian province of Hyrcania and admire the ancient wall that Muslims and Christians believed Alexander the Great had built to keep out the monstrous races of Gog and Magog. Just weeks later he arrived at Shirvan and met its Shi'a *begler-beg* (governor), Abdullah-Khan Ustajlu, Shah Tahmasp's cousin and one of his closest advisers, whom Jenkinson called "Obdolowcan." Yet again the Englishman appears to have made a good impression on his Muslim host, who provided lavish entertainment, including feasting and hawking. And as usual Jenkinson assiduously itemized every opulent fabric and object he saw, including the golden silken garments "of that country fashion" which he wore for the rest of his time in Persia.

When Abdullah-Khan asked "whether we of England had friendship with the Turks or not," Jenkinson's response was consummate. "I answered that we never had friendship with them, and that therefore they would not suffer us to pass through their country into the Sophy his dominions, and that there is a nation named Venetians, not far distant from us, which are in great league with the said Turks." Those awful Venetians had made a friend of the shah's sworn enemies, the Ottomans, and were responsible for blocking the honest English from reaching their obvious allies, the Safavids. When combined with Jenkinson's charm and plausibility, there was just enough truth in such claims given that the Venetians had a history of allying themselves strategically with the Ottomans, from just after the fall of Constantinople in 1453 to the renewal of trading privileges following the Ottoman conquest of Egypt in 1517. Abdullah-Khan was persuaded that the Englishman not only was to be trusted but could even be an asset to his cousin. When he pressed Jenkinson further, "touching religion, and also the state of our countries" and "whether the emperor of Almaine [Germany] or the great Turk were of most power," Jenkinson nimbly "answered as I thought most meet," probably evading the (rather tricky) questions and turning discussion toward the prospect of meeting the Sophy "to entreat friendship and free passage."[24]

Having secured the governor's "great favor" and being supplied with letters of safe-conduct, camels and horses, Jenkinson went on his way. On October 16, he reached Ardabil, another historically charged place where past and present collided, "wherein the princes of Persia are commonly buried, and there Alexander the Great did keep his court when he invaded the Persians." It was here that Jenkinson observed that the "late prince [Shah] Ismail lieth buried in a fair *Meskit* [mosque] with a sumptuous sepulcher," although he does not say if he managed to enter the mosque and see the shah's tomb.[25] Jenkinson was now at the very center of the ancient biblical (and Qur'anic) world, the holiest site of Safavid Shi'a belief. He was close to his ultimate goal of reaching the shah's court. Finally, on November 2, 1562, he arrived at Shah Tahmasp's imperial capital of Qazvin, ninety miles northwest of modern Tehran.

The shah that Jenkinson was about to meet was very different from his fanatical, charismatic father. Born just six months before Ismail's catastrophic defeat by the Ottomans at the Battle of Chaldiran, Tahmasp grew up in the shadow of a ruler whose followers believed he was the messiah, but who died a broken man when Tahmasp was just ten. During Tahmasp's turbulent minority he faced civil wars among his followers, as well as constant threats from the Ottomans to the west and the Uzbeks to the east. In the pursuit of more conciliatory and pious foreign and domestic policies, he signed the Peace of Amasya with the Ottomans (1555), followed by an Edict of Sincere Repentance (1556), which attempted to formalize Shi'a laws by banning painting, wine and many Sufi rituals that had been central to Safavid belief. In direct contrast to his father's fervent millenarianism, Tahmasp regarded himself as a pious king trying to consolidate his empire's political and religious boundaries, rather than expand them.[26] As Jenkinson arrived in Qazvin, the shah had recently completed an ambitious program of public works designed to transform it from a Sunni city into the center of Shi'ite political and religious power. Royal baths, cisterns and bazaars were built, as well as an entirely new royal garden complex to the north of the city, known as Sa'ādatābād, with palaces, promenades, canals and parade grounds for practicing polo and archery.[27]

When Jenkinson was finally granted an audience with the shah in his new palace on the afternoon of November 20, 1562, he was clearly unimpressed. Gone were his usual observations of sartorial elegance and domestic opulence. Instead he immediately pronounced the Safavid ruler—whom he called "Shaw Thomas"—as "nothing valiant," so that "through his pusillanimity the Turk hath much invaded his countries." What really fascinated him was the shah's Shi'a religion. "He professeth a kind of holiness," he wrote, "and saith that he is descended of the blood of *Mahomet* and *Murtezallie*," Murtezallie being Muhammad's cousin 'Ali ibn Abi Talib. He went on: "although these Persians be Mahometans, as the Turks and the Tartars be, yet honor they this false fained *Murtezallie*, saying that he was the chiefest disciple that Mahomet had, cursing and chiding daily three other disciples that Mahomet had called *Omar, Usiran* and *Abebecke*," Jenkinson's rather approximate transliterations of the names of the first three caliphs—Umar, Uthman and Abu Bakr. While confusing his early Islamic history in claiming that "these three did slay the said *Murtezallie*," Jenkinson grasped that it was this struggle between the Shi'a and Sunni branches of Islam, "and other differences of holy men and laws, [that] they have had and have with the Turks and Tartars mortal wars." This was apparently as far as Jenkinson could delve into the complex distinctions between Sunni and Shi'a theology. He concluded that to "entreat of their religion at large, being more or less Mahomet's law and the Alkoran, I shall not need at present."[28]

After charming Sultan Süleyman and Tsar Ivan, and spending nearly five years (on and off) in trying to reach the Persian Sophy, Jenkinson saw his luck with eastern potentates finally run out. Even his eloquence could not prevent the audience with Shah Tahmasp from turning sour. Upon entering the shah's presence, Jenkinson was given shoes so "I might not be suffered to tread upon his holy ground—being a Christian, and called among them *Gower* [from the Persian *gaur,* or non-Muslims], that is, unbeliever and unclean: esteeming all to be infidels and pagans which do not believe as they do, in their false filthy prophets *Mahomet* and *Murtezallie.*" Jenkinson presented the shah with Elizabeth's letter and spoke of his hope of "friendship, and free passage of our merchants and people, to repair and traffic within his dominions, for to bring in our commodities, and to carry away theirs, to the honor of both princes." The shah was having none of it. He demanded to know why Elizabeth's letter was written in Latin, Hebrew and Italian, when he claimed to "have none within our realm that understand those tongues." He also "demanded of me what country of Franks [Christian Europeans] I was, and what affairs I had there to do." The interview was going from bad to worse: nobody at the shah's court knew anything about this tiny place called England, its female ruler or its "famous city" of London. As with Abdullah-Khan, what interested Shah Tahmasp far more than insignificant England was "King Philip, and the great Turk, and which of them was of most power." Jenkinson judged that this was not the time to criticize the Ottomans, as he had in response to Abdullah-Khan's questions, answering the shah "to his contentation, not dispraising the great Turk." But then the shah's interrogation of Jenkinson took a dramatic turn:

> Then he reasoned with me much of religion, demanding whether I were a *Gower,* that is to say, an unbeliever, or a *Muselman,* that is, of Mahomet's law. Unto whom I answered, that I was neither unbeliever nor Mahometan, but a Christian. What is that said he unto the king of Georgia's son [the Muslim convert David XI of Kartli], who being a Christian was fled unto the said Sophie, and he answered that a Christian was he that believeth in *Jesus Christus,* affirming him to be the son of God, and the greatest prophet: doest thou believe so said the Sophie unto me: yea that I do said I: Oh thou unbeliever said he, we have no need to have friendship

with the unbelievers, and so willed me to depart. I being glad thereof did reverence and went my way.[29]

Thousands of miles from home, the plucky young mercer from Leicestershire stood his ground in front of two Muslim rulers—one the Shi'a shah Tahmasp, the other the Georgian king David XI, a convert from eastern Orthodox Christianity—and affirmed his belief in Christ as the son of God. It must have been a terrifying moment, and one that Jenkinson surely realized placed him in mortal danger. As he made his exit, he was followed by "a man with a basanet of sand, sifting all the way that I had gone within the said palace, even from the said Sophie's sight unto the court gate," in a symbolic erasing of the polluting presence of the unbeliever. Jenkinson must have imagined that his audience with Shah Tahmasp would have the triumphant culmination of a trading alliance between the two countries. Instead he found himself effectively banished from the shah's court, his life possibly in the balance, the Persian adventure wrecked as a result of insuperable religious differences. But he quickly learned that theology was not the sole cause of his expulsion.

Only four days before Jenkinson reached Qazvin, a Turkish ambassador had arrived "to conclude a perpetual peace betwixt the same great Turk and the Sophy." Nine years earlier, in November 1553, Jenkinson had watched as Sultan Süleyman marched into Aleppo en route to Persia just weeks after strangling his son Mustafa. The consequences of that murderous decision would eventually scupper Jenkinson's negotiations with Shah Tahmasp. Mustafa's death left Süleyman's sons Selim and Bayezid to fight over the right to succeed their father. The inevitable factionalism and intrigue culminated in Bayezid rebelling against his brother and father. Having been defeated by them at the Battle of Konya in May 1559, Bayezid fled and sought asylum at Shah Tahmasp's court in Qazvin. The shah was initially delighted to shelter such a prestigious rebel from his great enemy and used Bayezid as leverage in negotiating a favorable renewal of the peace treaty of Amasya. In return, Süleyman and Selim demanded Bayezid's rendition. Finally, in 1561 Shah Tahmasp agreed, and an Ottoman delegation was sent to

Qazvin. Bayezid and his four sons were handed over and summarily garroted the moment they left the city in July 1562.[30] An appalled Jenkinson reported that with Bayezid "being slain according to the Turk's will, the Sophy sent him his head for a present, not a little desired, and acceptable to the unnatural father." It would be inaccurate to say that the shah had ordered Bayezid's execution, but he certainly displayed murderous duplicity in sanctioning yet another act of political filicide.

As Jenkinson later discovered, the Ottoman ambassador who was in Qazvin to ratify the revised peace treaty with the shah had consulted resident Turkish merchants, who agreed that Jenkinson was bad for business, because his "coming thither (naming me by the name of Frank) would in great part destroy their trade." Sure enough, Jenkinson learned that the shah had been persuaded "not [to] entertain me well, neither dismiss me with letters or gifts, considering I was a Frank, and of that nation that was enemy to the great Turk his brother." If the shah persisted in pursuing an alliance with the Englishman and it came "to the knowledge of the Turk, it should be a means to break their new league and friendship." He was further dissuaded "because he had no need, neither that it was requisite for him to have friendship with unbelievers, whose countries lay far from him, and that it was best for him to send me with my letters unto the said great Turk for a present."[31] Having extracted trading privileges from Süleyman in Aleppo, Jenkinson now faced another possible audience with him, but this time as a gift from a rival Muslim ruler. Worse, it was quite possible that he might arrive in Constantinople dead, like Bayezid, rather than alive.

Fortunately, Jenkinson was saved by the intervention of Abdullah-Khan and his son, Shah Ali Murza, who persuaded the shah that "if he used me evil, there would few strangers resort into his country," which would adversely affect trade. With the Ottoman delegation gone, Shah Tahmasp agreed, and on March 20, 1563, "he sent me a rich garment of cloth of gold, and so dismissed me without any harm." Jenkinson immediately headed back to Shirvan and the relative safety of Abdullah-Khan's court. The governor explained that had it not been for Ali Murza's intervention on Jenkinson's behalf, he would have "been utterly cast away and sent to the great Turk." He also claimed that Shah Tahmasp would have granted him trading concessions "had not the peace and league fortuned to have been concluded between them and the great Turk."[32] For once in his short but charmed career, Jenkinson had been the victim of monumentally bad timing.

Extracting trading privileges from the ever hospitable Abdullah-Khan was better than nothing, and in May Jenkinson cut his losses and set off on the long journey back to Moscow. He arrived there in August 1563, presenting Ivan with a cache of silk and jewels, as well as "the apparel given unto me by the Sophy." In return he received enhanced trading privileges from the tsar. He wintered in Moscow before heading north to the White Sea, which he reached in July 1564. Embarking for England, Jenkinson faced what he described almost casually as "great and extreme dangers of loss of ship, goods and life" before finally arriving back in London on September 28, 1564, almost three and a half years after he had left.[33]

Over ten remarkable years, Jenkinson had traveled farther and achieved more than any other Tudor adventurer. He had met three of Asia's most powerful and terrifying rulers, survived to tell the tale, opened up trade with Russia and Persia and gained unprecedented insights into the region's Sunni-Shi'a conflict. Eventually, the commercial alliance he had cultivated with the Ottomans in the early 1550s carried no weight in his attempts to establish trade with Persia a decade later, as he stepped into a world of religious and ethnic complexity that he barely understood, and which nearly cost him his life. He probably owed his survival to Süleyman's and Tahmasp's utter indifference to Elizabethan England. They did not seem to know even where it was, dismissing it (if they ever thought about it at all) as a peripheral player on the world stage.

Over the next two decades, five more expeditions followed. In the late 1560s Jenkinson's immediate successor, Arthur Edwards, spent far longer at the Safavid court than he had, obtaining the prized trading privileges that had eluded his predecessor. Shares in the Muscovy Company, which had originally cost £25, now cost £200, but the trade failed to yield a consistent profit. The journey was too far, the returns too meager and the local conditions too volatile, with repeated skirmishes among Turks, Persians and Tatars leading to the kidnap, ransom, robbery and even murder of successive unfortunate English merchants working in the region.[34]

Jenkinson returned to Russia twice, in 1566 and for the last time in 1571. On both occasions his tact and skill were required to restore amicable trade agreements with Ivan, who took the opportunity of seeing his old friend again to propose a most unlikely marriage with Queen Elizabeth. The queen's court retained one further tangible legacy of Jenkinson's Persian adventure. Records from 1564 detailing Elizabeth's domestic servants describe "our dear and well beloved woman Ippolyta the Tartarian," who wore dresses made of Granadan silk and introduced the queen to the fashion of wearing Spanish leather shoes. Ippolyta is presumably "Aura Soltana," the "young Tartar girl" presented to Elizabeth by Jenkinson in 1560.[35] In the late 1570s Jenkinson returned to England, never to leave again, content to pursue his interests in commerce and property in Northamptonshire, where he died a very wealthy man in 1610.

Over three extraordinary decades, Anthony Jenkinson had met an Ottoman sultan, been sent out to travel to China, settled for Russia where he befriended a tsar, and ended up at the court of the Shah of Persia. Such was the nature of sixteenth-century travel and discovery. Jenkinson's success justified the connection of Russia with Persia in the minds of London's political and commercial elite and paved the way for further and even closer alliances with Muslims over the next four decades. Thanks to Jenkinson, the Islamic world had come just a little closer to England. In 1586 the poet William Warner issued a new edition of his celebrated history *Albion's England*, in which Jenkinson was extolled as one of England's greatest explorers, responsible for transforming the country's place in the world under Elizabeth's rule and within Warner's lifetime:

> But where shall we begin his laudes to tell,
> In Europe, Asia, Affrick? For these all he saw, in all
> Employed for England's common good: nor my rejoicing small,

That from Elizabeth to reign, and I to live begun,
Hath happened that commerce and fame he to his natives won.[36]

Such high praise might have endured, but even as these verses were being written, England's Persian trade was already a thing of the rapidly receding past, and with it Jenkinson's fame. Elizabeth and her merchants were looking closer to home for profitable alliances beyond Catholic Europe. The moment had come to turn their attention south. It was time to do business with the Moors from Barbary.

3

The Battle for Barbary

In the second edition of his *Principal Navigations,* Richard Hakluyt claimed that England's "first voyage for traffic into the kingdom of Morocco in Barbary" took place as early as 1551.[1] "Barbary" entered the English language from the amalgamation of Greek and Latin for "land of barbarians" and the Arabic word "Berber." The Elizabethans' vague geography understood Barbary as either the Moroccan kingdom or more usually the entire North African coast as far south as Guinea. What English merchants based in Spain knew was that shipping merchandise directly by sea down the Atlantic coastline, from one port (like Bristol) to another (usually Agadir) in relatively clement conditions at a distance of around eighteen hundred miles, was relatively easy.

From the late fifteenth century the Berber Wattasid dynasty ruled most of northern Morocco, but it was unable to oppose Portuguese incursions into its coastal regions. In the early sixteenth century a new dynasty emerged to the south. The Sa'adians, of Arab descent, claimed Marrakesh as their capital, defeating the Portuguese at Agadir in 1537 and finally overthrowing the Wattasids in 1554.

In 1551, as Wattasid control began to collapse, a group of English merchants financed Thomas Wyndham to sail to Morocco's southern ports, trading English linen, wool and "diverse other things well accepted by the Moors" in exchange for almonds, dates and the Moroccan sugar that would play such havoc with Elizabeth's teeth.[2] Most of Wyndham's backers regarded Barbary as a natural extension of their established business in Spain, though many also wanted to explore more distant eastern markets (four supporters of Wyndham's voyage soon became charter members of the Muscovy Company).

Not everyone was impressed by England's arrival. "The Portuguese were much offended with this our new trade into Barbary," admitted one English trader in 1552. The Portuguese still held Tangier, Mazagan near Casablanca, and El Mina in modern-day Ghana. Their claims to a trading monopoly on the three thousand miles of coastline in between seemed unrealistic, but this did not stop them from protesting at the English encroachment. The Spanish were also alarmed, their diplomats reporting that the first ships were loaded not just with linen and wool but also "pikes and armor," and that a subsequent expedition was "laden with all sorts of munitions of war."[3] The Protestant Edward VI and his regents were predictably uninterested in allaying Portuguese and Spanish anxieties that English weapons were arming their Moroccan adversaries, but with the marriage of Mary and Philip in 1554, the English crown agreed to Portuguese demands for a cessation of trade.

Elizabeth had few such qualms about trading with Morocco, and in 1559 her first Parliament drew up a series of economic reforms bracing the country for imminent international isolation by restricting imports, but encouraging overseas exports and a stronger navy based on "new navigations" into regions including "those to Guinea, to Barbary, to Muscovy." Within a decade England was importing 250 tons of Moroccan sugar each year, valued at £18,000, with imports overall worth over £28,000, nearly 25 percent more than the entire revenue for trade with Portugal.[4]

In 1562, as Portuguese warships and English merchant fleets began clashing off the African coast, the Portuguese ambassador protested to Elizabeth that her merchants were once again selling arms enabling the Moroccans to wage war on Portugal. Elizabeth replied airily in a memorandum drafted by William Cecil, Lord Burghley, her secretary of state, that "the more Christian people that shall resort to the Gentiles and Saracens, the more shall the faith increase," and that she "cannot allow that more regard should be had to the enriching of any particular person by monopolies and private navigations than to the public utility of the whole body of Christendom."[5] It was a wonderfully disingenuous answer, especially as it came precisely at the moment when Moroccan forces were besieging the Portuguese in Mazagan. Apart from Elizabeth's studiedly obtuse comment, the English hardly ever mentioned religion directly when pressed on their commercial incursion into Morocco. It was a sign of the trade's profitability—and Elizabeth's growing confidence—that when pressed by the Portuguese to ban it in 1571, she refused on the grounds that Morocco was not a Portuguese possession, and was therefore free to trade with whomever it wished.

There was good reason for Elizabeth to resist such political pressure. The Moroccan trade was becoming very profitable, and it involved over thirty of London's most powerful merchants, some acting alone, others in partnerships. In nearly every case, regardless of the commodities involved, the trade was conducted almost exclusively through Jewish intermediaries upon whom the new Sa'adian dynasty came to rely for everything from ransoming Christian captives to running the country's lucrative sugar farms. One of the most powerful of all the Jewish sugar barons in Morocco was Isaac Cabeça. Isaac and his brother Abraham came from a Sephardic family who had fled forced conversion in Spain for Morocco, where they reverted to Judaism and flourished under their Muslim patrons, first as translators and interpreters, then as merchants and bankers. By the late 1560s Isaac was selling sugar and buying cloth from a consortium of six English merchants led by Sir William Garrard. One of London's most influential cloth merchants, Garrard had been trading in Morocco since 1552, as well as supporting slaving voyages to west Africa and Richard Chancellor's ill-fated Russian voyage, which led to his appointment as one of the Muscovy Company's founding consuls.[6]

In 1568 Cabeça was pronounced bankrupt and was imprisoned by Sultan Abdullah al-Ghalib for unpaid rents of 50,000 ounces of silver owed on three royal sugar farms. Garrard's consortium was appalled: Cabeça owed them more than £1,000 for cloth bought on credit, a standard practice whereby payment—often with interest—was settled in either bills of exchange or sugar. As he had neither, the English merchants' factors struck a bargain with the insolvent Cabeça that "if he would promise unto them to discharge the old debt" of £1,000 and supplied the consortium with £16,000 of sugar, they would intercede on his behalf with the sultan.[7] They employed "a certain Moor being chief there about" called Tangarffe to petition Abdullah al-Ghalib to release Cabeça. But first Tangarffe insisted that the English factors had to "promise to become bound to him" for whatever costs he incurred in settling Cabeça's debts. Two of the English factors agreed, and Cabeça was released, but in the convoluted chains of debts and credits binding Christians, Jews and Muslims together, it became so difficult to establish who owed what that the English merchants began suing one another first in the High Court of Admiralty and then in Chancery in a series of tortuous and inconclusive cases that dragged on throughout the 1570s. It is symptomatic of these exchanges that in the depositions undertaken in his absence Cabeça was only ever referred to as "a famous and jolly merchant," whose religion was largely irrelevant to the financial machinations that threatened to engulf him.[8]

While English merchants traded with Muslims and Jews in Morocco, events thousands of miles away in London and Rome were about to transform England's position within Europe, and with it the country's relations with the Islamic world. In the early hours of May 24, 1570, John Felton, a well-known Catholic sympathizer living in Bermondsey, just south of the Thames, crossed London Bridge and nailed a printed document to the door of the Bishop of London's palace near St. Paul's Cathedral. It was a copy of a papal bull issued in Rome on February 25 by Pope Pius V, entitled *Regnans in Excelsis* ("Reigning on High"), declaring the excommunication of Elizabeth I.[9] The bull (so called after its lead seal, or *bulla*), named after its opening words, condemned "Elizabeth, the pretended Queen of England" for "having seized on the kingdom and monstrously usurped the place of Supreme Head of the Church in all England," reducing "the said kingdom into a miserable and ruinous condition, which was so lately reclaimed to the Catholic faith" under Mary and Philip. It cataloged a litany of perceived sins, based on Elizabeth's legislation of the late 1550s, including the abolition of "Catholic rites and ceremonies," the introduction of prayer books "to be read through the whole realm containing manifest heresy," and other "impious rites and institutions, by herself entertained and observed according to the prescript of Calvin." It concluded: "We do out of the fullness of our Apostolic power declare the aforesaid Elizabeth as being a heretic and a favourer of heretics, and her adherents in the matters aforesaid, to have incurred the sentence of excommunication, and to be cut off from the unity of the Body of Christ. And moreover We do declare her to be deprived of her pretended title to the kingdom aforesaid." The bull issued one last particularly divisive edict: "We do command and charge all and every noblemen, subjects, people, and others aforesaid that they presume not to obey her or her orders, mandates, and laws."[10]

For England's Catholics, the bull created a terrible dilemma, compelling them to choose between religion and country. For Felton, it proved fatal in the most gruesome manner. Within days of posting the bull he was arrested and imprisoned in Newgate, where he declared that Elizabeth "ought not to be the queen of England." Such treasonous statements landed him in the Tower of London, where he was put on the rack and became the first Englishman to be tortured by the state for his Catholic beliefs. He was found guilty of treason and sentenced to be hanged, drawn and quartered at the scene of his crime, in St. Paul's churchyard. On August 8 he addressed a hostile crowd and a hangman named Bull (a joke not lost on many Protestant observers), insisting that he had done nothing wrong other than promote a solemn papal edict. Refusing the ministrations of attendant Protestant clergy, Felton was hanged, cut down before losing consciousness, and then disemboweled; as the hangman pulled out his still beating heart he is said to have cried out "once or twice, 'Jesus,'" before he finally expired.[11]

There are several reasons it took the pope more than a decade to excommunicate Elizabeth. For starters her brother-in-law and former suitor King Philip II of Spain believed he knew England better than most, and he vetoed repeated attempts at excommunication, anxious to avoid pushing Elizabeth into the arms of the Calvinists in the Low Countries who were already causing him difficulties. So long as Elizabeth avoided persecuting English Catholics, Spain was reluctant to intervene. However, after the introduction of the Oath of Supremacy in 1559, which required public officials to swear allegiance to the queen as supreme governor of the Church of England, the country's religious reformers began to formulate a series of political and theological attacks on Catholicism. Defending the oath in 1566, Robert Horne, Bishop of Winchester, wrote that "the Pope is a more perilous enemy unto Christ, than the Turk: and Popery more idolatrous, than Turkery."[12]

As the religious rhetoric escalated and Europe started to divide along sectarian lines, Elizabeth found it increasingly difficult to remain neutral. In 1562 she began providing military support to the French Protestant Huguenots, and, though this venture failed, by 1566 she was also funding Calvinist rebels fighting Spanish rule in the Low Countries. Both policies soon ran into trouble. By the late 1560s the Catholic Guise faction in France appeared to be gaining the upper hand over the Huguenots. The Spanish finally lost patience with English privateers raiding Spain's American fleet and with Elizabeth's support for the Dutch Calvinist rebels, and in 1568 they impounded English goods in the economically vital port of Antwerp. That same year, Elizabeth's first cousin Mary Stuart, "Queen of Scots," fled the civil wars engulfing Scotland and sought refuge in England, where she became the focus of English Catholic hopes as a potential successor to Elizabeth. Within a year she was the catalyst for the Northern Rebellion, an uprising led by the powerful Catholic earls of Westmorland and Northumberland, who vowed to depose Elizabeth and enthrone Mary. Although the uprising was crushed, it finally galvanized Pius V to move against Elizabeth.

The pope's decision backfired almost immediately. He had neglected to consult an infuriated Philip, the only ruler with sufficient military might to enforce the bull's demand for Elizabeth's deposition. In England, the bull divided Catholics while strengthening patriotic support for Elizabeth and pushed her toward more aggressive Protestant policies at home and abroad. English suspicions of an international Catholic conspiracy seemed to be confirmed when the House of Guise carried out the infamous St. Bartholomew's Day Massacre on August 24, 1572, slaughtering more than three thousand Huguenots on the streets of Paris and thousands more in the rest of France. The news sent shock waves through Europe: Elizabeth's court went into mourning and condemned the "cruel murderers of such innocents." Rome openly re-joiced, and the usually phlegmatic Philip II announced that the massacre "was one of the greatest joys of my life."[13]

Emboldened by these developments and encouraged by the initial forays of London's merchant community into Russia, Persia and Morocco, Elizabeth and her advisers decided to extend their search for alliances beyond Europe. Ever since the eleventh century, unscrupulous Christian merchants had traded with the "Saracens," leading the Fourth Lateran Council in 1215 to threaten with excommunication "all those faithless and impious Christians, who against Christ Himself and the Christian people provide the Saracens with weapons, iron and wood."[14] This prohibition, reinforced in councils over the subsequent centuries, was quietly ignored by many Christian states and their merchants operating in the eastern Mediterranean. The Venetians continued to trade with the Ottomans before and after the fall of Constantinople in 1453, and France had proposed commercial agreements with the Ottomans granting its merchants trading privileges as early as 1535. These were known as the "Capitulations" (from the Latin for "chapter" or "paragraph," to describe an agreement with specified terms; the word developed its modern sense of "surrender" only in the seventeenth century). The treaties gave the French a significant advantage in the Levantine trade and cemented a more formal military and naval alliance with Sultan Süleyman, designed to check Habsburg imperial expansion.[15] England was generally too small and too far away to matter very much when it came to such edicts, but now, as a Protestant nation led by an excommunicated sovereign placed beyond papal sanction and with some experience of trade with Morocco, England and its merchants were suddenly freer than any other Christian country to trade with the Islamic world.

The dawning realization that England could pursue more significant commercial alliances with Muslim rulers was a circumstantial response to excommunication, exacerbated by the wider conflicts of the time. In September 1566, just months after the accession of the ultraorthodox crusading pope Pius V, Süleyman the Magnificent died, ending a forty-six-year reign of relentless Ottoman territorial expansion. His successor, Selim II, immediately set out to prove himself by turning away from renewed Ottoman conflict with Persia, choosing instead to confront Christianity in the Mediterranean. With an aggressive pope in Rome and a bellicose sultan in Constantinople, the naturally cautious Philip II was beset with challenges to his rule from all sides. In 1568, already struggling with a Calvinist Dutch revolt, he faced yet another challenge from the Morisco community in Granada. The Moriscos, or "New Christians," were Spanish-born Muslims forced to convert to Christianity after the *reconquista* (reconquest) of Iberia from Islam and the mass expulsions by the Catholic rulers of Castile in 1492. Angry at Philip's increasingly intemperate policy toward them, they offered to acknowledge Ottoman sovereignty if Selim provided them with military aid. An exasperated Philip regarded the Moriscos as akin to a fifth column aiding the Ottoman imperialists and the Protestant cause in northern Europe.[16] As prayers were offered in Constantinople's mosques supporting the Moriscos, the sultan began dispatching soldiers and weapons to Granada.

Like Elizabeth, Selim had designs on the Moroccan sultanate, although his interests were more territorial than commercial. From the time of his accession Selim tried to destabilize the Sa'adian dynasty, which had managed to retain its autonomy by playing the Spanish off against the Ottomans. Selim exploited the divisions between the kingdom's ruler, Abdullah al-Ghalib, and his younger brothers, Abd al-Malik and Ahmad al-Mansur, offering al-Malik and al-Mansur refuge in Algeria and Constantinople, where they made preparations to retake Morocco from their elder brother. Selim then turned his attention to Tunis. The city's fall to the Habsburgs in 1535 had always rankled his father, Süleyman, and in late 1569 Ottoman forces took the city back from its Spanish-backed Hafsid rulers. Selim was now in charge of the North African coast as far as Morocco and was poised to push into southern Spain should the Morisco uprising prove successful.

Having taken control of the southwestern side of the Mediterranean, Selim now looked east and planned an invasion of Cyprus, knowing that this would almost certainly result in war with the island's Venetian rulers. Legend has it that the decadent sultan wanted the island for the quality of its wine (questionable on many levels). Cooler heads among Selim's administrators knew that whoever held Tunis and Cyprus controlled the flow of trade across the Mediterranean basin, the geographical flash point for what one historian of the region has called the "forgotten frontier" between Latin Christian and Turkish Muslim communities in the sixteenth century.[17] In 1569, as Selim made preparations for the Cyprus campaign, he ratified the Franco-Ottoman Capitulations of the 1530s in a deft move aimed at ensuring French neutrality in any conflict that might unite Venice, the Papal States and possibly even Spain against him.

Ottoman designs on Cyprus inevitably led to a declaration of war against Venice in the summer of 1570, and in July a Turkish army of more than 60,000 invaded the island. Over the next sixteen months a brutal campaign was waged between Cyprus's Venetian defenders and the vastly superior Ottoman forces. In May 1571, as the Turkish army besieged the last stronghold of Famagusta, Pope Pius and the Venetian authorities finally agreed on a fragile Holy League, which also included Spain, the Knights of Malta (fêted since throwing off the Ottoman siege of their island headquarters in 1565) and most of the Italian city-states. The league hastily assembled a Christian fleet of more than 200 ships led by Philip II's half brother Don John of Austria, which set sail for Cyprus that August. It came too late for the defenders of Famagusta, who surrendered just after the fleet started out. When Don John learned of this, he headed for Lepanto near Patras in the Greek Peloponnese, where the Ottoman fleet of 300 ships lay at anchor. On the morning of October 7, 1571, the two sides engaged each other in what would come to be regarded as the greatest naval battle of the century. By 4:00 p.m. the Ottomans had been outgunned and defeated by the Holy League, losing around 210 of their ships and an estimated 15,000 soldiers and sailors.[18]

For a brief moment, Christendom forgot its divisions and united in celebration of its first victory in nearly a century over the seemingly invincible Turks. Across Europe the news was greeted with an extraordinary outpouring of delight and relief. Festivities, processions and church masses all celebrated the event as divine intervention just at the moment when Islam seemed poised to overwhelm Christianity.

Pamphlets, paintings and poems were published celebrating what the Venetian Pietro Buccio described as a "marvelous and glorious Christian victory against the infidels."[19]

When the news reached London, it sparked public celebrations there too, despite Elizabeth's recent excommunication. Sermons in St. Paul's thanked God for the victory, and the English chronicler Raphael Holinshed wrote that "there were bonfires made through the city, with banqueting and great rejoicing, as good cause there was, for a victory of so great importance unto the whole state of the Christian commonwealth." As far as Holinshed was concerned, the Ottomans were "that common enemy of us all, who regardeth neither Protestant nor Catholic."[20] Although this showed a limited understanding of Ottoman realpolitik—which had a very clear grasp of Protestant and Catholic divisions and how to exploit them—Holinshed's observation caught the popular mood. This was a moment, he intimated, when religious divisions could be set aside to unite Christianity against its biggest foe.

The victory at Lepanto would prove hollow within only a few years, and sympathy between England and the rest of Christendom evaporated almost immediately. Philip II and Pius V were now in a league that threatened to rid Europe of its Protestant "heresy," and both Elizabeth's allies and her adversaries knew it. One of England's spies in the Low Countries responded to the victory at Lepanto by reporting that Spain's "next enterprise shall be to subdue the English Turks,"[21] while another English spy, William Herle, wrote from the Low Countries in June 1573 that Philip II hated the English Protestants "with an immortal hatred never to be reconciled, esteeming them worse than either Turks, Marranos, Jews, or Infidels, the blasphemers of God's holy name and of his son Jesus Christ."[22]

Elizabeth turned to her most trusted counselors—William Cecil, Lord Burghley and Francis Walsingham, her ambassador to France and ruthless spymaster—who advised her to consider cultivating alliances at both ends of the Mediterranean, with Portugal and the Ottomans. The Portuguese might prove difficult, considering the recent rifts over Morocco, but there was at least a diplomatic presence in both countries that might allow some compromise to be reached. The Ottomans were a different case altogether. The 1570s represented the apogee of Ottoman imperial power and territorial reach—though Elizabeth and her counselors, from their limited perspective in London, could not have known it. To them the Ottomans seemed to be winning. Anyone who was able to take on the papacy and the Spanish was to be welcomed, whatever his religious persuasion. But at such a distance from London and with no resident English ambassador or merchants, any attempt to negotiate with the sultan would prove extremely difficult, even dangerous. So the proposal for an Ottoman initiative was quietly shelved and Burghley opened negotiations with Portugal, agreeing to sacrifice English commercial interest in Guinea to retain a foothold in Morocco. By 1576 an Anglo-Portuguese treaty had resolved most of the outstanding commercial disputes, but it failed even to mention Morocco, leaving the English free by omission to continue trading there with impunity.[23]

Even before the agreement was signed, English merchants were exploiting instability within the Sa'adian dynasty to pursue increasingly formal arms deals with the crown's tacit support. One of the key figures in the trade was Edmund Hogan, a member of the Mercers' Company from Hackney, who had commercial interests in Germany and Spain and was widely admired as one of "the wisest and best merchants in London."[24] In 1572 Hogan had sent a man named John Williams to Morocco to check reports of an abundance of high-quality potassium nitrate, or saltpeter, a key ingredient in making gunpowder, which was extremely scarce in western Europe and was imported at great expense from Persia and India. Attempts by the English to make saltpeter artificially were difficult, messy (involving urine and animal excrement) and low-yielding. As a result there was much excitement when Williams returned with Moroccan saltpeter, which he told Hogan was "far better than he could provide in any other place where he had traveled." The only problem was the new sultan, Abu Abdallah Muhammad II, Al-Mutawakkil, who had succeeded his father in 1574 after a brief power struggle with his uncle Abd al-Malik. Faced with al-Malik's continued opposition, Abdallah Muhammad was not interested in trading saltpeter for English cloth: he told Williams that "if we would take upon us to bring him bullets of iron for his great ordnance, we should have saltpeter." The sultan's counselors advised him against the trade, arguing that "although his law was to the contrary . . . no saltpeter should pass to the Christians, considering the commodity of pellets [iron shot or cannon balls] was as needful for him as saltpeter to the Christians."[25]

In 1575 Williams returned to England with saltpeter samples and took them to Killingworth Castle to show Burghley and Robert Dudley, 1st Earl of Leicester, who was entertaining the queen on one of her royal progresses. Both men were impressed with the quality and approved the export of shot, cannon balls and other munitions. But the order came too late for Abdallah Muhammad. As the arms arrived (and just as Burghley was concluding the Anglo-Portuguese treaty), Abd al-Malik marched into Morocco from Algeria at the head of an Ottoman army, defeating Abdallah Muhammad outside his capital city of Fez and proclaiming himself the fourth Sa'adian sultan of Morocco. Abdallah fled to Ceuta, where he sought the somewhat unlikely protection of his great adversary, the young Portuguese king Sebastian I.

Having spent many years at the Ottoman court, al-Malik was more urbane and cosmopolitan than his predecessor, and he was eager to reestablish links with the English as a bulwark against the Spanish. Assessing his depleted military supplies, he realized he needed to encourage Hogan's proposals. Although the English merchant found craftsmen initially willing to travel to Morocco to cast weapons, he reported that when they were about to embark from Harwich they took fright "and suddenly fled away."[26] Why they refused to leave is unclear, but not everyone was enthusiastic about trading with the infidel.

Despite these setbacks, the wily Hogan believed a deal was on offer from the new and inexperienced sultan. In a memorandum written to Elizabeth's advisers in March 1577, he claimed that al-Malik was prepared to offer the English an exclusive trade in saltpeter in exchange for weapons. According to Williams's intelligence, al-Malik claimed that, "being desirous of the honor I hear of your queen of England, and the good liking I have of the English nation," he was prepared to "enter in league as well as for the quiet traffic of her ships and subjects in to this country of Barbary." Hogan added one further intriguing observation:

al-Malik could provide a global market for English cloth by offering an alternative route into Turkey and the vast eastern markets beyond. He argued that "all Christian commodities that goeth out of Christendom through Germany and Italy to serve the Turk, shall pass through his country to Constantinople, being a nearer passage and less charge than the other way, with good safe conduct and passport." Hogan had watched the Muscovy Company struggle to sustain its Persian trade via the long and inhospitable Northeast Passage. He now seized this new opportunity to get at least as far as Turkey by going through Morocco, then east across North Africa. By transporting cloth "into Barbary by sea, which is as near as Spain, we shall cut off all strangers from transportation, and therefore maintain our navy to the enriching of the queen's majesty's subjects." This, Hogan insisted, "is a matter of great importance because there shall be saved two thousand miles of carriage, and a good direct passage, with danger of Portugal and Spain." He concluded by indirectly contrasting the Atlantic sea route to Morocco with the Muscovy Company's grueling northeast voyage to the Arctic Circle by noting that "in our time, since the trade hath been in Barbary, the passage is such by sea as no ship hath miscarried that way."[27]

Hogan's geography might have been questionable, but his determination was not. He managed to convince Burghley, Walsingham and Sir Thomas Gresham, the queen's financial adviser and founder of the Royal Exchange (who was always looking for new projects to enlarge Elizabeth's coffers), that he should travel to Morocco and meet the sultan as the queen's formal representative. Quite what he was to discuss has been a matter of intense conjecture. As we have seen, Elizabeth had been provided with outdated information back in 1561, when she had given Anthony Jenkinson a somewhat naive letter for Shah Tahmasp. She had no intention of repeating her mistake with another Muslim ruler, and on this occasion she furnished Hogan with a letter of introduction (since lost) and detailed instructions, probably drawn up by Burghley, explaining what he should say upon meeting the Moroccan sultan. Remarkably, the recently excommunicated queen appeared to reproduce the age-old papal line regarding trade in prohibited goods.

She ordered Hogan to thank al-Malik for allowing the English to trade in Morocco, but also to ask that he address English commercial grievances sparked by disputes with local Jewish merchants over the settlement of payments in "the matter of sugars." She told him to avoid any discussion of arms deals. If the sultan raised the issue of "artillery and munition as he shall from time to time have need of (a matter to which we can neither in honor or conscience yield unto), our pleasure therefore is that you make no mention thereof to him." If the sultan pressed Hogan about why the English could not supply him with arms, he was to say, "it is a matter that somewhat concerneth the service of our God," and that any attempt at such a trade would "draw the hatred of all Christian princes our neighbors upon us" and lead to war.[28]

Armed with his instructions and the dual role of private merchant and Elizabeth's first ambassador to Morocco, Hogan set sail from Portsmouth on May 6, 1577. Fifteen days later he landed at Safi, where he was met by a Moroccan delegation and English resident merchants. By the end of the month he had reached the outskirts of Abd al-Malik's royal court in Marrakesh. As he rode into the city "there met me all the Christians of the Spaniards and Portuguese to receive me, which I know was more by the king's commandment than of any good wills of themselves." Hardly stopping even to acknowledge his Christian adversaries, Hogan recounted somewhat petulantly that they "hung down their heads like dogs, and especially the Portuguese, and I countenanced them accordingly." On June 1 Hogan was finally ushered into a meeting with al-Malik, where he read out the queen's letter in Spanish, waiting patiently as it was translated into Arabic. The sultan responded cordially (via a Spanish interpreter), and "declared that he, with his country and all things therein, should be at your majesty's commandment." Over the next month al-Malik and Hogan developed a brief but intense friendship. They dined together, watched plays, listened to music until midnight, messed about on al-Malik's boat, baited bulls with what Hogan called the sultan's "English dogs" and even watched what the bemused Englishman described as "a Morris dance." In the midst of all the fun, Hogan managed to extract an agreement that "the Jews there resident" should settle their English debts, and he also obtained "300 quintals [13 tons] gross of saltpeter"—with no mention of any weapons in exchange.

Hogan gave an extremely positive assessment of al-Malik's rule in his correspondence with London. "I find him agreeable to do good to your merchants more than any other nation," he wrote to Elizabeth, although he acknowledged that the sultan still faced internal challenges from the deposed Abdallah Muhammad. "He is not yet all in quiet within his country," as Hogan put it, "for the black king keepeth in the mountains, being of small force." But what really caught Hogan's attention was al-Malik's apparent antipathy toward Spain and his support of England. He reported al-Malik as saying, "I make more account of you coming from the queen of England than of any from Spain," because Philip II "cannot govern his own country, but is governed by the Pope and the Inquisition. Which religion he doth wholly mislike of, finding him to be a very earnest Protestant of good religion and living, and well experimented as well in the Old Testament as New, bearing great affection to God's true religion used in your Highness's realm."[29]

Hogan's obviously partial report read more like Lutheran propaganda than the theological confessions of a Muslim ruler avidly reading the New Testament and embracing the "true" Protestant faith. Just as the Shi'a Safavids were cast by the Portuguese and Venetians as saintly crusaders akin to early Christian warriors, so Protestant English merchants refashioned the Moroccan king in their own theological image to assuage any qualms they may have felt about doing business with him.

After this apparent revelation of al-Malik's Protestant beliefs, Hogan went on to explain that the sultan was prepared to use his influence among the Ottomans to ensure that "all English ships that shall pass along his coast of Barbary, and through the straits [of Gibraltar] into the Levant seas" would be granted "safe conduct that the said ships and merchants with their goods might pass into the Levant seas, and so to the Turk's dominions." As far as Hogan was concerned, he was now dealing with a quasi-Protestant Moroccan ruler offering him free trade across his kingdom, and unfettered access to Ottoman dominions and markets even farther east. It was an assumption that sustained trade for the moment, but one that would not stand up to close scrutiny, or survive subsequent cataclysmic events in Morocco.

Hogan concluded his account by writing that "touching the private affairs entreated upon betwixt her Majesty and the Emperor, I had letters from him to satisfy her highness." It is most unlikely that Hogan would have left Morocco with a substantial consignment of saltpeter without exchanging it for the arms that the sultan craved, whose export Burghley, Walsingham and Gresham had already sanctioned. There is a long, undistinguished history of states, whatever their religious or ideological beliefs, being economical with the truth when it comes to selling arms to apparent adversaries, and the Elizabethans were no different. Formal written instructions are sometimes far from reliable guides to the truth, and it seems that Elizabeth, fearing that her letter to Hogan might be intercepted by Portuguese or Spanish spies, produced a set of written instructions elaborately condemning arms deals, while her verbal instructions authorized them.

When Hogan returned to London in late July, he carried letters for Elizabeth from al-Malik that acceded to all of Elizabeth's demands and proposed an exchange of ambassadors to formalize their new alliance. The Portuguese ambassador in London, Francisco Giraldi, was outraged and certainly believed that Hogan had exchanged English munitions for saltpeter during his visit. His formal complaint to Walsingham on August 9, 1577, provides insight into just how much Londoners knew about the Anglo-Moroccan trade. "I wish respectfully to inform you," he wrote tartly, "that this city is full of the reception given by that tyrant the Shereef [a corruption of the Arabic for "noble"] to her Majesty's ambassador; how he went to meet him, and honored him with this name by word of mouth, as has been more fully related to me by a Portuguese who came in the ship which brought the news. Also the thousands of stores and arms which that Ughens [Hogan] has taken in the galleon and in two other smaller vessels, which I am certain was little to the taste of the King, my master."[30] Elizabeth had to tread carefully. She wrote back to al-Malik in September saying she was happy to receive his ambassador, but would need great secrecy in the matter. A formal Anglo-Moroccan commercial and military alliance might be only a matter of months away.

• • •

Hogan's insistence that Morocco could provide access to the Ottoman markets had revived Walsingham's long-standing interest in establishing trade with Constantinople. He believed that Christian reports of the Ottomans' demise after the defeat at Lepanto were greatly exaggerated. The Holy League rapidly disintegrated as Pius died in May 1572 and Venice, desperate to reestablish commercial relations with the Ottomans, signed a peace treaty in March 1573 acknowledging Selim's sovereignty over Cyprus and even paying him a financial tribute. Sokollu Mehmed Pasha, the Ottoman grand vizier (in effect, the prime minister), conducted a massive naval rebuilding program and boasted that the "Ottoman state is so powerful, if an order was issued to cast anchors from silver, to make rigging from silk, and to cut the sails from satin, it could be carried out for the entire fleet."[31] As the Ottomans rebuilt, the Habsburgs seized Tunis in 1573. A year later a new Turkish fleet, now even larger than before Lepanto, retook the city and restored Ottoman domination of the eastern Mediterranean.

So far as Walsingham could tell, the Ottomans were more powerful than ever and they appeared likely to control access to Asia via the Mediterranean for the foreseeable future. Nevertheless, there were uncertainties: Selim died suddenly in December 1574 and was succeeded by his weak and capricious son Murad III, who retreated into his imperial palace and showed little appetite for taking on the might of Habsburg Spain. Undaunted, Walsingham was determined to foster an alliance.

The new sultan's first act was to have his five younger brothers strangled to prevent challenges to his accession. He notoriously allowed his *haseki,* or consort, Safiye Sultan, to exercise unprecedented political power from within the protected space of the Topkapi Palace's harem. Safiye, one of Ottoman history's most enigmatic figures, was believed to be of Albanian origin and had been presented to Murad as a teenager after being captured by Ottoman forces. Murad also gave his mother, Nurbanu Sultan, a Venetian noblewoman enslaved within the imperial household, the opportunity to adopt the role of queen mother and dictate rival policies to those of Sokollu Mehmed, with disastrous consequences.

One policy that particularly interested Murad was the desire to woo Protestants by stressing the commonalities between their faith and that of Islam. In an extraordinary letter written with Murad's approval by the Ottoman Chancery in 1574 and addressed to "the members of the Lutheran sect in Flanders and Spain," the Protestant reformers were praised because:

> you, for your part, do not worship idols, you have banished the idols and portraits, and bells from churches, and declared your faith by stating that God Almighty is One and Holy Jesus is His Prophet and Servant, and now, with heart and soul, are seeking and desirous of the true faith; but the faithless one they call Papa [the pope] does not recognize his Creator as One, ascribing divinity to Holy Jesus (upon him be peace!), and worshipping idols and pictures which he has made with his own hands, thus casting doubt upon the Oneness of God and instigating how many servants of God to that path of error.[32]

Rather like Hogan's fantasy of al-Malik being "nearly" Protestant, in the Ottoman appeal Lutherans become *almost* Muslim, apparently sharing their rejection of intercession and their belief that Jesus was a prophet, though not a divinity, a belief ascribed solely to the "faithless," misguided Trinitarian Catholic pope. Whether this was a calculated or an accidental misunderstanding of Protestant belief, its aim was clear: the Turks were eager to exploit the political divisions between Catholicism and what they referred to as the "Luterān mezhebi" ("Lutheran sect").

While Hogan was busy negotiating in Morocco, the Ottomans' attention was drawn away from Catholics and Lutherans back to the troublesome Shi'a dynasty in Persia. Wishing to exploit the internal turmoil following Shah Tahmasp's death the previous year, Murad declared war, beginning a long and attritional conflict that would define his reign. At a stroke the Turkish invasion of the Caucasus brought the Muscovy Company's faltering Persian trade to an abrupt halt. As far as Walsingham was concerned, the response required from England's merchants was obvious. The Ottomans were a powerful empire sympathetic to Protestants that needed to arm and clothe its armies. They were obviously crying out for two of England's staple commodities: cloth and guns.

Two of London's biggest commercial companies and their leading merchants had come to the same conclusion. In 1575 Edward Osborne and his trading partner Richard Staper, both members of the Clothworkers' Company, with extensive business interests in Spain, Portugal, Brazil and the Low Countries, proposed to open up Turkish trade through Poland. According to Richard Hakluyt, "about the year 1575 the foresaid right worthy merchants at their charges and expenses sent John Wright and Joseph Clements by the way of Poland to Constantinople, where the said Joseph remained 18 months to procure a safe conduct from the *Grand Signor* [the phrase used by the English to describe the Ottoman sultan] for Mr. William Harborne, then factor for Sir Edward Osborne, to have free access into his dominions, and obtained the same."[33] Hakluyt's praise was understandable, as he was in the pay of Osborne and Staper. They were instrumental in granting him a Clothworkers' scholarship at Oxford, which they continued to fund after he left. This was probably why Hakluyt omitted to mention that the rival Mercers' Company had financed an earlier Turkish venture, this time by sea.

In June 1577, because Clements was in Constantinople, Thomas Cordell of the Mercers' Company obtained an Ottoman license (or firman) ensuring safe-conduct to trade cloth, tin, lead and steel for a voyage bound for Tripoli, Alexandria and Constantinople. One of the ships that was then prepared for the voyage was the *Pelican*, a 120-ton galleon that did not in the end make it but was instead renamed the *Golden Hind* and became Sir Francis Drake's flagship when he left Plymouth in November 1577 on the first English circumnavigation of the globe. Cordell had probably obtained the license from French merchants trading under the Franco-Ottoman Capitulations, which had been ratified in 1569. Under the terms of the trade agreement the Ottomans regarded Christian merchants as *harbis,* alien non-Muslims, protected by an *aman,* or temporary license. They were then tolerated as *musta 'min,* a status similar to that of a *dhimmi,* a licensed non-Muslim, but they were exempt from paying taxes for one year.[34] There are no surviving records showing whether Cordell reached Constantinople, or how Clements obtained his precious license, but we do know that by the spring of 1578 the English were ready to do business with the Ottomans. Then, in July, news from Morocco sent shock waves throughout Europe and the Mediterranean.

Ever since al-Malik's accession in 1576, the ousted Abdallah Muhammad had been marooned in exile in Portuguese-occupied Ceuta. During his brief reign Abdallah Muhammad had been notorious for his hostility toward Christians, but now in extremis he made Sebastian a remarkable offer. If the young Portuguese king invaded Morocco, deposed al-Malik and restored him as ruler, Abdallah Muhammad promised to rule the kingdom as a Portuguese vassal state. Any experienced Christian ruler should have dismissed such a cynical proposal without a second thought, but to the astonishment of his counselors, the pious and naive Sebastian, desperate for an excuse to prove his mettle, could not resist. One of the sixteenth century's more misguided monarchs, Sebastian was both pompous and impulsive and had the great misfortune to succeed his grandfather, King John III, when he was just three, following the sudden death of his father, Prince John Manuel, two weeks before his birth. Under King John, the Portuguese Empire had reached its zenith, monopolizing the Far Eastern spice trade, colonizing Brazil and reaching China and Japan. But by the 1570s, after Sebastian reached his majority, the empire was already in decline, in direct contrast to the neighboring Spanish Empire ruled by his cousin Philip. The young Portuguese king's religious devotion and obsession with leading a crusade to rid Africa of the Moors blinded him to the folly of attacking, with a far smaller force and little backing from the rest of Christendom, a Moroccan army that had the tacit support of the Ottomans. By the spring of 1578 Sebastian began assembling a ragtag army of Portuguese conscripts, Moroccans loyal to Abdallah Muhammad, German Calvinist mercenaries and Castilian adventurers. Their number also included one of England's most notorious renegades, Thomas Stukeley—soldier, spy, pirate and informer.[35]

"Of this man," wrote Burghley, "might be written whole volumes." Even by the swashbuckling standards of Elizabethan England, Stukeley had an extravagant career. Rumored to be the illegitimate son of Henry VIII, he had fled England before he turned thirty to escape arrest for sedition and fraud. He fought with great bravery and distinction on the continent throughout the 1550s, before returning to England and gaining Elizabeth's favor as a privateer attacking Spanish and French shipping. In 1568 he was arrested on suspicion of treason and collusion with the Catholic Irish rebels. Having denounced Elizabeth, claiming scandalously that he "set not a fart for her, whore, nor yet for her office,"[36] he fled, first to Spain and then to Rome, arriving in the wake of the papal bull of excommunication. Loyal Elizabethans were appalled by Stukeley's behavior. Holinshed castigated him as "a defamed person almost through all Christendom, and a faithless beast," while the historian William Camden condemned him grandly as "a ruffian, a riotous spendthrift and a vapourer [boastful bully]."[37] Preaching open rebellion against Elizabeth, Stukeley encouraged first King Philip II and then Pope Pius V to finance his personal invasion of Ireland. In 1571 he captained Spanish galleys at the Battle of Lepanto, and by 1578 he finally obtained Pope Gregory XIII's begrudging support for his Irish adventure, receiving just one ship and 600 Italian soldiers.

When Stukeley arrived in Lisbon in May en route to Ireland, Sebastian was still desperately short of soldiers. He implored the Englishman to abandon his Irish adventure and join him on his equally improbable expedition into Africa. The king wrote to Rome with typical sententiousness, explaining that he had bigger plans for Stukeley, and that he "understood the business better than the pope, or any of us, or anyone else in the world, and *in fine* it was best not to go [to Ireland] at present." With characteristic opportunism (and the unattractive alternative of sailing on with a leaky boat and mutinous soldiers), Stukeley agreed, abandoning the papacy and Ireland, which he now claimed would have brought him only "hunger and lice." Throughout the summer of 1578 the English renegade watched as Sebastian assembled his fractious army of 16,000 soldiers, who were quickly outnumbered by an extraordinary array of noncombatants, described by one commentator as "an unsavory company of baggage" that included bishops, priests and "an infinite number of drudges, slaves, negroes, mulattoes, horse boys, laundresses, and those sweet wenches that the Frenchmen do merrily call the daughters of delight."[38] Finally, in late June, the fleet was ready. Sebastian was wisely advised that midsummer was no time to lead an army of armor-clad knights into a battle with an experienced standing army in the sweltering Moroccan heat. As ever, the impetuous king refused to listen, and on June 26 his armada of hundreds of ships left Lisbon.

On July 12, the fleet made a chaotic landing at Asilah, on Morocco's northwest coast. Rather than reembarking and sailing down the coast to his chosen landing site of Larache, Sebastian chose a suicidal week-long forced march inland to reach his objective. "A perilous overland march of some thirty-five miles to reach a point only twenty safe miles away by sea," observes one modern historian, was "an attraction which the scatter-brained youth could not resist."[39] On August 3, the exhausted and demoralized army, debilitated by marching for days on end in full armor in midday temperatures of over 100 degrees Fahrenheit and running low on rations, reached the Mekhazen River on a plain north of the town known locally as El-Ksar el-Kebir (in Portuguese, Alcácer-Quibir). There they met and were quickly encircled by al-Malik's formidable army of at least 60,000 experienced Berbers, Arabs, Turks and Moriscos, four times the size of Sebastian's pitiful force. Even worse, it soon became clear that Sebastian's decision to favor infantry with pikes over cavalry and arquebusiers (soldiers equipped with wheel-lock firearms) was a fatal mistake as they confronted al-Malik's 30,000 horse and 3,000 crack Morisco arquebusiers, many of whom were probably armed with English munitions. Facing almost certain annihilation, Sebastian's advisers gathered on the night of August 4, in a council of war. The consensus was to avoid disaster and beat a dignified retreat to the coast. Sebastian scorned this advice and ordered an engagement early the next day, in the hope of exploiting the element of surprise.

The following day, "the [fifth] day of August, which was Monday, in the year of our salutation 1578, the battle was begun between the two kings about twelve of the clocke." Once again Sebastian managed to disable his army, choosing to fight at the hottest time of the day and riding into the blinding sun. What he did not realize was that his adversary, al-Malik, was mortally ill even before he reached the battlefield. Those close to the ailing king suspected he had been poisoned by disaffected Turkish supporters, others feared the plague; but, whatever the cause, by the time he addressed his troops that morning he had only hours to live. The Moroccan artillery fired first, briefly halting the advance of Sebastian's infantry. Almost immediately "the arquebusiers on foot on both sides discharged as thick as hail, with such a horrible, furious, and terrible tempest, that the cracking and roaring of the guns did make the earth so to tremble, as though it would have sunk down to hell." The fighting quickly descended into hand-to-hand combat: Sebastian's German and Spanish regiments fought with such ferocity that they broke through the opposition, followed by the Portuguese cavalry. As the Moroccans buckled, al-Malik mounted his horse to rally his troops, but the effort was too much. He collapsed onto his litter and died within the hour. If the news had reached the rest of the battlefield, Sebastian might have won a most unlikely victory, but instead "his death was subtly dissembled" by the Moroccans and their troops rallied.

As the fighting raged on, a second king fell. Abdallah Muhammad had led an unsuccessful cavalry charge and seen the way the battle was going. He tried to escape across the Mekhazen, but he was thrown by his horse "and being unskilful to swim, was drowned and perished." Stukeley also suffered an ignoble end: having deserted his Italian troops at the Moors' first assault, "there came a piece of artillery that took off both his legs; and so he ended his days."[40] He might not have given a fart about Elizabeth, but it may have been one of her cannon balls that killed him. Finally, as the waves of Moorish infantry mowed down the last groups of exhausted soldiers, the third king fell on the battlefield. Sebastian had made every mistake possible in pursuing his dream of a crusade against the infidel, but at the last he proved a courageous, even inspirational warrior, who "forsaketh not his people: thinking it dishonorable to seek safety by flight, and with those few that followed him, behaved himself valiantly. He slew so many, he sent so many to hell, that many called him the lightning." He was last seen, even as all was clearly lost, charging once more into the heat of the battle, where he was cut down. He was probably unknown to his killers as the last undisputed king of the Portuguese House of Avis, which had ruled Portugal since 1385.

After six hours of brutal conflict the Battle of El-Ksar el-Kebir—referred to in Europe as the Battle of Alcácer-Quibir or the Battle of the Three Kings, known to the Moors as the Battle of Wad el-Mekhazen and reported in English diplomatic correspondence as the Battle of Alcazar—was over. Sebastian's army of 16,000 had been annihilated. Reports suggested that anywhere between 3,000 and 12,000 soldiers had been killed and no more than 200 had managed to escape. The rest, including the thousands of noncombatants, were carried off into captivity: the wealthy ones ransomed, the vast majority sold into slavery. Al-Malik was survived by his brother, Ahmad al-Mansur, who fought in the battle and immediately claimed the throne once victory was assured. He ordered the recovery of the bodies of the three dead claimants to his new crown:

> These dead bodies of three kings being brought into one pavilion, made a horrible spectacle, and wrung tears from the beholders. For what more sorrowful and horrible a sight could there be, than to behold three most mighty kings, that died in one battle, lying together. The army of one of whom was vanquished when he lived, and after he was dead did straight away overcome the army of the other two kings: and whereas all three did aspire to the kingdom of Morocco, none of them held it.[41]

When news of the defeat reached Lisbon the following month, a resident German merchant wrote home describing "how great were the lamentations, the despair and grief, not only in this city, but in all the land. The men went about as if dazed. . . . It is a woeful matter to lose in one day the king, their husbands, their sons, and all the goods and chattels they had with them. But what is even more terrible is that this kingdom must now fall under Spanish rule, which they can brook the least of all."[42] The humiliation was so profound that many Portuguese historians believe the country never recovered. Although Sebastian's body was eventually repatriated and buried in the church of Santa Maria in Belém, many refused to believe he was dead, claiming he had fled the battle and would one day return to save the country from its seemingly terminal decline. The messianic belief in "Sebastianism" was even evoked to defend the Brazilian monarchy in the late nineteenth century, and it is still part of the modern Portuguese concept of *saudosismo,* a yearning or nostalgia for what was lost and might yet be regained.

Across Europe, rulers assessed the significance of the battle. The Ottomans were annoyed at seeing another Muslim ruler (albeit one who paid them obeisance) destroy a Christian army, especially after their own failings at Lepanto, but they reassured themselves that al-Mansur would remain pro-Turkish and cement their dominion in North Africa. Philip II was officially distraught at the news of his cousin Sebastian's death, though he immediately saw an opportunity to exploit the subsequent power vacuum in Lisbon. Spain's papal nuncio wrote to Rome to blame Sebastian's defeat on Elizabeth's support of al-Malik: "there is no evil that is not devised by that woman who, it is perfectly plain, succored Mulocco [al-Malik] with arms and especially artillery," he thundered. Clearly shaken by the loss of their carefully cultivated Muslim ally, the English were dismayed by the prospect of Portugal falling into Philip's hands. That would give the Spanish king effective control over the vast wealth of the whole of Iberia, the Low Countries, the New World and the Portuguese possessions in southeast Asia. With no immediate heir, Sebastian was succeeded by his aged great-uncle Cardinal Henry. Henry's succession was contested by his nephew Don António, Prior of Crato, grandson of King Manuel I. Don António had fought bravely at Alcácer-Quibir, where he was captured, but had managed to ransom himself. Both England and France backed the Portuguese pretender in a forlorn attempt to stop Philip II, but such foreign support hardly helped his claim, especially when it included English "heretics" who were blamed for supplying the weapons that had defeated Sebastian. In August 1580 Philip's troops marched into Portugal, defeating Don António's forces at the Battle of Alcântara. Don António fled first to France and then to England, in the forlorn hope of building political opposition to the Spanish takeover. The following April Philip II of Spain was crowned Philip I, King of Portugal and the Algarve, creating (with the inclusion of Portugal's possessions in the New World) one of the greatest empires the world had ever seen.

Elizabeth's attempts to create an alliance with the Muslim world appeared to be in ruins, and her political isolation more complete than ever. Spain now had the heretic queen in its sights.

4

An Apt Man in Constantinople

As news of the events in Morocco began to reach London in the autumn of 1578, Francis Walsingham concluded that it signaled the end of the fledgling Anglo-Moroccan alliance, almost before it had begun. Ever the pragmatist, he turned his attention elsewhere—to the Ottomans. By the end of the year, the secretary of state and chief adviser on foreign affairs had written one of the most important documents in the early history of Anglo-Turkish relations, his "Memorandum on the Turkey trade," written for Elizabeth and her counselors, which would become the blueprint for all subsequent Elizabethan relations with the Ottoman Empire.

Characteristic in its attention to detail and unrivaled grasp of reasons of state, Walsingham's memo sought to justify the trade and to anticipate every eventuality. The English experience in Russia, Persia and more recently Morocco had taught him that it was vital to establish a trading presence before developing more formal political alliances, so he began by outlining "the profit that may ensue by trade into the Turk's dominions." He argued that it would strengthen the navy's role in national defense and international commerce, allow merchants to export English goods directly into Turkish markets rather than through costly middlemen, and enable the importation of duty-free Turkish goods, which could then be sold across Europe. The obstacles were manifold: Walsingham understood that all the great Catholic powers with an interest in Mediterranean commerce would attempt to stop the trade, "by finesse and by force." He observed drily that Spain, "being not the best

82

effected toward us," would undoubtedly concoct a strategic diplomatic and naval alliance with the French and Venetians to prevent the English trade. The difficulties would be all the greater once, as Walsingham correctly predicted, Philip "is possessed of the kingdom of Portugal."

Walsingham's solution was to "make choice of some apt man to be sent with her Majesty's letters unto the Turk to procure an ample safe-conduct, who is always to remain there at the charge of the merchants." It was a shrewd proposal. Whoever was chosen would exploit the blurred line between trade and politics, traveling under royal warrant but paid for by London's merchants, giving the queen maximum diplomatic returns on a minimum financial investment. He would remain in Constantinople indefinitely to thwart attempts by resident Venetian, French and Spanish merchants or diplomats to disrupt the English trade.

Walsingham stressed that the first visit was "to be handled with great secrecy" and undertaken overland initially to prevent news of a seaborne departure from London reaching the ears of Constantinople's resident ambassadors. The ambitious long-term plan was for twenty English ships to sail annually through the Mediterranean during the winter months, with sufficient commodities to turn a profit in Turkey. But Walsingham worried: Could the English supply enough cloth to load twenty ships? Would such a flotilla flood the Turkish market and cause prices to crash? He also wondered "whether there shall be that vent" or sale "of our kerseys during the wars between the said Turk and Sophy" at the same levels of profit that existed prior to the conflict. Finally, he took up Edmund Hogan's plan for connecting the Moroccan trade with Constantinople, believing that it would be vital "to procure the Turk's letters to the King of Barbary and the rest of the princes of Africa that the ports there may be free for our merchants."[1] Walsingham was clearly nervous about the Moroccan royal succession following al-Malik's death and hoped—rather optimistically—that he could use Ottoman leverage to ensure unimpeded English commerce through the region.

As Richard Hakluyt observed in his *Principal Navigations*, the "apt man" chosen to lead England's hazardous foray into the Turkish trade was William Harborne. Born in Great Yarmouth into a family of minor gentry, Harborne began traveling abroad as a factor in 1559. In 1577, with plans for a Turkish adventure already being mooted, he was named as one of the principal members of the newly formed Spanish Company, alongside Edward Osborne, Richard Staper and Anthony Jenkinson. Jenkinson's days of traveling to Russia and Persia were over by then, but if he and Harborne met during this period, the older man would surely have seen a kindred spirit in the younger. They certainly shared many of the attributes required to undertake such grueling and danger-ous long-distance travels into the Islamic world. Both men were char-ismatic, tenacious and resourceful, both dedicated mercers and both loyal servants of their Protestant queen. Neither was above speaking his mind, even when such frankness threatened his career or his life.

Like many English merchants of his time, Harborne was employed as a government spy before departing for Turkey, which suggests that his selection for the job resulted from the combined efforts of Osborne, Staper and Walsingham. Whatever the discussions behind his appoint-ment, in early August 1578, just before the Battle of Alcácer-Quibir, Harborne was several weeks into a four-month overland journey to Constantinople, accompanied by Joseph Clements and just one servant. They traveled through Germany to Poland, where Harborne met his brother-in-law in Lvov (possibly the English factor John Wright), to-gether with an Ottoman dragoman (a diplomatic translator and envoy) known as Mustafa Beg. It was his good fortune to arrive just at the moment when an Ottoman diplomatic delegation had come to renew a peace treaty between Poland and the new Turkish sultan, Murad III. Harborne joined Mustafa's diplomatic caravan as it headed back to Constantinople, taking a route advocated by Jenkinson back in 1561 through Moldavia, Romania and Bulgaria. He arrived in the Ottoman capital on October 28, 1578.[2]

What Harborne made of his arrival is not recorded, but as a Protes-tant English merchant from Norfolk he must have experienced some combination of exhilaration and trepidation. Constantinople, one of the world's greatest imperial capitals, had changed beyond all recogni-tion since it had fallen to Sultan Mehmed II in 1453. The new city of

Istanbul, from the Greek for "to the city," was also referred to in official Ottoman business for centuries as Kostantiniyye, or, as Christians would continue to call it, Constantinople, the name I have used in this book. The Ottomans had transformed a Byzantine city in decline with a population of just 50,000 into the capital of the Islamic world, a vibrant multiethnic and multidenominational city. By the time Harborne arrived its population was estimated at 300,000 to 500,000, much larger than London (200,000), Paris (220,000), Naples (280,000) or Venice (160,000). From sheer political and commercial necessity, Mehmed and his successors (including Murad) had made Constantinople into a cosmopolitan capital, repopulating it through the forced resettlement of merchants and craftsmen from various ethnic and religious backgrounds. Only 58 percent of the city was Muslim, with 32 percent Christian and 10 percent "Jews," a category that included Greeks, Armenians and various communities deported from the recently conquered Balkans.[3]

To Harborne, the city's skyline must have appeared alien and intimidating. At Mehmed's command, the iconic Greek Orthodox cathedral of Hagia Sophia had been transformed into a mosque, and an ambitious program of public building had begun. A new imperial palace, the Topkapi Sarayi, had been built overlooking the Golden Horn, as well as the Fatih Mosque and Külliye (a complex of buildings of characteristic Ottoman architecture) and a commercial district dominated by a *bedestan* (the marketplace known today as the Grand Bazaar) and a series of *khans* (urban caravanserais). On the northern side of the Golden Horn, Mehmed had repopulated Galata—still identified by its imposing Genoese tower—with Jewish and Christian merchants, and this is where Harborne lived during his time in Constantinople. Under Mehmed 190 mosques, 24 madrasas (schools), 32 *hamams* (bathhouses) and 12 markets were erected, transforming the city from a Greek Orthodox polis into a Muslim capital. Under Mehmed's grandson Sultan Süleyman, the urban transformation was even more pronounced, thanks primarily to the extraordinary achievements of the architect Mimar Sinan, who built some 120 buildings in Constantinople, many of which Harborne would have seen. Foremost among these were the Şehzade Mosque and the monumental Süleymaniye Mosque and Külliye, completed twenty years before Harborne's arrival.

Since his recent accession, in 1574, the young and pious new sultan Murad III had confined himself to proposing architectural projects outside his imperial capital. He commissioned a magnificent mosque in his birthplace of Manisa, but this would not be completed for another eight years. Perhaps befitting his mystical beliefs, he was more interested in leaving his mark on the holy sites in Mecca and Medina. He built a new arcade around the revered Ka'ba in Mecca, remodeled the Prophet's mosque in Medina and commissioned a range of new buildings in both cities, including madrasas, hospices and lodges for his beloved Sufi dervishes. Harborne could be forgiven for seeing little or no trace of the sultan he had come to court in Constantinople. Once installed as sultan, Murad rarely left his palace in Constantinople, surrounding himself with scores of advisers, mystics, astrologers, poets, calligraphers and musicians.[4]

Harborne's initial encounters with this intensely hierarchical and labyrinthine Ottoman political bureaucracy must have been completely bewildering. The first problem was one of communication. Harborne corresponded with his Ottoman counterparts in Latin or Italian (in which he appears to have been fluent), which was then translated into Turkish, leaving much room (as we have seen) for creative license and strategic misunderstanding. Then there was the difficulty of gaining appropriate formal access to the Ottoman court.

The French had developed the concept of the "Sublime Porte" or "High Gate" (in Turkish Bâbıâli), through which foreign dignitaries were allowed to enter the Ottoman state buildings in an elaborate and carefully orchestrated procession. Any breach of etiquette could prove disastrous. Once within the imperial complex, centered on the Topkapi Palace, visitors had to navigate through the many layers of the sultan's court.

The Inner Service, dominated by the harem, was responsible for the sultan's welfare. It included his wives, concubines and slaves. At the time of Harborne's arrival, the Inner Service was also, through the power granted to Murad's long-term lover or consort Safiye Sultan, exercising

considerable influence over imperial policy. Fiscal and diplomatic re-
sponsibilities were delegated to the Outer Service and the so-called
Scribal Institution, both of which were controlled by the grand vizier.
The grand vizier, appointed by the sultan, held executive powers over an
imperial advisory council (the *divan*) composed of viziers and pashas.
The *divan* had in turn to compete with the demands of various social
and economic ministries known as "institutions." These included the
Religious Institution and the Military Institution, the latter controlling
the sultan's feared and unpredictable fighting corps, the Janissaries. To
make matters even more confusing, the Ottoman ruling administration
was divided between the Turkish nobility and the *devşirme* (abducted
Christian youths), forcible converts to Islam who were loyal to the sultan's administrative or military institutions. Both groups claimed the
title "Osmanli" or "Ottoman" to signify their membership in the state's
ruling class, although in times of conflict each exploited the other's
weaknesses for political gain. The sultans had adopted the *devşirme*
system as a deliberate method of divide and rule, to play each group off
the other, but it was a volatile setup that baffled outsiders.

Harborne's first task was to establish a dialog with Murad's grand
vizier, the seventy-three-year-old Sokollu Mehmed Pasha. Bosnian by
birth, the wily Sokollu Mehmed was a *devşirme* who had risen rapidly
through the Ottoman ranks before being appointed grand vizier by
Süleyman in 1565. It was testament to his consummate political skill
that Sokollu Mehmed had not only survived but prospered in that role
for fourteen years under three different sultans; however, at the time of
Harborne's arrival he was locked in a bitter power struggle with Murad's consort, Safiye Sultan.

Harborne's disastrous start to his time in Constantinople was described in graphic detail in his earliest surviving correspondence, a
petition submitted to Sokollu Mehmed, the first ever written to a grand
vizier by a foreigner. Harborne submitted his petition, written in Italian, via a dragoman to the Ottoman Chancery, where it was translated
into Turkish with all the formal conventions (it was customary for the
plaintiff to write in the third person). Harborne complained that not
long after his arrival he had ordered the goods and money left in Lvov

to be sent to him by one of his servants, only for the servant to be "assassinated by thieves within one day's journey of this famous city, and they robbed him of his goods and money to the sum of 4000 ducats," which was around £1,300.[5] Considering that an average English ship's cargo was worth around £7,000, this was a substantial loss. The poor servant who lost his life remained anonymous, and was never mentioned again.

The goods involved were the ubiquitous coarse woolen kersey cloths, as well as tin and lead, a flagrant violation of the papal ban on the trade of all such merchandise with Muslims. Harborne complained that the grand vizier knew the whereabouts of his servant's assassins as well as of his goods, but his *chiauses* (Turkish sergeants) "have made no effort at all—they did not even wish to go to find the merchandise where the thieves confessed that it was but, rather, wasted their time." Despite the apparent delicacy of the situation, Harborne managed to end his petition with a request for safe-conducts to trade throughout the Ottoman-controlled eastern Mediterranean, and for permission to export surplus lead.

Neither Harborne's subsequent letters nor Ottoman Chancery records reveal if he received compensation for his losses, but he is unlikely to have been able to continue trading without some indemnity. Hakluyt certainly believed that Harborne turned his loss into broader profit, describing the canny Englishman as having "behaved himself so wisely and discreetly that within a few months after he obtained himself not only the great Turk's large and ample privilege for himself . . . but also procured his honorable and friendly letters unto her Majesty."[6] This was a very bland account of what really happened.

The imperial ambassador to Constantinople, Joachim von Sinzendorf, had been keeping a suspicious eye on Harborne ever since his arrival. He reported to the Habsburg court in Vienna that "this so-called merchant Harborne" had "begun to set this trade going here, with the foreknowledge of the Queen." Sinzendorf was appalled that, despite having no formal mandate from Elizabeth, Harborne had bribed Sokollu Mehmed "with a quantity sufficient for three robes of the best English cloth he had" to obtain commercial safe-conduct agreements. Having issued these agreements, the grand vizier had, Sinzendorf claimed, asked Harborne's interpreter, Mustafa Beg, "Does he also want to have a letter from the Sultan to the Queen?," to which a surprised and clearly delighted Harborne is reported to have said, "Yes, it would be nothing but good."

It seems that Murad was unaware of the proposed letter to Elizabeth, which was written by Sokollu Mehmed. Harborne had simply struck lucky, having obtained the precious commercial rights as well as the formal letter in return for a relatively cheap bribe. In demanding that the letter be written by the sultan's chancellor, Sokollu Mehmed ignored protocol that insisted the sultan would correspond only if a letter was first written to him. It was reported that the grand vizier told the chancellor, "Of course, write the letter, because they are Lutherans, and good people!"[7]

Sinzendorf's report was hardly impartial: he had a clear vested interest in claiming that Harborne's negotiations with the grand vizier were part of a broader Turco-Protestant conspiracy enabling Murad to establish "an open, safe port in England, by means of which to set his foot also into the western Empire."[8] However, Sinzendorf does seem to have understood that Harborne's maneuverings had formalized amicable commercial exchanges with the Ottoman authorities that put the other European representative in Constantinople on the defensive.

The letters that followed (which are discussed at the beginning of this book) were the first in an exchange of correspondence between an Ottoman sultan and an English monarch that would last for another seventeen years. The first letter, written in March 1579 on Murad's behalf and sent to Elizabeth, had been composed in the Diwani script, using a particular variant of Ottoman Turkish known as Fasih Türkce ("eloquent Turkish"), the language of poetry and imperial administration.[9] But with Mustafa Beg's assistance Harborne also had it translated rather more freely into Latin to be read out back in London. The Latin version began:

> In greatness and glory most renowned Elizabeth, most sacred
> queen, and noble prince of the most mighty worshippers of Jesus,

most wise governor of the causes and affairs of the people and family of Nazareth, cloud of most pleasant rain, and sweetest fountain of nobleness and virtue, lady and heir of the perpetual happiness and glory of the noble realm of England [Anletār] (whom all sorts seek unto and submit themselves) we wish most prosperous success and happy ends to all your actions, and do offer unto you such pleasures and courtesies as are worthy of our mutual and eternal familiarity: thus ending (as best beseemeth us) our former salutations.[10]

Buried within the letter's honorific rhetoric was some shrewd realpolitik. Murad was careful to describe Elizabeth as one of the Christian "worshippers of Jesus" and part of the "family of Nazareth," implying the possibility of a Protestant-Islamic alliance based on the mutual acceptance of Jesus as a holy figure. He also ensured that, in praising Elizabeth, she was to understand that he was the active partner doing all the wishing and offering, for which she and her subjects should be grateful. Acknowledging Harborne's arrival "in the name of your most excellent regal majesty," with "kindness, courtesy and friendly offices on your part," Murad was prepared to agree that "our country be always open to such of your subjects, as by way of merchandise shall trade hither: and we will never fail to aid and succor any of them that are or shall be willing to esteem of our friendship, favor and assistance." Murad assured Elizabeth he had commanded "all our kings, judges, and travelers by sea" throughout the Ottoman Empire to ensure that "such aforesaid persons as shall resort thither by sea from the realm of England, either with great or small vessels to trade by way of merchandise, may lawfully come to our imperial dominions, and freely return home again . . . straightly charging that they be suffered to use and trade all kind of merchandise as any other Christians do, without let or disturbance."

In case Elizabeth might feel she was receiving special dispensation, the letter reminded her that "our familiars and confederates the French, Venetians, Polonians, and the king of Germany, with diverse other our neighbors about us, have liberty to come hither, and to return again into their own countries, in like sort." The power and magnanimity of the Ottomans was so great they could accommodate anyone, from Catholic merchants and emperors to Protestant English sovereigns. However, in one final caveat, which seems to have been added by Harborne (with Mustafa's connivance), the Latin translation reminds Elizabeth that the alliance should be reciprocal, and that "you likewise bethink yourself of your like benevolence, humanity and friendship toward us, to open the gate thereof unto us . . . and that like liberty may be granted by your highness to our subjects and merchants to come with their merchandise to your dominions."[11] The original letter contained no such wish, because the Ottomans did not regard the English as a serious political power, an attitude that Harborne tried to mitigate but which was underscored by the method of delivering its letters to Elizabeth: they were transported in a satin bag tied with a silver capsule—the method used to write to Caucasian princes.[12]

Murad's letter was not the only one that arrived in London from Constantinople in September 1579. Harborne's dragoman, Mustafa Beg, also took the opportunity to break with convention and write an audacious letter to the queen. In it he encouraged Elizabeth to establish "a league and most holy alliance" between her and Murad, drawing yet again on the potential amity between Muslims and Protestants. "As I was negotiating in the presence of our Most Mighty Prince," writes Mustafa,

> it occurred to my mind that if by any means I could encourage some kind of understanding and friendship between our Most Mighty Prince and your Sacred Royal Majesty, not only as I know the Sacred Royal Majesty to hold the most Christian faith among all people and that, therefore, Christians throughout the whole world envy the Sacred Royal Majesty and, if they can, try to harm her in every way, but also because I considered it to be beneficial for your Sacred Royal Majesty to be able to establish an understanding with so great and so powerful an Emperor, with whom almost all princes and kings, of their own free will, wish to be closely allied.[13]

Despite its presumptuousness, the letter was taken seriously by Burghley, who filed and annotated it. Elizabeth regarded it as important enough to write back in October, just weeks after the letter arrived, imploring Mustafa to assist her in obtaining the release of English captives:

> Your letter of March 15 was handed to us by William Harborne, who at the same time recorded your kindness to our subjects. As it has taken the form of promoting the trade of our merchants to the dominions of his Imperial Highness it demands our gratitude and reciprocity of good offices. As by your good means matters are so far advanced that he has begun to incline to Harborne's request on behalf of himself and his partners, and we would not willingly be excluded from the conveniences granted to the subjects of other states, we have written to his Highness to testify our gratitude, and to ask him to allow to all our subjects the same permission that he has granted to a few; promising like liberty to his subjects in our dominions. We beg that you will aid us in obtaining this request. And as we have also dealt with him briefly for the freedom of certain of our subjects who are captive in his galleys we ask you to show your goodwill to us by promoting their cause.[14]

In requesting the captives' release, Elizabeth implicitly recognized Ottoman political legitimacy under (unwritten) international law.[15] It was unprecedented and highly significant for the future of any Anglo-Ottoman alliance, especially considering how far her excommunication by the papacy had isolated her from the rest of Europe.

The resident European merchants and diplomats in Constantinople were horrified by the sudden and apparently inexplicable success of the English interlopers. They were informed of developments by Mustafa Beg, who seems to have been playing both sides. In September 1579 Bernardino de Mendoza, Philip II's ambassador in London, wrote that Joseph Clements, Harborne's fellow agent, had "returned recently with a Turk, bringing a letter from his master [Murad] to the Queen, full of endearments, and offering unrestricted commerce in his country to

Englishmen if she, on her part, will give the same privileges here to his subjects. I will endeavor to get copies of the letter and their reply to send to Your Majesty."[16] Mustafa Beg presumably supplied these "copies," although not all Mendoza's intelligence was quite so accurate as he might have believed. It seems he read the Latin translation of Murad's letter, which had been embellished by Harborne and his associates to inflate the significance of the Anglo-Ottoman alliance, and its promise of closer trade relations. There is no record of the arrival in London of the Turkish emissary he mentions.

Nevertheless, both Sinzendorf's and Mendoza's responses reflect the alarm felt by the Habsburgs at the rise of English commercial influence in Constantinople. Just two months later, Mendoza reported to Philip that these fears appeared well founded. "This queen has received another letter from the Turk by way of France," he wrote on November 28. The letter has not survived, but Mendoza claimed that "in addition to many other offers," Murad "promises a favorable reception of Englishmen who come to his country, either by land or sea; both on account of his desire for her friendship as for that of the king of France, with whom he requests her to be as friendly as she can. He says that, by reason of his friendship to the king of France, he will be pleased to hear of her marriage with his brother [the Duke of Alençon], from which it may be seen that the French have made it their business to write to him about it."[17] Elizabeth was indeed embroiled in her famous on-and-off courtship with Alençon, which if successful threatened the Habsburgs with the prospect of an Anglo-Franco-Ottoman axis capable of dominating Mediterranean naval and commercial movements.

Mendoza went on to explain that "the Turks are also desirous of friendship with the English on account of the tin which has been sent thither for the last few years, and which is of the greatest value to them, as they cannot cast guns without it, whilst the English make a tremendous profit on the article, by means of which alone they maintain the trade with the Levant." His intelligence—presumably again gleaned from Mustafa Beg—was that five English ships were already en route to Constantinople, and "I am told that, in one of them, they are sending nearly twenty thousand crowns' worth of bar tin, without counting what the rest of them take. As this sending tin to the infidel is against the apostolic communion, and your Majesty has ordered that no such voyage shall be allowed to pass the Messina light [a watchtower built by Charles V in 1546 to protect Sicily from Turkish invasion] to the prejudice of God and Christianity, I advise the viceroy of Sicily of the sailing of these ships as I understand they will touch at Palermo, where the tin can be confiscated."[18] A month later he reported that even more ships were headed to Chios "carrying bell-metal and tin."[19] It was a symbolic act of alliance that conflated the iconoclastic faiths of Protestantism and Sunni Islam. With the queen's sanction, Protestant English merchants were removing metal from ecclesiastical buildings—including lead roofing and bell metal—and shipping it to Constantinople to arm Muslims fighting against Catholics.

By now events were moving fast. In late October 1579 Elizabeth had dispatched responses both to Murad's first letter and to Mustafa Beg's. The opening of her letter to Murad clearly took the hint about the superficial similarities between Protestantism and Islam by denouncing those Christians that "falsely profess the name of Christ."[20] Having learned that the Ottomans would give those they labeled "Lutherans" preferential commercial treatment, Elizabeth and her advisers obviously saw the advantages of presenting her as a religious ruler who rejected both idolatry and those who "falsely" professed Christ, attributes shared (according to the Catholic powers) by Protestants and Muslims. After establishing her theological credentials, the letter got down to business, asking for trading privileges to be "enlarged to all our subjects in general," and agreeing that Turks should be allowed "to come, and go to and from us and our kingdoms."

The letter concluded with a last request. Murad's "great affection to us and our nation, doth cause us also to entreat and use mediation on the behalf of certain of our subjects, who are detained as slaves and captives in your galleys," that "they may be delivered from their bondage, and restored to liberty, for their service toward us, according to their duty: which thing shall yield much more abundant cause to us of commending your clemency, and of beseeching that God (who only is above all things, and all men, and is a most severe revenger of all idolatry, and is jealous of his honor against the false gods of the nations) to adorn your most invincible imperial highness with all the blessings of those gifts, which only and deservedly are accounted most worthy of asking."

The galley slaves in question were probably the crews of the *Peter* and the *Swallow,* two English ships captured off Algiers two years earlier. The plea brought release and redemption, although it earned for the English a mortal enemy in the shape of the galley slaves' owner, the Turkish admiral Qilich Ali Pasha.

Sultan Murad and Queen Elizabeth seemed to be edging toward a closer commercial and political relationship when Harborne was faced with an unexpected crisis. On October 12, 1579, as Sokollu Mehmed Pasha was listening to petitions in the Topkapi's imperial council chamber, a Bosnian dervish suddenly leaped forward and stabbed him to death. Rumors abounded at court that Murad's powerful mother, Nurbanu Sultan, had ordered the assassination to resolve the courtly power struggle between her and Sokollu Mehmed. Whatever the motivation behind his murder, Sokollu Mehmed's death triggered a decisive shift in the balance of power within the palace. Over the next two decades the post of grand vizier would be progressively diminished, with eleven different incumbents unable to stop the sultan's harem from taking political matters into their own hands. Sokollu Mehmed's protégés were removed from government, and with them went his more emollient and westward-looking foreign and economic policy.[21]

It is testament to Harborne's determination and resourcefulness that he continued his dogged pursuit of an Anglo-Ottoman agreement. His time spent wooing—and probably bribing—subsequent grand viziers infuriated the other resident European diplomats, most especially Jacques de Germigny, the French ambassador. It was bad enough that Harborne lacked official diplomatic accreditation; even more galling was his skill in playing France off against Spain, while still trading under the cover of the French Capitulations. "I was informed," Germigny fumed in a report to Henry III in March 1580, "that this Englishman had represented to the Grand Vizier the seriousness of the increase of the power of the King of Spain, to the extent that he would take

possession of Portugal and the territories dependent on the said kingdom neighboring to this lord in the Levant."[22] He protested that, despite
Sokollu Mehmed's death, Harborne was "pursuing his negotiation ac-
tively in this Porte, and appears to be greatly favored, as much by reason
of the loads of steel, tin, and latten [copper alloys] which he has brought
them and promises to bring thereafter." In June, Germigny confessed
that it all "makes me fear that the said Englishman will soon realize his
aim" of obtaining full commercial privileges from the sultan. The
English advance, together with signs of a growing rapprochement between Murad and Philip II, threatened to leave France dangerously
isolated.

By then it was too late. Murad had already agreed to the terms of a
peace treaty with Spain, and at the end of May 1580, just days before
the dispatch of Germigny's letter, he signed a charter of privileges granting the English full commercial rights in Ottoman dominions. These
Anglo-Ottoman Capitulations would prove to be even more important
than Walsingham's Memorandum of 1578, and they endured for 343
years, until they were dissolved under the terms of the Treaty of Lau-
sanne in 1923, following the collapse of the Ottoman Empire and the
birth of the Turkish republic.

The agreement began by praising "Elizabeth Queen of England,
France and Ireland, the most honorable queen of Christendom," to
whom Murad agreed to "give license to all her people, and merchants,
peaceably and safely to come unto our imperial dominions, with all their
merchandise and goods without any impeachment, to exercise their traffic, to use their own customs, and to buy and sell according to the fash-
ions of their own country."[23] It listed in minute detail the privileges
granted to the English: their ships were guaranteed security and help in
the face of piracy (from Muslims or Christians), shipwreck or even debt;
in the event of death, goods reverted to the merchant's estate; in case of
commercial disputes both sides agreed to abide by the ruling of the local
cadi (judge) based on sharia law; English merchants were exempt from
paying *kharāj* (a local community charge) and were allowed to appoint
consuls in Alexandria, Damascus, Tunis, Algiers and Cairo; and if "any
pirates or other free governors of ships trading the sea shall take any

Englishman, and shall make sale of him . . . if the party shall be found to be English and shall receive the holy religion [Islam], then let him freely be discharged, but if he will still remain a Christian, let him then be restored to the Englishmen, and the buyers shall demand their money again of them who sold the man."[24]

For Harborne the Capitulations were the triumphant conclusion to nearly three years of tireless trade, diplomacy and bribery. For the French, they were a calamity. The English agreement was closely modeled on the Franco-Ottoman Capitulations of 1569, which had not been renewed since Murad's accession in 1574. Now the English had trading rights, the Ottomans were in league with the Spanish, and it was the French, preoccupied with their own internal religious strife, who were left politically and commercially isolated. Just weeks after signing the English Capitulations, Murad sent a terse letter to Henry III, rejecting any suggestion that Ottoman alliances with countries such as England violated prior agreements with France, assuring him somewhat disingenuously that "there is absolutely no refusing or repulsing to the coming and going of anybody," and "nothing whatsoever to preoccupy you concerning the ancient friendship with you and in the matters of precedence and pre-eminence over the other kings."[25] As European rulers of various theological persuasions queued up to court Murad, the French risked losing their long-standing influence at the Porte.

As the French floundered, Harborne prospered. From his residence in Galata, he exploited the Capitulations to consolidate a thriving commercial network across the Mediterranean. With the financial backing of Osborne and Staper, he traded with merchants as far north as Poland and the Baltic, as far west as Algiers, stretching all the way to Syria in the east, as well as with Turks, Egyptians, Greeks and Italians. He bought cotton, yarn and carpets from Turkey, flax from Egypt and the Black Sea, wine, oil and currants from Crete and Zante, all the time extending his trade in the ubiquitous English kerseys, lead, tin and copper. He was escorted everywhere by two Janissaries, a sign of the esteem in which the sultan held a man widely recognized, as one observer put it, as "the Queen's agent at the court of the great Turk, by whom he is held in the greatest credit."[26] Harborne even used this "credit" to visit

Ottoman-controlled Jerusalem on a pilgrimage that was probably as good for business as it was for his soul.

Just as it seemed that Harborne had achieved more than anyone in London could have hoped, disaster struck again. In September 1580, the *Bark Roe,* a merchant vessel carrying a cargo worth over £1,000 of kerseys, tin, brazilwood, madder, lead and broken "bell metal" from English Catholic churches, left London for the eastern Mediterranean. The ship's captain was Peter Baker, a servant of Edward de Vere, Earl of Oxford (one of Elizabeth's closest advisers and the man an eccentric minority still believe wrote Shakespeare's plays). Baker was already known in London merchant circles as a "greedy" and "evil man" with a reputation for robbing Christians, having seized a ship in the Mediterranean five years earlier laden with salt. He was responsible for a crew of around seventy, including two merchants, and a ship of 160 tons armed with twenty-four cannon. The crew would report much later that Baker had announced they were traveling "as merchants, though at sea the captain armed himself as a man-of-war," announcing that "we were sailing for Turkey to act as pirates." By January 1581, another crew member recalled, they were "laden with broken bells from England, and when we went to Malta" they made arrangements to sell the metal stripped from English churches to the Maltese Knights of St. John. After fifteen days anchored off Malta, Baker "summoned us on deck. It was bright moonlight; we had not yet unloaded any goods, and he informed us that he wanted to engage in cruising at a venture, plundering the Turks." The crew was divided, but one member admitted that "having unloaded the metal of the bells, we had to sail as corsairs."[27] It was a foolish decision that exposed their inexperience and cupidity—and threatened to wreck the Anglo-Turkish trade just as it began to flourish.

The following month the *Bark Roe* reached the island of Chios, which the Ottomans had taken from the Genoese in 1566. There by pure chance they met Harborne, en route to the Holy Land with a group of French and Flemish merchants. Fresh from his triumph in obtaining the English Capitulations, Harborne was oblivious to Baker's piratical plans. Instead he swaggered around the island, boasting of the terms of the Capitulations, much to the confusion of local Ottoman officials, who assumed that the new agreement ended English merchants' rights to trade under the lapsed French privileges. As the *Bark Roe* prepared to leave in early March 1581, Harborne reported that "the Jew customer of that port, alleging it unlawful for our nation to use of that [French] country banner and privilege coveted [tried] to embargo and detain" Baker's ship until he received clarification from his masters in Constantinople. Harborne hastily produced the new Capitulations, "not ever before showed," and the Jewish customs official allowed the ship to leave the island free of any charges.[28]

Having sold all his cargo, and possibly aggrieved at being detained on Chios, Baker bade farewell to Harborne and set off southward in pursuit of whatever bounty he could find. He chased Turkish and Greek vessels off Rhodes, then sailed westward across the Aegean, attacking two ships off Methóni in the Peloponnese at the end of March. "The ships we thought were Turkish," confessed one crew member, "but when we captured them we found out they were Greek and that they were carrying a cargo of camlets [woven fabric made of camel or goat hair] and raw silk."[29] To make matters worse, the cargo was owned by a consortium of Greek and Venetian merchants, and the ships' passengers included Greek Orthodox priests from Patmos, which lay under Ottoman jurisdiction, a jurisdiction that Baker had now violated.

In one foolish act Baker had brought the wrath of the Turkish, Greek and Venetian authorities down upon the English, confirming all their worst suspicions about these gauche interlopers. Seemingly unaware of the diplomatic crisis he was igniting, Baker quarreled violently with his crew over the spoils. They insisted that "he had no authority to take or rob any Christian," and forced him "to re-enter Malta to try for justice for fear that piracy would be laid to our charge."[30] By April 22 the *Bark Roe*, its crew and the two Greek ships were back in Malta, where they were imprisoned in Valletta by Monsignor Federico Cefalotto, the Maltese representative of the Roman Inquisition.

Over the next four months the Maltese authorities began building a case against Baker around claims made by the Greeks (who wanted their cargo back) and the Venetians (who demanded 12,000 ducats to cover their losses). Even worse, the captured Greek priests from Patmos lay within the jurisdiction of the Turkish admiral Qilich Ali Pasha, who was still smarting from having had to surrender English galley slaves to Harborne just two years earlier. The admiral immediately blamed the fiasco on the unsuspecting Englishman, condemning him as a spy and a pirate and demanding that the sultan imprison him and fine him 40,000 ducats and revoke the Capitulations. Horrified, Harborne rushed back to Constantinople to try to clear his name with the Ottoman authorities, from where he sent a letter to Lord Burghley on June 9, 1581, explaining the situation.

As he wrote, Harborne knew that the future of the Anglo-Ottoman alliance hung in the balance. For the first time in nearly three years, his usually cool and urbane demeanor gave way to fear and self-pity. "Behold," he wrote to Burghley, "in what pit of perplexity and snares of unluckiness (almost inevitable) I am entangled through the unchristian and detestable dealings of Peter Baker." Baker's actions had unleashed "the slanderous and hellish barking of the maliciously disposed Admiral," who threatened to ruin not only "our English traffic" in the region but also Harborne's personal reputation in "disgorging his long hidden poison against me." Baker's stupidity had driven Harborne to the brink of despair. "The intolerable grief of mind which these pirates have caused me, I cannot utter," he wrote. His greatest fear was how Sultan Murad would respond, and he invited Burghley to reflect on how such accusations would prejudice "this heathen prince against me, a worm."[31] Shorn of the usual honorific flourishes and verbose rhetoric that characterized Anglo-Ottoman correspondence, in this moment of extreme peril Harborne's veil slipped, and he was left calling Murad a heathen and seeing himself as little more than a parasite.

Harborne had good reason to panic. Arrested by the Ottoman authorities and subjected to relentless interrogation, he now admitted to Burghley that he had used credit to buy merchandise and send it back to London, but that as a result of Baker's piracy all his assets had been frozen and he had no money to settle his debts. To add to his humiliation, he had to beg the French ambassador to act as surety, which Germigny did with grace and, one imagines, some satisfaction, informing

Henry III of the remarkable turn of events and noting that Baker's and Harborne's behavior "gives a very bad smell to the said English here."[32] Harborne's pleading with the Ottomans was futile. Murad revoked the English Capitulations and signed new ones with the French. By July 1581 France was once again in control of European trade into Turkey, and Harborne's mission seemed in ruins.

In Malta, things were going from bad to worse. Baker and his crew were put on trial by the Maltese Inquisition. It focused, as usual, on heresy—an apparently straightforward issue when confronted with English Protestants—and the settlement of commercial debts was quickly subsumed by darker fears of plots and conspiracies involving those suspected of harboring reformist religious beliefs. Baker's arrest had coincided with a political crisis on Malta. Cefalotto had been appointed grand inquisitor by Pope Gregory XIII in late 1580 and immediately used his newfound power to accuse French members of the island's Knights of St. John of Huguenot sympathies. The crisis was compounded by the decision of a group of Knights in July 1581 to oust the octogenarian grand master Jean de la Cassière, just as Baker was being arraigned. Cefalotto's subsequent report to his superiors in Rome the following spring claimed to have uncovered not just an isolated case of piracy but a vast anti-Catholic conspiracy. "The plot of the capture of Malta was conceived," he wrote, "by the English Queen, the Duke of Alençon and the Turks through their intermediary, Peter Baker, who was captain of the English ship *Roe*." Cefalotto made lurid accusations that French Huguenots and English Protestants were in league with Muslim Turks to destroy what he called "the Catholic Commonwealth" and claimed he had uncovered letters proposing an Anglo-Ottoman invasion of Malta that would transform the political balance of power in the Mediterranean. He ordered that Baker and eight other Englishmen be dispatched to Rome, where they would stand trial for heresy.[33]

When the news reached London, Burghley advised Elizabeth to sacrifice Baker and apologize to Murad in a bid to salvage something of the imperiled Anglo-Ottoman trade. On June 26, 1581, she sent a letter to the sultan regretting "this unfortunate hap." Scrupulously avoiding specific names or details, she apologized for the "most injurious and grievous wrong which of late came unto our understanding . . . done unto certain of your subjects by certain of our subjects, as yet not apprehended." Choosing her words with care, Elizabeth regretted that Baker's actions "doth infringe the credit of our faith, violate the force of our authority, and impeach the estimation of our word faithfully given unto your imperial dignity." She implored Murad to "not withdraw your gracious favor from us . . . to hinder the traffic of our subjects."[34] Elizabeth must have been furious at having to grovel in this way to Harborne's "heathen prince," but unless she did so there seemed little chance that the Anglo-Turkish alliance would be renewed.

Even as Elizabeth wrote her letter, Harborne was battling to save his reputation, not to mention his liberty, in Constantinople. He accepted the humiliation of French diplomatic security to help contest the fines levied against him, and he used his dragoman, Mustafa Beg, to open communications with the current grand vizier, an unimpressed Koca Sinan Pasha. To his delight Mustafa reported that the Ottomans, perhaps in response to Elizabeth's letter, were prepared to do a deal. They would restore the English privileges on condition that the queen formalize trade and diplomatic relations and appoint an official ambassador to the Porte. Harborne decided to cut his losses, and on July 17 he fled Constantinople. He had spent three arduous and expensive years building up the Anglo-Ottoman alliance from nothing. Now Walsingham's "apt man" was returning to London hounded and impoverished.

5

Unholy Alliances

By the summer of 1581, events had conspired to frustrate Elizabeth's attempts to establish formal alliances with Muslim rulers in Morocco and Turkey. The death of Abd al-Malik at the Battle of Alcácer-Quibir had robbed Elizabethan merchants of one of their staunchest allies, and it was unclear whether his successor, Ahmad al-Mansur, would prove as receptive to English trade. Peter Baker's clumsy piracy seemed to have ended hopes of a commercial alliance with the Ottomans. At their trial before the Roman Inquisition, Baker and his crew were found guilty of heresy, for which most were consigned to the horror of the galleys, although it was reported that Baker had escaped before reaching Rome and was never heard of again, just another renegade who disappeared into the vastness of the Mediterranean. William Harborne, meanwhile, faced the likelihood, upon his return to London, of public disgrace and humiliation at his handling of the *Bark Roe* incident.

The unregulated nature of trade with Morocco had left the English merchants particularly vulnerable to sudden regime change, and Harborne's lack of diplomatic accreditation had always limited his ability to negotiate with both the Ottomans and the resident Christian emissaries. The Ottoman demand that Elizabeth appoint an official resident ambassador to the Porte if relations were to continue was the catalyst for a radical change in policy. Walsingham and Burghley had long favored tacit support for regulated trading companies without committing the state to full responsibility for their actions, primarily because they lacked the resources, but such a policy wasn't working in Russia, Persia, Morocco or—so it now seemed—Turkey.

Protests against unregulated commerce had been going on since the late 1560s, when the Muscovy Company had asked for a monopoly on trade in the northern region, asserting that "this Russian trade will be destroyed as the trade of Barbary is . . . through the greediness of the subjects of this realm carrying thither more of this country's commodities than that country was able to consume, and by that means also causing the Barbary commodities to rise excessively."[1]

In 1601, John Wheeler, the secretary of the Merchant Adventurers Company, published his *Treatise of Commerce* arguing in favor of joint-stock companies, and claiming that most of London's merchants believed that "it is most profitable both for the prince and the country to use a governed company, and not to permit a promiscuous, straggling and dispersed trade."[2] This may have been a self-interested view that lacked unanimity throughout the City, but it seemed to make sense when trading with particularly remote markets like those in Russia, Persia and the eastern Mediterranean. By the time Wheeler's book came out, London's mercantile community had proposed a series of initiatives to regulate trade in Muslim lands, from the joint-stock model pioneered by the Muscovy Company to regulated companies given exclusive trading rights by government charter in return for a percentage of customs duties on imports.

The shift in government policy precipitated by the *Bark Roe* crisis affected the Turkish trade especially: on September 11, 1581, the crown issued "The Letters Patents, or Privileges Granted by Her Majesty to Sir Edward Osborne, Master Richard Staper, and certain other Merchants of London for their trade into the dominions of the Great Turk." Under its terms Osborne was appointed governor of the proposed joint-stock company in recognition both of his "great adventure and industry" and of the "great costs and charges" incurred in establishing the Turkish trade. His knowledge of the cloth trade as well as his familiarity with markets as diverse as Brazil, Portugal and the Baltics made him an obvious choice. He would lead a team of merchants tasked with nominating up to twelve others who would be allowed "during the term of seven years from the date of these patents, freely [to] trade, traffic and use feats [transactions] of merchandise into, and from the dominions of the said Grand Signior."[3] The company was empowered to create its own internal regulations in return for agreeing to pay £500 of customs duties per annum into the Exchequer. It would call itself the Turkey Company. How its members could inveigle themselves back into the trust of the Ottoman Porte following the *Bark Roe* debacle and Harborne's departure was unclear.

After three decades of trading with Muslim powers, Elizabethans were beginning to express increased interest—and some unease—at what was happening in Morocco and Turkey. One outlet for such interests was London's theater. Ever since the first commercial playhouses had opened in 1576, the stage had quickly become a touchstone for popular hopes and fears concerning everything from witchcraft to adultery and cross-dressing. Throughout the 1580s and 1590s new theaters were being built across London, and, alongside other arenas for public spectacle such as executions, floggings and royal progresses, the Elizabethan public were learning to enjoy their leisure time in the rich and fascinating world of contemporary drama. The various theater companies running the playhouses boasted some of the country's most powerful aristocrats as their patrons, and their plays were regularly performed at Elizabeth's court. Yet public drama was also regarded with suspicion by London's civic and religious authorities. Preachers condemned theaters as breeding idleness, lust and vanity, and worried that, as institutions driven by profit, and as places where hundreds of people met regularly, they offered a potentially subversive alternative to the church. Writing in 1579, Stephen Gosson, a former playwright and one of the theater's earliest and sharpest critics, attacked what he saw as its alien and worthless commercial nature, arguing that "were not we so foolish to taste every drug, and buy every trifle, players would shut in their shops, and carry their trash to some other country."[4] Gosson, who was also a failed actor, condemned theater as "the invention of the devil, the offerings of idolatry, the pomp of worldlings, the blossoms of vanity, the root of apostasy, the food of iniquity, riot and adultery."[5]

In response to such attacks, Elizabeth appointed a master of the revels in 1581 to censor any play performed in the city deemed offensive to the church or state. Wary of such opprobrium, the early theater impresarios built playhouses outside London's ancient Roman walls, in the so-called liberties, areas free from the oversight of the city's civic authorities and usually instead under relatively lax royal or aristocratic control. The Rose, the Hope and the Swan were all open-air playhouses erected on the south bank of the Thames—or Bankside—an area known for its dangerous yet also glamorous atmosphere. People crossed over to the south bank to visit a brothel or a bear pit—or to see a play. In the minds of many Londoners the three activities were interchangeable. When Philip Henslowe first bought the lease of the Rose tavern it was a brothel, whose activities continued to provide a profitable supplement to the theater that he erected in the building's backyard.[6] He also built the Hope Theatre on the site of a bear garden, where up to a thousand spectators could come and pay a penny to see a play, then return the next day and spend the same amount to watch a bear tied to a stake, whipped and attacked by dogs.[7]

The theater inhabited a precarious position in Elizabethan London: it was a vibrant new industry, a contributor to London's financial prosperity, watched by thousands from all walks of life. Yet it was also subjected to relentless attack from the authorities. Its practitioners lived and worked in London's poorest areas alongside volatile and marginalized communities of prostitutes, servants, artisans and "strangers"— people escaping religious persecution and slavery from the Low Countries, North Africa, the Ottoman Empire and even the New World. The theater was drawn to the stories reaching London from the Islamic world of enslavement, conversion, piracy and heroic adventure because they held a mirror up to its own practices and people.

In the summer of 1581, a play appeared that dramatized the issues of trade, money, religion and national differences generated by recent events in and around Turkey. Its author, Robert Wilson, was a talented young actor and playwright attached to a company financed by Elizabeth's favorite, Robert Dudley, the Earl of Leicester. The play was called *The Three Ladies of London*. In 1583 Wilson would subsequently transfer his allegiance to the theatrical company called Queen Elizabeth's Men and forge his reputation producing plays for the Rose Theatre, which opened six years later. But in the early 1580s he was still learning his trade with Leicester's Men and writing plays indebted to the medieval morality tradition and classical Roman city comedy whose sobriety might even have satisfied Stephen Gosson.

The Three Ladies of London centers on the struggle between personifications of Love, Conscience and Lucre. It begins in London, with Lady Love and Lady Conscience complaining that Lady Lucre and her employees, the vice characters of Dissimulation, Fraud, Simony and Usury, have destroyed the traditional civic virtues and replaced them with the pursuit of money. The problem is identified as foreign goods coming into England purchased with money borrowed at excessive interest rates—a practice known as usury and condemned as immoral. Lady Love complains:

> For Lucre men come from Italy, Barbary, Turkey,
> From Jewry: nay, the pagan himself
> Endangers his body to gape forth her pelf [money].
> They forsake mother, prince, country, religion, kiff and kin,
> Nay, men care not what they forsake, so Lady Lucre they win.[8]

The overseas trade practiced in Muslim kingdoms like Morocco and Turkey by merchants such as Hogan and Harborne is identified as the source of the problem, responsible for eroding England's time-honored social relations.

As the play progresses, Usury and Simony begin their work on behalf of Lady Lucre. Both vices are represented as nefarious Italian Catholics infiltrating virtuous Protestant England. Usury explains that he left his birthplace in Venice to come to London because "England was such a place for Lucre to bide."[9] Simony admits that his "birth, nursery and bringing up hath hitherto been in Rome, that ancient religious city" where he had been selling ecclesiastical privileges (including papal indulgences) before English merchants smuggled him into London— where, he tells Lucre, "I heard in what great estimation you were."[10] Wilson then introduces an effete, villainous Italian merchant called

Mercadorus with a ludicrous accent. He tells Lady Lucre—addressed as "Madonna"—"me do for love of you tink no pain too mush."[11] Lucre orders him to "go among the Moors, Turkes, and pagans" to sell English grain, leather and beef. In return "for these good commodities" he must bring back exotic oriental "trifles to England" such as amber, jet, coral "and every such bauble,"[12] expensive objects with little intrinsic value. With comic relish Mercadorus acknowledges the widespread awareness of—and concern with—the English trade with Morocco and Turkey:

> Tink ye not dat me have carried over corn, ledar, beef and bacon
>   too all tis while,
> And brought hedar many baubles dese countryman to beguile?
> Yes, shall me tell you Madonna? Me and my countrymans have
>   sent over
> Bell-metal to make ordnance, yea and ordnance itself beside,
> Dat my country and oder countries be so well furnished as dis
>   country, and has never been espied.[13]

The play invites its audience to laugh at England's weakness for fripperies and its willingness to arm Muslims with metal taken from churches. The country is seen as sick, exporting its resources and absorbing unhealthy "baubles," and even arming its opponents.[14] As Mercadorus pursues his villainy, Usury murders the character personifying Hospitality to ensure that money is spent on "trifles" rather than the poor, Love is forced into a marriage with Dissimulation, and Conscience falls into debt and turns to running a brothel.[15]

Meanwhile, Mercadorus arrives in Turkey, where he is confronted by Gerontus, described as a "Jewish usurer in Turkey," who has lent him money to buy goods in London. Gerontus complains that Mercadorus has broken the terms of his bond. "You know I lent you two thousand ducats for three months' space," he tells Mercadorus, but the unscrupulous Italian "fled out of the country." Gerontus complains that if Jews behaved like this they would never be trusted, "But many of you Christians make no conscience to falsify your faith and break your day"[16] (that is, a contractually agreed settlement date). He claims the original capital plus the accrued interest, but Mercadorus deceives him, promising to settle in a few more days, while asking Gerontus for "toys" or "some fantastic new knack," because "da gentlewomans in England buy such tings for fantasy."[17] Seduced, Gerontus offers him perfumes, precious stones and "many more fit things to suck away money from such green-headed [covetous] wantons,"[18] suggesting yet another group to blame for England's consumerism, this time women.

When Mercadorus defaults yet again, Gerontus swears "by mighty Mahomet" to have him arrested and brings him before a "Judge of Turkey" to resolve the dispute. The judge is the first Turk recorded on the English stage. Gerontus fears that Mercadorus will appear "in Turkish weeds to defeat me of my money"[19] by converting to Islam. This is based on a principle pronounced by the Turkish judge, who warns Gerontus that "if any man forsake his faith, king, country and become a Mahomet," then all his "debts are paid."[20] Sure enough, Mercadorus enters wearing a turban, announcing repeatedly, "me will be a Turk,"[21] and agrees to swear upon the judge's holy book, possibly the Qur'an. Gerontus is horrified and, fearing that he will be blamed for Mercadorus's apostasy, cancels the debt. A jubilant Mercadorus accepts, but then refuses to "turn Turk," leaving the judge to offer the following homily before he departs: "Jews seek to excel in Christianity, and Christians in Jewishness."[22] Mercadorus exits with his own vicious little moral:

> Me be a Turk? No. It will make my Lady Lucre to smile
> When she knows how me did da scald [scurvy] Jew beguile.[23]

In this convoluted three-way exchange, it is the Catholic Mercadorus who is seen as the villain, not the Turk or the Jew, who both try to behave honorably by pursuing the debt in question. Eventually they are all corrupted by money, but this is a Protestant morality play that trades in bad faith: Wilson ends up blaming the Italian Catholic merchant for the play's ills, while exculpating the Muslim and the Jew.[24] In the final scene a judge named Nemo arraigns Ladies Lucre, Love and Conscience and imprisons them in a forlorn attempt to ensure that "we be not corrupted with the unsatiate desire of vanishing earthly treasure."[25] Nemo's name means "no one" in Latin, which hardly inspires confidence that London's rampant materialism will be curbed.

A clumsy melodrama, caught between the two-dimensional personifications of medieval morality plays and the more dynamic verisimilitude of later Elizabethan drama, Wilson's play has not stood the test of time. It is rarely studied and never staged these days, but in late 1581 its topicality was unquestionable. It addressed the hopes and anxieties of a Turkish trade that was enriching England, that aligned it with the Ottomans and their Jewish commercial intermediaries, and that cemented Protestant opposition to Catholicism. If lucre could corrupt a Catholic into converting to Islam, and enable a Jew to worship Muhammad, then how easily might Protestant Englishmen be seduced into embracing Judaism—or even Islam?

For Wilson, the corrupting influence of international trade was symptomatic of the larger problem of usury. On May 19, 1581, a proclamation had been issued "Reviving the Statute against Usury" in response to public "doubts and questions" regarding the Act of Usury passed in 1571, which had fixed the legal limit at which interest could be charged on loans at 10 percent. The "doubts" being raised clearly related to moneylenders trying to exceed the set rate, partly in response to the growing volume of overseas trade, including with Morocco and Turkey. The statute was therefore not "against" usury, but simply sought to redefine its terms. Wilson's play exploited a general confusion about usury. Having been regarded for centuries as an immoral practice condemned by scriptural authority, it was now increasingly seen as a necessary evil, mainly due to the expansion of overseas trade. The traditional ways of doing business face-to-face at market time, with goods bartered or exchanged on the spot for hard currency, were giving way to an international credit network over vast distances and time, where bills of exchange were required to transact goods, and where currency and interest rates dictated profit (or loss).[26] Elizabethan England's economic prosperity depended on usury, but nobody liked to admit it: hiding behind a Catholic, a Jew or even a Muslim was infinitely preferable.

Protestant merchants like Anthony Jenkinson, Edmund Hogan and William Harborne had all needed to obtain credit to purchase goods from Muslim merchants, and they invariably turned for help to Jewish brokers. Although Christian and Islamic theology officially forbade the practice, the Torah and Talmud tolerated the use of financial loans, so the Englishmen could ask Jewish merchants or moneylenders to lend to them. These religious distinctions over usury lay at the heart of anti-Semitic prejudice in the period. In times of peace and profit, Christian merchants and their Muslim counterparts accepted Jewish merchants and moneylenders as integral to their trade: but when times were bad and losses mounted, the Jews became scapegoats. Wilson's play finds it is easy to blend the usurious and credulous Jew Gerontus with Turkish Muslims, and encourage his Protestant English audience to laugh as he is duped by the Catholic Mercadorus, but over the next decade the portrayal of Jews and international finance on the Elizabethan stage would become darker and more complicated in the hands of Christopher Marlowe and William Shakespeare.

In September 1582 John Aylmer, Bishop of London, wrote a letter to Thomas Blanke, lord mayor of London, complaining about the fate of "certain miserable captives in Turkey." Aylmer hoped that these Englishmen could be ransomed with the help of collections held in London's churches, and "redeemed out of that hellish thralldom where they be, to the great danger of their souls." Aylmer went on to make the first known attack on the Anglo-Ottoman Capitulations:

> Surely in mine opinion it is very strange, and dangerous, that the desire of worldly and transitory things should carry men so far, with such kind of traffic, which neither our ancestors before us knew of, nor can be attempted without selling of souls for purchasing of pelf to the great blemish of our religion and the shame of our country. Wherefore if your Lordship and the rest of your brethren could by your authority stay such intercourse with infidels and save the souls of our people from the Gulf of Mahomet, I think you should do a gracious deed and win an everlasting remembrance.[27]

Complaints like Aylmer's had little discernible impact on the City's merchants or on Elizabeth's advisers, who seem to have had no qualms about entering the "Gulf of Mahomet." On the contrary, even as Aylmer was writing, plans were being hatched to expand commerce with Turkey and Morocco by securing commercial monopolies in both regions. When it came to trade, material interests prevailed over religious ones.

Where the English saw a new commercial opportunity, the Spanish saw a serious threat to their geopolitical interests. Mendoza, the Spanish ambassador to London, had already written a long memorandum to King Philip II in 1582 outlining the commercial and geopolitical dangers of England's alliances with Shi'a and Sunni Muslim kingdoms. "The English," he wrote,

> settled through the Muscovite with the Tartars on the banks of the Volga to allow the free passage of their merchandise down the river to the Caspian Sea; whilst the Persian, building large ships in Astrakhan, should give them leave to trade and distribute their merchandise, through Media and Persia, in exchange for goods which reach the Persians by the rivers that run from the East Indies to the Caspian Sea. This privilege was granted to the English by the Persian.

He went on to express anxiety about the Anglo-Ottoman trade, reiterating that it was "extremely profitable" for the English, "as they take great quantities of tin and lead thither, which the Turk buys of them almost for its weight in gold, the tin being vitally necessary for the casting of guns and the lead for purposes of war. It is of double important to the Turk now, in consequence of the excommunication pronounced *ipso facto* by the Pope upon any person who provides or sells to infidels such materials as these."

Mendoza warned that the English were in discussion with the Ottomans to import merchandise from Persia through Constantinople and overland via Russia, "without their having to pass, as at present, by Italy." Mendoza added that with the Ottomans' collusion the English "might monopolize the drug and spice trades," thus "weakening the forces of your Majesty, by diverting the English trade from Italy."[28] In fact, the English had nowhere near the resources to achieve such a global monopoly, but Mendoza's letter was a sign of how far their success in the east had rattled the Spanish. As far as Mendoza could discern in the spring of 1582, the scale of their diplomatic achievements in Russia, Persia, Morocco and Turkey suggested that anything was possible.

Nobody was more surprised by Elizabeth's renewed interest in Ottoman trade than William Harborne. Having arrived back in London as Wilson's play was being performed, the disgraced Englishman must have assumed that his Turkish career was over. He was not mentioned in the articles establishing the Turkey Company that September, but Burghley, Osborne and Staper decided that his experience outweighed his humiliation and proposed to send him back to Constantinople. A hugely relieved Harborne waited patiently as Osborne and Staper haggled with Burghley over his formal commission as the queen's first Turkish ambassador. They also wrangled over the financial terms of the Turkey Company's establishment, requesting that the crown settle Harborne's outstanding debts of £600 and cover his travel costs and salary for a five-year tenure, and provide an annual budget of £1,000 for buying the sultan lavish "presents" (thinly veiled bribes).

Burghley demurred, knowing that Elizabeth wanted all the financial and political benefits of overseas trade without incurring any of its costs.[29] The queen may also have hesitated to take such a momentous step toward formalizing a diplomatic *and* commercial alliance with the Ottomans. Osborne and Staper were interested in trade, not politics, and stood their ground. They reminded Burghley of Elizabeth's promise to Murad "to send thither her ambassador to gratify his goodwill . . . whose presence is hourly expected." Any delay risked alienating Murad, who might "think himself deluded" and refuse to sanction new English Capitulations.[30] Burghley would not relent, and the new company's governors were forced to foot Harborne's bills.

The queen seemed pleased to save the cost of paying for Harborne's embassy, and on November 20, 1582, she issued a formal commission to Harborne "to be her majesty's ambassador or agent in the parts of Turkey." Praising the "trustiness, obedience, wisdom and disposition of this our beloved servant William Harborne," the commission ordained him "our true and undoubted orator, messenger, deputy and agent." He was also given a letter to present to Murad, reiterating his diplomatic credentials, in the hope that his appointment would cement the "perfect and inviolable" league between England and Turkey, and that "a noble traffic will flourish between these nations."[31] Within weeks Harborne was aboard the Turkey Company's ship *Susan*, bound for Constantinople. In less than eighteen months he had gone from being a self-confessed "worm" fearing for his life, to England's first ambassador to the Ottoman Empire and the newly formed Turkey Company's official representative.

As Harborne set sail, London's merchants were also reassessing Moroccan trade in response to the sudden interest of a new and powerful investor: Robert Dudley, Earl of Leicester. The earl was one of Elizabeth's most devoted servants and for many years a suitor for her hand in marriage. In 1562 he was appointed to her Privy Council and subsequently made lord steward of the royal household. In addition to his keen support of the arts and patronage of Robert Wilson and his acting company, Leicester was an enthusiastic advocate of trade and exploration, having invested in the Merchant Adventurers and the Muscovy Company and having acted as the principal promoter for Francis Drake's global circumnavigation in 1577–1578. By 1581, with the Muscovy trade struggling and the Turkey Company about to receive its royal charter, Leicester turned his attentions to Morocco.

The earl had good reason to be interested. Morocco's commercial possibilities were obvious, although still relatively undeveloped in the aftermath of the Battle of Alcácer-Quibir. Equally tantalizing was the possibility of a political and military alliance between Elizabeth and al-Mansur. A year earlier, in June 1580, al-Mansur had exchanged letters with Elizabeth (many since lost), in which he flattered her as the greatest adherent of the "religion of Christ," labeling her "the majesty in the lands of Christ, the sultana Isabel," and promising a mutually beneficial coalition. "As you are doing the best to facilitate our affairs," wrote al-Mansur, "so we will do the same for you here."[32] If Leicester could broker an Anglo-Moroccan alliance it would fulfill two of his most cherished ambitions: getting closer to Elizabeth and antagonizing the Spanish.

In June 1581 Elizabeth issued a license to John Symcot, a "merchant trading into Barbary," allowing him to sell six hundred tons of English timber "and to bring into this our realm so much saltpeter as he shall have in exchange in Barbary for the same wood."[33] Symcot was Leicester's agent, and Leicester had persuaded Elizabeth to grant him this lucrative concession that promised to reopen the trade in saltpeter. The commission did not escape the attention of the Spanish ambassador Mendoza, who naturally informed Philip. "Some Englishmen have arrived in this country," he informed Philip in October 1581, "having arranged with the king of Morocco to take him timber from here ready cut to build his galleys. The quantity is so large that, although Leicester is mixed up in the affair for the sake of profit, they have had to send to Holland for some of the wood, as it could not be furnished here."[34]

Unfortunately for Leicester, the whole venture was a disaster from beginning to end. Symcot was already in trouble with the lord mayor and sheriffs of London, who arrested him on suspicion of fraud. Leicester was furious and demanded his immediate release, insisting that Symcot was "bound to her majesty in the sum of two thousand pounds for the bringing over hither certain quantities of saltpeter and other commodities for the maintenance of her majesty's munitions from the country of Barbary."[35] This appeal scarcely concealed the earl's personal interest, but his closeness to the queen meant that it worked. In October 1582 Symcot was released and allowed to sail for Morocco.

The English merchants pursuing respectable if unregulated trade in Morocco were unimpressed by Symcot's arrival. They had quietly sought trade in sugar, cloth and timber with Ahmad al-Mansur ever since his accession in 1578. Symcot immediately started to use his royal license and Leicester's influence as though they were a monopoly, playing on Elizabeth's imprimatur to obtain an agreement from al-Mansur to grant him control of the trade in iron, lead and tin. He detained certain merchants' cargoes destined for England and was even accused of opening their letters and sharing them with al-Mansur. An almighty row ensued. A group of English merchants wrote to Walsingham complaining of the "sinister and undirect dealings of John Symcot and his adherents," to which Symcot responded by protesting against the "lewd practices and speeches" he claimed were being directed at him, insisting he was only doing the queen's and Leicester's work.[36]

As the dispute escalated throughout the summer, the English merchants wrote again to Walsingham, demanding he redress their grievances. Their position was difficult: as legitimate but unregulated merchants, they were furious with the fly-by-night English traders flooding the Moroccan market with goods, driving prices and hence profits down, but they were also opposed to a creeping state monopoly that threatened their dissolution. With their future in jeopardy, the merchants justified their complaints by turning to religion. Having shown few qualms hitherto about trading with Muslims, they now told Walsingham that the "undirect and hard dealing" of unscrupulous English merchants in "forbidden commodities" into "the heathen country of Barbary" was causing "great clamors to be spread in other countries, that out of England there should be suffered to go munitions and other furniture to the aid of the infidels, which causeth our most true and pure religion to be brought into question." Arming the infidel only strengthened Moroccan pirates and threatened "captivity to others who profess Christianity, but even also to her majesty's subjects that tradeth [in] Spain."[37] According to this nervous claim, forbidden Moroccan trade was putting English Protestants in double jeopardy—captivity by armed Muslims and insolvency from antagonized Spanish Catholics.

The complaint painted a halcyon picture of harmonious and profitable Anglo-Moroccan trade "until the first shippers of unlawful commodities spoiled the same." This was an illusion, but a powerful one nonetheless: these interlopers were described as inveigling their way into the Moroccan ruler's affections, obtaining from him a "grant to the Jews, renters of the sugar houses, to give unto them other men's sugars long before paid for, by which hard dealing the Jews bankrupted [them], and thereby her majesty's subjects lost very near £40,000, the circumstances whereof would be tedious to trouble your honor."[38]

A three-way trade among English merchants, Muslim rulers and Jewish intermediaries had been going on in Morocco for decades, with hardly a murmur of dissent, but once the private trade came under threat, the regulars opposed the monopolists by playing their trump card, religion, disclosing lurid tales of unscrupulous English merchants in league with villainous Muslims and greedy Jewish moneylenders. The problem, however, was not really caused by Muslims or Jews, but by Symcot, who was condemned in the merchants' complaint for trading in "forbidden commodities, with such others that there doth associate them about some new and secret contract" that threatened to end commercial competition and by extension the unregulated trade. The complainants begged Walsingham to write to Symcot and to apply pressure on Leicester to stop both men's high-handed interference.

As a close associate of Leicester's, Walsingham was unlikely to uphold a protest against the queen's favorite. Besides, he was more interested in the news coming out of Constantinople, where William Harborne had arrived safely on March 29, 1583.

It was a wiser and more circumspect Harborne who returned to Constantinople that spring. He rented a house he called Rapamat (a corruption of "Ahmad") from a man named Ahmad Pasha in the Findikli district along the Bosporus, a safe distance from the prying eyes of the other European ambassadors up the hill in Galata. This time he established a formal embassy consisting of his secretary, Edward Barton, as well as interpreters, servants, stables and a Janissary guard.[39] He lost no time in paying due obeisance to the grand vizier, Kanijeli Siyavuş Pasha, and his old adversary, Admiral Qilich Ali Pasha. He also visited Hagia Sophia, which he acknowledged respectfully as "the chief see and church of primacy of this Turk."[40]

On April 24 Harborne was given a formal audience with Murad III at Topkapi Sarayi. He presented an array of gifts, described by the incensed Venetian ambassador as "a most beautiful watch set with jewels and pearls, ten pairs of shoes, two pretty lap dogs, twelve lengths of royal cloth, two lengths of white linen, and thirteen pieces of silver gilt."[41] Having this time ensured that he presented the right credentials as ambassador, Harborne was rewarded with the renewal of the Anglo-Ottoman treaty that had been canceled in 1581. This allowed him to begin appointing consuls across the Ottoman territories to represent English commercial interests. He boasted of his immediate success in renegotiating the customs duties charged on English goods. "In my oration to the Grand Signior upon my first arrival for her majesty I obtained of him for the company the release of almost half his custom," he recalled, reducing the Ottomans' customs duty rates from 5 percent to 2 percent, giving the Turkey Company a crucial advantage over its European rivals.[42]

The day after his audience with Murad, Harborne appointed Harvie Millers as "our consul in Cairo, Alexandria, Egypt and other places adjacent, for the safe protection of body and goods of her majesty's subjects."[43] Two months later Richard Forster was appointed to Aleppo, Damascus, Amman, Tripoli (in Lebanon) and Jerusalem. Other appointments followed on Chios and Patras, as well as in Algiers and Tunis, creating an impressive network of English residents across the Mediterranean in a vast arc from the Straits of Gibraltar to the Holy Land and into the Ionian Sea. Harborne reported that Murad had agreed to "the delivery of captives," English galley slaves, "freed *gratis* at our request."[44]

Having thought he had seen the back of Harborne, the Venetian ambassador Gianfrancesco Morosini was infuriated by the Englishman's sudden reappearance. He shared the French ambassador's anger at the "breach" of their treaty with the sultan, "which provides that all ships, except those of Venice, must sail under the French flag." He reported that Harborne "was escorted by no Christians, only by the Turks," adding rather petulantly that "even the Turks in contempt call him a Lutheran, and show that they are far from pleased to see him."[45] However, he confessed that Harborne "has been well received by his majesty [Murad], who is flattered that such a powerful queen should have sent from four thousand miles away to tell him that she is all for him and desires his friendship. He considers also that she is a very fit instrument to damage the Christians, toward whom in her letters she shows an open ill-will."[46]

Against all expectations, Harborne had built a network of agents loyal to Walsingham dotted across the Mediterranean, able to facilitate smoother commercial relations (and hopefully avoid incidents like the *Bark Roe* debacle) as well as to provide vital military intelligence about

Spanish and Ottoman activities. He was now far more experienced in countering the strategies adopted against him by the resident Catholic ambassadors, most especially the French and the Venetians, who, he reported, "have the uttermost opposed themselves against us, but their malice contraried, the Venetian denieth such his proceedings, and dissemblingly pretendeth friendship, having personally visited us," while the French swore "to renew former amity."[47]

Staper and Osborne were no doubt relieved to hear of Harborne's success, as they had recently funded another team of merchants to head east with even greater ambitions to reach Persia, the Mughal court of Akbar the Great, in India, and even China. In February 1583 a group led by Ralph Fitch and John Newberry left London on board the *Tiger*, bound for Syria, with letters from Elizabeth addressed to Akbar, or "Echebar king of Cambaya," and the "King of China." They arrived in Tripoli in April and traveled overland to Aleppo, then on to Basra and Hormuz, where they were arrested by the Portuguese authorities and shipped off to Goa. Having obtained their release thanks to the intercession of local Jesuits, they fled to Agra, where they claimed to have been given the first English audience with Akbar in the late summer of 1585, although what if anything passed between them remains unknown. From here the team split up, and Newberry disappeared. But the intrepid Fitch traveled on, visiting Bengal, Burma and Malacca before making his return to England in April 1591.[48] The news of Fitch's epic adventures remained in vogue for long enough for Shakespeare to allude to them in *Macbeth* (1606), where one of the witches plots against a sailor's wife, saying, "Her husband's to Aleppo gone, master o' th' Tiger."[49] Although the venture failed to yield any concrete commercial breakthrough, it was another sign of the growing confidence of London's mercantile community.

Harborne's good fortune in Constantinople was in stark contrast to the undignified squabbling in Morocco following Symcot's arrival. His success diverted the queen's attention from Morocco, giving Walsingham a space to consider his response to the increasingly intemperate petitions of the regular merchants. Symcot died suddenly in the summer of 1583, as he was traveling back to England. This took some of the pressure off Walsingham to censure him, but the larger question of whether to introduce a commercial monopoly remained. Leicester lobbied ruthlessly for the creation of a regulated company capable of imposing a monopoly on the Moroccan trade—strictly on his own terms, of course. In April 1585, Elizabeth wrote to al-Mansur thanking him for the favor shown to Leicester over the Symcot affair, a tacit seal of approval for her favorite's Moroccan policy. It was a preemptive decision motivated by the knowledge that London's merchants were already drafting petitions arguing for and against a monopoly.

On July 15 the petitions were published. Those against a regulated company once again invoked religious differences, arguing that it would be ineffective because the "King of Barbary and all his subjects are barbarous infidels and without any knowledge of the true God; and his magistrates govern by tyranny; and therefore the danger will be great to execute any ordinance of this corporation within his kingdom, if it shall be understood to him or any of his magistrates." Their case rested on a question of trust: How could a Christian trust a Muslim, and if the Muslim's ruler refused to abide by the new corporation's terms, how could it work? Finally, they invoked the classic laissez-faire economic philosophy: Why was regulation needed when there was already a long-standing "freedom of traffic" in the region where each merchant "standeth upon his own devise"?[50]

Leicester's pro-regulation merchants adopted a more optimistic common-law approach to regulating trade, believing the statutes they proposed would "keep reasonable men in order and bridle unreasonable men trading into Barbary, by incorporating them." They pointed to the oversupply of English commodities "being sold there to much lost advantage," in contrast to the demand for Moroccan goods "viz. sugar much advanced there," that could be restrained by the creation of a regulated company (an organization with a government charter giving it exclusive rights to trade in a particular region). They also proposed that any English transgressions in Morocco could be "restrained by order and fear of punishment at home," and that if anyone impeached his countrymen in Morocco "he must of a Christian become an infidel and abandon his country, which cannot be entered." Finally, they argued that regulation was a direct response to "seeing the commodities of that country is in so few men's hands as a few wily heads, with great stocks."[51] It took an even wilier head, like Leicester's, to argue that a monopoly was required to oppose monopolization.

The result was a foregone conclusion. On the same day, July 15, 1585, the "letters patent or privileges granted by her majesty to certain noble men and merchants for a trade to Barbary" were proclaimed, providing a charter for the foundation of what would become known as the Barbary Company. Most of them were copied almost verbatim from the privileges granted to the Turkey Company less than four years earlier. But there were two important differences. The first was that the new initiative was not a joint-stock but a regulated company (the former allowed members to trade on their individual capital and at their own risk, whereas the latter formalized and shared collective investments, profits and losses). The second was that Leicester was given unprecedented executive powers so far as a commercial company was concerned. Alongside Leicester and Robert Rich, 1st Earl of Warwick, forty London merchants trading in Morocco were named who, the patent claimed, "have sustained great and grievous losses." The way to avoid such losses was to stipulate that "none others, shall and may, for, and during the space of twelve years, have and enjoy the whole freedom and liberty in the said traffic or trade, unto or from the said country of Barbary," aside from those named. Although there was no official governor, all ordnance was subject to "the consent of the said earl of Leicester," making the privilege little more than Elizabeth's gift to Leicester and his cronies to run the Moroccan trade as they liked.[52] Leicester could now ship timber and munitions to Morocco with impunity, and in return Elizabeth was guaranteed a resident company agent, at no cost to the crown, capable of pursuing a diplomatic alliance with al-Mansur against the growing threat of Spain.

The wisdom of appointing a resident agent was exhibited by the continued effectiveness of another English agent operating in the Muslim world, more than two thousand miles from Morocco, the rejuvenated William Harborne. In January 1585 Harborne had intervened successfully in yet another maritime incident that threatened Anglo-Islamic relations, but this time one committed against the English. In May 1584 the Turkey Company's ship *Jesus* had been seized, its cargo confiscated and its crew imprisoned in Tripoli (Libya). The local authorities believed that a factor had boarded the ship owing a local Turkish merchant 450 crowns, and promptly seized the ship, hanging its master and one of its crew. The vessel's fate might have remained unknown had it not been for the *Jesus*'s resourceful boatswain, Thomas Sanders, who managed somehow to smuggle a letter out of captivity in Tripoli to his father in Tavistock in Devon. Sanders provided one of the earliest English accounts of life as a galley slave. He described his "miserable bondage and slavery" in vivid detail, with lurid stories of how he was sold into the Turkish galleys, where "we were chained three and three to an oar and we rowed naked above the girdle," raiding Greek vessels trading African slaves. He wrote that some of his compatriots had been compelled to "turn Turk," graphically describing their forced circumcision.[53]

When the news reached London, the Turkey Company's directors were outraged by what they saw as a flagrant breach of the resurrected Anglo-Ottoman Capitulations by a Turkish client state. They petitioned Elizabeth successfully to raise the matter with Sultan Murad, who in turn wrote to the Kaid Ramadan Pasha, ruler of Tripoli, demanding that he release the ship, cargo and crew immediately. Emboldened by such royal support from queen and sultan, Harborne himself wrote to Ramadan Pasha in January 1585 demanding immediate restitution. The Englishman condemned the Pasha's actions as "contrary to the holy league sworn by both our princes," and warned him that unless he redeemed the crew and cargo he would "answer in another world unto God alone, and in this world unto the Grand Signior, for this heinous crime committed by you against so many poor souls, which by this your cruelty are in part dead, and in part detained by you in most miserable captivity."[54]

Harborne's argument anticipated the calls for a regulated Moroccan trade back in London; here was a Christian demanding that a Muslim abide by the terms of the contractual agreement set out in the

Capitulations, regardless of faith or personality. The authoritative tone Harborne now adopted toward a Muslim ruler was in stark contrast to the fretful, self-pitying figure pleading his case during the *Bark Roe* fiasco. It helped that he could use the Ottoman sultan as diplomatic leverage, but there was no doubting that he had finally mastered his brief, and that the English were starting to pull their weight in the Levantine trade. The letter succeeded: the captives were released and mostly melted away into the Mediterranean littoral, never to be heard of again.

Once Harborne had firmly established himself as ambassador with control of a network of English consuls across the Mediterranean, he took on a more explicitly political role. He was in regular correspondence with Walsingham, who was now briefing him to entice Murad into a desperately needed anti-Spanish alliance. By early 1585, relations with Spain were virtually on a war footing, and England was perilously isolated from the rest of Europe. As a consequence Elizabeth had finally sided with those of her counselors advising a more aggressive approach toward Spain. Walsingham, foremost among them, drew up "A Plot for the Annoying of the King of Spain," which advocated using Sir Francis Drake to launch a preemptive attack on the Spanish fleet. Elizabeth approved, unleashing Drake's squadron of twenty-five ships in a series of assaults on Spanish shipping across the Atlantic and Caribbean. On August 10, she signed the Treaty of Nonsuch with Dutch Calvinists fighting the Spanish in the Low Countries. Under its terms the queen offered the Dutch £125,000 as well as the support of an expeditionary English army led by Leicester, still preening over the successful establishment of the Barbary Company and eager for an opportunity to prove himself on the battlefield. Philip II interpreted the treaty as a declaration of war against Spain, and in October he informed Pope Sixtus V of his intention to invade England. It was a momentous decision. By December 1585 a plan for a massive fleet to sail against the English was being prepared.[55]

Keenly aware of the inevitability of a Spanish attack, Walsingham had been corresponding with his agents in the Low Countries and with Harborne in Constantinople about the need to create an Anglo-Islamic alliance against the Spanish threat. That December the spy William Herle wrote to Elizabeth from Antwerp, insisting that the English policy of arming Muslims to fight Catholics was not only expedient but righteous. "Your majesty in using the King of Fez &c," he wrote, "doth not arm a barbarian against a Christian, but a barbarian against an heretic [Philip II], the most dangerous that was in any age, the usurper of kingdoms, and the subverter of God's true religion, which you are bound as defendresse of the faith, to defend."[56] Such arguments added credence to Walsingham's Ottoman policy.

Throughout the autumn of 1585, Walsingham encouraged Harborne to agitate for Ottoman military aggression against the Spanish, adding Elizabeth's voice in the matter. "I did advise you," he wrote on October 8,

> of a course to be taken there for procuring the Grand Seigneur, if it were possible, to convert some part of his forces bent, as it should seem by your advertisements, from time to time wholly against the Persians, rather against Spain, thereby to divert the dangerous attempt and designs of the said King from these parts of Christendom. So am I at present, her majesty being, upon the success of the said King of Spain's affairs in the Low Countries, now fully resolved to oppose herself against his proceedings in defense of that distressed nation, whereof it is not otherwise likely but hot wars between him and us, wills me again to require you effectually to use all your endeavor and industry in that behalf.[57]

If Harborne could persuade Murad that it was in his interests for the Ottomans to attack the Catholic Spanish fleet in the Mediterranean, it might hamper Philip's English invasion plans. Ever the realist, Walsingham appreciated that this was an ambitious request and concluded his letter by advising Harborne that "if you shall see that the sultan cannot be brought altogether to give ear to this advice," then "procure at least that, by making show of arming to the sea for the King of Spain's dominions, hold the King of Spain in suspense, by means whereof he shall be the less bold to send forth his best forces into these parts."[58]

Like Walsingham, the Venetian Morosini understood that a pragmatic approach to religion played its part in all this subterfuge, and he wrote to the Venetian Seignory in 1585 that Murad "places especially great worth on the friendship of the Queen of England, because he is convinced that, owing to the religious schism, she will never unite against him with other princes in Christendom; she will, on the contrary, always be an excellent instrument for disturbing and thwarting such alliances."[59] Both Sunni Muslim and Protestant Christian rulers had told each other only half the reasons for their mutual association.

Even as Walsingham was turning a merchant into a spy versed in military matters, Leicester was dispatching a soldier to oversee commercial matters in Morocco. Having established the Barbary Company's privileges on terms of his choosing, it was incumbent upon him to appoint England's first official ambassador to Morocco. The man he chose was Henry Roberts, a very different kind of ambassador than William Harborne. Roberts was a client of Leicester's, a soldier with experience fighting in Ireland and privateering against the Spanish, but little knowledge of trade or diplomacy. He would later claim, "I was forced to take this voyage full sore against my will, for the which cause I was forced to yield up my place where I was settled in Ireland," saying that his forced relocation had cost him five hundred pounds.[60]

Whatever the truth, Roberts's appointment was closely linked to his association with Don António, Prior of Crato, who since losing the Portuguese crown to Philip II in 1580 had used Elizabeth's backing to support his claim to the throne. Elizabeth and Leicester appointed Roberts with a view not only to establishing formal trade relations through the Barbary Company but also to securing al-Mansur's support for Don António's claim to the Portuguese throne, yet another policy that put Protestant England and its Muslim ally Morocco on a collision course with Philip II's Spain.

Roberts left England with three ships on August 14, 1585, and arrived at Safi, on the west coast of Morocco, exactly a month later. He was met "with all humanity and honor" by the local authorities as the first official English ambassador to Morocco. He dined with the resident English, French and Flemish merchants before setting out on the ninety-mile journey inland to the capital, the "Red City" of Marrakesh.[61]

Marrakesh, which Roberts entered in the stifling September heat, was Morocco's second great city, home to nearly twenty thousand people and the gateway to the trans-Saharan caravan trade in salt, ivory, spices, gold and slaves. Founded in the eleventh century by the Berber Almoravid dynasty, it had maintained an abiding rivalry with the much older city of Fez, 280 miles to the north, whose madrasas were known throughout the Muslim world, securing its fame as one of the great centers of theological and legal scholarship. Until the 1550s Fez had remained Morocco's capital city, but with the rise of the Sa'adian dynasty power had shifted south, and by the time Roberts reached Marrakesh, al-Mansur was transforming the city into one of Islam's great imperial capitals.

In 1578 work began on a palatial complex known as the Dar al-Makhzen, designed to rival the Moorish Alhambra Palace in Granada and Philip II's Escorial, then under construction northwest of Madrid. Where Philip's palace was paid for with New World gold and silver, al-Mansur's was built on profits from Moroccan sugar. Carrara marble was imported from Tuscany and two thousand captives were brought from Fez (including many Portuguese survivors of the Battle of Alcácer-Quibir) to build the palace and new mosques, madrasas, hospitals, factories and even funerary tombs for the new sultan's ancestors. Antonio de Saldanha, a Portuguese nobleman captured by the Sa'adians who wrote a chronicle of al-Mansur's reign, claimed that the rebuilding included premises for Christian merchants, and that "in the streets set aside for their shops, all the goods of France, Italy, England and Spain were sold at lower prices than in the lands where they were produced. . . . The town of Marrakesh then attained such greatness as it had never attained before nor ever would again."[62]

Upon his arrival in Marrakesh, Roberts reported, "I was lodged by the emperor's [al-Mansur's] appointment in a fair house in the Juderia or Jurie, which is the place where the Jews have their abode, and is the fairest place, and quietest lodging in all the city."[63] Another walled Juderia, more commonly known as the *mellah*, was the first Jewish quarter established in the salt marshes outside Fez in 1438. It took its name from the Arabic *mallah,* or "salty soil."[64] Marrakesh's *mellah* had been established in the late 1550s on the same principles as Fez's, but it was very different from the Jewish ghettos created in the Christian cities of Venice (1516) and Rome (1555). In Europe the religious persecution of Jews led to severe restrictions on their rights of employment, property ownership and freedom of movement. Under Muslim rule, Jews were granted the status of a protected minority (*dhimmi*) and acknowledged to hold important positions in government and finance, as well as the monopolies over trade in sugar and Christian captives. The vast majority were Sephardic Jews, thousands of whom had started to arrive in Morocco following the expulsions in 1492 of both Muslims and Jews from the Iberian Peninsula. Their cosmopolitan experience and ability to broker international political, cultural and commercial deals on behalf of Morocco's new rulers ensured that al-Mansur was assiduous in building a *mellah* in Marrakesh with grand mansions, its own *funduq* (markets) and synagogues, as well as Christian chapels for other exalted foreigners, like Roberts, who found themselves lodged there.

To a soldier like Roberts, used to the monoglot world of England and Ireland and its stark religious divisions between Protestant and Catholic, the multiconfessional and polyglot world of Marrakesh must have come as a massive shock. Marrakesh was a multicultural city, containing Berbers, Arabs, Sephardic Jews, Africans, Moriscos and Christians, many of them merchants and diplomats, others slaves and captives hoping to be ransomed and each professing one or another of a variety of religious persuasions. Walking through the city, Roberts would have heard Arabic, Hebrew, Spanish—the lingua franca of most of the resident Europeans—Portuguese, Italian, French and even German. Marrakesh was also becoming known as a home for a new community that was caught between religions: the *renegadoes.* The Spanish *renegado* (from the Latin *renegare,* "to deny") was an apostate, specifically a Christian who had converted to Islam, although the term could also refer to Jewish and Muslim apostates. The word first entered English in the early 1580s, usually with a Spanish inflection—suggesting that it was a phenomenon associated with Spanish Catholicism rather than English Protestantism.[65]

Roberts, who was more used to quashing Catholic insurrection in Ireland than to moving in cosmopolitan communities, suddenly found himself living alongside individuals like Estêvão Dias, a Portuguese *converso*—a Jew forcibly converted to Christianity. When, in 1564, Dias had been denounced as a crypto-Jew by the Lisbon Inquisition, he immigrated to the Low Countries, where he lived for a time as a merchant. He traveled throughout Italy before settling in Marrakesh in 1581 and reconverting, adopting the name of Rabbi Joseph, at which point he began writing an extraordinary defense of his Jewish faith. Known as the "Marrakesh Dialogs," Dias's apologia is couched in the form of a dialog between two Flemish brothers. Both are merchants: one is Catholic; the other, Bernard, converts to Judaism while on business in Morocco and takes the name Obadia Ben Israel. The two brothers debate their respective religions. Obadia criticizes Catholic beliefs ranging from Trinitarianism to idolatry and denounces the recent rise of Lutheranism and Calvinism, which he identifies as a sign of the need for Christianity to embrace Judaism.[66]

In his brief account of his time in Marrakesh, Roberts expressed no interest in describing encounters with individuals like Rabbi Joseph. Instead he limited himself to prosaic details of his domestic arrangements. He occupied a spacious house alongside three resident English factors, Robert Lion, Miles Dickonson and Edmond Mastidge. It included two countinghouses, two warehouses and a study, rented for £14 a year. On top of his salary of £100, Roberts could reclaim from the company various expenses ranging from lodging, food and clothes to furniture, laundry, horses and a Moroccan groom. Lion even claimed the medical costs of treating his "leg bitten by a dog" (£1 5s 3d). In such a remote and unfamiliar country these expenses were unsurprising, but they would soon begin to diminish the Barbary Company's profits.

Within three days of his arrival, Roberts was given an audience with al-Mansur. He "delivered my message and her Majesty's letters, and was received with all humanity, and had favorable audience from time to time for three years," whose content, "for diverse good and reasonable causes, I forbear here to put down in writing."[67] Such circumspection was understandable. Roberts spent part of his three years trading munitions on Leicester's behalf (with Elizabeth's tacit support), even though he was officially allowed only to act as the crown's representative overseeing the company's commercial activities. The rest of his time was spent trying to persuade al-Mansur to join an anti-Spanish league in support of Don António's claim to the Portuguese crown.

By now both Leicester and Walsingham were exploiting their alliances at either end of the Mediterranean in a concerted effort to disrupt Spanish military preparations against England. Just as Roberts in Marrakesh was ordered to press Don António's claims on al-Mansur, in Constantinople Harborne was pursuing a more directly anti-Spanish approach with Murad.

By July 1586 Philip had finalized his plans for the invasion of England by a huge Spanish armada, and the antagonism between the two countries spilled over into Morocco. That October, an English ship called the *Dolphin* arrived in Safi and unloaded its commercial cargo of cloth and metal worth an estimated £5,000. Then, in a piratical act reminiscent of the *Bark Roe* incident, the *Dolphin*'s captain, John Giles, suddenly attacked and captured a Spanish caravel, confiscating all its goods. The Spanish crew escaped and fled to Marrakesh. Fearful of alienating the Spanish and inviting retribution, al-Mansur condemned Giles's piracy and threatened to confiscate the *Dophin*'s goods and levy further penalties against the English merchants unless the Spanish caravel and its cargo were released. Roberts dispatched two English merchants to Safi to instruct Giles to return the caravel. To the new ambassador's obvious embarrassment, Giles refused, claiming that the Spanish ship had been lawfully captured on the high seas. In response al-Mansur immediately arrested all English merchants with goods on board the *Dolphin*. Roberts again attempted to reach a resolution by asking those involved to stand the cost of the goods on board the Spanish vessel, but as in the case of Isaac Cabeça in 1568, the English merchants began squabbling over their respective contributions.

One of the merchants' servants was "imprisoned among a number of heathens" in "the infidel's prison" in Taraoudant, 180 miles south of

Safi, but managed to write a letter to the Privy Council back in London begging them to intervene in the whole "unnatural dealing." The letter was a terrible indictment of Roberts as the crown's agent and of the Barbary Company more generally. Both were condemned as unable to address either the English merchants' factionalism or the complexities of working successfully with al-Mansur. The servant claimed that a "malicious and envious" faction among the English mercantile community led by William Gore (one of the merchants involved in the Cabeça dispute) were "affectioned more to the Spaniards" and refused to bear any of the costs involved in settling the dispute, thus "disobeying the commandments of her majesty's servant," the hapless Roberts.

Under duress and facing the prospect of confinement in a Moroccan jail unless the Spanish claim was settled, the unfortunate servant began by complaining about "what small account these heathen people make of us and our English commodities, which proceedeth of the disorderly dealing of the Barbary Company, by overlaying this wicked country of late with abundance of goods." He then listed the "great injuries and abuses" that were "daily offered by the king [al-Mansur] in favor of the Spaniards," which included "detaining our goods ashore, imprisoning merchants, our masters and mariners of our ships, at the departure of any ship laden by the Spaniards and threaten us that, if their ships miscarry, we shall answer for it, in such cruel manner that no Christian heart would suffer, if we could otherwise remedy it." He concluded that "the Barbary Company regardeth little the wrongs and intolerable injuries we abide among those cursed people."[68]

The fate of the poor servant is unknown, and the Spanish caravel's cargo was never returned, but the *Dolphin*'s cargo was nonetheless restored. (The Barbary Company claimed that this was due to a letter written by the lord admiral Charles Howard of Effingham to al-Mansur, while Roberts maintained that it was all his own doing—another example of how far internal relations within the company had deteriorated.) Technically it seemed like a victory for the English, but the political tensions between England, Morocco and Spain were now greater than ever. The financial balance sheet of Roberts's years in Marrakesh was even less impressive.

Leicester had never really tried to make the Barbary Company a going commercial concern: his interests were more political, primarily to monopolize the Moroccan arms trade and by extension to persuade al-Mansur to enter into an anti-Spanish alliance. As a result, the terms of the company's trade were extremely irregular when compared with those of the Muscovy and Turkey companies. By allowing its agents to claim lavish expenses, the company compromised its chances of profitability, a problem that was compounded by Leicester's agreement to pay al-Mansur £4,000 worth of cloth, lead, iron and tin in the first year's trading, in order to ensure his subsequent monopoly over the import of metals, mainly for munitions. Excluding the £4,000 paid in goods, sales in 1586 amounted to just £2,994. By shipping more than two thousand cloths a year, the company had saturated the Moroccan market, driving down prices. Worse still, those importing Moroccan sugar, almonds and gold all registered losses, mainly due to the expense of transportation. Seven tons of raw sugar were bought at £5 8s a pound, but they cost over £9 to transport back to London, where they sold at £9 a pound, a loss of over £5 a ton.[69] The initial excitement over importing saltpeter soon evaporated as the costs of refining and transporting it (not to mention the bribes and presents required to sustain the trade) proved prohibitive and led to further heavy losses. Yet the trade mission was bearing other dividends.

By 1586, it seemed that the Barbary and Turkey companies were helping to weaken the threat of Spanish aggression. Both companies had been established with the dual purpose of trade and politics, to exploit a strategic and potentially profitable commercial alliance, and to cultivate military alliances in the face of Catholic aggression. While the political alliances had borne some fruit, the commercial results were decidedly mixed. In contrast to the Moroccan trade, the Turkey Company was thriving. The company had put £45,000 into start-up costs, exporting cloth and metal in return for silk, spices, cotton, currants, mohair, carpets, indigo and drugs of various kinds. At the height of Harborne's embassy, it was dispatching nineteen ships weighing between 100 and 300 tons and crewed by nearly eight hundred seamen on an average of five voyages a year to trade in ten Ottoman-controlled

Mediterranean ports. The profits on some voyages were estimated at more than £70,000, producing returns of nearly 300 percent.[70] Both Murad and Elizabeth were benefiting enormously from the trade, and the strategic alliance that came with it. The Spanish were furious with Harborne's success, as were the other Catholic powers, but diplomatically there was little they could do. In 1586 the new French ambassador in Constantinople, Jacques de Savary Lancosme, reiterated his predecessor's long-standing demands that Murad expel Harborne. The Englishman coolly quipped, "I think he won't be quite strong enough to turn me out."[71] He was right: in Constantinople at least, the English were there to stay.

6

Sultana Isabel

By the late 1580s hundreds, perhaps thousands, of Elizabethan merchants, diplomats, sailors, artisans and privateers were plying their trade throughout the Islamic world, from Marrakesh to Qazvin in Persia. Slowly the consequences of their adventures began to have a discernible public impact in England, particularly in London. One of the most startling came on October 2, 1586, when a Welsh minister named Meredith Hanmer preached a sermon at St. Katharine's Church, near the Tower of London, entitled "The Baptizing of a Turke." This homily was the first recorded example of a Muslim converting to English Protestantism, which was all the more remarkable given the circumstances. In his sermon Hanmer explained that Chinano (possibly a garbled Anglicization of the Turkish "Sinan") was a forty-year-old native of "Nigropontus" on the Greek island of Euboea, which had fallen to the Turks in 1470. "This Turk," Hanmer claimed, "was taken captive by the Spanish, where he continued in great misery the space of twenty-five years, whom the most worthy knight Sir Francis Drake found at Carthaginia."[1] Drake had set off for the Spanish colonies in the Americas in 1585 with seventeen ships and two thousand men, pillaging his way across Florida, the Caribbean and the northwest coast of South America. By February 1586 he had reached Cartagena in modern-day Colombia. There he burned its monasteries, ransomed resident Spaniards and captured local Indian, Moorish and Turkish slaves, including Chinano.[2]

Drake's return to England that July led the Privy Council to write to the Turkey Company's directors, asking how "the hundred Turks brought by Sir Francis Drake out of the West Indies (where they served as slaves in the Spanish galleys)" might be "conveyed home and presented by the ambassador [Harborne] unto the Grand Seigneur, whereby their lordships are persuaded that they may both draw on greater favor and liberties unto them selves than they yet enjoy, and also procure the release of some of the captives of the English nation there."[3] Both council and company knew that trading repatriated Turkish slaves for English ones in the Ottoman territories made good diplomatic and financial sense.

Harborne spent much of his time negotiating the release of English galley slaves throughout the Mediterranean, and he later claimed that he had spent £1,203 during his five-year residence in having "redeemed at Constantinople, Algiers, Tripoli in Barbary and other places fifty four of her subjects [Englishmen] from long miserable captivity."[4] Over the next few years, many of the Turks returned home on Turkey Company ships. But some, like Chinano, stayed in London; and within a matter of weeks Chinano had come to Hanmer's attention.

The motivations and sincerity of his conversion are unclear, but these were of little interest to Hanmer, who seized on the case of what he called "this silly Turk and poor Saracen" as a way of justifying English Protestantism, refuting Islam and stoking the anti-Catholic and anti-Spanish sentiment that was gripping London. "I have purposed by God's help, to lay before you," Hanmer proclaimed, "first the original of Mahomet, that false prophet with the nations of Moors, Saracens and Turks; secondly their false doctrine and wicked religion, wherewith they have bewitched infinite souls: with a brief confutation thereof." What followed was a fairly standard (and very long) denunciation of the Prophet Muhammad and the Islamic faith, riddled with the usual Christian errors, fears, myths, stereotypes and fantasies.

According to Hanmer, the Prophet was born to a "heathen" father and an "Ishmaelite" mother. Ridiculed by Hanmer as a drunken epileptic, Muhammad is described as using magic to "bewitch the people" and spread "the law of Mahomet" throughout Arabia, Persia and North Africa. The minister claimed that Muhammad "patched together his Alcoran of the laws and doctrines of heathens, Indians and Arabians, of superstitious Jews, of Rechabites, of false Christians and heretics," producing a confused theology that denied the Christian Trinity and Jesus as the son of God but approved of the Gospels. In Hanmer's mind Muhammad's beliefs betrayed a devilish confederacy with the Jews, who "continually prick him forward against the Christians." But the minister reserved his real venom for what he saw as a conflation of Islam and Catholicism. In the "flocking to tombs and sepulchers, worshipping of dead corpses, bones and relics" and other "feigned miracles of Romish idolatry . . . , we need not say it is popish," railed Hanmer, "nay, it is Turkish and Mahometicall." While Elizabeth's merchants and diplomats strategically allied themselves with Muslims in opposition to Catholic power, her preachers took a less flexible position, compounding Islam and Catholicism as two variants of the collective sin of idolatry.

From Hanmer's perspective, Chinano's conversion was a chink of light in the theological darkness. When questioned on "what should move him at this present to receive the Christian faith," Hanmer reported that Chinano identified "his misery and captivity under the Spaniards, his travel hither, and the view of this land, [which] had beaten into him (as he said) the knowledge of the true God. And further he said, that if there were not a God in England, there was none nowhere." The image of Chinano having knowledge of the "true" Protestant God "beaten into him" suggests that his conversion may not have been the joyful and spontaneous decision that Hanmer would have had his congregation believe. Warming to his theme of Protestant England's beneficence, the minister identified two further reasons for Chinano's conversion: "before his coming, the virtue, the modesty, the godliness, the good usage and discreet government of the English Christians, and among others (as he chiefly noted) he was most beholden unto the right worshipful knight, Sir Francis Drake, and that worthy captain W[illiam] Hawkins, terming them most worthy Christians."

Drake's and Hawkins's worthy characters were in fact rather dubious: Drake was a licensed pirate, a "corsair," and Hawkins a notorious slave trader, whose recent rampage through the Caribbean had brought death, imprisonment and enslavement to countless Spaniards, Native Americans and *renegadoes*. Hanmer seemed unconcerned that Chinano's conversion may have been coerced, claiming that upon his arrival in England the Turk "saw courtesy, gentleness, friendly salutations of the people, succor for him and his countrymen, pity and compassion of the Englishmen, and withal he learned that the poor, the aged, the impotent, the sick and diseased Christians were provided for, whereas in his country and where he had been in captivity, the poor and sick and diseased were scorned, despised, and accounted of as dogs." When pressed on why he had never converted to Catholicism in twenty-five years of Spanish servitude, he (or more likely Hanmer) gave the reasons every Elizabethan Protestant wanted to hear: the Spaniard's "cruelty in shedding of blood, and his idolatry in worshipping of images."

The rest of the sermon descended into a fantastical celebration of Protestantism and a denunciation of Catholicism. Hanmer maintained that Chinano's conversion showed that it was only the political might of Catholic Spain and the papacy that prevented Muslims—who "know not the purity of religion in the reformed churches"—from converting en masse to Protestantism. "Let the Church of God be swept then will the heathens, the Jews, the Turks and Saracens the sooner come in," he declared. Hanmer even used his selective knowledge of the first letters exchanged between Elizabeth and Murad seven years earlier to support his millenarian belief in the mass conversion of Jews and Muslims. He even went so far as to quote one version of the letters from the Turks after describing how they came to England:

> Mustafa Beg, secretary to the great Turk of Constantinople that now is writing to the Queen of England as appeareth by his letters bearing date the 15 March, and in the year of great Jesu (so he writeth) 1579 sheweth the great affection his master the Turk together with himself beareth to this land and of our religion as it is interpreted he sayeth thus:
>
> "We know that your sovereign majesty among all the Christians have the most sound religion, and therefore the Christians throughout the world envy your highness."

Hanmer's account was a clearly misleading interpretation of Mustafa Beg's letter, but the preacher had no interest in such subtleties; the political and commercial dimensions of the Anglo-Ottoman rapprochement were of negligible significance when set against what the preacher saw as the Ottoman ruler's obvious acknowledgment of the theological superiority and inevitable triumph of English Protestantism over Catholicism.

The sermon ended with a moment of pure Elizabethan theater: "the Turk confessed in the Spanish tongue before the face of the congregation," while from the pulpit Hanmer performed a catechistic dialog with Chinano, "propounding the questions and receiving the answers by skillful interpreters." Chinano "renounced Mahomet the false prophet of the Moors, Saracens and Turks," embraced the Trinity and "believeth verily that Jesus Christ was and is the son of God," and finally "desired he might be received as one of the faithful Christians, and be baptized." At the conclusion of the service Chinano was led to a table with a basin in the middle of the congregation where he was baptized, having "desired his name might be William," the Christian name of his liberator, Captain Hawkins.

Throughout Hanmer's oration, the voice of Chinano (or William) was mediated by others, and once the sermon was finished he would disappear from the historical record. Like many other sixteenth-century converts and *renegadoes* his life flickered into public view suddenly for one reason or another, and disappeared again just as quickly. Chinano presented a justification for Hanmer's virulent anti-Catholic position at a moment when a Spanish invasion seemed imminent. The sermon does however reveal that a small but visible group of Chinano's Turkish "countrymen" were moving around London, and that many Londoners knew about the Anglo-Ottoman alliance and their queen's cordial correspondence with the sultan. While it used Chinano's conversion as a sign of Protestantism's growing ability to redeem its rival religions of the Book, it left other concerns about religious conversion unanswered. How genuine was Chinano's baptism, and what could prevent him from reverting? How sincere and enduring was anyone's religion in the face of the sheer variety of forced, strategic or spontaneous conversions taking place between various faiths at this time? This included Protestantism, a theology barely seventy years old, now riven with its own factionalism and fighting for its survival in late-sixteenth-century Europe.

Such anxieties were compounded by a growing number of cases in which conversion went the other way, with English Protestants embracing Islam—often coerced, at other times strategic and sometimes willing converts. Thomas Sanders's sensational account in 1584 of how the *Jesus* and its crew had been imprisoned by the ruler of Tripoli and eventually released thanks to Harborne had also described how English cabin boys "voluntarily turned Turk." As Sanders reported, when the dey's son tried to persuade two of the *Jesus*'s crew to convert to Islam, he turned to one of his father's servants, "a son of a yeoman of our Queen's guard, whom the king's son had enforced to turn Turk; his name was John Nelson. Him the king caused to be brought to these young men, and then said unto them, 'Will you not bear this, your countryman, company, and be Turk as he is?'" Sanders and his crew resisted such demands at their peril: several were forcibly circumcised and dressed "in the habit of a Turk," while others were thrown into the galleys.[5] But the case of Nelson and the anonymous cabin boy suggests that there were growing numbers of English converts to Islam.[6]

Reports of even more visible English converts to Islam were also beginning to reach London. In June 1586, just four months before Hanmer baptized Chinano in St. Katharine's Church, William Harborne dispatched a letter from Constantinople addressed to "Hassan Aga, Eunuch and Treasurer to Hassan Bassa king of Algier." Hassan Aga was better known to Harborne as Samson Rowlie, a fellow merchant from Great Yarmouth who had been captured by Turkish pirates off Algiers in the *Swallow* in 1577. Most of the crew had been imprisoned, but Rowlie had been castrated and either willingly or forcibly converted to Islam. Over the next decade he took the name Hassan Aga and rose to become chief eunuch and treasurer of Algiers as well as one of the most trusted advisers to its Ottoman governor, Harborne's old adversary Qilich Ali Pasha ("Hassan Bassa").[7] Like Rowlie, Ali Pasha was himself a Christian convert to Islam. Born a Catholic in Calabria but captured and enslaved in the 1530s by one of Kheir ed-Din Barbarossa's captains, he converted and became renowned as "the greatest corsair of them all," and by 1568 had been appointed Ottoman governor of Algiers.[8]

Harborne asked Hassan Aga to use his influence to secure the release of the surviving members of the *Swallow*'s crew, still imprisoned in Algiers, many of whom had lived and worked with him in his previous life as Samson Rowlie. In direct contrast to Hanmer's account of Chinano's conversion, Harborne acted as though Hassan Aga's was a calculated act of survival that belied his true and unshakable Protestant faith. He presumed that Rowlie still professed a "fervent faith" in "our lord Jesus Christ, by whose only merits and blood-shedding you together with us and other good Christians shall be saved, and also for your faithful obedience like a true subject of Her Majesty, naturally loving your country and your countrymen." Harborne believed that his "true" religion would compel him to intercede with Ali Pasha on behalf of the English captives in "procuring their redemption," which he assured him would "manifest to all the world, especially to her majesty and me her ambassador, your true Christian mind and English heart . . . that notwithstanding your body be subject to Turkish thralldom, yet your virtuous mind [be] free from those vices."[9]

A portrait of Samson Rowlie that appeared in a traveler's book just two years after Harborne wrote his letter offers little to support the ambassador's conviction that Rowlie's conversion was a superficial act driven by self-preservation. Dressed in opulent robes and wearing the white turban of a convert, he reclines on a gilt throne, the picture of a confident, prosperous and successful young Muslim. Like many other contemporary Christians who "turned Turk" in the Mediterranean during this period, Rowlie gives the impression that, on balance, a career as a rich and powerful member of the Algerian ruling elite was more appealing than life as a struggling, peripatetic Protestant merchant from Norfolk.

Whether Harborne's petition for the release of the *Swallow*'s crew was successful is unknown, although his failure to mention it in subsequent correspondence suggests that it was not. What happened to Hassan Aga is also unclear: Harborne's letter is the last we hear of him.

With other matters to attend to, Harborne was unable to act on every single captive, ransom and conversion brought to his attention during his time in Constantinople.

One English traveler who did have Harborne to thank for saving him was Edward Webbe. One of the most colorful of all the Elizabethan adventurers in the eastern Mediterranean, Webbe obtained a degree of fame with the publication of his picaresque memoir *The Rare and Most Wonderful Things Which Edward Webbe an Englishman Born, Hath Seen and Passed in His Troubelsome Travails* (1590). He was born around 1553 near the Tower of London, the son of a master gunner, and by 1566 he was in the service of Anthony Jenkinson. He spent five years traveling throughout Russia with Jenkinson, and in 1571 he was captured and enslaved by Crimean Tatars. After being ransomed, he returned to England and sailed to Alexandria, where his ship was attacked by Turkish galleys. Following a fierce fight in which most of his crew was killed, Webbe described how he and ten survivors were "sent to Constantinople, and committed unto the galleys, where we continued the space of five years."

Somehow Webbe managed to persuade his captors of his "good skills in the gunner's art" and traveled with the Ottoman army to Persia, Damascus, Cairo, Jerusalem, Goa and Ethiopia, and along the Red Sea coast, "to do the Turk's service in the field." Returning to Constantinople, he organized what he described as "a cunning piece of firework, framed in form like to the Ark of Noah," for the circumcision ceremony of the sultan's sons. However, as a Christian with no immediate military usefulness, Webbe became once more a "prisoner in the Turk's dungeons" and was pressed "to forsake Christ, to deny him, and to believe in their God Mahomet: which, if I would have done, I might have had wonderful preferment of the Turk, and have lived in as great felicity as any lord in the country." He managed to resist, despite being "grievously beaten naked" and "reviled," until "it pleased God to send thither for the release of me and others, a worthy gentleman of this land, named Master Harborne." Webbe praised Harborne, who "did behave himself wonderfully wisely, and was a special means for the releasement of me and sundry other English captives."[10] Unfortunately,

Webbe's freedom was short-lived: traveling home through Italy, he was imprisoned and tortured as a heretic in Rome and Naples before finally returning to England in 1587.[11] He was last heard of in 1592, living in Blackwall, having been made a cannoneer for life, presumably living off his pension and his tall traveler's tales.

Despite Harborne's success in negotiating the release of captives like Webbe, his time in Constantinople steadily darkened because of what he rather dramatically called "the subtle secret devices of my many mighty enemies both Christian and heathen."[12] His memoirs (written sometime after Francis Walsingham's death in April 1590, and never published) conceded that throughout the second half of 1586 he was under intense pressure from London. "I being certified by the late Right Honorable of worthy memory Mr. Secretary Walsingham, of the said Spaniard his great preparation to invade this realm." According to Harborne, the Spanish were prepared to pay the Venetians 160,000 ducats "to break off our intercourse and expel us" from Constantinople, as well as to encourage the Venetian ambassador to use his influence over Murad's imperial harem to conclude a nonaggression treaty that would free Philip to concentrate on attacking England. It was now clear to Harborne that the "said Spaniards and adherents' jealous suspicion of my proceedings since my second arrival there" went far beyond commercial protectionism, and that he needed to use what influence he had to "restrain the Venetians from entering the cursed league" with Spain.[13]

Harborne maintained that his strategy drew on his reformed religious beliefs. "I performed my utmost endeavor," he wrote, "by setting one enemy of god his church against the other to impair the same." In a pragmatic echo of Hanmer's denunciation of Catholics and Muslims, Harborne claimed to have set Spaniards against Turks to get what Walsingham wanted. His anti-Catholic Protestantism was clearly useful in creating an alliance with the Ottoman court, although privately he was frustrated by the way the sultan and his court teased him about his religious beliefs. "Everyone, for a joke," wrote Morosini, "calls him Lutheran—even the very Pashas—much to his disgust, as he is a most desperate Calvinist."[14]

Putting aside such annoyances, Harborne's first objective was to build a network of alliances close to Murad. He cultivated his friendship with the sultan's tutor, the great Turkish historian Seadeddin Muhammad Ben Hassan, and made his peace with his old enemy Qilich Ali Pasha, presumably by giving them both substantial "presents." This secured their opposition to any plans within the harem for a nonaggression pact with Spain. Harborne's machinations appear to have been at least partially successful, as he was able to report that "the Spaniard dares not withdraw his total forces out of Sicily, Naples and other ports of the Levant Seas," which could then be turned against England.

The "cursed league" was blocked, and Harborne was triumphant. "I performed my uttermost endeavor," he boasted, "not only to break of the same but further to procure the said Turkey navy against him [Philip II], which when (for the streightness [violence] with Persia) I perceived could not be, I yet notwithstanding through god his assistance so prevented his crafty devices in that count, that neither his travel or much exhausted treasure prevailed."[15] Although he had persuaded Murad to reject an alliance with the Spanish, Harborne believed that any attempt to convince the sultan actually to join with Elizabeth in turning his navy against Philip II was unlikely to succeed, mainly because of the financial and military cost of the Ottoman campaigns in Persia, which had recently led to the occupation of the former Safavid capital of Tabriz.[16]

On June 24, 1587, Walsingham congratulated Harborne on "how carefully and discreetly you have proceeded in your negotiations with the sultan and his counselors." He also told him that the queen was delighted with his success in preventing the peace treaty, and that

> her pleasure is that you let the Grand Signor understand that she most thankfully taketh this his stay, by you signified, of renewing the truce desired by the King of Spain which you shall in her name not only persuade him to continue but also show unto him how necessary it is for him to attempt somewhat presently for the impeachment of the said Spaniard's greatness, much more in truth to be doubted than of Persia, against whom his forces seem to be altogether bent, and may be performed by setting such princes as are

in Barbary at his devotion upon the King of Spain, furnishing them for the purpose with some number of galleys, which with small cost shall give him great annoyance, whereunto her majesty's hand will not be wanting.[17]

Walsingham then made one final tantalizing offer: "You may signify unto the Grand Signor that her Majesty hath lying upon the coast of Spain a fleet of very strong, well furnished ships under the conduct of Sir Francis Drake, which the last year spoiled and burned Cartagena and other places in the West Indies, who hath already entered diverse ports of Spain and Portugal." The implication was clear: England was a naval power to be reckoned with, and if Murad joined forces, they could wipe out Spanish maritime influence in the Mediterranean. Not that Elizabeth *really* needed Murad's help, as Walsingham was at pains to explain: "Although her Majesty needeth no assistance of other princes yet shall it be a great encouragement and contentation to her Majesty as a more terror to the King of Spain, they having like interest, use like endeavor to abate his power. All which," concluded Walsingham, "as well to satisfy and stir up the Grand Signor as also to disgrace your adversaries in that court and country, I leave to yourself to be published, urged and enlarged as you shall see cause."[18]

Having successfully resurrected his career as ambassador to Constantinople and single-handedly wrecked Spain's détente with the Ottomans, Harborne was now faced with the colossal task of engineering an Anglo-Ottoman naval attack on Philip's Mediterranean fleet. He clearly believed that the undertaking was impossible, and the strain soon began to tell. In November 1587, when war between England and Spain seemed assured, Harborne wrote an extraordinary letter to Murad, complaining about his reluctance to ratify an Anglo-Ottoman military alliance. The letter shows how Harborne used religious concordance between Protestants and Muslims to justify a military coalition:

Do not let this moment pass unused, in order that God, who has created you a valiant man and the most powerful of all worldly princes for the destruction of idol-worshippers may not turn his utmost wrath against you if you disregard his command, which my mistress, only a weak woman, courageously struggles to fulfill. The whole world, with justice, will accuse you of the greatest ingratitude if you desert in her danger your most trusting confederate, who, in the confidence of the friendship and the promises of Your Highness, has placed her life and her kingdom in jeopardy that cannot be greater on this earth. For the Spaniard, since my mistress had declined him peace, is determined to destroy her completely, relying on the maximum assistance of the pope and all idolatrous princes. And when, finally, there will not remain any other obstacle in Christendom, he will direct his invincible military forces toward your destruction and that of your empire and will become the sole ruler of the world. For the pope, whom they consider as their God on earth, does not cease to persuade him with his false prophecies that he can and will achieve it. If, however, Your Highness, wisely and courageously, without delay, will undertake jointly with my mistress war upon the sea (which the Almighty God, the pledged faith, the favorable moment, the fame of the glorious house of Othman, and the salvation of your empire unanimously advise), then the proud Spaniard and the mendacious pope, with all their adherents, will not only be cheated of their cherished hope of victory but will also receive the penalty for their audacity. Since God protects only his own, he will through us in such wise punish these idol-worshippers that those of them who might still remain will be converted by their example to worship the true God in unison with us. You, however, who are fighting for his true fame, he will grant victory and shower with other favors.[19]

Harborne's argument is a selective combination of Hanmer's theology and Walsingham's realpolitik. Where Hanmer saw Catholicism and Islam as idolatrous faiths, Harborne proposed an antipapal coalition between Protestant and Islamic iconoclasm. The rest of his arguments are a succinct précis of the brief that Walsingham had urged him to publish and "enlarge" back in June.

The letter to Murad was an official (if clandestine) statement of Elizabethan foreign policy designed to flatter and cajole the Ottoman sultan into action. Harborne's memoir of this fraught period, written toward the end of his life, is altogether more revealing about his attitude toward the unholy alliance he was charged with proposing. He grumbled about "the perverse condition of those Turkish infidels with whom forcedly so long I was conversant," and admitted that it was "my continual earnest prayer to god, which blessed be his holy name he granted, that her Majesty in her just defense might never need this heathen tyrant his assistance, as also that during my residence there he might never make him the executioner of his fierce wrath and scourge of Christendom for their sins."[20] Whatever his public statements, privately Harborne felt deeply uneasy about trafficking with the "infidel."

In early 1588 Harborne began to petition Walsingham and his Turkey Company paymasters for a recall. His five-year embassy was coming to an end. His situation was exceptionally stressful, but his request appears to have been exacerbated by the company's failure to pay him his £200 annual salary with any degree of regularity. "I disbursed there more than I ever charged to account in the advancement of her majesty's service," he complained.[21] All told, by his count he had been paid just £400 over his ten years in Constantinople. The surviving accounts reveal that his expenditure was covered not only by the Turkey Company but also by the sultan himself. Of the £15,341 Harborne spent on wages, household costs, redeeming captives and "presents" (£1,442), the company covered £13,246; the remainder had come out of "the allowance of the emperor [Murad] in the time of his being in Constantinople."[22] Such costs were much higher than those incurred by Henry Roberts in Marrakesh, but this reflected the far greater commercial and political investment that Elizabeth's advisers were prepared to make in Constantinople. Although Harborne would claim that such expenditure had contributed to an alliance between Elizabeth and Murad and the wrecking of that between the sultan and Philip, it had not produced the firm military axis that Walsingham had hoped for. No Ottoman attack on the Spanish fleet in the Mediterranean was forthcoming, and without it there would be no delay in the launching of Spain's armada against England.

In late April 1588, as Harborne was about to be recalled to London, a Spanish armada of 130 ships, 8,000 sailors and 18,000 soldiers prepared to sail out of Lisbon bound for the English Channel. It raised its banner in a ceremony reminiscent of that used before the Battle of Lepanto, against another of Spain's "infidel" enemies, the Ottomans. In July 1588, the English fleet led by the lord high admiral Charles Howard, Francis Drake and John Hawkins engaged the Spanish off Plymouth. By the beginning of August, after a series of engagements in different parts of the English Channel, the English were in the ascendant, scattering the Spanish fleet and pursuing it up the eastern coast of England. Much of what remained of the Armada was destroyed in stormy weather on the rocky coasts of Scotland and Ireland. Against all odds, the English had prevailed in the face of the overwhelming might of Catholic Spain.

On August 1, 1588, as the remains of the Spanish fleet limped around the Scottish coast in a desperate attempt to reach home, Harborne wrote his final dispatch to Walsingham from Constantinople. Disillusioned and frustrated by the sultan's persistent broken promises of a formal military alliance, Harborne told Walsingham that he was ready to "depart presently." He enclosed his final petition to the sultan, offering the same accusations and justifications as before. He believed the Ottomans remained more interested in war with Persia than with Spain, and offered the forlorn hope that Don António could lead an anti-Spanish force to recapture the Portuguese throne, diminishing Spanish power in Iberia, North Africa and beyond.[23]

Twelve days later, after putting his twenty-five-year-old secretary Edward Barton in temporary charge of the embassy (partly because he was a fluent Turkish speaker), Harborne left the sweltering heat of Constantinople for the last time. When he reached Hamburg on November 19, he learned of "her majesty's victory over the Spaniard."[24] It must have been a bittersweet moment for the tenacious Englishman. After ten years in Constantinople, he had retrieved a commercial agreement with the Ottomans when all seemed lost, established England's first official embassy in the Muslim world, founded an extensive network of English factors across the Mediterranean and negotiated the release of scores of English captives from the horrors of galley slavery. Although he had failed to clinch a deal that would have set Turkish Muslims against Spanish Catholics, his diplomacy had played its part in unsettling the Spanish and their preparations for invasion—or so Harborne would insist upon his return to England. A life of peaceful, obscure retirement in Norfolk now awaited the former ambassador, who lived for nearly three more decades before his death in 1617.

In Marrakesh, Henry Roberts had been facing a similar struggle to persuade another reluctant Muslim ruler of the wisdom of backing Elizabeth in her struggle with Spain. Like Murad, Sultan al-Mansur seemed unconvinced that the English were worth the risk: they just did not appear to have the military power and diplomatic status to match their rhetoric. Don António was coming to the same conclusion. In the spring of 1588, he had appealed directly to al-Mansur for help in persuading Elizabeth to attack Spain. But the wily al-Mansur prevaricated, waiting to see what would come of the Spanish invasion of England.

On July 12, 1588, Roberts wrote to Leicester informing him that "here came news that the king of Spain's armada is departed for England; the which I well perceive is the case that this king [al-Mansur] doth prolong the times, to know how they speed: for, if the king of Spain should prosper against England, then this king would do nothing; and, if the king of Spain have the overthrow, as by God's help he shall, then will this king perform promises and more."[25] Don António and Elizabeth were powerless to act in Morocco, or anywhere else for that matter, until the outcome of the Spanish invasion was known.

Across the capitals of Europe and North Africa, statesmen eagerly awaited news of the fate of the Spanish Armada. In Marrakesh, the Spanish circulated rumors that their fleet had triumphed. In a letter dated August 5, Elizabeth wrote to al-Mansur informing him of her victory. The letter reached the small community of English merchants in Marrakesh at the beginning of September. The news sparked extraordinary scenes of celebration. The merchants set off fireworks and organized impromptu street banquets and dancing. They led a procession through the city center; according to eyewitness reports, some flew standards showing Elizabeth standing in triumph over a prostrate

Philip, while others carried effigies of the Spanish ruler and Pope Sixtus, which they set on fire, much to the consternation of the watching Italian and Spanish merchants. The procession then entered the *mellah,* where three men challenged them. The first, Diego Marín, was a Spanish diplomat; the other two, the Portuguese nobleman Joao Gomes de Silva and the Spaniard Juan de Heredia, a survivor of the Battle of Alcácer-Quibir, were living in the city in a state of limbo after having been ransomed. What exactly happened next is disputed, but what is clear is that the three men drew their swords and attacked the English merchants, knocking several from their horses, killing between three and seven of them and wounding many more. The *mellah* descended into chaos, with Jews and Muslims watching in horror as Catholics murdered Protestants, Europe's Christians replaying their sectarian conflicts on the streets of Marrakesh.[26]

Al-Mansur was appalled that such violence should threaten the peace and commercial stability of his capital city, and he immediately arrested the assailants. What happened to de Silva and Heredia is unknown, but Marín would spend the next twenty years in prison. For some of the English merchants, the Armada celebrations had proved fatal, but the Spanish defeat at the hands of the English naval forces had finally convinced al-Mansur of two things: that the mighty Spanish were not as invincible as he believed, and that England and her female ruler could no longer be dismissed as peripheral to the commercial and diplomatic world of the Mediterranean. The Armada's failure prompted Spain's enemies to reassess their alliances: suddenly an Anglo-Moroccan alliance seemed like a very real possibility, one that might transform the delicate balance of power in North Africa.

The shift in al-Mansur's approach to relations with England is recorded in the writings of his court scribe and historian, Abd al-Aziz al-Fishtali, who provided the earliest known non-European commentary on the English queen. In his account of events, al-Fishtali pitted Elizabeth, whom he called "sultana Isabel," against Philip, whom he described as "the enemy of religion, the infidel (may God increase his sorrow and weaken his hold), the tyrant [*taghiya*] of Castile [Qishtala] who is today against Islam and who is the pillar of polytheism [*shirk*]."

According to al-Fishtali, once the Armada approached the English coast, "God sent a sharp wind [*reehan sarsaran*] against the fleets of the tyrant that broke up their formation and pushed them onto the enemy's lands, bringing down their flags and banners."[27] Al-Fishtali's use of the term *reehan sarsaran* is particularly telling: it is taken from the Qur'an (4:16), where it describes the divine winds sent against the polytheistic people of Aad. God punished the Spanish for their sins just as he punished the people of Aad.[28]

The English agreed: the commemorative medal struck to celebrate the English victory bore the similar inscription *Afflavit Deus et dissipati sunt* ("God blew and they were scattered").[29] Al-Fishtali interpreted the Armada's defeat as a sign that God was on the side of the English. This provided al-Mansur with a pretext for contemplating a reconquest of Al-Andalus (the Arab name for the mainland of Spain, which had been under Muslim rule for many centuries). "These actions," continued al-Fishtali, "were, thanks be to God in this dear matter, the harbingers of success and conquest, and a sign for him [al-Mansur] to fulfill his awaited promise, in taking possession, by God's will, of his [Philip's] lands and territories, and in confronting him with the victorious soldiers of God on his own turf."[30]

Al-Mansur was now convinced of England's military capabilities and signaled his willingness to discuss an alliance that would strike against Spain and install Don António on the Portuguese throne. Unfortunately, nobody seems to have told Henry Roberts, whose patron, the Earl of Leicester, died suddenly, on September 4, after a short illness, just weeks after marshaling the country's defenses against the Spanish invasion. Leicester's death left Elizabeth utterly distraught, and seems to have acted as a catalyst for Roberts's decision to leave Morocco. The record of Roberts's time in Morocco was hardly impressive. As well as failing to conclude a political alliance with al-Mansur, he had overseen only small and irregular profits on exported goods, mainly cloth, but a significant loss on imports, primarily of sugar. Roberts was not sufficiently versed or interested in business to avoid falling into the traps of selling English cloth too cheaply and buying Moroccan sugar too expensively. The diplomatic strategy of drawing al-Mansur into an anti-Spanish alliance had failed, and Leicester's death left Roberts more exposed than ever.

Having been almost completely ignored by al-Mansur during his time there, Roberts was promptly adopted as a pawn by the canny sultan as soon as the latter learned of the Armada's defeat. Roberts was staying outside Marrakesh in one of al-Mansur's garden palaces, presumably oblivious of the attack inflicted on his fellow English merchants in the city's *mellah*. On September 14 he left Morocco "at the king's charges, with forty or fifty shot attending upon me for my guard and safety," bound for England.[31]

In the terse account of his embassy, "written briefly by himself" following his return to London, Roberts recalled that he had left Marrakesh and traveled 150 miles southwest to the port of Agadir. "In this port," he wrote, "I stayed forty three days, and at length the second of November I embarked myself and one Marshok Reiz [his real name was Ahmad Bilqasim], a captain and a gentleman, which the emperor sent with me upon an ambassage to her majesty."[32] His own embassy at an end, Roberts was now accompanying Morocco's first-ever ambassador to England. What he did not know was that the embassy was just one element in a carefully choreographed exchange of diplomats destined to lead to an Anglo-Portuguese-Moroccan military axis. As Roberts and Bilqasim sailed for England, the Portuguese pretender Don António had agreed to send his brother Don Cristóbal to al-Mansur's court as a hostage to secure the sultan's commitment to a proposed military alliance.

On November 10, Don Cristóbal left London with four warships and six merchant ships, bound for Morocco. Having passed Roberts and Bilqasim en route, the Portuguese arrived in Marrakesh in January 1589 and immediately petitioned al-Mansur to support Don António in reclaiming his throne. The irony of the situation was not lost on al-Fishtali, who wrote that Don Cristóbal needed "our swords, made triumphant by God, to regain his lost kingship . . . although our imamate swords with their sharp blades had earlier destroyed the edifice of his kingship" at the Battle of Alcácer-Quibir, and "only with our hands would he recover it."[33]

Just as Don Cristóbal arrived in Morocco, Roberts and Bilqasim landed in England. As usual, Roberts made a meal of it, complaining that "after much torment and foul weather at sea, at New Year's Day I came on land at St. Ives in Cornwall." From there the two men traveled "by land up toward London." Roberts reported: "We were met without the city with the chiefest merchants of the Barbary Company, well mounted all on horseback, to the number of forty or fifty horse, and so the ambassador and myself being both in coach, entered the city by torchlight, on Sunday at night the 12 of January 1589."[34] The Moroccan ambassador's dramatic arrival in London concluded in a suitably theatrical way a turbulent episode in Elizabethan England's relations with the Islamic world, which had witnessed the success of Harborne's embassy to Constantinople, the birth of the Barbary Company and the defeat of the Spanish Armada. It set the stage for another to be played out over the next decade, this time in London's public theaters.

7

London Turns Turk

In the summer of 1588 London was braced for a Spanish invasion that, if successful, would open up the possibility of a victorious Philip II returning in public triumph to the city he had ridden through thirty-four years earlier as consort to the queen. Six months later, with Philip's armada in ruins, instead of a Catholic conqueror, Londoners watched a Muslim ambassador riding in state through the capital. The sight of Ahmad Bilqasim—or Marshok Reiz, as his English hosts Anglicized his name—entering London at the head of an entourage that included the Barbary Company's most senior merchants signaled an important shift in Elizabethan foreign policy toward the Islamic world. Both the Moroccan and Ottoman rulers had watched tiny, insignificant England overcome the mighty war machine of "the great tyrant of Castile" and now regarded her queen as an important political player on the international stage. Elizabeth and her advisers understood that a strategic alliance with these Muslim rulers was more important than ever to combat the inevitable attempt by King Philip to recover from his recent humiliation.

Little documentary evidence remains of where the Moroccan ambassador stayed and whom he met during his time in London, but the official diplomatic correspondence suggests what both sides hoped to achieve from his mission. A remarkable memorandum written by Bilqasim in late January 1589 outlined the scale of al-Mansur's projected alliance. It proposed:

> To offer unto your majesty not only to employ in her assistance men, money, victuals and the use of his ports, but also his

own person, if your majesty should be pleased to require it; and to desire, for the better withstanding of the common enemy the King of Spain, there might [be] a sound and perfect league between them.

To let her understand that for the better furtherance of her princely purpose to restore Don António to the kingdom of Portugal, he thought it a good course that the army by sea that she should send with him, should enter into the Straits [of Gibraltar], and there to ship such assistance as he should send; whereby the King of Spain, for the defense of those parts of Spain within the Straits, that coast upon Barbary, should be constrained to withdraw his forces out of Portugal; whereby Don António, finding the country unfurnished of foreign forces, may be better able to recover his country.

Lastly, to offer, when the 100 ships should come upon the coast of Barbary, whereby he might in his own person go into Spain, he would deliver unto her majesty 150,000 ducats.[1]

Acting through Bilqasim, al-Mansur was proposing an audacious joint military campaign against the Spanish that would put Don António on the Portuguese throne and enable him to reconquer the lost Muslim lands of Al-Andalus, in return for which he would pay Elizabeth 150,000 ducats. With his subtle but emotive emphasis on "recover" and "restore," the sultan offered a "perfect league" between the English and the Moroccan rulers that was as much an ideological as a geographical union of the two countries. In the uncertain aftermath of the Spanish Armada's defeat, al-Mansur was proposing an extraordinary identification of Muslim aims with Protestant ones.

This plan was not solely of al-Mansur's making. It was in fact part of a much larger anti-Spanish axis, developed by Elizabeth and her advisers in the immediate aftermath of their victory, that became known as the Portugal Expedition. In September 1588 plans were being drawn up to launch a bold counterstrike against Spain, with Sir Francis Drake appointed admiral and Sir John Norris as general. Elizabeth approved a military campaign to capture Lisbon, which it was hoped would trigger a popular uprising to put Don António on the throne, and to strike at Seville and establish a naval base in the Azores to attack the remnants of the Spanish fleet. Elizabeth's problem was that she was virtually bankrupt. Drake and Norris therefore proposed that the expedition be financed as a joint-stock operation: Elizabeth would contribute £20,000, and £40,000 would be raised from London merchants, who would see a return on their investment in booty. The Dutch Calvinists were further asked to provide troops, ships and supplies to the value of £10,000.[2] When Elizabeth learned that al-Mansur was prepared to pay 150,000 ducats toward the costs of the expedition—at sixteenth-century exchange rates, that was approximately £70,000, or the campaign's entire budget—the possibility of an alliance must have been extremely attractive.

With Francis Walsingham ailing and unable to fulfill his role on the Privy Council (he would die in April 1590), it was left to Lord Burghley to lead the negotiations with Bilqasim. He proceeded with his usual caution, worrying as to how Elizabeth should advise Don António to respond, the exact nature of Moroccan military support and "when the money shall be paid." He also expressed concern that Elizabeth would risk losing her newfound prestige by throwing in her lot with a Muslim ruler, writing, "Her majesty is loath to hazard the honor achieved last year." Eventually Elizabeth agreed to al-Mansur's offer, albeit with some reservations, being "most ready to requite the same, so far forth as may stand with her honor and conscience."[3] In January 1589, as Bilqasim settled into his London residence, Drake and Norris were in the Low Countries recruiting Calvinist troops to join their fleet and sail for Lisbon the following month.

Bilqasim was secure enough in his diplomatic role to lodge a series of further requests with Elizabeth's advisers. He asked that, should al-Mansur need to defend his realm against other Muslim states while attacking Spain, he be permitted "to hire for his money certain ships and mariners within this realm," as well as carpenters, shipwrights and "such provision and commodities" as he required. Bilqasim also requested that Elizabeth "bestow her reward on the poor man of Bristol, who brought him out of Ireland and had his ship cast away in the

A silver "Geuzen" ("revolt") medal coined during the sixteenth-century Dutch Revolt, with the inscriptions "Rather Turkish than Papist" (*left*) and "In spite of the Mass" (*right*), dated 1574.

voyage." This seems to be a reference to the unfortunate Henry Roberts, England's first ambassador to Morocco, who was now reduced to receiving royal handouts. Roberts's fall from grace was all the more humiliating for his having spent more than a year embroiled in an undignified and ultimately unsuccessful squabble with the Barbary Company's directors over outstanding pay.[4]

Had the Moroccan ambassador taken time out that winter from his political negotiations, he could have done what so many diplomats have done in London ever since and gone to the theater. What he would have seen might have startled him, as the city's commercial playhouses were in the grip of a fascination for staging scenes and characters from Islamic history with which Bilqasim would have been very familiar, though he might not have recognized their version of events.

London's most fashionable and popular play at this time was *Tamburlaine,* a play in two parts first performed in late 1587 by the Admiral's Men (named after their patron, the lord high admiral Charles Howard of

Effingham) at the Rose, the open-air playhouse built by Philip Henslowe. The play's full title was *Tamburlaine the Great, who, from a Scythian shepherd, by his rare and wonderful conquests, became a most puissant and mighty monarch, and (for his tyranny and terror in war) was termed the scourge of God*. It was written by a precocious young playwright barely out of Cambridge by the name of Christopher Marlowe.

Variously accused in his short yet brilliant life (1564–1593) of being a spy, an atheist, a sodomite and (worst of all) addicted to tobacco, Marlowe quickly saw the limitations of plays like Robert Wilson's *Three Ladies of London,* with their heavy-handed morality and abstract characters who bore little relation to the dynamic and exciting world that he saw around him. His response, in subject matter and language, would change the entire direction of Elizabethan drama. Marlowe's inspired choice for his hero was Timur, a Turkic-Mongol warlord and founder of the Timurid dynasty. In just over thirty years at the end of the fourteenth century, Timur led a series of spectacularly successful and brutal campaigns, laying waste to central Asia, conquering Persia, invading Russia and capturing the Delhi sultanate. In 1402 he marched into Syria, defeating the Egyptian Mamluks and taking Aleppo and Damascus before overcoming and capturing the Ottoman sultan Bayezid I at the Battle of Ankara in 1402. Timur's imperial aspirations were ended only by a fever that killed him in February 1405 as he marched on Ming China.

Timur provided Marlowe with a violent yet seductive hero, bestriding a vast global panorama of the postclassical world in which rival Tatar, Persian, Turkish and Christian empires contended for global sovereignty. In Marlowe's hands much of Tamburlaine's life is fictional (including his name, which Marlowe adopted from the Latin sources he had read, unaware that "Tamburlaine" was originally a contemptuous nickname referring to the warlord's lameness from a youthful injury, a disability he lacks in Marlowe's play). He is transformed into a lowly Scythian shepherd, a brilliant orator and charismatic overreacher who delights in humbling the mighty, whatever their beliefs. Tamburlaine's ceaseless and apparently amoral appetite for conquest simultaneously appalled and enthralled Elizabethan audiences.

Marlowe's play dramatizes the extraordinary ambition and will to power of its hero. In the opening scene, Tamburlaine is threatened by the Persian emperor Mycetes, but he is shown quickly seducing, fighting, commanding and conquering his way to lead one of the most powerful empires in history. Marlowe wanted to create a heroic character in which his audience could believe. Despite the challenge of staging a play with such a vast geographical range (from Persepolis through Africa to Damascus), *Tamburlaine* succeeds due to the unprecedented force of its hero's language. Here is an utterly captivating orator who can perform terrible acts of cruelty and violence while simultaneously persuading the audience of his love for his wife and his absolute commitment to imperial success. In Part Two, finally conquering Babylon and hanging its governor from the city walls, Tamburlaine performs his most audacious and controversial act and burns the Qur'an, claiming to be greater than any god. He falls ill shortly after and commands his sons to conquer what is left of the world before he dies.

Marlowe's riveting drama hinged on an innovative combination of language and action. Before him, most English poets and dramatists wrote rhyming verse whose structure was dictated by the number of syllables in each line. Marlowe's great innovation was to transform one such rhythmic technique, iambic pentameter, previously used in stiff and repetitive rhyming couplets, into a vehicle for creative expression. In *The Three Ladies of London,* Wilson had used what is known as "Poulter's measure," rhyming couplets alternating between twelve and fourteen syllables. The resulting lines in the "Prolog" sound flat and trite:

> To sit on honor's seat, it is a lofty reach,
> To seek for praise by making brags, oft times doth get a breach.[5]

Marlowe chose to use unrhymed iambic pentameter, what we now call blank verse. From the very first lines of *Tamburlaine,* the difference was electrifying:

> From jigging veins of rhyming mother-wits,
> And such conceits as clownage keeps in pay,
> We'll lead you to the stately tent of War,
> Where you shall hear the Scythian Tamburlaine

Threat'ning the world with high astounding terms
And scourging kingdoms with his conquering sword.
View but his picture in this tragic glass
And then applaud his fortunes as you please.[6]

It sounds like a manifesto, which is what Marlowe intended. He tells his audience audaciously to forget the artificial "jigging" rhymes of clowning of plays, leading them halfway across the world into the heart of battle, where the hypnotic beat of the blank verse allows them to "hear" Tamburlaine declaiming in "astounding terms" how he will match his words with deeds.

Ben Jonson captured the power and originality of Marlowe's verse when he wrote of "Marlowe's mighty line," but he also mocked Tamburlaine's "scenicall strutting and furious vociferation," vulgar entertainment that did no more than pander to the playhouse's poorly educated audience.[7] Thomas Nashe ridiculed Marlowe's innovations as "the swelling bombast of a bragging blank verse," dismissing his new technique as "the spacious volubility of a drumming decasillabon."[8] Marlowe's great rival Robert Greene went even further, complaining that Marlowe's innovation was putting him out of business, "for that I could not make my verses jet upon the stage in tragical buskins, every word filling the mouth like the faburden of Bow-Bell, daring God out of heaven with that atheist Tamburlaine."[9]

Tamburlaine's grand, declamatory style was notorious for its theatrical impact and the provocative views it conveyed. It allowed Marlowe to question some of his audience's most cherished beliefs—including their attachment to religion. As the classical writers of ancient Greece and Rome had shown, the ability to persuade was one of the most highly regarded attributes of public figures. Marlowe was as skillful an orator as Cicero but as dangerous as Satan, who had shown in the book of Genesis that artful persuasion could change the fate of mankind. Is Tamburlaine the brave hero who conquers the Turkish, Persian and Egyptian enemies of Christianity in Part One, or the tyrannical atheist who will even march against heaven in Part Two?

In Part One, as Tamburlaine prepares to go into battle with the

Ottoman sultan Bajazeth (Bayezid I), he congratulates his lieutenant Theridamas for his rousing anti-Turkish rhetoric:

> Well said Theridamas! Speak in that mood,
> For "will" and "shall" best fitteth Tamburlaine,
> Whose smiling stars give him assurèd hope
> Of martial triumph ere he meet his foes.
> I that am term'd the scourge and wrath of God,
> The only fear and terror of the world,
> Will first subdue the Turk, and then enlarge
> Those Christian captives which you keep as slaves.[10]

Tamburlaine sounds and acts like a Christian agent sent to vanquish the Ottoman Turks, promising to release the captives enslaved in Turkish galleys. Just as Marlowe was writing, William Harborne was struggling to free Christian galley slaves, albeit using more peaceable methods. Within two scenes Tamburlaine defeats Bajazeth and imprisons him in a cage, adding to his humiliation by using him as a footstool to step onto his throne. Bajazeth asks in vain that the "holy priests of heavenly Mahomet"[11] poison Tamburlaine, who responds by declaring,

> let the majesty of heaven behold
> Their scourge and terror tread on emperors.[12]

The moral ambiguity of Tamburlaine made him a captivating hero: simultaneously tormentor and savior. Marlowe had created a man who was more than a type—he made a character.

Trampling an enemy underfoot held powerful and immediate religious associations for Marlowe's audience, who would have heard in Marlowe's lines the verse from the Psalms, where God says, "Sit thou at my right hand, until I make thine enemies thy footstool" (Psalms 110:1). The 1583 edition of John Foxe's hugely popular *Acts and Monuments* gave a particularly English twist to this concept with a woodcut showing Henry VIII in the guise of Solomon, using Pope Clement VII as a footstool. Marlowe knew that many Protestant theologians—including Foxe—conflated the pope with the Turk as two incarnations of the Antichrist, but Tamburlaine was no reformed Christian. At every turn Marlowe confounds his audience's expectations as to where their sympathies should lie, by creating a hero who is simultaneously antagonistic toward Christianity and a liberator of Christians.

Perhaps Greene was right that Tamburlaine and his creator were both atheists. In Part Two, Tamburlaine spends much of his time taunting any and all deities, including the Prophet Muhammad. Marlowe shows extensive knowledge of recent reports about Islamic theology. Indeed, his mention of the "Zoacum" tree in Act II, scene 3, suggests that he may

Henry VIII using Pope Clement VII as a footstool in John Foxe's *Acts and Monuments* (1583).

even have read the Qur'an, where the tree is mentioned in surah 37.[13] In the opening scenes of Part Two, Tamburlaine's lieutenant Orcanes signs a peace treaty with Sigismund, King of Hungary, promising:

> By sacred Mahomet, the friend of God,
> Whose holy Alcoran remains with us,
> Whose glorious body, when he left the world,
> Clos'd in a coffin mounted up the air,
> And hung on stately Mecca's temple roof,
> I swear to keep this truce inviolable.[14]

Tamburlaine himself proves less respectful. Much later in the play, after he captures Babylon and orders the slaughter of its inhabitants, he asks Usumcasane, King of Morocco:

> where's the Turkish Alcoran,
> And all the heaps of superstitious books
> Found in the temples of that Mahomet
> Whom I have thought a god? They shall be burned.[15]

Boasting that "I live untouch'd by Mahomet," Tamburlaine then taunts the Prophet, calling out as he watches the Qur'an burn:

> Now, Mahomet, if thou have any power,
> Come down thyself and work a miracle.
> Thou art not worthy to be worshippèd
> That suffers flames of fire to burn the writ
> Wherein the sum of thy religion rests.[16]

Continuing his diatribe, he asks:

> Why send'st thou not a furious whirlwind down
> To blow thy Alcoran up to thy throne
> Where men report thou sitt'st by God himself,
> Or vengeance on the head of Tamburlaine,
> That shakes his sword against thy majesty
> And spurns the abstracts of thy foolish laws?[17]

He tells his soldiers that "Mahomet remains in hell," unable to respond to such mockery, and they should "seek out another godhead to adore."[18] Less than twenty lines later, Tamburlaine feels "distemper'd suddenly," and two scenes later he is dead. Is it just coincidence or is Marlowe finally bringing down the wrath of God upon his antihero? As he enters the play's final scene, Tamburlaine addresses his general Techelles and other close advisers and rails against all religions:

> What daring God torments my body thus
> And seeks to conquer mighty Tamburlaine?
> Shall sickness prove me now to be a man,
> That have been termed the terror of the world?
> Techelles and the rest, come, take your swords,
> And threaten him whose hand afflicts my soul.
> Come, let us march against the powers of heaven
> And set black streamers in the firmament
> To signify the slaughter of the gods.
> Ah, friends, what shall I do? I cannot stand.
> Come, carry me to war against the gods,
> That thus envy the health of Tamburlaine.[19]

Marlowe makes it quite clear here that his hero is the scourge of *any* divinity, not just the God of Islam or Christianity. Here, finally and majestically, the body of the man and the mind of God collide: the "terror of the world" has a soul but he will die in "war against the gods." Only God, Marlowe suggests, can defeat such a man.

Marlowe was fully aware of Elizabethan England's close relations with the rulers of Persia, Morocco and the Ottoman Empire that people his play. While he was studying at Cambridge and writing *Tamburlaine,* he was already associating with the intelligence networks run by Burghley and Walsingham, and he might well have been privy to aspects of the ambiguous and conflicted policy of Elizabeth's advisers toward the Islamic world.[20] Marlowe's play had little interest in either celebrating or condemning the crown's strategic alliances with Islam. It explored the contradictory and ambivalent emotions inspired by a traditional enemy that could be—and had been—quickly transformed into an ally, and possibly even a savior. The result was a new kind of drama that embraced duality and encouraged the audience to revel in both the horror and the delight of identifying with a charismatic outsider. The play created a shiver of pleasure rather than a somber moral lesson; it asked the audience to make up their own minds about its eastern hero and "applaud his fortunes as you please." Judging by the "sundrie times" the play was "showed upon stages in the city of London," his audience could not get enough of it.[21]

Tamburlaine's success spawned a new generation of playwrights, eager to exploit Marlowe's style and exotic settings. One of the first was Thomas Kyd, a close friend and former roommate who soon became embroiled in the murky world of Elizabethan espionage. Kyd would subsequently be arrested, tortured and imprisoned on charges of blasphemy arising from documents that he said in fact belonged to Marlowe. The two died within little more than a year of each other, Marlowe in May 1593, Kyd in August 1594. Kyd probably wrote his celebrated revenge play *The Spanish Tragedy* within months of *Tamburlaine*. The backdrop for Kyd's violent and bloody drama was the political struggle between Spain and Portugal, a prescient issue in the late 1580s. It featured a play within the play dramatizing the Ottoman sultan Süleyman the Magnificent's fictional pursuit of the Greek beauty Perseda. *The Spanish Tragedy* was so successful that in 1592 Kyd rushed out a follow-up, *Soliman and Perseda,* which focused exclusively on the Ottoman sultan's invasion of Rhodes, his capture of Perseda and his eventual downfall.

Around the time of the Armada's defeat, another of Marlowe's contemporaries, George Peele, turned to an earlier moment of conflict involving Iberia for inspiration. If Bilqasim, the Moroccan ambassador, had seen Peele's *Battle of Alcazar* on one of the many occasions it was performed by Lord Strange's Men at the Rose Theatre in Bankside, he would have been perplexed to see his sovereign, Ahmad al-Mansur, renamed "Muly Mahamet Seth." Peele took the innovative decision to dramatize a recent historical event, drawing on publications that described the battle. The result was more like war reportage than epic drama. It was the first play in English history to use a Presenter to introduce each act, and the first set exclusively in Morocco to put a Moor on the English stage. What Peele did with his "Moorish" characters would have a profound effect on subsequent Elizabethan drama.

Peele referred to the ruling sultan, Abd al-Malik I, as "Abdelmelec, also known as Muly Molocco, rightful King of Morocco." His scheming nephew, the exiled Abu Abdallah, Peele called "Muly Mahamet, the Moor" (not to be confused with Muly Mahamet Seth). While Abdelmelec is represented as the legitimate "brave, Barbarian lord Muly Molocco," Abu Abdallah is "the barbarous Moor, / The negro Muly Mahamet," a "tyrant," "Black in his look and bloody in his deeds."[22] The term "Moor" was derived from the Greek word Μαῦρος, which had two distinct meanings: an inhabitant of Mauretania (the ancient land covering today's Moroccan coast) and "dark" or "dim." During the Middle Ages the Latin derivation "Maurus" took on an ethnographic sense and, following the Islamic conquest of North Africa, came to be used as a synonym for "Mahomet's sect" (Muslims).[23] The word was thus an explosive mix of religion and ethnicity that Peele exploited to the full as he contrasted the two contenders for the Moroccan throne. He drew on contemporary sources to argue that Moors "are of two kinds, namely white or tawny Moors, and Negroes or black Moors."[24] His face made up with burned cork and oil and wearing black gloves, the actor playing Muly Mahamet was easily transformed into the devilish, scheming "blackamoor," while Abdelmelec was his complete antithesis, a virtuous "tawny Moor," a suitable figure for English merchants to do business with.

The son of Peele's Abdelmelec would inherit the kingdom and establish an alliance with Elizabeth. But this is where the play began to run into problems. Despite their apparent differences, both Abdelmelec and Muly Mahamet are acknowledged as Muslims and "descended from the line / Of Mahomet."[25] Although Abdelmelec is seen as the legitimate ruler, he announces, "I do adore / The sacred name of Amurath the Great,"[26] the Ottoman sultan Murad III, with whom he was in league. Muly Mahamet, by contrast, allied himself with a Christian king, Sebastian I. From this point in the play onward, Peele has to work hard to portray Sebastian as a courageous but tragic figure, flawed by his Catholicism and therefore easily manipulated by the scheming Muly Mahamet.

The play's anti-Catholic bias intensifies with the introduction of Thomas Stukeley, surrounded by Irish clergy and Italian soldiers, heading for Ireland and hoping to "restore it to the Roman faith."[27] Sebastian persuades Stukeley to join his Moroccan crusade, but the bombastic Englishman's thundering speeches reveal him to be a pale, opportunistic shadow of Tamburlaine:

> There shall be no action pass my hand or my sword
> That cannot make a step to gain a crown,
> No word shall pass the office of my tongue
> That sounds not of affection to a crown,
> No thought have being in my lordly breast
> That works not every way to win a crown.
> Deeds, words and thoughts shall all be as a king's,
> My chiefest company shall be with kings,
> And my deserts shall counterpoise a king's.
> Why should not I then look to be a king?
> I am the Marquess now of Ireland made
> And will be shortly King of Ireland.
> King of a mole-hill had I rather be
> Than the richest subject of a monarchy.[28]

The vain and conceited Stukeley lacks the ambition and linguistic prowess of Tamburlaine. He is blandly fixated on the pursuit of a crown.

At the end of Peele's play, his sources dictated that everyone should die. This duly happens in a climactic battle scene, in which Muly Mahamet demands: "A horse, a horse, villain, a horse," prefiguring the demise of another tragic villain, Shakespeare's Richard III, four years later. The only man left standing is Muly Mahamet Seth, Elizabeth's future ally, but even he does little more than order the mutilation of Muly Mahamet's body followed by a Christian burial for Sebastian (which did not happen historically). Like Marlowe's *Tamburlaine*, there is no obvious lesson from Peele's play. It ends with no Chorus to provide a simple moral and offers no character with which the audience can identify. One is left to choose between the pompous Abdelmelec, the pious Sebastian, the scheming Muly Mahamet and the mercenary Stukeley.[29]

This lack of simple identifications was in part a reflection of the contradictory nature of England's relations with the Muslim world in the late 1580s. These contradictions provided an alternative to the prescriptive histories of classical Rome and Greece, allowing Elizabethan dramatists to develop their own idiom, addressing their audiences' hopes and fears by staging them in a faraway land where the horrors of warfare, murder, atheism and tyranny could be explored in relative safety, free from the suspicious eyes of censors. We might think the play recommends the avoidance of Catholic-Muslim conflicts, while counseling Elizabeth against pursuing an alliance with al-Mansur, but Tudor dramatists were not moralizing priests or foreign policy advisers. They wanted to exploit the ambivalent emotions created by English experiences in the east as spectacular, captivating drama.

The Battle of Alcazar was not Peele's only foray into contemporary events. He also produced a poem entitled "A Farewell Entitled to the Famous and Fortunate Generals of our English Forces," dedicated to Sir John Norris and Sir Francis Drake, written in anticipation of the Portuguese Expedition's departure in the spring of 1589. Where *The Battle of Alcazar* had shown Catholic Portugal destroyed by its ill-fated Moroccan adventure, Peele's poem imagined an English Protestant crusade taking on the might of Spanish Catholicism. He describes the fleet leaving "England's shore and Albion's chalky cliffs" as they head for "the spacious bay of Portugal" and the "golden Tagus." Bidding farewell to all they hold dear, Peele glances backward at his own recent play alongside those of Marlowe and Greene:

> Bid theaters and proud tragedians,
> Bid Mahomet's poo, and mighty Tamburlaine,
> King Charlemagne, Tom Stukeley, and the rest,
> Adieu. To arms, to arms, to glorious arms!
> With noble Norris, and victorious Drake,
> Under the sanguine cross, brave England's badge,
> To propagate religious piety.[30]

Peele invokes the evocative image of a "sanguine" red cross, the traditional symbol of Christian militancy since the time of the

Crusades, in anticipation of an English victory as part of a wider religious crusade that will "propagate religious piety." Clearly, the hope was that Drake and Norris's heroic exploits would eclipse those of Tamburlaine.

By January 1589, preparations for the Portuguese Expedition were beginning to show signs of strain. The Dutch and English commanders in the Low Countries quarreled over how many troops could be spared. The final number of 1,800, excluding cavalry, was half of Norris's original request, as was the eventual supply of arms and munitions. Popular enthusiasm for the venture throughout the southeast of England swelled the army's numbers to nearly 20,000, but many of these were inexperienced adventurers who all needed feeding, adding to the financial headaches. Running out of money but determined to continue, Drake and Norris issued the order for their fleet of 180 vessels to leave Plymouth on April 18, 1589, with provisions to last them less than a month.[31] On board were Don António and the returning Moroccan ambassador Bilqasim, disguised as a Portuguese nobleman. It was yet another awkward alliance of Portuguese Catholics and Moroccan Muslims, with echoes of Alcácer-Quibir, but this time the intention was to overthrow Lisbon rather than Marrakesh.

Things went wrong almost immediately. Despite Elizabeth's orders to attack the Spanish fleet at Santander, Drake and Norris plundered La Coruña on the northwestern Spanish coast instead, wasting valuable time and manpower and alerting the Spanish. Elizabeth was furious, complaining bitterly that "they went to places more for profit than for service," but she was powerless to change their course.[32] By the time the fleet reached Lisbon in May, the city was heavily defended. The promised revolt in support of Don António never materialized and the siege soon turned into a fiasco, as the English forces dwindled to just 6,000 in the face of sickness and desertion. In late June the English withdrew and made their way home, having failed to achieve any of their objectives after losing a huge number of men (an estimated 11,000 died) and a great deal of money. Drake and Norris were in deep disgrace and Don António returned to England yet again, his last opportunity to regain the Portuguese throne apparently gone, while Bilqasim exploited the chaos to discard his Portuguese outfit and slip away to Marrakesh.

Elizabeth's best chance of ending the Spanish military threat for a generation failed, lost in the face of mismanagement, greed and mutual recriminations. The queen blamed everyone for the expedition's ignominious end, including al-Mansur, who was accused of duplicity in failing to support the fleet during the critical attack on Lisbon. In August al-Mansur wrote to Drake and Norris, protesting weakly that he had not been informed of the fleet's departure from England, and so was unable to help them. The truth was that al-Mansur's support could not have saved the disastrous campaign and that his sudden withdrawal was not duplicitous but pragmatic, as it transpired that the Moroccan was not the only ruler holding hostages. After the Battle of Alcácer-Quibir, Philip II had taken charge of two Moroccan princes who had fled the fighting: Mulay al-Shaykh, the son of Abu Abdallah Muhammad II, and al-Mansur's nephew Mulay al-Nasr. As news of the Anglo-Moroccan alliance reached Philip, he moved the princes to Seville, a veiled threat to send them back to Morocco, where they would undoubtedly have unleashed a civil war. In the face of such an imminent challenge to his rule, al-Mansur's dream of *reconquista* dissolved almost immediately. To reward him, Philip agreed to return the strategically important towns of Asilah and Larache on the Moroccan coast.[33] By the autumn of 1589, Catholic Spain, Protestant England and Muslim Morocco were locked in a three-way power struggle, each side playing off the others in a complex dance of politics, religion, money and military one-upmanship, with the first round going to the wily Philip.

Still, the English refused to give up on a Moroccan alliance. Faced with the collapse of the Portugal Expedition, Don António had sent an envoy named John de Cardenas (alias "Ciprian") to Marrakesh in order to plead with al-Mansur to give him money to support his claim to the Portuguese throne. Cardenas was a double agent who was also working for Walsingham, and in October 1589 he wrote a long letter to his English paymaster providing a remarkably frank assessment of the political situation and of al-Mansur's intentions. He appears to have been made of far sterner stuff than predecessors like Hogan and Roberts. As a spy rather than a merchant or a soldier, he had greater experience of the slipperiness of rulers, although he was not without his own braggadocio.

Cardenas reported to London that he had been kept waiting nearly a month before meeting al-Mansur, complaining that when the Moroccan sultan finally entered his presence, he was "twice or thrice interrupted in the midst of my tale; which had been clean cut off, if I had not resolutely insisted to be suffered to say what I had to say. I delivered my message to the Moor, urging him, by all the reasons I could, to the performance of his promise" to assist Don António and Elizabeth in their anti-Spanish league. Al-Mansur responded by offering what Cardenas dismissed crisply as "his pretended forward disposition to assist the king of Portugal." As far as Cardenas was concerned, al-Mansur had failed "to perform what he had promised" and "went about to fill my ears with wind only."

Cardenas claimed rather grandly to have issued the Moroccan ruler with an ultimatum: unless he committed to financing another military strike against Portugal by the winter, "I would take his delay thereon for a plain refusal." Boasting that he had "driven him to the wall," he extracted al-Mansur's agreement "to take a final resolution in the matter." Subsequent events suggest that Cardenas's bluster had absolutely no effect on al-Mansur. Just days later the frustrated spy reported that the Moroccan's "former promise made to me was performed only by sending his Jew without unto us," an unnamed official offering yet more vague assurances of political support.[34]

Cardenas then turned on al-Mansur for the way he conducted business. "The Moor," he protested, "doth rob the Jews" by demanding that they run the sugar mills for hardly any profit, leading them to default on their contracts with English merchants. The English were not exempt from criticism. In a withering attack, Cardenas excoriated the English merchants for having "been the causes of their own harm and spoiling of the trade," because they had "bred a glut of and discredit of their commodities, and partly also by outbidding one another in the price of Barbary commodities through the envy and malice that reigneth among them." He took a swipe at Protestant Elizabethan foreign policy by reflecting that it was "to be lamented that Christians should furnish the sworn enemies of Christ with iron, with brimstone, handguns, with firelocks, with swordblades, and such like."[35]

Although Cardenas had been sent to Marrakesh to resurrect the faltering Anglo-Moroccan alliance, he had a cynical view of al-Mansur's promises. As far as he was concerned, "the Moor doth not purpose the performance of his promise, I judge by his ill usage of me . . . whereunto I may add the natural hatred he beareth to Christians, and his cowardly and extreme covetous disposition." He denounced al-Mansur for trying to draw Elizabeth into a war in which he never had any intention of participating: "the proof hereof appeareth both by the untruth of some of his promises, which his country cannot perform, and by the consideration of his own estate and disposition: for how can it agree with reason that the cowardliest man in the world, another Sardanapalus in life, a man generally hated of his subjects, should hazard himself and his fortune at home to undertake a needless and endless war abroad?"[36] Sardanapalus was a semifictional Assyrian ruler renowned for his licentiousness and indolence—a byword for oriental despotism who could have stepped right out of a scene from Marlowe's *Tamburlaine*. Cardenas's insistence on calling al-Mansur "the Moor," and his repeated references to his ability to "perform" his "role,"[37] suggest that he had been watching Scythians, Turks and Moors on London's stages before he left for Marrakesh. What is certain is that by the beginning of the 1590s, the concept of "the Moor" had infused the language not just of Elizabethan theater but of diplomacy too.

When Cardenas's report reached London, Elizabeth reacted with a fury born of impotence. In August 1590 she wrote to al-Mansur complaining about his bogus friendship. Not only had he failed to support the English during the disastrous attack on Lisbon, but his promise of money and offer to free English captives had failed to materialize. In an uncharacteristic fit of pique, Elizabeth threatened to go over his head to the Ottoman sultan. "If you would not grant us what we so reasonably ask from you, we will have to pay less attention to your friendship," she wrote in exasperation. "We know for sure also that the Great Turk, who treats our subjects with great favor and humanity, will not

appreciate your maltreatment of them in order to please the Spaniards."[38] Sounding more like a childish taunt than a diplomatic maneu-
ver, it was nevertheless a revealing comment: she assumed that
al-Mansur dreaded the Ottomans far more than he feared Spain.

Elizabeth had in fact already written to Murad, but the wily Moroccan ruler brushed off the threat of an Ottoman intervention, writing
back a delightfully patronizing letter mollifying the queen and assuring
her of his love and friendship. By January 1591 even Murad was becoming annoyed by al-Mansur's behavior. In one of his letters to Elizabeth
he confided his irritation with the "faithless prince of Fez."[39]

Al-Mansur seemed to be indifferent to such threats. He was far too
preoccupied with the fulfillment of a messianic project that had exercised
him since his accession: extending his empire into the Muslim kingdom
of Songhai, in modern-day Niger. When Elizabeth's letters reached him
in the autumn of 1590, his army of 5,000 soldiers including Moriscos,
renegadoes and European mercenaries had already set off to cross two
thousand miles of the Saharan desert to march on Gao, on the Niger River.
On March 13, 1591, the Moroccan troops, equipped with muskets, mas-
sacred 80,000 Songhai warriors armed with only lances and javelins. As
the Songhai soldiers fell, they reportedly shouted, to no avail, "We are
Muslims, we are your brothers in religion."[40] The Moroccan victory
brought al-Mansur vast wealth. He now controlled a key stretch of the
trans-Saharan trade route, generating an annual tribute from the Songhai
of 1,000 slaves and 100,000 gold pieces.[41] European merchants flocked
to Marrakesh in droves as gold poured into the imperial capital. Politically and financially, al-Mansur seemed more secure than ever. He wrote
to Elizabeth apologizing casually for not having done so earlier, excusing
himself due to the small matter of the invasion of Songhai, but promising
her that the money rolling into his imperial coffers would help their joint
effort to defeat the Spanish. His victory was chronicled by his court historians in terms that illuminated his rivalry with the Ottomans: al-Mansur
was now regarded as the Mahdi, the legitimate heir of the caliphate
descended from the Prophet Muhammad (unlike the Ottoman sultan),
who would unify Islam and lead a holy war against Christianity. If New
World gold and silver had enabled Catholic Spain to fight Protestants and

Muslims throughout Europe and the Mediterranean, gold from central Africa would be used to confer imperial and religious legitimacy on al-Mansur. The English were of course oblivious to these quasi-spiritual claims, but Elizabeth appreciated that al-Mansur's success in Songhai, in contrast to her own military failure, meant she needed his support more than ever.

While Elizabeth struggled to impose her will in Marrakesh and made more lasting inroads in Constantinople, London's printing presses lit up with diplomatic reports, travelers' tales and sermons chronicling epic military victories and heroic defeats far from home. Stories of gold plundered from fabled African empires, captive princes, ransomed slaves, political skulduggery and apocalyptic claims of universal empires were the raw material that quickly became a recipe for theatrical success in London's commercial playhouses. A mixture of faith, ambition and exoticism was staple theatrical fodder, as almost every Elizabethan dramatist attached to an acting company began to include despotic sultans, deceitful Moors, renegade Christians, murderous Jews and vulnerable princesses in his plays. An endless variety of pagans, converts, apostates and atheists paraded the power of their beliefs (or lack thereof) onstage, as these formerly marginal characters became a ticket to commercial success.

Of the more than sixty plays featuring Turks, Moors and Persians performed in London's public theaters between 1576 and 1603, forty were staged between 1588 and 1599, more than ten of which acknowledge explicit debts to Marlowe's *Tamburlaine*.[42] The line between imitating Marlowe and exploiting the new fascination with the Islamic world became increasingly blurred as playwrights drew on a growing body of diplomatic, commercial and religious writings. Robert Greene, who had suggested that Marlowe was an atheist, now offered up his own play set in the east for the Queen's Men. *The First Part of the Tragicall Reign of Selimus, Sometime Emperor of the Turkes, and Grandfather to Him that now Reigneth* (c. 1588–1590) was an explicit attempt to imitate *Tamburlaine* by envisaging a two-part play chronicling the life and reign of the Ottoman sultan Selim I.[43] Selim was the first sultan to get his own play on the English stage. A combination of Tamburlaine (who is mentioned on three separate occasions) and Machiavelli's prince, he is shown poisoning his father, Bayezid II, and murdering his brothers in pursuit of absolute power. Greene's Selim has little interest in what he calls "the holy Prophet Mahomet," the "sacred Alcoran" or "gods, religion, heaven and hell," which he dismisses as "mere fictions" and "bugbears to keep the world in fear."[44] In keeping with medieval Christian stereotypes, Greene portrays him as a pagan drawn to idolatry. Selim buries his father at the "Temple of Mahomet" as Greene tries every theatrical trick to compete with *Tamburlaine*'s success, from exotic settings and epic battles to deathbed conversions, poisoning, strangling, the severing of one character's hands and even a graphic eye-plucking scene that anticipates a similar moment in *King Lear* (1606). The play ends much like the first part of *Tamburlaine,* with "victorious Selim" preparing to march against the Egyptian sultan, as Greene's Chorus angles for a sequel:

> If this first part, gentles, do like you well,
> The second part shall greater murthers tell.[45]

Unfortunately, it seems the audience did not like it well at all. Greene lacked Marlowe's rhetorical flair: he put a murderous and unsympathetic Turk in Tamburlaine's clothing, with none of his epic allure. There would be no second part.

Greene tried again with *Alphonsus, King of Aragon,* which purported to chronicle the life of Alfonso V, King of Aragon and Naples, and his defeat at the hands of a fictional Ottoman sultan, the bombastic Amurack. In a theatrical flourish designed to trump the burning of the Qur'an, the "God Mahomet" is brought onstage as a brass idol, "a brazen head set in the middle of the place behind the stage, out of the which cast flames of fire, drums rumble within."[46] Mahomet's false prophecy leads to Amurack's defeat at the hands of Alphonsus. The sultan offers his daughter Iphigina to the Spanish king, promising in a bizarre fantasy of Christians triumphing over the Ottomans that for her dowry he "shall possess the Turkish empery."[47]

Many attempted to outdo Marlowe. They failed not because their audience's appetite for the exotic had diminished, but because they were unable to reach beyond stereotypes and create believable characters. Writers like Thomas Dekker, Fulke Greville, John Day and William Haughton all tried, each one producing ever more overblown plays featuring despotic characters strutting, stamping, ranting and bellowing their way across the stage as they conquered and murdered their way to power. They wore turbans (also known as "Turkish caps") or flowing robes, carried ostentatious scimitars and boasted elaborate "moustachios." The result was an outlandish parade of histrionic orientalism whose affected performance has become an enduring characteristic of English theatrical tradition. This convention first developed when Marlowe's "mighty line" was yoked to contemporary reports reaching London from merchants and travelers living and working throughout Africa, the Ottoman Empire, Russia, Persia and even India.[48]

But as Marlowe's followers churned out ever more lurid imitations of *Tamburlaine*, the mercurial young playwright followed that work's success with a complete change of direction: in 1589–1590 he wrote *The Jew of Malta*. While *Tamburlaine* was a recognizable figure from world history, this new play was an explosive and unprecedented leap of the imagination. There are no direct (or at least obvious) sources for the play. Its central and wholly unscrupulous character was taken from the Bible, where Matthew tells the story of how Barabbas, a violent mobster, was released from prison by Pilate instead of Jesus (Matthew 27:15–26). Marlowe's Barabas is one of the most outrageously immoral characters in Elizabethan drama: a wealthy Jewish merchant who relishes the riches of trade and has no qualms about murdering those who threaten it. Out went the epic, restless geographical sweep of *Tamburlaine* and in came the insular setting of Malta, a Mediterranean island so apparently insignificant that Tamburlaine never even mentioned it in his thundering speeches of imperial conquest. Gone too was Tamburlaine's mighty rhetoric and military ambition, replaced by a middle-aged Jew who first appears onstage counting his "infinite riches" and confessing that his people "come not to be kings."[49]

Within two scenes the island's Christian authorities confiscate Barabas's wealth to settle the annual tribute demanded by the Ottomans.

Barabas embarks on a gleeful rampage of deception and murder to recover his wealth. He buys a Turkish slave called Ithamore and forms a
murderous alliance with him based on their shared religious identities.
Barabas tells Ithamore, "Both circumcised, we hate Christians both."[50]
He proceeds to poison his own daughter Abigail (as well as a convent
of nuns) when she converts to Christianity and plays the Maltese Christians and the invading Ottoman army off against each other to ensure
his own survival, before they both realize what he is up to and turn on
him, boiling him alive in a cauldron as he rails against them:

> had I but escap'd this stratagem
> I would have brought confusion on you all,
> Damn'd Christians, dogs, and Turkish infidels![51]

Marlowe's play drew on recent events, from the unsuccessful Ottoman siege of Malta in 1565 to the *Bark Roe* incident of 1581 and the
wider role of Jewish merchants as commercial intermediaries between
Christian and Islamic interests. What interested him as a dramatist was
not the mechanics of trade, but the deeper underlying issues of trust and
betrayal, faith and apostasy, conversion and cultural exchange. These
were problems that English merchants like Hogan, Harborne and Roberts had been struggling with for decades, but it took Marlowe's genius
to give them voice. Here was a play that put the three religions of the
Book onstage, with each found to be more rapacious, duplicitous and
hypocritical than the next. In a wonderful declaration of self-confessed
villainy, Marlowe set Barabas up to revel in the prejudices of an Elizabethan audience:

> As for myself, I walk abroad a-nights
> And kill sick people groaning under walls;
> Sometimes I go about and poison wells;
> And now and then, to cherish Christian thieves,
> I am content to lose some of my crowns,
> That I may, walking in my gallery,
> See 'em go pinioned along by my door . . .
> And with extorting, cozening, forfeiting,

And tricks belonging unto brokery,
I filled the jails with bankrupts in a year,
And with young orphans planted hospitals,
And every moon made some or other mad,
And now and then one hang himself for grief,
Pinning upon his breast a long great scroll
How I with interest tormented him.[52]

Marlowe evokes every myth associated with anti-Semitism, focusing on the holy trinity of apostasy, murder and money. The pun on "interest" would not have been lost on his audience: Jewish "interest" was never far from the public imagination. Although Jews had been officially expelled from England in 1290, a small but significant community still lived in London.[53] As he picks over his riches, Barabas declares:

Give me the merchants of the Indian mines,
That trade in metal of the purest mold;
The wealthy Moor, that in the eastern rocks
Without control can pick his riches up,
And in his house heap pearl like pebble-stones,
Receive them free, and sell them by the weight.[54]

The rich and exotic world of imperial conquest comes to rest "as infinite riches in a little room."[55] In this play more than any other, Marlowe demonstrated how charismatic characters like Barabas could transcend established boundaries of morality, religion and ethnicity. Marlowe himself had little interest in the specific nature of Barabas's Jewish faith, or Ithamore's Islamic beliefs; he wanted to show that in many respects their duplicitous behavior (though perhaps not their appetite for murder) could be just as rapacious and unprincipled as that of his audience.

The Jew of Malta was another great success, but Marlowe's dominance was tragically cut short. On May 30, 1593, he was stabbed to death in a house in Deptford, ostensibly after a dispute concerning the settlement of a bill. The exact circumstances of his murder are shrouded in mystery; what cannot be doubted is that his death brought to an end the career of one of Elizabethan theater's most promising talents.[56] Marlowe's genius was to take the fear, hypocrisy and greed surrounding Elizabethan England's relations with the Islamic world and transmute them into electrifying theater. Conflict, doubt and anxiety always make for better drama than moral absolutism. Five extraordinarily creative years had forever altered the course of English theater. It was difficult to imagine that any of his imitators would ever manage to surpass his brilliance. But one man, born like Marlowe in 1564, had been quietly learning his stagecraft by observing his fellow playwright, absorbing his style and working out how he might take things in a new direction. His name was William Shakespeare.

8

Mahomet's Dove

In his diary entries for the Rose Theatre's spring season in 1592, Philip Henslowe noted that Marlowe's *Jew of Malta* was a popular hit, performed on at least ten occasions, but its success was soon eclipsed by a new play called *Henry VI*. Henslowe recorded that the play's first performance took place on March 3, 1592, and during the rest of the season it was performed on fifteen occasions, often on alternate days with *The Jew of Malta*.[1] Today few people read Shakespeare's earliest forays into English history, but during the first half of his career the three parts of *Henry VI*, written in rapid succession in the early 1590s, were enormously popular with audiences, offering a distinctive new style that challenged Marlowe's theatrical supremacy.

Shakespeare did not try to compete with Marlowe by imitating his "high astounding terms" and exotic settings. Instead he looked closer to home, to the Plantagenets, the flawed line of medieval kings who preceded the Tudors. London's commercial theater had never been secure enough to put recent English history onstage, let alone to humanize it by considering the vulnerabilities and frailties of weak kings and transforming them into tragic figures. Marlowe emphasized his characters' relentless will to power. Shakespeare, by contrast, succeeded in making historic failures into figures of empathy, insight and pathos.

The first act of *Henry VI, Part 1* opens much as *Tamburlaine* ends, with the death of a fabled warrior—in this case, Henry V—with no obvious successor strong enough to fulfill his legacy.[2] What follows is a catalog of woe, as the infant king and his advisers prove powerless to prevent civil strife and the loss of French territories so valiantly conquered by his father. Central to the play are its portrayal of the French mystic and warrior Jeanne La Pucelle, known in Britain as Joan of Arc, and the death of the famous English warrior John Talbot, Earl of Shrewsbury, in a scene said to have caused the shedding of "the tears of ten thousand spectators" when the play was first performed.[3]

In Act I, scene 2, the French dauphin Charles tries to raise the siege of Orleans but is beaten back by the English. He is then introduced to Joan, who,

> by a vision sent to her from heaven,
> Ordained is to raise this tedious siege
> And drive the English forth the bounds of France.[4]

Marlowe's ghost was never far from Shakespeare's early plays, and Joan describes herself as "by birth a shepherd's daughter," who is "black and swart."[5] Challenged to single combat to prove her worth, she wins, whereupon the heir to the French throne boldly chooses to make her the leader of the French army. Looking on this self-confessed visionary, Charles exclaims:

> Was Mahomet inspirèd with a dove?
> Thou with an eagle art inspirèd then.
> Helen, the mother of great Constantine,
> Nor yet Saint Philip's daughter's, were like thee.
> Bright star of Venus, fall'n down on the earth,
> How may I reverently worship thee enough?[6]

The dauphin struggles to understand Joan's strength and capabilities before he alights on an analogy that expresses her singular power: if Mahomet had a mystical dove, then she must have been inspired by an eagle. Both the eagle and the dove have obvious symbolic resonance in a play about war: peace has no place in the dauphin's ideology, and Joan, famed for her prowess on the battlefield, is associated with a spectacular bird of prey. But, more significantly, the allusion to Islam puts France within a context of holy war. Joan is recruited because she demonstrates divine powers, and it is this divinity that establishes her role in French history as a crusader.

This is Shakespeare's only explicit reference to the Prophet Muhammad, an allusion to the widely held Christian belief that Muhammad was a fraudulent apostate mimicking divine intercession. In his sermon "The Baptizing of a Turke" (see chapter 6), Meredith Hanmer proclaimed that Muhammad "taught a dove to feed at his ear, wherein he was wont to put grains of corn [and] persuaded his wife and others that he was a prophet, that the spirit of God fell upon him and that the Angel Gabriel, in the form of a dove, came to his ear and revealed him secrets."[7] Sir Walter Raleigh also peddled this myth in his voluminous *History of the World* (1603–1616), denouncing "Mahomet persuading the rude and simple Arabians, that it was the Holy Ghost that gave him advice" as a fraudulent mimicry of the apparition of the Holy Spirit as a dove at Jesus' baptism.[8] Thomas Nashe, widely regarded as one of Shakespeare's collaborators on *Henry VI,* also wrote about Muhammad's dove in *The Terrors of the Night* (1593), which refers to "the dove wherewith the Turks hold Mahomet their prophet to be inspired."[9] Nashe may in fact have had a hand in drafting the exchange between Charles and Joan.

In the English chronicles, Joan is an impostor, but in French history she is a saint. From the perspective of a Protestant English audience watching the play in 1592, it made sense to compare the Catholic French with the Prophet Muhammad. The "false" prophecy of Muhammad is followed by Charles's invocation of more obvious Catholic prophets—John the Apostle and his eagle, St. Helen and the True Cross, and Philip the Apostle's daughters (known for prophesying the "true" word of God among "heathens"). The parallel between Islam and Catholicism damns the French in the Protestant English audience's eyes. Charles then promises Joan a grander urn than that given to "the rich jewell'd coffer of Darius"—a reference to the last ruler of the Achaemenid Empire of Persia. Darius was of course not a Muslim, but to the Elizabethan audience he conjured up an image of oriental absolutism. Marlowe had exploited Islamic characters and settings to create a suitably epic drama; Shakespeare's use of them now highlighted the religious differences confronting the Elizabethans in the early 1590s.

1600

ABDVLGVAHID.

ÆTATIS:42.

LEGATVS REGIS BARBARIÆ
IN ANGLIAM.

Muhammad al-Annuri, the Moroccan ambassador who
arrived in London in August 1600 with a large delegation to
propose an Anglo-Moroccan alliance and twice met the queen.
Shakespeare started to write *Othello* around six months later.

Willem de Pannemaker's tapestry showing Catholic Habsburg forces triumphantly sacking Tunis in 1535. These scenes of slaughter and enslavement were first displayed in London following Mary Tudor's marriage to Philip of Spain in 1554.

fueron muertos. toman los soldados aprissen ypor esclauos todala gente que delos
a presa de buir los moros noauian podido lleuar consigo niblen esconder. hallanse enla
barcoes quesepusiesen en prisson todos los esclauos quepudiesen tomar armas conlos
ces detodas naciones. Los quales estedia son puestos enlibertad. Da el emperador su
el emperador: aceptando debuenagana las condiciones quele quiso poner.

VICTOREM CAROLVM TER GRATA VOCE SALVTANT.
HASAMVM CAESAR QVAMVIS NIL TALE MERENTEM
OMNIA POLLICITVM CVM RE NEC IVVERIT VLLA.
RESTITVIT MISERVM SOLIOQVE REPONIT AVITO

A double portrait of Philip of Spain and Mary Tudor painted in 1558. It shows Philip ruling England alongside Mary, who died in November that same year.

NON SINE SOLE
IRIS.

The "Rainbow Portrait" of Elizabeth I, c. 1600. The jewels and fabrics are all recognizably oriental, a reminder of the extensive Anglo-Islamic trade.

Diogo Homem's map of the Mediterranean from the Queen Mary Atlas (1558), showing Ottoman flags flying over North Africa.

The idealistic but naive king Sebastian I of Portugal, whose defeat and death (alongside two rival Moroccan rulers) at the battle of Alcácer-Quibir in 1578 sent shock waves throughout Europe.

A view of Marrakesh, the capital city of the Sa'adian dynasty, from a seventeenth-century engraving by the Dutch artist Adriaen Matham.

Hans Eworth's 1549 portrait of Sultan Süleyman the Magnificent on horseback, one of many pictures of Islamic rulers owned by the Elizabethan elite.

Sultan Selim II, surrounded by his army, receiving homages
after the death of his father, Sultan Süleyman, in 1566.

Samson Rowlie, a Norfolk merchant captured by the Turks in 1577. As the Latin inscription states, he was castrated, converted to Islam, and was renamed Hassan Aga; he then became chief eunuch and treasurer of Algiers.

Below: A needlework hanging showing a personification of Faith—looking remarkably like Queen Elizabeth—and Muhammad, commissioned by Elizabeth Talbot, Countess of Shrewsbury, at the height of the Anglo-Ottoman accord.

A portrait of Sultan Murad III from an Ottoman album of 1588–1589. Murad and Queen Elizabeth corresponded about politics and commerce for more than two decades and established an unprecedented alliance. When Ottoman forces were confronting Spain and challenging the Holy Roman Empire, Elizabeth's merchants were supplying them with guns.

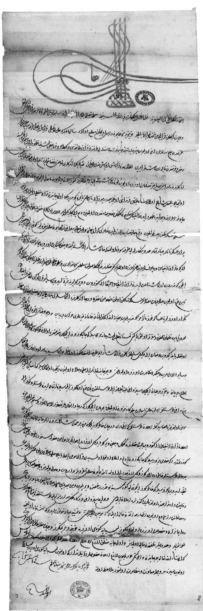

A copy of a letter from Sultan Murad III to Queen Elizabeth dated June 20, 1590, in praise of the queen, with the Ottoman calligraphic monogram at the top.

Nicholas Hilliard's Heneage Jewel, c. 1595, made of gold, diamonds, crystal, and rubies. Elizabeth sent jeweled portraits like this to the Ottoman court in the 1590s.

Sir Anthony Sherley and his rival ambassador, the Persian cavalryman Husain Ali Beg Bayat, engraved by Aegidius Sadeler during their joint embassy to Emperor Rudolf II in Prague in 1600 to propose a Euro-Persian alliance. The two men quarreled violently before Ali Beg finally abandoned Sir Anthony and returned to Persia.

Sir Robert Sherley and his wife, Teresa, painted in an opulent oriental style by Sir Anthony Van Dyck during Sherley's embassy to Rome in 1622. The daughter of a Circassian chieftain, Teresa was baptized into the Catholic faith.

The Persian shah Abbas I, Safavid ruler of Iran, from a seventeenth-century Mughal painting. Falconry was one of his passions, shared by his friend Sir Anthony Sherley.

Constantinople, the Ottoman capital, in the early seventeenth century. The skyline is dominated by minarets, characteristic of the Ottoman architecture that redefined the Byzantine city after it fell to Mehmed II in 1453.

A conference at Somerset House in 1604 brought about reconciliation with Spain and marked the end of Elizabethan engagement with Islam. The English delegates are on the right, the Spanish and Flemish on the left; on the table between them is an Ottoman rug.

• • •

The anxious and seditious atmosphere of *Henry VI* captured the mood of a nation whose optimism since the victory over the Spanish Armada in 1588 had evaporated. The failure of Drake and Norris's Portuguese Expedition in the summer of 1589 was the first of several foreign policy setbacks that suggested Elizabeth, who was now in her midfifties and had ruled for more than three decades, might be on the wane. Walsingham was in the last months of his life and Leicester was dead, as were many of her other most trusted advisers. Only Burghley remained, but he was in his seventies. The news from France was also bad. King Henry III's attempt to mediate between the Catholics and Huguenots had provoked his murder in August 1589 and the contested succession of the Huguenot Henry of Navarre as King Henry IV.

Henry of Navarre's elevation split France, and the outraged French Catholic League rose up against him as he marched on Paris. The possibility that the French capital would fall into Protestant hands was too much for Philip, who ordered Spanish forces to invade France through the Low Countries. Elizabeth could not countenance the thought of a Spanish-controlled northern France being used as a launching pad from which to invade England again, so she dispatched an English army of 3,600 men to support Henry's campaign in Normandy. In May 1591, when Shakespeare would have been working on *Henry VI,* she sent another 4,000 soldiers under the command of the rehabilitated veteran Sir John Norris. Once again, Norris was compromised by the vagueness of his orders. He spent the next twelve months at Henry's whim tied up in pointless sieges and skirmishes, his force dwindling by the spring of 1592 to just 600 sick and hungry men. *Henry VI* described in graphic detail the political mismanagement of an English campaign in France in the 1420s. Its audience was painfully aware of the disastrous campaigns of the last three years, which had left thousands of English soldiers dead or returning home as invalids, with nothing to show for their support of the French Protestant cause.[10]

The turmoil in France was felt as far afield as Constantinople, where Harborne's successor, Edward Barton, assiduously exploited divisions within the French diplomatic community. Ever since his appointment, the industrious if somewhat intemperate Barton had proved remarkably successful, thanks to his cultivation of a close personal relationship with Murad's powerful consort, Safiye Sultan. In a letter sent to Burghley in July 1591 Barton boasted, "Such an eyesore I am to the Christians here resident and so well esteemed by the Turks." His proximity to the sultan was such that it was assumed Murad was preparing a new Turkish fleet to sail against the Spanish in league with Elizabeth.[11] The resident French ambassador, Jacques de Savary Lancosme, a firm supporter of the Catholic League, now found himself compromised by the accession of the Huguenot Henry IV. Barton accused Lancosme of working for Philip II and had him arrested by the Ottoman authorities. When Lancosme was finally released into Barton's charge, the triumphant Englishman sent him as a prisoner to Henry IV.[12]

Just as Barton believed he had cemented a three-way alliance among France, England and the Ottomans, Henry IV was making plans to break the religious stalemate in France by converting to Catholicism. Throughout the spring of 1593, the king was locked in discussions with theologians about how to present his conversion to both sides of the religious divide. His Catholic advisers finally agreed solemnly that "His Majesty was not a Turk . . . that he should be led gently from error to truth."[13] An oath abjuring his Huguenot faith and embracing Catholicism was agreed, and on July 25, before entering the capital, Henry celebrated high mass in the Abbey of St.-Denis, just outside Paris. Elizabeth had feared that Henry would try to cement his political position by choosing what one of her counselors called a religious "metamorphosis," and she responded to the news of his conversion by refusing him any further military support.[14]

In March 1592, the English Catholic propagandist and exile Richard Verstegen had circulated a pamphlet entitled *A Declaration of the True Causes of the Great Troubles, Presupposed to be Intended against the Realm of England,* in which he attacked Elizabeth's privy counselors, Burghley in particular, for England's political difficulties. He criticized the advisers for "the assisting of the Huguenots of Navarre," which was just one aspect of England's "general discord with all the Catholic Christians of the world." He continued:

Thus the realm of England, being brought into breach of amity, not only with the Church of God, but with all their old allies and friends, if we now consider with whom they are joined in true friendship, we shall find them to be so few as none at all, since they have neither spared, to offend friend nor foe. But if we look what new confederates they have chosen, instead of the old, we shall see them to be the great Turk, the kings of Fez, Morocco, and Algiers, or other Mahometains and Moors of Barbary, all professed enemies to Christ.[15]

Having condemned Elizabeth's alliance with the Turkish and Moroccan "Mahometains," Verstegen mocked English support for a variety of Protestant groups across northern Europe. "They are also in league with a few beer-brewers and basket-makers of Holland and Zealand," he wrote jeeringly, as well as "a company of apostates and Huguenots of France."

Verstegen was fully aware of Walsingham's and Harborne's attempts to draw the Ottomans into a closer military alliance during the previous decade. He warned his readers,

The great Turk and his consorts, may be by the English excited to invade some parts of Christendom, near unto them adjoining (as already upon such persuasion they have attempted) but good unto England they can do none albeit the English would exchange their Geneva Bible for the Turkish Alcoran, because their situations are so far distant.

The attack on England's Protestantism was clear enough: "the English thus leagued with infidels, heretics and rebels" would only make them increasingly isolated within Christendom.[16] The religious accommodation of the Anglo-Ottoman Capitulations had come back to haunt Walsingham and their English adherents.

Elizabeth's counselors were so concerned about the possible damage of Verstegen's pamphlet both at home and abroad that they commissioned Burghley's nephew, the philosopher, scientist and future lord chancellor Francis Bacon, to write a refutation, entitled "Certain

Observations made upon a Libel Published this Present Year, 1592."
Toward the end of his lengthy response Bacon directly addressed
Verstegen's claim that "England is confederate with the great Turk."
First, he asked rhetorically:

> If he mean it because the merchants have an agent in Constanti-
> nople, how will he answer for all the kings of France since Francis
> I which are good Catholics; for the Emperor; for the King of Spain
> himself; for the Senate of Venice; and other states, that have long
> time ambassadors liegers [residents] in that court? If he mean it
> because the Turk hath done some special honor to our ambassador
> (if he be so to be termed) we are beholding to the king of Spain for
> that; for that the honor we have won upon him by opposition hath
> given us reputation through the world.

This was a standard justification, based on commercial exigency,
which had been used ever since William Harborne's arrival in Constantinople: every Christian ruler had ambassadors and merchants in the
city, and England's opposition to Spanish aggression in the region had
won rather than lost friends.

Bacon's next claim was more theologically ambiguous: "If he mean
it because the Turk seemeth to affect us for the abolishing of images, let
him consider then what a scandal the matter of images hath been in the
church, as having been one of the principal branches whereby Mahu-
metanism entered."[17] As far as Bacon was concerned, Islamic aniconism
was not responsible for Protestant iconoclasm; instead, the flagrant
idolatry of Catholicism had enabled heresies like Islam to thrive. His
argument went right back to Erasmus's claim in his essay "On the War
Against the Turks" (1530) that Islam had flourished because of Catholic disunity, and was a scourge sent by a Christian God to punish the
church's sins. This had some resonance, but it was hardly a convincing
justification for the deeply entrenched alliances that Elizabeth had cultivated with the Islamic world over the previous three decades. Then as
now, ideological differences could always be put to one side in pursuit
of trade.

Bacon had good reason for his reticence. Even as he wrote, Elizabeth's relations with "the great Turk" were taking on a new dimension. Rumors were circulating through Europe's royal courts that Elizabeth was providing financial and military support "to help the Great Turk to invade Christendom," partly inspired by the success of Barton's embassy.[18] Barton was also petitioning Burghley to send Murad gifts from the queen to endorse his appointment.

In September 1593 Burghley relented, and the *Ascension* of London docked in Constantinople laden with offerings for the sultan. Barton presented gifts of gold plate, cloth and satin to Murad and his entourage while also conferring gifts upon Safiye Sultan, whom he described as "the Sultana or empress who (by reason that she is mother to him which was heir to the crown imperial) is had in far greater reverence than any of his other queens or concubines." One of Barton's retinue described the gifts "sent in her majesty's name" as

a jewel of her majesty's picture, set with some rubies and diamonds, three great pieces of gilt plate, ten garments of cloth and gold, a very fine case of glass bottles silver and gilt, with two pieces of fine Holland, which so gratefully she accepted, as that she sent to know of the ambassador what present he thought she might return that would most delight her majesty: who sent word that a suit of princely attire being after the Turkish fashion would for the rareness thereof be acceptable in England. Whereupon she sent an upper gown of cloth of gold very rich, an under gown of cloth of silver, and a girdle of Turkey work, rich and fair, with a letter of gratification.[19]

The whole exchange was conducted by the two royal women's intermediaries: Barton represented Elizabeth while Safiye delegated everything to her *kira* (a Jewish agent), the Spanish-born Esperanza Malchi, whose power in the imperial harem was second only to her own. A delighted Barton valued the sultana's gifts at £120 before sending them on to England.[20] No record of Elizabeth's bejeweled portrait remains, but other surviving examples provide some clue to the kind of object she sent. They include Nicholas Hilliard's magnificent golden locket of the queen encrusted with diamonds and rubies, which showed her as

"Defender of the Faith," a title she had used repeatedly in her correspondence with Murad.

The exchange of these luxury items was a carefully rehearsed diplomatic act designed to celebrate the Anglo-Ottoman alliance, a point underlined by a translation of Safiye's "letter of gratification," which reached Greenwich Palace with her presents in August 1594. The letter provided an unequivocal statement of Ottoman political supremacy. It began by praising God and "the pure soul of Lord Muhammad" before listing Murad's numerous titles as "emperor of the seven climates and of the four parts of the world," then reminding the queen that the correspondence was initiated "on the part of the mother of Sultan Murad Khan's son," Safiye, the sultan's consort and mother of his presumptive heir. The letter then managed to praise Elizabeth while also stressing her subservience to Murad:

> Sultan son of Sultan from all the sons of Adam to this time, the shadow of God, the protector of faith and state, Khan Murad, the support of Christian womanhood . . . who follow the Messiah, bearer of the marks of pomp and majesty, trailing the skirts of glory and power, she who is obeyed of the princes, cradle of chastity and continence, ruler of the realm of England, crowned lady and woman of Mary's way—may her last moments be concluded with good and may she obtain that which she desires![21]

As far as Safiye was concerned, regardless of the presents exchanged between them, Elizabeth came under Murad's imperial and theological protection. Her letter unwittingly confirmed the accusations leveled against Elizabeth and her Protestant counselors by Verstegen and the exiled English Catholic diaspora: England was being treated as a vassal state of the Ottoman Empire, prepared to trade anything from cloth to its faith.

In late 1593, just as this exchange of gifts and letters began, London learned of the outbreak of war between the Ottomans and the Habsburgs, following the sultan's invasion of Hungary that July. This conflict would drag on for thirteen years with no decisive outcome, and news of its campaigns would dominate English publications for the rest of Elizabeth's reign. Reports of the conflict coincided with the reopening of London's playhouses after a year of closures prompted by a particularly severe outbreak of plague.

On January 24, 1594, a new play by Shakespeare was performed at the Rose Theatre by the Earl of Sussex's Men: *The Most Lamentable Roman Tragedy of Titus Andronicus*. Having found early success by staging the prehistory to the triumph of the Tudors, now Shakespeare cast his creative net further back to the decline of the Roman Empire and the brutal, bloody tragedy of a fictional general.

The play shows Titus returning to Rome in triumph after a ten-year campaign against the Germanic Goths, in which twenty-one of his sons have died. As tradition demands, he attempts to appease the gods by sacrificing the son of the imprisoned Tamora, Queen of the Goths. The new Roman emperor Saturninus makes Tamora his empress, and she vows revenge on Titus for her son's death. Tamora's sons rape Titus's daughter Lavinia, leading to a grisly and unrelentingly violent cycle of atrocities that culminates in Titus feeding Tamora her dead sons in a pie before killing her, his own daughter and himself. By the end of the play fourteen killings have been shown or described (ranging from ritual murder to infanticide and suicide), there are six severed body parts (including heads, hands and tongues), a rape, one live burial, one bout of madness and one case of cannibalism. Shakespeare adapts Lavinia's rape and Tamora's enforced cannibalism from the story of Tereus and Philomel in book six of *Metamorphoses*. The sixteenth-century translation of Ovid's Latin poem used by Shakespeare begins with the line "Of shapes transformed to bodies strange I purpose to entreat."[22] For Shakespeare, Ovid's stories of transformation and mutability were an endless source of inspiration. He reveled in the ability to miraculously transform the stage and its humble actors into myriad protean characters, places and situations. But Shakespeare was not content with emulating Ovid; he was determined to surpass him. In *Titus Andronicus,* instead of one rapist there are two, where Ovid has one murdered child Shakespeare has five, two children are eaten rather than one, and Lavinia has not just her tongue severed but also her hands.

Shakespeare also borrowed from his contemporaries. Robert Greene's *Selimus* gave him the idea for the sickening scene where Titus is tricked into cutting off his hand to ensure the release of his sons, unaware that they have already been beheaded. This leads to one of the grisliest stage directions in all of Shakespeare: "Enter a messenger with two heads and a hand."[23] Titus is an aged and tragic version of Tamburlaine, a histrionic antihero railing about his military valor and honor, yet blind to the consequences of his intransigence for him and his family. If the play begins by mimicking Tamburlaine's humorless swagger, its spectacular violence owed something to *The Jew of Malta* with the murderous exploits of Barabas. When Titus's brother Marcus discovers the raped and mutilated Lavinia, he says, "Cousin, a word,"[24] before realizing she has no tongue. Titus later tells the messenger, "Lend me thy hand, and I will give thee mine."[25] At the play's climax Titus appears dressed as a cook about to feed Tamora her sons in a pie, a gruesome joke about getting your "just deserts."

Shakespeare's bloodiest and most violent play, *Titus Andronicus* has had a mixed critical history. Despite its initial success it fell out of favor in the later seventeenth century, and from the eighteenth its extreme violence led many critics to dismiss its "bad taste." These included T. S. Eliot, who in 1927 called it "one of the stupidest and most uninspired plays ever written, a play in which it is incredible that Shakespeare had any hand at all."[26] (The pun was probably unintentional.) Later in the twentieth century the atrocities of the Second World War left many directors and critics agreeing with the British theater reviewer Harold Hobson's verdict that "there is absolutely nothing in the bleeding barbarity of *Titus Andronicus* which would have astonished anyone at Buchenwald."[27] Since the 1980s it has experienced an extraordinary theatrical and critical revival. Today it is as popular as when it was first performed in 1594, and in 2014 the English press reported with some relish that a new Globe Theatre production had seen five members of its audience faint.[28]

In a play where violence seems to be the rule rather than the exception, the distinction between civilization and barbarism becomes increasingly tenuous. Initially Rome represents everything that is civilized, but once it allows the barbarian Goths inside its gates, it too can turn on itself and, as Titus says, become "a wilderness of tigers." Distinguishing between civilization and barbarism was a problem that had preoccupied Elizabethan Protestants in their relations with the Islamic world for decades. To Elizabeth and her advisers, it was difficult to see who was more barbaric: idolatrous Catholics trying to eradicate heretical Protestantism, or Muslim infidels offering military and religious salvation.

One of the most striking characters in the play is without question Aaron the Moor. Aaron is the ultimate outsider, an amoral and unrepentant villain who unlike the Goths refuses to be assimilated into Rome or any other society. He first appears as part of the triumphal procession of Goth prisoners that Titus leads into Rome, though why a North African Moor should be in league with Germanic Goths is never explained. Aaron is Tamora's lover, a relationship that continues after her marriage to Saturninus, which leads to the birth of a "blackamoor" child, described as "a joyless, dismal, black and sorrowful issue."[29] Once Tamora is established as Roman empress, Aaron is allowed to go on a murderous spree of "murders, rapes and massacres / Acts of black night, abominable deeds,"[30] encouraging Tamora's sons to rape Lavinia, framing Titus's sons for murder, and tricking Titus into cutting off his own hand. Aaron's only loyalty is to his "first-born son and heir."[31] At the end of the play, the surviving Romans deem death too good for him: he is buried "breast-deep in earth"[32] and left to die.

Classical texts by writers such as Seneca and Ovid often allowed for the intrusion into civilized society of a destructive barbaric outsider who causes chaos, but Shakespeare invigorated and developed this tradition by drawing on Elizabeth's fraught relations with North Africa's Moors. Recent stylometric analysis of *Titus Andronicus* suggests that, like *Henry VI,* he was not alone in writing it. Several key scenes—including many featuring Aaron—appear to have been written by George Peele.[33] To what extent Peele was involved may never be known, but Aaron was clearly modeled on his evil, duplicitous blackamoor Muly Mahamet in *The Battle of Alcazar.* Like Peele's character, Aaron is a "blackamoor," an "irreligious Moor"[34] who conflates his own skin color with villainous relish. As he plots Lavinia's rape he compares himself to a snake, his "fleece of wooly hair that now uncurls" like "an adder when she doth unroll / To do some fatal execution."[35] As he helps Titus to chop off his hand, Aaron laughs:

> Let fools do good, and fair men call for grace
> Aaron will have his soul black like his face.[36]

Aaron is one of the earliest Elizabethan representations of black men as duplicitous, lustful and evil. By naming him Aaron, Shakespeare associates his character with more immediate anxieties about Muslims and Jews. Aaron, the Old Testament prophet and elder brother of Moses, is common to all three Abrahamic religions. The Qur'an venerates him as related to the Virgin Mary, while Judaism celebrates his descendants as upholders of Jewish ritual law. Many in Shakespeare's audience would know that the biblical Aaron's youngest son was called Ithamar, an obvious allusion to the villainous Turk Ithamore in Marlowe's *Jew of Malta*.

While Aaron's name and ethnicity recall Marlowe's Turk/Moor, his speech and actions bring to mind Barabas. Toward the end of the play, when he is confronted with his crimes and asked if he is "not sorry for these heinous deeds," Aaron responds:

> Ay, that I had not done a thousand more.
> Even now I curse the day—and yet I think
> Few come within the compass of my curse—
> Wherein I did not some notorious ill,
> As kill a man, or else devise his death,
> Ravish a maid, or plot the way to do it,
> Accuse some innocent and forswear myself,
> Set deadly enmity between two friends,
> Make poor men's cattle break their necks,
> Set fire on barns and haystacks in the night,
> And bid the owners quench them with their tears.
> Oft have I digg'd up dead men from their graves,
> And set them upright at their dear friends' doors,

Even when their sorrows almost were forgot;
And on their skins, as on the bark of trees,
Have with my knife carved in Roman letters,
"Let not your sorrow die, though I am dead."
Tut, I have done a thousand dreadful things
As willingly as one would kill a fly,
And nothing grieves me heartily indeed
But that I cannot do ten thousand more.[37]

The relish with which Aaron recounts his brutality is reminiscent of Barabas's attitude to his own villainy. Even when he is buried in the ground, Aaron mocks those who would turn to conscience or prayer:

I am no baby, I, that with base prayers
I should repent the evils I have done.
Ten thousand worse than ever yet I did
Would I perform, if I might have my will.
If one good deed in all my life I did
I do repent it from my very soul.[38]

Aaron encapsulates all the fears associated with his non-Christian character. He is black, a Moor, but also "irreligious"; however, by associating him with Barabas and Ithamore, Shakespeare also conflates him with Turks and Jews as well as Moors and atheists. He is everything the audience should despise; and yet they are drawn irresistibly to him. Then as now, we listen to Aaron—as he speaks directly to us in soliloquy or asides—powerless to intervene, mute accomplices, colluding in his outrageous villainy.

To create such a formidable character, Shakespeare exploited every available stereotype; he asks his audience to see the Moor as an embodiment of the failings of the "civilized" Roman world. By incorporating Tamora and by extension Aaron into their body politic, the Romans invite their own destruction. As much as the Elizabethans aspired to emulate the Roman Empire, it was also the citadel of Catholicism, which since the Reformation had represented the barbaric idolatry of the papacy. Such a double perspective emerges toward the end of the play, when Roman soldiers capture Aaron while he is hiding with his new-born son in "a ruinous monastery."[39] When he is presented to Titus's sole surviving son, Lucius, Aaron promises to confess everything if the Roman will "swear to me my child shall live." Lucius refuses, saying, "Who should I swear by? Thou believest no god."[40] Aaron responds:

> What if I do not?—as indeed, I do not—
> Yet for I know thou art religious
> And hast a thing within thee called conscience,
> With twenty popish tricks and ceremonies
> Which I have seen thee careful to observe,
> Therefore I urge thy oath; for that I know
> An idiot holds his bauble for a god,
> And keeps the oath which by that god he swears,
> To that I'll urge him: therefore thou shalt vow
> By that same god, what god soe'er it be
> That thou adorest and hast in reverence.[41]

In a sudden moment of metamorphosis, the audience is transported from imperial Rome to post-Reformation England, in a scene from Henry VIII's dissolution of the monasteries, with a Moor captured by "popish" Roman Catholic soldiers and condemning their idolatrous "tricks and ceremonies." The audience is put in an invidious position, agreeing with Aaron's dismissal of Catholicism, only to realize that it is identifying with an "irreligious Moor" who regards faith as nothing more than a "bauble."

Titus Andronicus is not a play designed to elicit sympathy for Aaron the Moor. His villainy remains indebted to an older tradition of medieval morality plays, but Shakespeare adds a new dimension by making him ethnically different, funny and, crucially, unrepentant. The play manipulates its audience's profound ambivalence about the role of such "barbarians" in a confused post-Reformation world of shifting political and theological alliances. Shakespeare combined classical fears about outsiders with Elizabethan England's ambiguous relations with Moors and Turks to create gripping drama filled with conflicts and contradictions. Nobody really cares about Barabas, because he kills his own children and gleefully attacks any religious belief, but Aaron is a sadistic, murderous atheist who nevertheless cares for his child and offers a familiar critique of Catholicism, leaving the audience then as now confused about whether to admire or revile him.

Even as *Titus Andronicus* played to large crowds throughout the 1594 season, negotiations between Elizabeth and al-Mansur were under way for a second Moorish delegation to visit England. In May 1595 Edward Holmden, master of the Grocers' Company and a prominent merchant in the Turkey Company, wrote to the Privy Council from Morocco and reported that it "is still given out that the king's ambassador shall go for England, being a man of account, and two alcaids [military governors or chiefs] with him, and carrieth a retinue of twenty-five or thirty persons . . . he will be here before Michaelmas [September 29]. The cause is not known."[42] Although Holmden claimed that the embassy's "causes" were unknown to him, its leader was clearly on his way to England to discuss further Anglo-Moroccan military operations against the Spanish.

Diplomatic tensions between England and Spain were once more leading both sides toward open conflict. Tit-for-tat naval raids throughout 1595 led Philip II to sanction yet another invasion of England, which this time involved landing a Spanish army in Catholic Ireland ahead of a full-scale military assault on the English mainland. When news reached London, Elizabeth's Privy Council authorized a preemptive strike at Cadiz, Spain's main Atlantic seaport and home to the Indies fleet. The Moroccan delegation was designed to negotiate logistical support for Elizabeth's naval operations, including Moroccan ships and soldiers, and the creation of a fort at Agadir from which the English could attack the Spanish gold fleet en route to and from the Americas. No records survive of the delegation reaching London that autumn, but although al-Mansur eventually refused English access to Agadir, he sent several galleys and supplies to support the English attack on Cadiz.

Having coordinated an unlikely alliance involving Muslim Moroccans and Dutch Calvinists, Elizabeth's fleet of 150 ships and 6,000 soldiers left Plymouth in June 1596 under the joint command of the loyal veteran Charles Howard, lord high admiral of England, and the queen's new favorite, the dashing thirty-year-old Robert Devereux, Earl of Essex. Others involved included Sir Walter Raleigh, who was seeking political rehabilitation after returning empty-handed from a long and dangerous voyage to Guyana. There were younger men too, in search of booty and adventure, including the royal physician Roger Marbeck and the twenty-four-year-old poet John Donne.

In late June the fleet reached Cadiz and attacked immediately, first by sea, then by land.[43] In the short but fierce naval exchange that followed, the English destroyed several Spanish galleons including the *St. Philip,* which Marbeck watched being blown up by a "Moorish slave" who set fire to the ship's gunpowder store before seeking refuge alongside thirty-eight other Moroccans among the English forces. Marbeck wrote that Howard and Essex agreed

> to furnish them with money and all other necessaries, and to bestow on them a bark and pilot, and so to have them freely conveyed into Barbary, willing them to let the country to understand what was done and what they had seen. Whereby I doubt not but, as her majesty is a most admirable prince already over all Europe and all Africa, Asia and Christendom, so the whole world hereafter shall have just such cause to admire her infinite princely virtues.[44]

The English also captured two Spanish galleons, the *St. Matthew* and the *St. Andrew,* both of which had run aground, although the Indies fleet laden with a cargo worth an estimated 12 million ducats of bullion was destroyed before the English could reach it. They then sacked the city, ransomed hostages and sailed away on July 4, leaving Cadiz on fire and a large part of Philip's Indies fleet at the bottom of its harbor.

News of the English victory spread quickly across Europe and North Africa. Although the expedition had failed to capture the vast wealth of the Indies fleet, its commanders celebrated it as a great triumph. William Monson, one of the English naval commanders, proclaimed, "Spain never received so great an overthrow, so great a spoil, so great an indignity at our hands as in that journey to Cadiz."[45]

The English did not have a monopoly in claiming victory. When the "Moorish slaves" reported back to Marrakesh, al-Mansur was quick to insist on his part. In characteristically astounding terms his court historian al-Fishtali described how "the sky darkened with dissension against the tyrant of Qishtala [Philip II], and the kings of the nations of the Christians attacked him like wild dogs. The most ferocious against him, and the one most daring in attacking his kingdoms and tightening the noose around him, was Isabella the sultana of the kingdoms of the lands of England."

Al-Fishtali claimed that the Cadiz victory was thanks to al-Mansur's diplomatic and logistical support. It was al-Mansur who "had lured her with his support and sharpened her will against him [Philip II]; he showed her his willingness to confront him by supplying her with copper to use in cannons, and saltpeter for ammunition which he permitted her to buy from his noble kingdom. . . . With God helping him, he pitted her against the enemy of religion."[46] It is unclear just what the Moroccan galleys had achieved during the battle, but according to al-Fishtali's account, England and Morocco were now joined in a holy war against Catholic Spain.[47]

Philip II responded by preparing yet another armada, this time one that would land first in Ireland and exploit the Catholic rebellion there before invading England. A fleet of more than sixty ships carrying over 10,000 soldiers left Lisbon for Ireland on October 25, 1596, but off the northwest Spanish coast it ran into a terrible storm, losing half its ships and thousands of lives. Defeated at home and overstretched abroad, Philip II was forced to declare his kingdom bankrupt just weeks later. He would try to raise another armada the following year, but the weather wrecked his plans once more.[48] Some of Philip's Spanish advisers felt that, when it came to invading England, Divine Providence had deserted them. It seemed that on this matter God was indeed on the side of the English.

Although a second Moroccan delegation never materialized, another Moor did appear in London—not at London's royal court, but on its stage. In late 1596 Shakespeare wrote *The Merchant of Venice*, or to give it its full title when it was first published in 1600, *The Most Excellent History of the Merchant of Venice with the Extreme Cruelty of Shylock the Jew.* Shakespeare's portrayal of Shylock, the Jewish moneylender who demands a pound of flesh from a Venetian merchant, Antonio, in settlement of a bad debt, has divided audiences for generations. Antonio borrows the money to help his feckless friend Bassanio pursue the wealthy heiress Portia, who is in turn being wooed by a series of suitors, including the Prince of Morocco. The play reaches its climax with the famous courtroom scene where Shylock prepares to cut out a pound of Antonio's flesh, only to be prevented by Portia, disguised as a lawyer, who argues that "if thou dost shed / One drop of Christian blood, thy lands and goods"[49] will be confiscated by the Venetian state. Unable to act, Shylock is then condemned as an "alien" who has sought the life of a Venetian. He is stripped of his wealth and required to "presently become a Christian,"[50] leaving the stage a broken man and agreeing to all the Christians' terms.

Shakespeare had several inspirations for writing this play. The Cadiz expedition was clearly on his mind as scholars base their dating of the play on an explicit reference to the captured Spanish galleon *St. Andrew* in the play's opening lines. The Venetian merchant Salarino talks about "my wealthy Andrew dock'd in sand"—the ship had run aground when it was captured in Cadiz, and nearly did so again when it was brought back to England in the summer of 1596. In terms of dramatic precedents, Shakespeare was responding to Marlowe's *Jew of Malta* and Wilson's *Three Ladies of London* with their contrasting depictions of Jewish merchants—as well as Muslims.

Another recent event may also have inspired Shylock's creation. In January 1594 Elizabeth's personal physician, Dr. Roderigo Lopez, a Portuguese-born Jewish convert to Protestantism, was arrested on charges of treason and conspiring with the Spanish to poison the queen. Although Lopez had indeed been paid to spy for the Spanish, the charges of attempted murder were completely fabricated by the Earl of Essex, who was eager to prove his loyalty to the queen and gain an advantage over his great rival Burghley. Lopez was a pawn caught up in court machinations, and he never stood a chance. At his trial he was accused of accepting 50,000 crowns from Philip to poison Elizabeth. One of his prosecutors, Sir Francis Bacon, captured the suspicion that Lopez's conversion had generated by describing him as "of nation a Portuguese, and suspected to be in sect secretly a Jew though here he conformed himself to the rites of Christian religion."

Lopez was sentenced to death and executed that June. According to the historian William Camden, he protested from the scaffold "that he loved the Queen as well as he loved Jesus Christ; which coming from a man of the Jewish profession moved no small laughter in the standers-by."[51] For those who watched Lopez being hanged, drawn and quartered, his profession of innocence was seen as a comically equivocal admission of guilt, the duplicity of a convert who spoke of love when he meant hate.

The cruel but uneasy laughter that accompanied Lopez's violent demise permeates Shakespeare's play. It seems that Shakespeare intended it to be a comedy (which is how it was listed when published in the Folio of 1623), and at various times over the past four hundred years audiences have felt able, or perhaps incited, to laugh at Shylock's downfall and the anti-Semitic abuse from Portia and Antonio that comes with it. But the laughter is not the same as that associated with Shylock's direct predecessor, Marlowe's Barabas. Like Barabas, Shylock watches his daughter, Jessica, convert to Christianity, but despite his murderous designs on Antonio, he never engages in the wicked depravity of Marlowe's character. Shakespeare provides Shylock with a depth of humanity not out of some secret liberal desire to express toleration toward the Jewish faith, but to sharpen the dramatic ambiguity and the power of his character.

Shylock appears in only five of the play's scenes, but in one of the most significant he utters a resounding plea for a common humanity. "I am a Jew," he tells Solanio and Salarino:

Hath not a Jew eyes? Hath not a Jew hands, organs, dimensions, senses, affections, passions; fed with the same food, hurt with the same weapons, subject to the same diseases, healed by the same means, warmed and cooled by the same winter and summer, as a Christian is? If you prick us, do we not bleed?[52]

The speech's conclusion also reminds the audience that Shylock is a creation of Venice's society and its Christians, and he is no better or worse than they are:

> If you wrong us, shall we not revenge? If we are like you in the rest, we will resemble you in that. If a Jew wrong a Christian, what is his humility? Revenge. If a Christian wrong a Jew, what should his sufferance be by Christian example? Why, revenge. The villainy you teach me, I will execute, and it shall go hard but I will better the instruction.[53]

Shylock is just as vicious and acquisitive as Antonio, a point made inadvertently by Portia when she enters the courtroom dressed as a lawyer and, unable to distinguish between them, asks, "Which is the merchant here, and which the Jew?"[54]

Portia refers to Shylock contemptuously as "Jew" on no fewer than ten occasions during the courtroom scene. But he is not the only alien who feels her wrath. Under the terms of her father's will, she can only marry the man who identifies which of three caskets of gold, silver and lead contains Portia's portrait. The play's second scene opens with her recalling those suitors who have already failed, including an arrogant Italian, a drunk German, a capering Frenchman, a badly dressed Englishman and a quarrelsome Scot. It is then announced that a new suitor is about to try his luck: the Prince of Morocco. Upon hearing this Portia immediately recoils, joking, "If he have the condition of a saint and the complexion of a devil, I had rather he should shrive me [hear confession] than wive me."[55]

But when Morocco enters he is not what the audience might expect. He is a tawny Moor dressed in white, who sounds more like Tamburlaine than Aaron. In a speech that anticipates Shylock's plea for humanity he asks Portia:

> Mislike me not for my complexion,
> The shadowed livery of the burnished sun,
> To whom I am a neighbor and near bred.
> Bring me the fairest creature northward born,

Where Phoebus' fire scarce thaws the icicles,
And let us make incision for your love
To prove whose blood is reddest, his or mine.[56]

Having created an evil blackamoor in the shape of Aaron, Shakespeare now produced his opposite, a virtuous, heroic tawny Moor, one who has no apparent qualms about marrying into the Christian world of Portia's fictional Belmont. His religion is never mentioned, but he retains an element of sexual frisson sometimes associated with Moors, boasting to Portia:

I tell thee, lady, this aspect of mine
Hath fear'd the valiant; by my love I swear
The best-regarded virgins of our clime
Have loved it too: I would not change this hue,
Except to steal your thoughts, my gentle queen.[57]

His virile boastfulness turns into fantasy when he swears to win Portia:

By this scimitar
That slew the Sophy and a Persian prince
That won three fields of Sultan Solyman.[58]

The audience would have known that nobody had been able to slay a Persian ruler and defeat the Ottoman sultan Süleyman the Magnificent. Nevertheless, here was a Moroccan warrior claiming to have defeated Ottoman and Persian forces, bearing a striking resemblance to al-Mansur. Officially al-Mansur's diplomatic and military overtures were known only to Elizabeth's innermost circle, but one wonders how far awareness of the Anglo-Moroccan rapprochement had spread into the public domain.

In any event, Morocco's suit fails: he chooses the wrong casket and Portia ushers him hastily off the stage and out of the play with the devastating couplet:

A gentle riddance. Draw the curtains, go.
Let all of his complexion choose me so.[59]

There is no real reason that a Prince of Morocco should be in a romantic comedy about Venetian merchants and Jewish moneylenders. But Shakespeare had at least two precedents for putting Muslims into plays about conflicts between Jews and Christians. In Wilson's *Three Ladies of London,* the honorable Jewish moneylender Gerontus complains to a Turkish judge about the hypocrisy of the villainous Christian merchant Mercadorus, while in Marlowe's *Jew of Malta* Barabas forms a murderous alliance with the Turkish Ithamore. As usual Shakespeare took the middle way, putting a Jew and a Moor onstage who are not saints, but are expelled ruthlessly as soon as they threaten to challenge the status quo.

At a theological level, Christendom had always seen Muslims and Jews as apostates who denied Christ as the son of God, heretics representing two sides of the same religious error. At a commercial level, they were intimately related too: Jews acted as mediators in most mercantile transactions with the Muslim courts in Morocco, Turkey and Persia. In fact, the English had much greater experience of Jewish merchants, moneylenders and political intermediaries in Morocco in the 1590s than in Venice. The highly publicized case of the Moroccan Jewish sugar baron Isaac Cabeça's insolvency in 1568 and the subsequent trials in the High Court of Admiralty and Chancery would have been far more familiar to Londoners watching Shakespeare's play than any Venetian merchant's activities. Shylock is not an attractive character, but Shakespeare deliberately chose to move away from purely villainous stereotypes with the more ambiguous Shylock and Prince of Morocco. The exigencies of politics and trade made alliances with Jews, Turks and Moors necessary. While everyone profited, everything was fine, but when trouble arrived, the laughter stopped and one side was often pitted against the others. By the end of Shakespeare's play, the audience is in the uncomfortable position of being as repelled by its self-righteous Christians as by its haughty Moroccan and vindictive Jew. Within just over two years of Marlowe's death, Shakespeare had modulated his murderous eastern characters to produce a far more subtle theater of complicity, where Moors, Jews and Christians—and even the audience—were all equally culpable.

In July 1597, a year after Shakespeare wrote *The Merchant of Venice,* the Barbary Company was quietly dissolved. Its charter had expired and the regulated trade seemed to have made little difference to the trade's uneven profitability. It was proving difficult to recover debts from the Moroccan merchants, and the English merchants had flooded the market with cloth in return for expensive sugar. The Levant merchants were already complaining about the effect of the badly organized Barbary trade on English commerce across the Mediterranean. As early as 1591, one group had written to Burghley complaining that the Barbary merchants "have brought our English cloth there into contempt, and advanced their dross and base sugars to high price, and so not only spoiled and overthrown that trade, but undone themselves and many an honest merchant."[60] Regulation had clearly failed, and private trade seemed to promise better returns.[61] The dissolution of the company made no discernible difference to the Barbary trade throughout the late 1590s as it returned to private hands operating outside state control. It was now every man for himself in Morocco. With the plans for a formal alliance stalled and the crown's interest in the trade waning, Elizabeth and her advisers turned their attention more fully toward the Ottoman Porte in Constantinople.

9

Escape from the Seraglio

On January 15, 1595, Sultan Murad III died in the Topkapi Palace in Constantinople. In keeping with Ottoman tradition, his death was kept secret until his heir, the crown prince Mehmed, could reach Constantinople and ensure a smooth transition of power. Four weeks later Edward Barton forwarded a letter to Lord Burghley from a man whom he called a "curious Jew" describing "what here hath lately passed," the "death of the late Sultan Murad III and success to this empire of Sultan Mehmed III."[1] The letter was written by a Portuguese Jew named Alvaro Mendès, better known to the Ottoman court as Salomon Aben Yaèx, an associate of Barton's with privileged access to the imperial *divan*. Mendès reported that on January 27 Mehmed had arrived from Manisa near the Aegean coast to claim the throne and bury his father in Hagia Sophia. What followed next has became one of the most terrible and reviled acts in Ottoman imperial history:

> That night his nineteen new brothers were conducted to the king Sultan Mehmed, they were the male children then living of his father, by several wives; they were brought to kiss his hand, so that he should see them alive; the eldest of them was eleven. Their king brother told them not to fear, as he did not wish to do them any harm; but only to have them circumcised, according to custom. And this was a thing that none of his ancestors had ever done, and directly they had kissed his hand they were circumcised, taken aside and dexterously strangled with handkerchiefs.[2]

The Venetian ambassador added to the horror with a story of even greater pathos. "They say," he wrote, "that the eldest, a most beautiful lad and of excellent parts, beloved by all, when he kissed the sultan's hand exclaimed, 'My lord and brother, now to me as my father, let not my days be ended thus in this my tender age.' The sultan tore his beard with every sign of grief, but answered never a word. They were all strangled." Salomon acknowledged that such a brutal act of political succession "certainly seems a terrible and cruel thing, but it is the custom"; he also conceded that the sight of all nineteen coffins—some no bigger than a doll's—when placed next to their father's, brought forth "the tears of all the people."[3]

Barton had taken great pains to obtain Salomon's report for Burghley because Murad III's death was a critical moment in Anglo-Ottoman relations. Most of Elizabeth's diplomatic and commercial relations with the Ottomans were based on a cordial personal correspondence with Murad that stretched back over seventeen years, and more recently with Safiye Sultan, who with his death was now elevated to the role of Valide Sultan (Queen Mother). It was unclear whether Mehmed would be as sympathetic toward the English as his father had been, but the signs were not promising. Mehmed vowed to pursue the flagging Ottoman military campaigns in Hungary, but he hardly seemed like a warrior. One English merchant described him as "a prince by nature of wit and courage: but by accident, dull, timorous, and very effeminate."[4]

Barton needed to act quickly if he was to retain Ottoman favor. He hoped that by sending Salomon's letter to London, Burghley would see the wisdom of dispatching a suitable gift to the new sultan to cement his diplomatic position. Unfortunately, the Privy Council was somewhat dilatory in its response. With no present forthcoming, Barton felt obliged to show his support for the new sultan by accompanying him on a military campaign the following year against Archduke Maximilian's Catholic armies in Hungary.

Barton set out for Hungary with Mehmed's army in June 1596, accompanied by a large retinue paid for by the sultan. He observed the Ottoman campaign and even sent Burghley a detailed account of the dramatic victory over the Austrian-Hungarian Habsburg forces at Keresztes, in northern Hungary, in October 1596.[5] When news of Barton's presence spread throughout Europe and Russia, Elizabeth was forced to go on a diplomatic charm offensive, sending embassies as far as Prague and Moscow to deny that she had "incited the most loathsome enemy of the Christian name to wage war on Christian princes."[6]

Nevertheless, the alliance with the Ottoman Porte endured because of its importance. Qualms about the relationship ranged from the obvious religious differences to fears about Ottoman imperial ambitions and distaste for their fratricidal approach to political succession, but none of this was enough to derail it. The partnership had far-reaching consequences both diplomatically and economically. While the sultans acted as a powerful if capricious bulwark against Spain, trade with the Ottoman Empire had a marked impact on England's domestic economy. In contrast to the uneven profitability of the Barbary Company, the Turkey Company was successful—so much so as to prompt a merger with the Venice Company in 1592. Many of London's merchants felt that separating the Venetian and Turkish trade made little sense, so when a new charter was proposed most of the Turkey Company's members petitioned the government for an extension of its jurisdiction to include Venice, as well as expanding membership to fifty-three merchants, with space for more. To acknowledge the geographical expansion of its operation, the organization renamed itself the Levant Company, and in acknowledgment of his achievements in establishing the Ottoman trade, Edward Osborne was appointed its governor. It was an immediate success and by the end of the decade had twenty ships exporting cloth worth £150,000 annually to the Mediterranean.[7]

The impact of all this trade could be seen at various levels back home. If printed books are anything to go by, there was a notable surge of interest in the Muslim world toward the end of the sixteenth century. The registers of the Company of Stationers of London reveal that an estimated sixty books were published in Elizabeth's reign on subjects relating to the Ottomans, over half of them in the 1590s, though the true figures are likely to be much higher.[8]

Portraits of the Ottoman sultans could at this point be found in many of England's great houses.[9] The inventories of the art collections of London's lord mayor Sir Ralph Warren, the Virginia Colony's governor John West and the Oxford scholar Thomas Key all listed pictures of the "Great Turk."[10] In 1575 the poet, courtier and soldier Sir Philip Sidney had been delighted to receive a Venetian "portrait of Murad the new Emperor of the Turks" from one of his correspondents in Strasbourg.[11] This portrait had a significant influence on Sidney's poetry and prose. Sidney invoked his knowledge of the Ottomans in his *Defense of Poesy* (1579), in which he argues that in contrast to England, "even Turks and Tartars are delighted with poets."[12]

Elizabethan portraiture reveled in reproducing the growing volume of oriental imports flowing into London. These included opulent fabrics, rugs, carpets, embroideries and even Iznik pottery made in Bursa in Turkey. The pearls, diamonds, sapphires, silks, brocades and damasks that feature in so many Elizabethan paintings—including those of the queen herself—were self-conscious displays of the success of Anglo-Islamic trade. Ownership of "Turkey carpets," quilts and Anatolian rugs containing Kufic (Arabic) script were also statements of personal wealth and connections to the Islamic world. Robert Dudley the Earl of Leicester's various household accounts show that at the time of his death in 1588 he had amassed a collection of more than eighty carpets described as either Turkish or Persian, worth hundreds of pounds.[13] The inventory of another Elizabethan nobleman, John, Lord Lumley, and his household goods in Nonsuch Palace and Lumley Castle similarly lists more than a hundred "Turkey carpets of silk." Like many other noblemen, Lumley also owned depictions of the Ottoman capital Constantinople.[14]

This luxuriousness was not confined to kings, queens and noblemen. Cotton wool from Turkish merchants stimulated a burgeoning textile industry in Lancashire, and by the end of Elizabeth's reign the manufacture of raw silk from Iran provided employment for hundreds of workers who produced clothes "in the Turkish manner" and household furnishings for middle-class consumption.[15] The resulting objects were such a common feature in wealthy Elizabethan homes and domestic life that Shakespeare felt confident enough to make casual references in his comedies written in the 1590s to "Turkey cushions bossed with pearl," in *The Taming of the Shrew*,[16] and to "Turkish tapestry," in *The Comedy of Errors*.[17]

The English even began to imitate the textiles they were importing: in 1579 Richard Hakluyt had sent the dyer Morgan Hubblethorne to Persia to find "carpets of coarse thrummed [twisted] wool, the best of the world," asking him to return with "the art of Turkish carpet making." It is unclear if Hubblethorne complied, but by the 1590s English craftsmen (and women) were copying Persian and Turkish carpets with cheaper and simpler "Turkey work," which involved tying woolen knots onto linen or hemp.[18]

The Muscovy, Turkey and Barbary imports enabled Elizabethans to wear silk and cotton in new designs, drink sweet wines and incorporate myriad condiments into their diet, including aniseed, nutmeg, mace, turmeric and pistachios. The demand for currants alone from Ottoman-controlled Greek islands was so great that at the height of Elizabeth's reign 2,300 tons were being imported annually.[19] The activities of John Sanderson, a Levant Company merchant working in the Ottoman territories from 1585, suggest how far oriental goods percolated through Elizabethan society. Sanderson gave his sister Grace a wedding present of "a Turkey carpet, more worth than £1.10.0," and his clergyman brother received "six Turkey painted books" (probably a reference to Ottoman costume books), worth £3, and "Four Turkey carpets" worth over £5.[20]

Nor was the display and consumption of objects and artifacts from Muslim lands limited to London. By 1601 Elizabeth Talbot, Countess of Shrewsbury, better known as Bess of Hardwick, had amassed a collection of oriental embroidery, tapestry and needlework of a quality and size to rival those of Leicester and Lumley, which she displayed in her two great Derbyshire homes, Chatsworth House and Hardwick Hall. It included forty-six "Turkey carpets," as well as a remarkable set of three large embroidered wall hangings depicting personifications of the cardinal virtues and their opposites dating from the 1580s.[21] The first of these showed Hope triumphing over Judas, the second Temperance prevailing over Sardanapalus (to whom Cardenas had compared al-Mansur, as we have seen), while the final hanging shows Faith subduing her contrary, the unfaithful "Mahomet." All three were based on a series of Dutch engravings of traditional Christian "Virtues and Vices" dated 1576, which had been adapted by the embroiderers to suit the prevailing theology of the day and, more practically, to fit the best bedchamber in Hardwick Hall, where they can still be seen on public display.

The hanging of Faith and Mahomet shows Faith modeled closely on Queen Elizabeth. She stands in front of a backdrop of ecclesiastical architecture, next to a large crucifix, holding a Bible in her right hand with the word "Faith" picked out on its spine in gold twist, a communion chalice in her left hand, and "Fides" embroidered on her arm. She towers over Muhammad, a turbaned, mustachioed figure crouching down as if in subjection at her feet, resting his face on his hand in a melancholy pose of apparent despair at his faithlessness, with a copy of the Qur'an ("Acoran") on the floor in front of him. Above him are what appear to be scenes from the life of Muhammad. In the foreground two groups of turbaned Turks with scimitars are shown in deep discussion, while in the background Muhammad appears again in what seems to be a sixteenth-century English idea of a mosque. He stands holding a book (presumably the Qur'an) in a canopied arch resembling a Gothic church. Angels float above, pulling back the curtains in a moment of religious revelation—surprising for a scene involving the Prophet Muhammad, as such iconography was usually reserved for Catholic images of Christ or the Virgin and Child. Perhaps the embroidery was meant to suggest the idolatry that many Protestants believed united the papacy and the Prophet Muhammad.[22]

The Hardwick embroidery captures Protestant English ambivalence toward Islam, and the Ottomans in particular, as the sixteenth century drew to a close. Bess of Hardwick wanted to display her wealth by acquiring expensive and elaborately crafted Turkish rugs and carpets, but she also wanted to show off her Christian piety, offering the faithless Muhammad in the foreground the possibility of salvation through the cross and communion. As with so much of Elizabethan visual art, the embroidery was a carefully crafted delusion. Protestants across North

Africa and the Mediterranean like Samson Rowlie were more likely to bow down before the Qur'an and convert to Islam than Muslims were to embrace Christianity. Like many other Elizabethan misrepresentations of Islam, the Hardwick embroidery was a wishful fantasy.

Unlike many of his contemporaries, Shakespeare never put a Turkish character in any of his plays (with one peculiar exception, which we shall discuss later). But throughout the mid-1590s, he wrote a series of plays mainly about English history that are haunted by the specter of the Turk. He refers to Turks in thirteen plays written in this decade, with more than a third of these references appearing in his history plays. Having established his reputation with a first tetralogy about the reigns of Henry VI and Richard III in the early 1590s, in the latter half of the decade he began a second series of four plays dramatizing the lives of Richard II, Henry IV (in two parts) and Henry V. He wrote about this turbulent period of English political history, characterized by conflicts over royal succession, deposition, rebellion and civil war against the backdrop of a new genre of English "war books" dramatizing the conflicts between Christians and Muslims in central Europe, and, in particular, the Ottoman incursions into Hungary. Inevitably the specter that came to Shakespeare's mind time and again was the tyrannical, fratricidal, faithless yet inscrutable Turk.[23]

The second group of plays begins with *King Richard II*, probably written in 1595. The play culminates in the climactic moment of Richard's deposition by Henry of Bolingbroke, the future King Henry IV. In the fourth act, as Bolingbroke prepares to accept the crown after forcing Richard to stand down, the Bishop of Carlisle warns his followers of the dire consequences of dethroning a legitimate king. He utters a prophecy that reverberates through the rest of the tetralogy:

> My Lord of Hereford [Bolingbroke] here, whom you call king,
> Is a foul traitor to proud Hereford's king;
> And, if you crown him, let me prophesy
> The blood of English shall manure the ground,
> And future ages groan for this foul act.

> Peace shall go sleep with Turks and infidels,
> And in this seat of peace tumultuous wars
> Shall kin with kin and kind with kind confound.[24]

The Bishop of Carlisle condemns Bolingbroke's attempt to seize the crown as a form of political apostasy, the kind of murderous and illegitimate behavior that was all too familiar to Elizabethan theatergoers who had watched various eastern potentates strutting, murdering and conquering their way across London's stages throughout the early 1590s. Carlisle's point is that to depose a king breaks the bonds and laws of nature, defined and decreed by God. He identifies "Turks and infidels" as similarly unnatural: the Turk is political shorthand for a breakdown in the natural order of things.

Carlisle's prophecy is ignored. Bolingbroke is crowned and Richard II murdered. Over the two parts of *Henry IV*, Carlisle's prediction is fulfilled as the country descends into a series of civil wars. *Henry IV, Part 1* (1596) begins with Bolingbroke as the new king bemoaning the way his kingdom is being torn apart by "the intestine shock / And furious close of civil butchery."[25] To atone for his sins, Henry promises to launch a crusade:

> As far as to the sepulcher of Christ—
> Whose soldier now, under whose blessed cross
> We are impressed and engaged to fight—
> Forthwith a power of English shall we levy,
> Whose arms were molded in their mother's womb
> To chase these pagans in those holy fields
> Over whose acres walked those blessed feet
> Which fourteen hundred years ago were nailed,
> For our advantage, on the bitter cross.[26]

Henry announces himself to be a crusader using the language of Christian righteousness. He is not the least bit convincing, but he conveys Shakespeare's vision of national identity shaped by faith and belonging. It does not matter that Jesus never actually walked on the "holy fields" through which Henry's army will chase their enemies:

what is important is that the king develops national unity by invoking a shared faith, and a common enemy. Having overthrown Richard and pitched England into a Turkish hell, the new king seems to be acting like a pious Christian prince, trying to exorcise his sins by recovering the Holy Land from what Carlisle had earlier called "black pagans, Turks, and Saracens." The ending of *Richard II* had Henry associated with usurping Turkish sultans; now, at the opening of this new play, the first of his reign, he appears to be either the penitent Christian ruler or the scheming prince.

Shakespeare was becoming increasingly adroit at manipulating contradictory impulses to exploit the audience's allegiances. He was also beginning to exorcise the ghost of Marlowe. In *Part 1* the leader of the rebellion against Henry IV is Henry Percy (nicknamed Hotspur), the Earl of Northumberland's son. As his nickname suggests, Hotspur is an impetuous warrior who uses the hyperbolic language of Tamburlaine, declaiming before one battle, "we live to tread on kings"[27]—an explicit reference to Tamburlaine's treatment of Sultan Bajazeth. But speaking in a tavern in London's Eastcheap, Hal (Henry IV's son) mocks Hotspur's bombastic pretensions, observing drily, "I am not yet of Percy's mind, the Hotspur of the north; he that kills me some six or seven dozen of Scots at a breakfast, washes his hands, and says to his wife 'Fie upon this quiet life! I want work.'"[28] Viewed from London's taverns and brothels, Hotspur starts to look like a throwback to an older world of pagan heroes and heroic conquests that has been supplanted by the opportunistic cunning of Henry IV and his even more inscrutable son.

In both parts of *Henry IV* Shakespeare moves between the elite courts and London's murky underworld, the taverns and fleshpots of Eastcheap, where Prince Hal consorts with Sir John Falstaff, Mistress Quickly and their confederates. In *Henry IV, Part 2* he goes so far as to parody the vogue for exotic stories and characters. In Act II, scene 4, the cowardly soldier Pistol mangles a series of mock-heroic references to Peele's *Battle of Alcazar* and his lost play *The Turkish Mahamet and Hiren the Fair Greek*. "Have we not Hiren here?" he asks of Doll, before telling Mistress Quickly to "feed and be fat, my Calipolis," a direct quotation from *The Battle of Alcazar*.[29] Shakespeare was wittily show-ing Marlowe and Peele the exit, building on their portrayal of Moors and Turks to create his own characters: charismatic but withdrawn, ironic yet violent. In the shape of Hal, he depicts a leader who is unfath-omable, perhaps even to himself.

Toward the end of *Henry IV, Part 2*, with his father dead and him-self about to succeed to the throne, Hal suddenly makes a striking comparison with an Ottoman sultan that has puzzled critics. As he enters Westminster Palace dressed as the new king, he turns to his three brothers and tells them:

> This new and gorgeous garment, majesty,
> Sits not so easy on me as you think.
> Brothers, you mix your sadness with some fear.
> This is the English, not the Turkish court;
> Not Amurath an Amurath succeeds,
> But Harry Harry.[30]

Hal's first pronouncement as king seems straightforward enough. He assures his brothers that his accession is as strange to him as it is for them and that they have nothing to fear. Hal promises his younger brothers that they will not be murdered like Murad's five younger brothers or his nineteen sons. But perhaps the prince doth protest too much. The speech's awkwardness betrays the problem. Hal claims he will imitate his father, not Murad, but the audience has already expe-rienced one version of Henry IV as the calculating pretender whose political usurpation triggers civil war. If young Harry is just the same as old Harry, then perhaps he will reproduce the same sectarian divi-sions. By trying to erase associations between his family and despotic Turks, Hal succeeds only in reminding us of the comparison. Everyone hopes the reformed son will metamorphose into the perfect Christian prince, but the fear remains that he might still turn Turk.

The anxiety recurs throughout the final play in the series, *Henry V*, written in the summer of 1599. For generations of English-speaking readers, the play has represented England's greatest warrior king, a patriotic celebration of Henry's plucky English "band of brothers" triumphing over the French at Agincourt in the face of impossible odds. But perceptive critics have identified a more ambivalent side to Henry. The great essayist William Hazlitt saw in Hal "a very amiable monster, a very splendid pageant,"[31] who preferred brute force over right or wrong. More recently the American critic Norman Rabkin argued that the play points in two different directions: Henry can be seen as the militant Christian warrior, or as the scheming Machiavellian prince.[32] Today, in an age when the idea of a crusade is more problematic than ever before, audiences are similarly attuned to Henry's slipperiness.

This ambivalence was built into Henry's character from the moment Shakespeare first conceived him. As he leads the English into a morally questionable war with the French, the young English king begins to reveal a latent "Turkish" aspect to his character. In the scene where his forces are besieging Harfleur, Henry warns the town's inhabitants that failure to surrender will lead him to unleash rape and murder:

> Your naked infants spitted upon pikes,
> Whiles the mad mothers with their howls confused
> Do break the clouds, as did the wives of Jewry
> At Herod's bloody-hunting slaughtermen.[33]

The threat is reminiscent of Tamburlaine's massacre of the virgins of Damascus. The image of infants spitted on pikes would have brought to mind the stories of Turkish atrocities in central Europe published in pamphlets across the continent at this time. But it also drew on a much older theatrical traditional: fourteenth-century mystery plays such as Coventry's *The Pageant of the Shearmen and Taylors,* depicting the Slaughter of the Innocents. The play shows Herod, King of Judaea, slaughtering Bethlehem's newborn infants to prevent a future King of the Jews from threatening his position. By associating Henry with Herod, Shakespeare presents him as a raging pagan tyrant. The *Pageant,* which Shakespeare may well have watched as a child, showed Herod embracing idolatry, or *"maumetrie"*—worshipping and swearing by Muhammad—while dressed in "Saracen" clothing.[34] Through these associations Henry is given many faces: he is simultaneously the heroic English king defeating the French, the pagan Herod menacing the Jews and the idolatrous Muslim threatening to slaughter innocent Christians "spitted upon pikes."

Of course unlike Tamburlaine, Herod or Murad, Henry does not slaughter the innocents of Harfleur. Our qualms are soon alleviated by his adoption of that most quintessential of English icons, St. George. Before Harfleur, after exhorting his soldiers to adopt the ruthless "action of the tiger," he combines patriotism with religion in his famous rallying call, "Cry God for Harry, England and St. George!"[35] His transformation from the dissolute Prince Hal seems complete. But even his adoption of George's militant purity would not have convinced everyone.

St. George offers a perfect example of how far Christian and Islamic traditions were entangled in the late sixteenth century. Influential Protestant theologians such as John Calvin and John Foxe frequently attacked the veneration of saints as yet another example of popish "idolatry." In his *Institutes of the Christian Religion* (1536), Calvin condemned those who regarded God's "intercession as unavailing without the assistance of George and . . . other such phantasms."[36] Foxe was similarly dismissive. In his chapter on the "History of the Turks," published in the 1570 edition of the *Acts and Monuments,* he argued that "if God have determined his own Son only to stand alone, let not us presume to admix with his majesty any of our trumpery. He that bringeth St. George or St. Denis, as patrons, to the field, to fight against the Turk, leaveth Christ, no doubt, at home."[37] Henry denied any association with "Amurath," but in his invocation of St. George he may have fallen into another trap, this time of Catholic idolatry.

To make matters even more complicated, St. George is not an exclusively Christian saint: he is also a key figure in the Islamic faith. In Christian iconography St. George is shown as a resurrected martyr who appears, from the Crusades onward, slaying the heretical "dragon" of Islamic militarism.[38] But in Islam he is associated with Al Khidr, identified in the Qur'an as a servant of God who meets Moses, and as an associate of Elijah in the Hadiths. In Sufism he is known as "the Verdant One," a mystical warrior whom some sources claim to have been an officer in the army of Alexander the Great. Some versions of his life declare that, like St. George, Al Khidr was resurrected after his death at the hands of a pagan king. In the 1550s the Habsburg diplomat Ogier Ghiselin de Busbecq traveled through the Ottoman Empire, recounting stories of a similar figure revered by Turkish dervish communities in central Anatolia, "a hero called Chederle, a man of great physical and mortal courage, whom they declare to be identical with our St. George and to whom they ascribe the same achievements as we ascribe to our saint, namely, that he rescued a maiden by the slaughter of a huge and terrible dragon."[39] Busbecq observed that "the Turks are much amused at the pictures of St. George, whom they declare was their own Chederle, in the Greek churches," and that when they saw such pictures "they prostrate themselves in adoration and imprint kisses all over it, not omitting even the horse's hoofs. St. George, they declare, was a man of might, a famous warrior, who often in single combat fought with the Evil Spirit on equal terms and was victorious."[40]

Although he went under various names, St. George was shared widely among various Christian and Muslim communities, and it was only around the time that Shakespeare wrote *Henry V* that he began to have a more recognizably English identity. The likelihood is that Shakespeare had no idea of the Islamic version of St. George, but many of his contemporaries placed the saint in a nebulous Muslim context even as they tried to reclaim him for a more parochial version of English Protestantism. Richard Johnson, a popular writer of prose romance now largely forgotten, in his *The Most Famous History of the Seven Champions of Christendom* (1596)—a source for *Henry V*—transferred St. George's origins from Cappadocia in Turkey to, perhaps surprisingly, Coventry. In Johnson's hands St. George is somewhat clumsily turned into an "English Champion," even though his enemies remain Persian Muslims. Johnson's St. George travels east in search of adventure and is offered the hand of Sabra, daughter of the Egyptian king, but he insists, "I am a Christian, thou a Pagan: I honor God in heaven, thou earthly shadowes below: therefore if thou wilt obtaine my love and liking, thou must forsake thy Mahomet and be christened in our Christian faith." Sabra agrees, but they are betrayed by the jealous "Almidor the blacke knight of Moroco."[41] George is sent to Persia to be executed.

Johnson depicts George as a militant Protestant iconoclast: "Upon the day Saint George entred the sultan's court when the Persians solemnly sacrificed to their Gods Mahomet, Apollo, Termigaunt, the unchristian procession so moved the impatience of the English champion, that he took the ensigns and streamers whereon the Persian gods were pictured, and trampled them under his feet."[42] As a consequence George is condemned by a "Soldan" who swears by "Mahomet" and hands him over to his "Janissaries" to be executed. As he is martyred, George vows:

> Let tyrants think if ever I obtain,
> What now is lost by treason's cursed guile:
> False Egypt's scourge I surely will remain,
> And turn to streaming blood Moroco's smile.
> The damned dog of Barbarie shall rue,
> The baleful stratagems that will ensue.
> The Persian towers shall smoke with fire,
> And lofty Babylon be tumbled down:
> The Cross of Christendom shall then aspire,
> To wear the proud Egyptian triple crowne,
> Jerusalem and Juda shall behold,
> The fall of Kings by Christian Champions bold.[43]

Johnson's St. George has to go through a series of encounters with Muslims in the Holy Land before he can be martyred and adopted as England's patron saint.

Much of what Johnson wrote about St. George's complex heritage finds its way into Shakespeare's *Henry V*, culminating at the end of the play in one final striking identification between Henry and St. George. After his victory at Agincourt, Henry makes peace with the French by marrying their princess, Catherine. His rather awkward wooing concludes with his proposal: "Shall not thou and I, between Saint Denis and Saint George, compound a boy, half-French half-English, that shall go to Constantinople and take the Turk by the beard?"[44] It is hardly a romantic proposal, but rather one of militant Christian expansion, where the compound French and English heir can establish his power at the heart of Islam. As Henry augments his power through a dynastic marriage with the French princess, he reveals himself a strategic polyglot.

Yet the audience knows there will be no crusade. As the Epilog points out:

> Henry the Sixth, in infant bands crowned king
> Of France and England, did this king succeed,
> Whose state so many had the managing
> That they lost France and made his England bleed.
> Which oft our stage hath shown.[45]

In a moment of self-promotion, Shakespeare reminds his viewers that eight years earlier they had seen what had happened to Henry VI. Henry's great victories were all for nothing. The boy would not conquer Constantinople—quite the contrary, he would lose France, and England would sink into yet another civil war. The dynastic cycle of conflict will begin all over again, and the specter of Carlisle's prophecy of internecine strife where "Peace shall go sleep with Turks and infidels" will return like a ghost that cannot be exorcised. Shakespeare intimates that even at the core of England's greatest ruler there is a touch of Turkish tyranny. Perhaps, he suggests, a Christian is not so very different from a Turk after all.

By 1600, the ghost of Marlowe was gone, consigned to the occasional parody of largely ineffectual characters. The process of exorcism had given Shakespeare a fascinating new compound figure, the Moor-Turk. Shakespeare had no interest in making moral judgments about such characters. Gradually he transformed the stereotype of the eastern antihero as a murderous villain into something subtler, yet also tragic and conflicted. Shakespeare's Moors were exotic yet unsettling. Standing on the threshold between Rome and Venice, they threatened to invade the domestic economy, and to pollute English women and bloodlines. For an Elizabethan audience accustomed by now to an extensive exchange of goods and people between England and Morocco, such face-to-face encounters were a distinct possibility. In contrast, Shakespeare's Turks were more spectral figures, metaphors more than roles, archetypes rarely seen on England's shores.

• • •

Even as Shakespeare finished *Henry V* with its unlikely proposal of a crusade against the Turk, a group of Englishmen were involved in a far less heroic but no less extraordinary adventure in Constantinople that would put Elizabeth's relationship with the Ottomans back at the top of the international political agenda. In January 1598 Edward Barton had died of dysentery, abruptly ending his colorful tenure as English ambassador to the Porte. He was buried with little fanfare in a Christian cemetery on the island of Heybeli Ada, a short boat ride away from Constantinople. Sultan Mehmed had never officially ratified Barton's position. His controversial Hungarian adventure had further delayed the dispatch of royal presents. It was left to Barton's successor, Henry Lello, to renegotiate England's commercial Capitulations in the face of renewed French opposition.

Lello possessed neither the tact nor the dynamism of his predecessors. His colleagues nicknamed him "Fog" and could hardly restrain their glee in reporting his shortcomings. During one of his earliest audiences with the sultan, he stood "like a modest midwife, and began a trembling speech in English . . . sounding like the squeaking of a goose divided into semiquavers."[46] Although he struggled to adapt to his position in Constantinople, he managed to convince London that if reasonable Anglo-Ottoman relations were to continue, gifts and letters confirming his position must be sent immediately.

As Elizabeth's advisers debated what to send to Mehmed, Richard Hakluyt was in the final stages of preparing the publication of the second edition of his *Principal Navigations*. Hakluyt had dedicated the first edition to his patron, Walsingham, and would soon dedicate the second to Burghley's son Robert Cecil, who became one of Elizabeth's leading ministers in 1596 following his father's incapacitation due to ill health (he died two years later).

Hakluyt's dedicatory epistle drew on Bacon's earlier defense. It turned first to ancient history, arguing, "If any man shall take exception against this our new trade with Turks and misbelievers, he shall show himself a man of small experience in old and new histories, or wilfully lead with partiality, or some worse humor. For who knoweth not, that king Solomon of old, entered into league upon necessity with Hiram the king of Tyrus, a gentile?" It was a carefully chosen Old Testament analogy. Just as King Hiram of Tyre had provided Solomon with the timber needed to build the Holy Temple of Jerusalem, so Elizabeth would do business with whoever enabled her to erect the Protestant Temple of God in England. Turning to the hypocrisy of England's Catholic opponents, each of whom had merchants based in Constantinople, Hakluyt went on: "Who is ignorant that the French, the Genoese, Florentines, Ragusans, Venetians, and Polonians are at this day in league with the Grand Signior, and have been these many years, and have used trade and traffic in his dominions?" He concluded by taking a global perspective:

> Who doth not acknowledge, that either hath traveled the remote parts of the world, or read the histories of this later age, that the Spaniards and Portugales in Barbary, in the Indies, and elsewhere, have ordinary confederacy and traffic with the Moors, and many kinds of Gentiles and Pagans, and that which is more, do pay them pensions, and use them in their service and wars? Why then should that be blamed on us, which is usual and common to the most part of other Christian nations?[47]

In other words, nobody could blame the English for working with the Turks or the Moors because everyone was at it.

Nevertheless, as news began to circulate in January 1599 that a ship carrying a consignment of gifts was ready to leave London for Constantinople, many onlookers expressed their anxiety. The inveterate gossip and diarist John Chamberlain wrote that a "great and curious present is going to the Grand Turk, which will scandalize other nations, especially the Germans."[48] Elizabeth chose the gifts personally and they were indeed "curious." One was a coach worth £600 intended for Safiye Sultan, a shrewd decision that not only continued their reciprocal exchange of gifts but also enabled Elizabeth to cultivate the woman who it was believed had wielded ultimate power at the Turkish court since her son's accession. The other gift was even more elaborate—a clockwork musical organ, built and already played before the queen (much to her satisfaction) by a musician and blacksmith from Warrington in Lancashire named Thomas Dallam. Edward Barton had written to Elizabeth back in 1595 suggesting she send Mehmed a "clock in the form of a cock." Elizabeth clearly felt that a clockwork organ was better than a cock, and along with the coach, a consignment of cloth and a team of artisans, including Dallam himself, the organ was packed up and put on board the *Hector,* a 300-ton Levant Company ship bound for Constantinople.

On August 28, 1599, the *Hector* reached its destination. The Venetian *bailo* (resident ambassador) Girolamo Capello's report on its arrival was mixed. He noted that the ship's cargo "consists of an organ very cunningly designed, which serves as a clock and can play several airs by itself, of a carriage and fittings for the sultana, of some silver vases and many suits of cloth which they say are moldy and ruined."[49] The reality was even worse. Lello was horrified to discover that Dallam's organ had been damaged on the long sea journey, alongside the consignment of ruined cloth, and with it possibly his hopes of receiving Mehmed's formal blessing as ambassador. Dallam saw that the "gluing work was clean decayed on the organ" and "his metal pipes were bruised and broken." He blamed "the working of the sea and the hotness of the country."

Lello's French and Venetian counterparts had turned up to laugh at the pile of broken pipes. Aside from the fuss over the presents, the Venetian *bailo* remained concerned about Lello's longer-term ambitions to establish a Protestant church in Constantinople. Several weeks after Dallam's arrival, Capello wrote to his superiors:

> The English Ambassador will kiss hands tomorrow morning. He goes working away at various chimerical schemes, principally the idea of asking the Grand Signor to give him one of the churches in Galata for the use of a preaching minister whom he has brought with him. Both the French Ambassador and myself considered this design of his to be obviously important in its effect on the honor of the Holy Church, and we accordingly approached the poor Mufti on the matter. He promised us every support; but now we

have had recourse to the Chief Eunuch; nor shall we fail to make every effort in order to thwart this excessive and arrogant pretension of the English, who would endeavor to sow even here the perversity and impiety of Calvin.[50]

While the French and Venetians worried about Lello's religious ambitions, the prickly Englishman was more concerned about Dallam. It must have been with mixed feelings that he watched the industrious Lancastrian quickly overcome the initial setback with his organ, spending the next month repairing, then reassembling it in front of a curious and increasingly expectant Turkish audience at the Topkapi Palace. At least the coach had arrived unscathed and proved to be a success. Lello later described the somewhat incongruous sight of the sultan and his mother riding around the city in it. When the organ's repairs were complete, Dallam was called to perform before the sultan. On September 25 he and his organ were ushered into the inner sanctum of the Topkapi. As the sultan entered he demanded silence, and the twenty-four-year-old blacksmith from Lancashire began to play the organ in front of the most powerful ruler in the world. Dallam recounted what happened next:

> All being quiet, and no noise at all, the present began to salute the Grand Signor [Mehmed]; for when I left it I did allow a quarter of an hour for his coming thither. First the clock struck 22; then the chime of 16 bells went off, and played a song of 4 parts. That being done, two personages which stood upon two corners of the second story, holding two silver trumpets in their hands, did lift them to their heads, and sounded a tantara. Then the music went off, and the organ played a song of 5 parts twice over. In the top of the organ, being 16 foot high, did stand a holly bush full of black birds and thrushes, which at the end of the music did singe and shake their wings. Diverse other motions there was which the Grand Signor wondered at.[51]

Mehmed was so enchanted that he demanded Dallam play for more than two hours, while the humiliated Lello was left outside, fuming, as he waited in vain to kiss the sultan's hand.

The recital was a triumph for Dallam. He was given gold worth £20 by Mehmed and was implored by the sultan's advisers "to stay with them always, and I should not want anything, but have all the content that I could desire." Then he was taken into Mehmed's "privy chambers," where he was allowed to draw his sword in imitation of the sultan and was offered the pick of the sultan's harem, "either two of his concubines or else two virgins of the best I could choose my self." To whet his appetite, he was even allowed to see the harem women by spying on them through "a grate in a wall," where he saw "thirty of the Grand Signor's concubines," and "very pretty ones indeed."

Dallam was clearly delighted to report that the concubines wore "fine cloth made of cotton wool, as white as snow and fine as lane [muslin]; for I could discern the skin of their thighs through it." It all proved too much for his furtive guide, who "stamped with his foot to make me give over looking; the which I was very loath to do, for that sight did please me wondrous well."[52] Dallam was the first recorded Englishman ever to see the sultan's harem. It must have all seemed a long way from Warrington.

Somewhat surprisingly, none of these enticements persuaded Dallam to stay, and he made plans to leave. Both Mehmed and Lello were determined to keep him, and removed him from the *Hector* as it was about to sail for England in December 1599 with Safiye's gifts and diplomatic correspondence for Elizabeth. The furious organist eventually persuaded the ambassador to let him slip away under pretense of illness and travel to Zante, where he could rejoin the *Hector*. As he left Constantinople never to return, Dallam had one final poignant encounter. To guide him through Ottoman territory he was assigned a dragoman, whom he described as "an Englishman, borne in Chorley in Lancashire; his name Finch. He was also in religion a perfect Turk, but he was our trusty friend."[53] As he reached the Greek coast, Dallam took his leave of Finch: two men from Lancashire, briefly united as friends, standing together on the Greek coast, one, a Christian, headed west, the other, a Muslim convert who had "turned Turk," headed back east. Dallam had spent nearly a year traveling more than thirty-five hundred miles from London to Constantinople and through Greece to meet a man born in Chorley, not much more than twenty miles away from his hometown of Warrington. We will never know what they discussed on their ten-day trek, or whether they spoke of their lives, their beliefs and the choices they had made that separated them.

In May 1600 the *Hector* docked in England, with Safiye's gifts and letters to Elizabeth. At first, all seemed well. Safiye's translated letter acknowledged that "you sent us a coach; it has arrived and has been delivered. It had our gracious acceptance." It also itemized the gifts sent in response: "a robe, a sash, two gold-embroidered bath towels, three handkerchiefs, and a ruby and pearl tiara." Even more important, the elaborate exchange of gifts seemed to have had its desired diplomatic effect of persuading Mehmed to ratify the Anglo-Ottoman Capitulations. Safiye assured Elizabeth:

> I will take action in accordance with what you have written. Be of good heart in this respect. I constantly admonish my son, the Padishah [Mehmed], to act according to the treaty. I do not neglect to speak to him in this manner. God willing, may you not suffer grief in this respect.[54]

Unfortunately, on closer inspection it transpired that the original letter had been so hastily written in Constantinople that it was addressed to "the king of England, may his last moments be concluded with good."[55] Safiye's gifts paled in comparison with the lavish coach and organ sent to Constantinople. Safiye's *kira*, Esperanza Malchi, who it transpired had already been accused of withholding some of the gifts dispatched to Elizabeth six years earlier, had the temerity to address a letter directly to the queen, asking whether she could send Safiye "rare distilled waters of every kind for the face and odiferous oils for the hands" and offering her services, despite being "a Jewess by faith and of a different nation from your Majesty."[56] Perhaps unsurprisingly, no record survives of any response from Elizabeth to this request for perfume and hand lotion.

The exchange would prove to be the zenith of Anglo-Ottoman relations under Elizabeth. Although the Capitulations were agreed and

Lello's embassy was ratified, the querulous Englishman failed to reproduce the kind of friendship the increasingly pro-Venetian Safiye Sultan had enjoyed with Barton. He was also persistently outwitted by his French opposite number. He struggled on until 1607, when he was recalled to England and replaced by the more capable Thomas Glover, who was promptly accused by his vindictive predecessor of bigamy, adultery, sodomy, domestic violence and—worst of all—wearing too many jewels and feathers in the sultan's presence.[57]

In Constantinople, Esperanza Malchi's luck ran out even before the *Hector* reached London. Fed up with the political control and financial corruption exercised by the harem, the Turkish imperial cavalry rose up against the Safiye Sultan and vented their fury on her confidante Esperanza. A Levant Company official named Humphrey Conisby described what happened. The cavalry

> drew the *kira* out of her house (this was a Jew woman most dear to the Sultana, who by such grace, with her accomplices, governed in effect, the whole empire; and was worth at her death millions). Her they hauled through the streets, forth at Adrianople Gate, and there killing her (after she had offered more for her life than their pay came to) they cut her into small pieces, every one, that could get, carrying back through the streets to their houses a piece of her flesh upon his knife's point.[58]

Safiye had sacrificed Esperanza to the mob to protect her own life, although the incident severely diminished her influence. She lived for another five years, during which she conspired with Mehmed to have his son Mahmud strangled when the youngster began to question his grandmother's continued influence over his indolent father.

Nothing quite so dramatic awaited Thomas Dallam back home. He got married, had six children and spent the next thirty years building some of the period's finest organs for King's College Chapel in Cambridge, St. John's College in Oxford, Eton College, the Scottish Chapel Royal and the cathedrals in Norwich, Worcester and Bristol. According to his entry in the *Oxford Dictionary of National Biography,* Dallam's greatest achievement was "the consolidation of the two-manual 'double organ' with twelve to fourteen flue stops (without reeds, mixtures, or pedals) as the norm for English cathedrals and for larger collegiate churches during the pre–civil war period."[59] Perhaps. But he probably never forgot his grand performance in front of the sultan, his glimpse of the harem or his escape from the seraglio.

10

Sherley Fever

By the end of the sixteenth century, many Londoners had heard stories of English merchants, diplomats and artisans like Edmund Hogan, William Harborne and Thomas Dallam and their adventures throughout the Muslim world. Their accounts were often circulated in random and unreliable ways, by gossip and word of mouth, in private diplomatic correspondence or handwritten manuscripts passed from hand to hand. Few of these men had sufficient social standing or financial resources to publish printed books about their travels. Dallam may not have forgotten his time in Constantinople, but there is no evidence that Shakespeare ever met this modest Lancastrian artisan or read about his organ. There was, however, one Englishman living in Islamic lands at the turn of the century who had sufficient stature to broadcast news of his exploits so widely that he could be casually mentioned in a Shakespearean comedy and everyone knew who he was. This was Sir Anthony Sherley, an English knight whose notoriety epitomized the desire and peril associated with English relations with the Islamic world in the final years of Elizabeth's reign.

Sherley's name first appears on the London stage in Shakespeare's *Twelfth Night*, early in 1601. *Twelfth Night* is one of Shakespeare's most accomplished comedies and a world away from the crusading rhetoric of *Henry V*. The play is set in Illyria, on the Dalmatian coast (stretching from modern-day Croatia down to Albania). It seems to be a never-never land where near identical twins Sebastian and Viola are shipwrecked and spend their time trying to find each other in a comical reworking of Shakespeare's earlier *Comedy of Errors* (set in Ephesus, an Ottoman possession since the fifteenth century). Viola cross-dresses as "an eunuch,"[1] a young male page named Cesario, to secure a position of service at the court of Countess Olivia, who employs her as a go-between with Orsino, Duke of Illyria. Olivia falls in love with Viola, who in turn falls for Orsino. In the chaos of mistaken identity that ensues, the delusion of Olivia's pompous steward Malvolio that he could marry his mistress is comically yet brutally exposed by her roguish kinsman Sir Toby Belch and his friends. The play ends with betrothals and reconciliation, though not for the humiliated Malvolio, who exits comparing himself to a bear baited by dogs, warning "I'll be revenged on the whole pack of you."[2]

For all its wit and humor, *Twelfth Night* is full of unrequited love, loss, mourning, melancholia and tragedy. Some critics have explained its darker side by noting that it was written at the same time as *Hamlet,* but it contains a surprising number of references to the "Orient" and the Islamic world that had preoccupied Shakespeare and his contemporaries throughout the 1590s. At the time Illyria was no fantasy, but a region of the Ottoman Empire, which controlled most of Hungary, the Balkans, Mesopotamia (modern-day Syria, Iraq and Kuwait), Egypt, Palestine, western Arabia, much of the Caucasus and western Iran. Its tributary states and semi-autonomous principalities included Transylvania, Moldavia, the Crimea, Tripoli, Tunis and Algiers.

The reach and extent of the Ottoman Empire were clearly on Shakespeare's mind as he wrote *Twelfth Night,* a play replete with references to Egyptian thieves, "the gates of Tartar," "notable" pirates, a "renegado," heathens and even a "new map with the augmentation of the Indies."[3] This was a reference to the Cambridge mathematician Edward Wright's world map, made to illustrate the second edition of Richard Hakluyt's *Principal Navigations.* Wright's map was widely celebrated as the most up-to-date of its time, incorporating the latest Spanish, Portuguese and Dutch discoveries in the East and West "Indies."[4] Shakespeare also alluded to the Ottomans in the loaded reference to Viola early in the play as "an eunuch," a phrase the audience would have associated with Ottoman customs and mores.

Halfway through the play, Sir Toby, his cowardly friend Sir Andrew Aguecheek and Fabian the clown deceive Malvolio with a fake letter from Olivia proclaiming her love for him. Fabian is so pleased with the trick that he says, "I will not give my part of this sport for a pension of thousands to be paid from the Sophy"—a reference to the Shah of Persia.[5] Later in the play, when Sir Toby goads Sir Andrew into a duel with the cross-dressed Viola, he teases him with dire threats about his adversary:

> Why, man, he's a very devil, I have not seen such a virago. I had a pass with him, rapier, scabbard and all, and he gives me the stuck in with such a mortal motion, that it is inevitable, and on the answer, he pays you as surely as your feet hit the ground they step on. They say he has been fencer to the Sophy.[6]

The terrified Sir Andrew is tricked into believing he is about to face a deadly warrior renowned for teaching swordsmanship to the fearsome Persian emperor, rather than the equally petrified Viola dressed as Cesario, who the audience knows is of course a young female servant, hardly capable of holding a rapier. Shakespeare's audience would have recognized the allusion to two real rogues, Sir Anthony Sherley and his brother Robert, and they would have heard immediately that he was punning on the brothers' name—"surely"—and evoking their adventures in Persia.

By early 1601, thanks to many books and pamphlets printed with the tacit support of the vain and ambitious Sir Anthony Sherley, the Sherleys' adventures were the subject of gossip throughout London. Sir Anthony had left England in the summer of 1598 bound for Italy, but within months he appeared with his brother Robert at the court of Shah Abbas I, the fifth Safavid ruler and grandson of Anthony Jenkinson's old adversary, Shah Tahmasp. The Sherleys' extraordinary enterprise was described in several travel books published just before Shakespeare wrote *Twelfth Night,* works that claimed (among many other things) that their mission was so successful that Robert was appointed the shah's fencing master and Sir Anthony was given a substantial pension of thirty thousand crowns a year to train the shah's army.[7]

The Sherleys were famed for their escapades and misdemeanors. Their father, Sir Thomas Sherley, was a notorious courtier who embezzled hundreds of thousands of pounds from Elizabeth's military campaigns in the Low Countries, for which he was declared bankrupt and imprisoned in the Fleet debtors' prison. His estate of Wiston, in Sussex, was sequestered by Elizabeth. His eldest son, named Thomas as well, an almost comically incompetent soldier and a terrible pirate, was also imprisoned for various misdemeanors in London and Constantinople. He tried (but failed) to poison himself before being elected a member of Parliament later in life. Robert, the youngest brother, was held hostage in Persia for a decade after being abandoned by Anthony. Despite such travails, Robert managed to convert to Catholicism, marry a princess, return to Europe, work for the papacy and have his portrait painted by Sir Anthony Van Dyck wearing full Persian dress before dying in Qazvin and being buried in Rome.

Between them, over five decades, the brothers visited the Low Countries, Ireland, Scandinavia, Italy, Spain, Turkey, Africa, Persia, India, Greece, Russia, Newfoundland, the Caribbean, Mexico, the Azores and the Cape Verde Islands. At various times they worked for English monarchs and earls, French kings, Persian shahs, Russian tsars, Ottoman sultans, Habsburg emperors (one Spanish, the other Austrian), Moroccan kings and the Venetian state. All three were knighted outside England in dubious circumstances: Thomas in Ireland, Anthony in France and Robert in Prague. Each one was associated with recusancy and embraced Catholicism at some point in his life.

The brothers' exploits were celebrated throughout their lifetimes and beyond in a vast number of plays, pamphlets, magazines and books. In 1625, Samuel Purchas, Richard Hakluyt's successor as the great chronicler of England's voyages and discoveries, wrote, "Among our English travelers, I know not whether any have merited more respect than the honorable, I had almost said heroic gentlemen, Sir Anthony & Sir Robert Sherley." For Purchas, their adventures exceeded those of classical myth, because "if the Argonauts of old, and Graecian worthies, were worthily reputed heroical for European exploits in Asia, what may we think of the Sherley brethren, which not from the nearer

Greek shores but from beyond the European world, *Et penitus toto divisus Orbe Britannia* [Even to Britannia, that land completely separated from the world], have not coasted a little way (as did those), but pierced the very bowels of the Asian seas and lands, unto the Persian center."[8]

By using a quotation from Virgil's *Aeneid,* Purchas hoped to wrap the Sherleys in the mantle of heroic empire-builders, spreading the word of English decency and common sense across the globe. He saw their support of Persian military expansion as ridding the world of the troublesome Turks: "The mighty Ottoman, terror of the Christian world, quaketh of a Sherley fever, and gives hopes of approaching fates. The prevailing Persian hath learned Sherleian Arts of War, and he which before knew not the use of ordnance hath now 500 pieces of brass and 60,000 musketeers."[9] It was an early example of the belief that superior Christians brought technology to the backward orientals. Unsurprisingly, the Victorians embellished Purchas's sentiments with romantic gusto. The *Gentleman's Magazine* of 1844 lauded "those three brave Sherleys! Each separate history a romance! How proud must the old knight their father have been, living at Wiston with his noble sons! What heart-breaking partings; what sorrowful misgivings as son after son left the paternal home to seek honor and renown in distant lands!"[10]

Such praise was precipitated by the Sherleys' genius for self-promotion in their memoirs and correspondence and by the patronage of various printed publications extolling their adventures. Not everyone was impressed. Accusations of flagrant personal aggrandizement and corruption began to circulate as early as the 1580s, and more sober recent biographical studies have uncovered a dizzying trail of betrayal, debt, embezzlement, dishonesty, espionage, heresy, privateering, incarceration, treason, drunkenness, elopement and murder wherever the brothers went.[11] Of all the attacks leveled at the Sherleys, none were more consistent and vituperative than those directed at Sir Anthony. Even his biographers find it hard to admire him. One of the earliest, the renowned orientalist scholar and linguist Sir Edward Denison Ross, conceded that he possessed great courage and charisma, and "rare insight into the Oriental mind," but concluded that he was "an inveterate and unscrupulous intriguer, being incapable of single-minded devotion to any person or cause. He had all the natural instincts of a buccaneer, and his cupidity was only equaled by his extravagance." He "passed without compunction or regret from one employment to another and surely it is seldom that one man has served so many monarchs." These came to seven, according to Ross's calculations: three Protestants, two Catholic, one Sunni and one Shi'a Muslim. Not only was Sir Anthony "quick-tempered and quarrelsome," he gave "no evidence of possessing a sense of humor."[12] A subsequent biographer managed to go even further, condemning Sherley as "a born intriguer, a complete opportunist, a man whose word could never be relied on and whose personal dishonesty leaves us gasping."[13]

The garrulous Sherley was himself partly responsible for these damning assessments. Unlike so many anonymous travelers to the Muslim world, he left behind a mountain of correspondence, pamphlets, and even a rambling vainglorious memoir entitled *Sir Anthony Sherley His Relation of his Travels into Persia* (1613). Although it is often difficult to extract the facts from Sherley's fanciful self-fashioning, supporting evidence reveals his opportunism from an early age. Like most young aristocratic Elizabethan men, Anthony Sherley went to fight the Spanish in the Low Countries, along with his father and elder brother Thomas. By 1586 they were all serving there under the Earl of Leicester, but his father began embezzling money from the war effort, and the Spanish slaughtered his brother's company one night after the foolish Thomas had spent all day drinking with them. With his father and brother in disgrace, Anthony went on to distinguish himself in battle— bravery was one virtue he did not lack—and after Leicester's death he attached himself to Elizabeth's new favorite, the equally intemperate Earl of Essex.

In 1591 he joined Norris's expeditionary force to France, where the French king Henry IV awarded him a knighthood of the Order of St. Michel. Sherley was delighted, but when Elizabeth heard he had accepted a foreign honor without her permission she threw him in jail. Sherley refused to relinquish the title with characteristic verbosity, insisting that "this matter concerned his reputation, more dear to him than his life, and that his life and all that he had was at Her Majesty's commandment, and that he had rather lose his life than lose his reputation, desiring rather to die than live with disgrace, which he accounted the yielding up of this would bring him."[14] He was marched straight back to jail. A compromise was reached and he was released, but from then on he would only ever answer to the title of Sir Anthony.

A spell in prison seems to have done nothing to temper Sherley's ambitions. Almost immediately he incurred the queen's wrath again by secretly marrying Essex's cousin, in 1594, and he was exiled from court. He turned to privateering and in 1596 persuaded his father to channel an exorbitant amount from the war effort in the Low Countries to outfit a fleet of ships to attack the Portuguese island of São Tomé in the Gulf of Guinea. It was an ill-fated expedition from the outset. Bad weather and illness forced Sherley to abandon his initial plans and launch a feeble attack on the Cape Verde Islands. Fearing a Portuguese counterattack, he made the ludicrous decision to cross the Atlantic and head for the Caribbean. In early 1597 the fleet tried unsuccessfully to plunder Dominica and Jamaica, but was beset by mutinies and limped home empty-handed via Newfoundland. By June Sherley was back in England, poorer than when he had left and overshadowed by Essex's success in Cadiz. In an attempt to recoup some money and escape from his estranged wife, he joined Essex and Raleigh's unsuccessful summer expedition against the Spanish-held Azores, alongside the young poet John Donne. He returned in October 1597, impatient for his next escapade.

As one adventure ended, another opened up. Late that year, Essex sent Sherley to Ferrara in a misguided scheme to help Cesare d'Este, the last surviving member of the city's ruling dynasty, hold on to the duchy in the face of Pope Clement VIII's claims. Essex hoped to tie up Spanish and papal forces in the crisis that would otherwise be turned against England. Sherley was the obvious choice to bribe, flatter and generally cause chaos, and in early 1598 he slipped out of London without the queen's permission, leading a party of twenty-five volunteers. He would never set foot in England again. Not satisfied with a substantial budget of £8,000 from Essex, before he left Sherley duped his father out of jewels worth more than £500. Sir Thomas, having only just been released from debtors' prison, wrote to the ailing Lord Burghley on December 30, declaring that "against my will I am driven to complain of the cruel dealing of Anthony Sherley toward me" and protesting about the theft of the jewels. "When my man called then, Anthony had gone out of town, we hear, with purpose to go beyond the seas, but whether with the Queen's license, or not, I do not know. After wounding my estate by his voyage [for São Tomé] he has now the more undone me in my present desperate state by thus cozening me of the money which I am in no way able to repay. . . . For this indeed is wickedness to add to the affliction of his poor aged parents."[15] So much for the proud old knight and his noble sons.

In January 1598 Sherley crossed the Channel and traveled with his party on to Germany, where he learned that Don Cesare had fled Ferrara, which was now under papal control, apparently bringing his mission to an end before it had begun. Seemingly unconcerned, Sherley made instead for Venice in search of even greater opportunities. The city's network of spies and informants was abuzz with the arrival of the pompous Englishman and his intentions. In March 1598 one wrote:

> Here, one finds a gentleman named Sherley. . . . He passed through Holland while on his way here, and he was (or so he says) well-regarded and received there. Nevertheless, he hardly speaks better of the Estates [the Dutch Calvinists], and, on the contrary, he unceasingly extols the greatness of Spain, and even more that of the Pope, and says that he has received great offers from the one and the other. . . . If he were wise and of good counsel, he would talk less and would be more feared. . . . He is a spendthrift who has spent all his means, and those of his father who he has ruined, and he lives here on what he has borrowed.[16]

These comments distilled the characteristics that Sir Anthony displayed throughout his life: the profligacy, boastful claims, suspect religious and political allegiances, empty threats and unscrupulous opportunism.

It did not take long for Sherley to spot an opportunity. Venetian overland trade with southeast Asia had been hit hard by the Portuguese discovery of a sea route to the same markets following Vasco da Gama's voyage to India in 1497–1499. Since Portugal's annexation by Spain in 1580, Philip II's empire had monopolized the seaborne eastern trade. Its Portuguese fortress at Hormuz on the Persian Gulf controlled maritime traffic in and out of the gulf and much of the Red Sea, which was ruining Venice. However, in 1597 news reached London and Venice that a Dutch fleet had broken the monopoly by sailing to Java via the Cape of Good Hope and returning to Holland with a consignment of spices and pepper. Essex, always keen to develop an international strategy that would expand his political influence and challenge Spain, began to explore the feasibility of an Anglo-Dutch maritime alliance that could establish seaborne and overland relations with Persia and break the Iberian stranglehold over the region. The result was an Anglo-Dutch-Persian coalition capable of challenging the dominance not only of the Spanish and Portuguese but also of the Ottomans.[17]

This put Essex at odds with Elizabeth's pro-Turkish policy, but his more militant advisers were pushing him to challenge the queen's foreign policy. The Essex faction's increasingly bellicose strategy would, as we will see, culminate in one of the most serious crises faced in the course of Elizabeth's reign; however, it also found itself in an unlikely alliance with Catholic sympathizers like the Sherley family, unhappy with Elizabeth's Anglo-Ottoman friendship. It was this unlikely association that gave the restless Sir Anthony his next glorious opportunity: in the late spring of 1598, he would strike out for Isfahan and befriend the Shah of Persia.

It is unclear who first proposed the venture. In his *Relation* Sherley naturally claimed that it was his idea, sanctioned by Essex, who, he wrote, "proposed unto me (after a small relation, which I made unto him from Venice) the voyage of Persia." He described the decision in his characteristically prolix and neologistic style as "a profitable experience of my seeing those countries, limiting upon the king of Spain's uniall [united] parts, and answering to her majesty's merchants' trade in Turkey and Muscovy; and besides, being not unlikely but some parts might have been found fit for the Indian navigation, then principiated [initiated] in Holland, and muttered of in England." He could not resist adding that he was plotting "some more private designs, which my fortune, being of the condition, which my persecutions have brought it unto, counselleth me not to speak of."

Other evidence suggests that the wily Venetians had planted the seed of a Persian adventure in Sherley's overactive imagination. Using the hyperbolic terms Sherley loved, the Venetian statesman Giacomo Foscarini encouraged him to go because it would be "beneficial to all Christendom and in particular to Venice, which by the traffic overland from thence was mightily enriched before the Portugals were lord of those parts." It was undoubtedly no accident that Sherley was subsequently introduced to a Persian merchant who told him about "the royalty of the Sophy, his king, which pleased Sir Anthony very well." He also met "a great traveler, newly come from to Venice from the Sophy's court, whose name was Angelo [Corrai], born in Turkey, but a good Christian, who had traveled sixteen years, and did speak twenty-four kind of languages." Corrai also appealed to Sherley's vanity, telling him "of the worthiness of the King of Persia, that he was a gallant soldier, very bountiful and liberal to strangers, and what entertainment he had at his court; assuring Anthony that, if he would go thither, it would be greatly for his advancement."[18]

Sherley needed little further encouragement, and in May 1598 he left for Persia. His small entourage included Angelo Corrai as guide and interpreter, a Frenchman named Abel Pinçon (a spy working for Burghley), several English gentlemen, including George Mainwaring and William Parry (both of whom survived to write about their adventures), and his brother Robert. Their elder brother, Thomas, was unavailable, having extracted money from his long-suffering father and Burghley to fund a privateering adventure off the Portuguese coast that was to prove disastrous.

Even before he left Falmouth, one of Thomas's six ships sprang a leak, another was damaged and several of its crew were killed by a botched cannon salute. A mutiny in which four hundred sailors absconded forced him to sell four ships and sail with just two. If his departure was a farce, the outcome was an embarrassment. He tried to attack the southwest coast of Spain but anchored too far offshore and the landing party got stuck on a sandbar at the entrance to the bay. He finally abandoned the whole humiliating affair and returned home—to the scorn of the diarist John Chamberlain, who sneered that Thomas Sherley's only achievement was "two or three peasants to ransom, of whom when he saw he could raise nothing [for them] he would not bring them away for shame."[19]

A talent for logistics clearly did not run in the family. As Sir Anthony left Venice, he left behind him the inevitable debts. He also failed to muster sufficient provisions (although the two may have been related). Within weeks of his departure for Zante, he ran out of food. He begged for provisions from the Italian passengers, but it was a group of Persians who came to his rescue and shared their food. The enraged brothers took their revenge on one unfortunate Italian, accusing him of slandering the queen. Sir Anthony ordered him to be beaten brutally, and when the captain intervened, Sir Robert attacked him. It was symptomatic of their behavior all the way to Persia. On arrival in Zante, Sir Anthony wrote to "foggy" Henry Lello in Constantinople, insisting that he was heading for the Red Sea on the queen's official business while posing as an English merchant. He demanded that the hapless ambassador send him passports and money to enable him to travel unmolested through Ottoman territory.

Over the next six months Sherley lied, bullied and borrowed his way across Ottoman territory, traveling through Crete, Tripoli and Aleppo, where he obtained more money from the English consul. News of his behavior was already reaching London, where in December 1598 John Chamberlain noted, "Sir Anthony Sherley has wrung £400 from our merchants at Constantinople, and has scraped together £500 more at Aleppo, with which he has charged Lord Essex by his bills, and is gone away to seek his fortune."[20] As old Levant hands like William Harborne knew, Sherley's route was a dangerous one, and his retinue faced repeated harassment from the Turks they met along the way. While in Aleppo, George Mainwaring recounted that "to my hard fortune, I met with a Turk, a gallant man he seemed to be by his habit, and saluting me in this manner: took me fast by one of the ears with his hand, and so did lead me up and down the streets." As onlookers watched, laughed and threw stones at Mainwaring, the Turk "gave me such a blow with a staff, that did strike me to the ground." Once Mainwaring had returned to the safety of the English consul's house bloody and beaten, the resident Janissary sought out the Turk, and "ran fiercely at him, and threw him on his back, giving him twenty blows on his legs and his feet, so that he was not able to go or stand." Such attacks, a reflection of the fragile nature of English relations with the Turks, occurred, so Mainwaring claimed, "diverse times."[21]

In early September 1598, as Sherley's retinue prepared to leave Aleppo, they were probably unaware of events at the other end of the Mediterranean that would have a significant impact on Europe's balance of power and Sir Anthony's own future. The seventy-one-year-old Philip II lay dying in the Escorial just outside Madrid, riddled with fever, gout and septicemia. With characteristic diligence the king worked up until the end, signing one peace treaty with France and proposing another with England even as he lay dying. He finally expired on September 13 after ruling Spain for more than forty years. His undistinguished son, Philip III, succeeded him. The new king possessed little appetite or ability to match his father's tireless global vision of Spanish imperial reach and oversaw a period of drift and decline in imperial affairs.

As Philip II passed away, Sherley's entourage struck out eastward, traveling through Al Fallujah before reaching Ottoman-controlled Baghdad at the end of the month. News of his unofficial embassy quickly spread, and English merchants refused to honor his debts unless assured that Elizabeth or Essex had sanctioned his trip. Even worse, Baghdad's suspicious Turkish governor impounded Sherley's goods, and in November the Englishman and his party fled after a tip-off from a sympathetic Florentine merchant that they were about to be arrested on orders from Constantinople. They were pursued by a party of Ottoman Janissaries whom they shook off as they traveled toward Persian territory with a group of Shi'a pilgrims returning from Mecca. As they went, George Mainwaring reported, they "saw many ruinated places which Tamberlane had conquered, as we were told both by the Jews and the Turks, for his name is had in memory among them to this day."[22]

They traveled through Raqqa, where they had a run-in with some Turks, before reaching Babylon. William Parry assessed that its tower, which he called "Nebuchadnezzar's Tower," was "about the height of St. Paul's." When they finally crossed into Persian dominions, Parry "thought we had been imparadised, finding our entertainment to be so good and the manner of the people to be so kind and courteous, far differing from the Turks."[23] Finally, on December 1, 1598, the group reached the Safavid Persian city of Qazvin.

Sherley could not have timed his arrival better. Thirty-six years earlier, when Anthony Jenkinson was the first Englishman to enter the city, Shah Tahmasp had just concluded a peace treaty with the Ottomans and thus had no interest in an alliance with Christians. Jenkinson was promptly expelled. Sherley arrived just as Shah Tahmasp's grandson, Shah Abbas, ended years of internecine conflict by defeating the Safavids' sworn enemies the Uzbeks. The shah was now ready to confront the Ottomans once more. He had overseen a remarkable transformation of the Safavid Empire since his accession in 1588, at seventeen. Ottoman expansion in the west and Uzbek depredations in the northeast meant that he had inherited a kingdom riven with factional rivalries and reduced drastically in size and stature since the glory days of Shah Ismail. A pragmatic and ruthless leader, Shah Abbas understood that if he was to survive and his kingdom to prosper, he must somehow end division, reorganize the army and recover lost territory. He immediately made a strategic peace treaty with the Ottomans, quashed internal dissent and created a new standing army with musketeers and an artillery corps. He also took the bold decision to move his imperial capital from Qazvin to the more central Isfahan. That city underwent a period of enormous urban renewal: Shah Abbas supervised the building of one of Islam's greatest capitals at a time when other great Muslim cities like Marrakesh were being redesigned on a grand scale. Isfahan's transformation included new palaces, mosques, bazaars, madrasas, baths, forts, gardens and public avenues, earning it the epithet *Esfahān nesf-e jahān ast* ("Isfahan is half the world"—the other half being paradise).[24]

In the spring of 1598, as work began on his new capital, Shah Abbas had made his move against the Uzbeks. He marched out of Isfahan in April, and on August 9 his army of 10,000 soldiers defeated the Uzbeks at the Battle of Rabat-i-Pariyan, seizing Herat, Nishapur and Meshed. As he returned to Isfahan at the head of a triumphal procession, he heard of Sherley's arrival. He ordered a steward by the name of Marjan Beg to present Sherley with twenty gold pounds to sustain him until he was called for. Mainwaring observed with relief that Marjan Beg was pleased with Sherley's typically contemptuous response: "Sir Anthony, according to his princely mind, turning the money over with his foot, returned this answer: 'Know this, brave Persian, I come not a-begging to thy king, but hearing of his great fame and worthiness thought I could not spend my time better than come to see him, and kiss his hand, with the adventure of my body to second him in his princely wars.'"[25]

Sherley's rhetoric of fame, adventure and contempt for wealth seems to have captured the ethos of the Persian court. Mainwaring notes that Marjan Beg responded to Sherley's bravado, "Pardon me, brave stranger, for now I see thou art a prince thyself, for so it seemeth by thy princely answer." Sherley demurred, but was finally being given the regal treatment he felt he deserved. Equally thrilling, it was time to dress up. His party was "furnished with apparel and horses" and prepared for a meeting with the shah.[26]

At the very end of December, Sherley's party was summoned to a royal audience four miles outside Qazvin. The Sherley brothers were attired in lavish Persian outfits, "Sir Anthony himself in rich cloth of gold, his gown and his undercoat, his sword hanging in a rich scarf to the worth of a thousand crowns, being set with pearls and diamonds, and on his head a turban according, to the worth of two thousand [Spanish] dollars, his boots embroidered with pearl and rubies."[27] As they approached, Abel Pinçon was given a sickening insight into the shah's ruthlessness. Shah Abbas was making a "triumphal entry" into Qazvin: "He caused to be carried on the end of strong and heavy spears twenty thousand heads of Tartars whom he had defeated in Uzbek." Mainwaring estimated that it was only twelve hundred, but whatever the number it was "a hideous spectacle" designed to impress Qazvin's inhabitants, which also unsurprisingly intimidated the newly arrived Christians.[28]

At this point, Shah Abbas appeared. Pinçon described him as "about thirty years of age, small in stature but handsome and well proportioned, his beard and hair is black . . . he has a strong and active mind and an extremely agile body, the result of training."[29] Mainwaring claimed that "at our first encounter of the king, Sir Anthony and his brother did alight off their horses, and came to kiss the king's foot; for it is the fashion of the country. . . . After that was performed the king did look upon them both very stately, and afterward did look upon us all, giving never a word unto Sir Anthony."[30] Sir Anthony glossed over such servility, recalling he "kissed his stirrup; my speech was short unto him, the time being fit for no other." He was keen to stress that Abbas told him that the Englishman "had done him infinite honor, to make such a journey for his sake."[31] Other sources say he delivered a more fulsome and obsequious oration to Abbas, which sounds more in keeping with his characteristic verbosity. "I am a soldier whose profession is clean contrary to words, which shall sooner fail me," he is reported to have begun. He then offered to act as "a subject for your majesty's most excellent virtues, if my devotion and observances were not sealed with my blood, the which I do humbly and freely offer at your majesty's feet, to be shed and spent, at the least sign and token of your majesty's pleasure."[32]

Again, accounts differ as to Abbas's response, but as they were all from Sherley's party they were unanimous in stating that it was positive. Mainwaring claimed that the shah embraced and kissed the brothers, "and taking Sir Anthony by the hand, swearing a great oath that he should be his sworn brother, and so he did call him always."[33] Parry went so far as to claim that Sherley immediately "possessed the king with such a burning desire to invade the Turk's dominions" that he threatened to launch a campaign there and then.[34]

Whatever the truth of these accounts, the English were certainly welcomed royally. They received sumptuous entertainment, spending over two months feasting, drinking and hunting with the shah's court. Gifts of horses, camels, mules, weapons and jewels were exchanged, and if the reports are to be believed, Sir Anthony and Shah Abbas became virtually inseparable "in sporting and banqueting," walking arm in arm through the city's streets. The Englishman was even made a *mirza*, a title originally reserved for Muslim princes. It was hardly surprising that in return Sir Anthony extolled Abbas's virtues, describing him as "excellently well shaped, of a most well proportioned stature, strong and active . . . his mind infinitely royal, wise, valiant, liberal, temperate, merciful, and an exceeding lover of justice." He even praised the Persian ruler's approach to political succession: in contrast to the Ottomans, rather than strangling his siblings upon his accession, the magnanimous Abbas only blinded them.[35]

It is difficult to assess the genuineness of the two men's friendship. There are no known records from the Persian archives to tell us what Shah Abbas thought of Sir Anthony, while the Englishman's memoir and the reports of his supporters are either too vague or deeply biased. Nevertheless, though doubtless exaggerated, subsequent events suggest that Sherley and Abbas's closeness went beyond that of any other Elizabethan Englishman and Muslim ruler. Certainly men like Jenkinson, Hogan and Harborne had never managed such a personal rapport with a Persian, Ottoman or Moroccan ruler. But they had been lowly merchants pursuing ignoble commercial agendas. Sherley would have recoiled in horror at such a comparison. His diplomatic brief was unofficial, possibly not even sanctioned by Essex, but he reveled in proclaiming his aristocratic status. The relationship between the two men was closer in spirit to that of the Portuguese king Sebastian and the English renegade Sir Thomas Stukeley. Both Sherley and Stukeley regarded themselves primarily as warriors with little time for unseemly discussions of money or commerce.

Religion was a far more complex matter. Sherley's party certainly progressed beyond Anthony Jenkinson's limited grasp of the distinction between Shi'a and Sunni Islam. William Parry understood that the Safavid faith was "as the Turk's, but somewhat different in religion. As the Persian prayeth only to Mahomet and Mortus Ally ['Ali ibn Abi Talib], the Turk to those two and to three other that were Mahomet's servants. Against which three the Persian still inveighs."[36] Parry also learned that "their conceit of Christ is that he was a very great prophet and a most holy and religious man, but in no way comparable to

Mahomet: for Mahomet (say they) was that final prophet by whom all things were and are to be perfected and consummated." Parry did not condemn this belief; he only observed, "They further say that because God never had wife, therefore Christ cannot possibly be his son."[37]

Pinçon felt that his Christian readers were familiar with the schism between Sunni and Shi'a and it was thus "unnecessary to treat of the hatred and discord which exist between them [the Persians] and the Turks over the explanation of the Alcoran and over the precedence and dignity of their false prophets," only saying that "the Persians hold the Turks in great abomination." He also made a token gesture to reclaim Abbas for Christianity, acknowledging that he was a "Mahometan" but that "round his neck he always wears a cross, in token of the reverence and honor which he bears toward Jesus Christ." Pinçon's attempted assimilation only went so far: just a few paragraphs earlier he had succumbed to more familiar stereotypes, damning Abbas as a tyrant who tormented his subjects, "behaving toward them inhumanely and cruelly, cutting off their heads for the slightest offense, having them stoned, quartered, flayed alive and given alive to the dogs, or to the forty Anthropophagi [a mythical race of cannibals] and man-eaters that he always has by him."[38]

Sir Anthony of course had his own view on Abbas's religion. He had already found the shah's "government differing so much from that which we call barbarousness" that he compared it flatteringly to Plato's *Republic*.[39] After many weeks in his company, conversing in a mix of Latin, Persian (Farsi), Italian and possibly even Spanish, he reflected on Abbas's theological beliefs, which he saw as positively Machiavellian:

> For the king knowing how potent a uniter of men's minds the self-same religion is for the tranquility of an estate: and the like dis-uniter several religions are for the disturbance of the peace of an estate, he is exceeding curious and vigilant to suppress through all his dominions, that religion of Mahomet which followeth the in-terpretation of Ussen [Uthman] and Omar [Umar], and to make his people cleave to that of Aly: not (as I judge) through any con-science, which carrieth him more to the one than the other; but

first to extirpate intrinsic factions, then to secure himself the more firmly against the Turks.[40]

It made sense for Sherley to conclude that the shah's Shi'a beliefs were as politically strategic as his suppression of the Sunni followers of Uthman and Umar, but his judgment may have revealed more about his own religious predisposition than about that of Shah Abbas.

After Sherley's party had spent nearly three months reveling in Qazvin, the shah invited them to accompany him to his new royal capital of Isfahan. When they arrived, Sir Anthony began the delicate task of finding a way to broach the subject of his political mission. For once in his life, he seems to have grasped the sensitivity of a Christian proposing an alliance with a Persian shah "to move him to war in so fit a time against the Turk," and he prevaricated while Abbas showed him the splendor of his new city. Finally, "taking the opportunity of the king's being alone with me and my brother in a garden" and using increasingly cryptic and periphrastic language, Sherley raised what he called "the enterprise." He argued that "the extreme tyranny of the Turk" continued to threaten the Persians, and that if Abbas wanted "the recovery of that which was by force and violence usurped from his state," there was a solution: "If it pleased him to invite the princes Christian to his amity," Abbas could forge a Shi'a-Christian alliance that would defeat the Ottomans and give the shah control over central Asia.[41]

Once the shah's advisers heard of Sherley's proposals, they were furious, and a protracted debate ensued. Many warned Abbas that "these Christians . . . were sent to disquiet your majesty's tranquility of your state." He should not jeopardize a hard-fought peace with the Turks nor intimate any military weakness by having to "beg an amity of the Christian princes." Besides, despite Abbas's recent victory over the Uzbeks, his army was still not strong enough to face the mightier Ottomans.

Others were more supportive of Sherley's proposals. One counselor pointed out that "this Christian hath brought with him a founder of artillery: let him be useful to your majesty"—although there are no records of such an expert in Sherley's team. As weeks went by without agreement, Sherley complained that talk of the proposals "did aggravate both the grief of my mind, and unquiet of my body," and he took to his bed.[42] As he did so, a Turkish ambassador arrived in Isfahan, warning Abbas to respect their truce and demanding that he cede territory to Mehmed III and acknowledge his servility by sending one of his sons as a hostage to Constantinople. It seemed that like Jenkinson, Sherley might soon be unceremoniously ejected from Persia in the face of the Ottomans' overwhelming political and military superiority.

At this point Shah Abbas paid Sherley an unexpected visit on his sickbed. If Sherley is to be believed, an extraordinary conversation ensued. The shah began by saying "he had no great inclination" to demean himself by allying with a divided group of Christian powers, "God having given him so ample, so rich and so warlike a dominion" as Persia. Sherley responded by arguing that Abbas would have to confront the Turks sooner rather than later, as their political demands and military campaigns against Persia "were likely rather to increase than diminish." He conceded that the Christians were divided, but contended that many, including the Spanish and the papacy, were already fighting the Ottomans, and would "embrace the amity, honor the name of your majesty, and unite themselves in any terms of princely alliance." He also suggested that the shah could strike at Ottoman hegemony in another way: "In giving liberty of Christian religion, so much abhorred of their part, and security of trade, goods and person to Christians," Abbas would circumvent Constantinople's control over commercial and pilgrimage routes in the region, and he would gain access to European "founders of ordnance, makers of all sorts of arms, and munitions."[43]

Sherley's proposals were optimistic to say the least, but, remarkably, Abbas responded to them. He agreed "to write to as many of the Christian princes as are greatest among them" to "apply themselves to our purpose" and allow "their merchants to repair to our dominions." Abbas made it clear that it was Sherley's responsibility to implement the initiative. "And because you have been the mover and persuader of this business, you also shall be the actor of it, assuring myself that my honor cannot be more securely reposed in any man's hands, than your own." Sherley was ecstatic: he now claimed the right to represent the shah's interests in Europe and to act like a Persian *mirza* with the authority to mingle with kings and emperors. Having left England in 1598 in the service of the Earl of Essex, intent on disrupting Spanish and papal policy in Italy, Sherley was now proposing to broker a grand anti-Ottoman alliance between Persia and Europe's Catholic rulers. Considering that official Elizabethan policy remained broadly pro-Ottoman, this was an extraordinary turn of events. As Sherley took on the mantle of the shah's ambassador to Europe, he must have known he was turning his back on any possible rehabilitation with the queen or her counselors. Perhaps he believed he could single-handedly change the queen's foreign policy. Perhaps his arrogance and hubris was such that he no longer cared.

As before, it is difficult to assess the veracity of Sherley's claims as little or no evidence has been found from the Persian side. The shah may have already decided to dispatch an embassy to Europe following the Turkish ambassador's provocative demands. Mainwaring recalled that Abbas immediately "sent away the Turk's ambassador . . . commanding him to tell his master the Turk [Mehmed III] that he would never rest until he were in the field with him."[44] Whatever actually passed between Sir Anthony and the shah at the Englishman's bedside, in April 1599 Abbas began a lavish round of feasting in preparation for the departure of Sherley's embassy. The shah prepared formal "Letters of Credence from the Great Sophy to the Christian Princes," stating that Sherley had come "of his own free will, out of Europe, into these parts," and that "when this gentleman comes unto your Christian princes, you shall credit him in whatsoever you demand or he shall say, as mine own person." Sherley was also given commercial privileges by Abbas "for all Christians to Trade and Traffic into Persia." These stated that Persia was "open to all Christian people and to their religion," and included a "patent for all Christian merchants, to repair and traffic in and through our dominions, without disturbances or molestations."[45] These were remarkable concessions that, if set beside Elizabeth's alliances with the Ottoman and Sa'adian rulers, gave England unprecedented commercial and diplomatic relations with the Islamic world, stretching over 4,300 miles from Marrakesh via Constantinople to Isfahan.

Sherley, now drunk on his own grandeur, began planning his

embassy. He agreed blithely with Abbas that his brother Sir Robert should stay behind in Persia, ostensibly to aid the shah in his military preparations, but obviously as a hostage to ensure that Sir Anthony would return. Perhaps as further insurance Abbas appointed a member of his trusted tribal cavalry, Husain Ali Beg Bayat, to join the embassy as an ambassador with Sherley, alongside four Persian secretaries, including Ali Beg's nephew Uruch Beg. The most surprising member of the party was a Portuguese Augustinian friar named Nicolò de Mello, who had arrived in Isfahan claiming to be not only the Spanish procurator to the Indies (an agent responsible for liaising between the Curia in Rome and its missionaries in the Indies), but the long-lost brother of the dead Portuguese king Sebastian I. De Mello intrigued Sherley, who introduced him to the shah, but the friar promptly denounced the Englishman and his mission. Moving quickly to defuse the situation and "stop this priest's mouth," Sherley explained to him that he "was sorry that he had not understood my purpose which was the general service of all Christendom, and that he might make himself great, by bearing a part in such a holy service."[46] While acknowledging that it was a risky plan to travel with a hostile Augustinian friar as well as a Persian cavalry officer, Sherley invited de Mello to join his party.

By May 1599, after spending five months in Persia, Sherley and his embassy were ready to leave. It was an ill-assorted crew of at least twenty-four, excluding servants, boasting two ambassadors (Sherley and Ali Beg), Augustinian and Franciscan friars, a retinue of Persians and the long-suffering Mainwaring, Parry and Pinçon, along with thirty-two crates of gifts for the Christian princes. Their political mission made returning via Ottoman territory impossible, so with Abbas eager to foster closer commercial relations with the new Russian tsar Boris Godunov, the embassy headed north toward the Caspian, and from there up the Volga toward Moscow. Divested of his semiregal status at the Persian court, Sir Anthony started behaving badly almost immediately, although on this occasion it seemed with some justification. Almost as soon as they departed, Parry learned that de Mello had "confessed he was but an ordinary Augustine friar, and in a gamesome vein he further confessed how he would bring men's wives, after he had shriven them, to his bent." He said he liked nothing more than to be "with a whore at night." When the Franciscans revealed further details of de Mello's duplicity, Sherley kept him under armed guard for the rest of the journey. He was also soon quarreling violently with Ali Beg and the Persians over various unspecified "misdemeanors." When they reached the Caspian Sea, bad weather threatened to capsize the entire ill-tempered mission. As the storm hit, "one heard a dreadful medley of voices and prayers," recalled Pinçon. "We of the [Protestant] religion prayed in one way; there were some Portuguese monks who threw figures of the *Agnus Dei* into the sea to appease it, and muttered certain words, repeating 'Virgin Mary,' 'St. John' and the *In Manus* [Evening Prayer]. The Mahommedans invoked 'Ali, Ali Mahomet,' but instead of all these I feared that the Devil would come to carry this rabble to Hell."[47] They survived to reach Moscow in November, but the mood in the party remained tense.

If the plan was to incorporate the new tsar as the first member of a grand Euro-Persian alliance, it was a miserable failure. Godunov, a shrewd and capable politician, had succeeded to the tsardom following the collapse of the Rurik dynasty, and was suspicious of any diplomatic initiatives that might threaten his questionable accession to power. Upon his arrival Sherley was promptly arrested for ten days by a "crew of aqua-vitae-bellied fellows, clad in coats of cloth of gold." When he and Ali Beg were granted an audience with the tsar, an ambiguity relating to the ambassadors' status arose, causing the first of many diplomatic incidents. By appointing two ambassadors, neither with precedence over the other, Abbas had invited obvious confusion, which resurfaced when the tsar requested to see the Persians before Sherley, who "utterly refused to go in that order . . . especially he being a Christian and they pagans."[48] Sherley's notorious sensitivity in matters of protocol alienated him from both the tsar and the Persian ambassador; Godunov "vexed and molested" him, while Ali Beg goaded de Mello into accusing Sherley of being a lowborn spy, with no desire to further anyone's interests other than his own. Boris's officials seized Abbas's letters of introduction, whose studied vagueness seemed to confirm the Russians' suspicions; once again Sherley was placed under arrest.

Not for the first time, the Englishman's reckless behavior managed to save him. When summoned by Boris to answer de Mello's charges, "being by that graceless and ungrateful friar further provoked, he, not able, though instantly he should have died for it, to suppress his heat, gave the fat friar such a sound box on the face, his double cause of choler redoubling his might, desire of revenge withal augmenting the same, that down falls the friar, as if he had been struck down with a thunderbolt."[49] Remarkably, instead of arresting him for such violent behavior, the Russians were impressed by Sherley's "courage and high resolution," and promptly dropped the charges against him. In response he mentioned that de Mello had been secretly celebrating the Roman Catholic mass during his stay in Moscow. Catholicism was detested and outlawed by the Russian Orthodox tsar, who immediately banished de Mello to the Solovetsky Monastery on the White Sea (which in the 1920s became one of the earliest labor camps in the infamous Soviet gulag).

His honor partly restored, Sherley wintered in Moscow and prepared to leave in the spring of 1600. He now wrote to his supporters back in London, justifying his actions and positioning himself for a return to England. In February he sent a letter to the counselor of his patron the Earl of Essex, Anthony Bacon, elder brother of the queen's counselor Francis. In his letter Sherley boasted of his achievements in Persia. "I have opened the Indies for our merchants," he fantasized, with the result that "they shall have more power than the Portuguese, through Persia they may bring as secure as between London and St. Albans." Spinning ever more fanciful and grandiose schemes, Sherley professed to be in correspondence with "the King of Tabur [Lahore]," the "mightiest king of the Indies," the Mughal emperor Akbar the Great. He claimed Akbar "hath desired of me some man which knows the wars to discipline his men," and that he was ready to send a Captain Thomas Powell, at that time in Persia with his brother Robert, to assist him in attacking the Portuguese. Sherley's extravagant plans did not end there. He had an even crazier scheme to conquer the Indies that involved the illegitimate children of the unfortunate Portuguese pretender Don António (who had died in poverty in Paris in 1595). He suggested that "if any of Don António's sons will come into his [Akbar's] country he shall be assisted with money and men, for the recovering of the rest of the Indies." Unsurprisingly, Bacon did not rise to this lurid fantasy of an alliance between Portuguese renegades and Mughal Indians dislodging the Habsburg-controlled Portuguese in the Indian Ocean.

In any case, back in London Anthony Bacon was facing far more pressing matters. The previous year his master Essex had been appointed Lord Lieutenant of Ireland with the task of defeating the country's Catholic chieftains, who were led by Hugh O'Neill, Earl of Tyrone. The subsequent military campaign was a complete disaster. Essex agreed to a humiliating peace with O'Neill against the queen's explicit orders and then fled Ireland for London in September 1599. His reckless actions left him in deep disgrace with Elizabeth, who placed him under house arrest in London over the winter of 1599–1600. As Sherley spun ever more improbable tales of grand political strategy, one of the few men capable of ensuring his honorable return to England was losing the capacity to do so.

In June 1600 Sherley and his party abandoned Moscow and retraced Anthony Jenkinson's steps toward Arkhangelsk on the White Sea. There he wrote to Essex, clearly having been informed of the earl's arrest and political isolation, telling him, "I am plunged in grief to hear of your Lordship's misfortunes, but my devotion to you is as great as ever."[50] This did not prevent him from meeting Muscovy Company merchants and writing to Essex's rival Robert Cecil, much to the dismay of the Essex faction. Sherley knew he was in disgrace for leaving England without royal permission and, even worse, brokering a Persian alliance that now threatened to upset Elizabeth's cordial relations with the Ottomans (the queen was currently preoccupied with the elaborate exchange of gifts with Safiye Sultan). With his habitually florid and unintentionally comical style he tried to be contrite: "Yet do I upon the knees of my heart acknowledge the greatness of my fault in departing from her majesty without the blessedness of her gracious favor," he began. But then he bragged, "I have laid open the treasures of other countries for her subjects," adding, "I have only used the favor and love of the king of Persia for her glory." He then apologized for further delaying his return home. "Neither is it my will," he maintained unconvincingly, "that I am first gone to the Emperor of Germany," the

Habsburg Holy Roman Emperor Rudolf II. Still, he could not resist offering the queen a little advice, pointing out that Tsar Boris had a daughter and if Elizabeth could find a suitable "gentleman of spirit whom she will vouchsafe to call cousin" then an Anglo-Russian marriage would be "to the infinite benefit of her merchants."[51]

Robert Cecil was unimpressed. He wrote to Ambassador Henry Lello in Constantinople, another victim of Sherley's duplicity, complaining of Sir Anthony's arrogance in having "taken upon him to be an ambassador to the princes of Europe, to unite themselves in a league with the Persian, for which purpose he came through Muscovy." Cecil reported that the queen's fury over Sherley's reckless scheme had been intensified as he had had "the audacity to write to the queen for leave to come to her. . . . Hereupon her majesty increased her former displeasure toward him . . . as by no means she will suffer him to come into the kingdom."[52]

The way home was now closed. Perhaps Sherley knew, because his behavior became even more impulsive and erratic. As the embassy prepared to leave Arkhangelsk, the Persians accused him of stealing the shah's thirty-four cases of presents for the Christian princes and selling them off through the local Muscovy Company agents. Sherley denied this, claiming that he had opened the cases and found that the gifts were an embarrassment, and worth only a fraction of their estimated value of 400,000 crowns. Rather than risk humiliation by presenting them to Europe's rulers, Sherley said he had quietly sent them back to Persia. Whatever happened, they were never seen again, and the imputation that Sherley had profited from them blighted the rest of the embassy.

In late June the embassy sailed out of Arkhangelsk, traveling first to Stade, then to Emden on the German coast, which they reached on August 30, 1600. Over the next three months they traveled in state through Germany, entertained by delighted and astonished princes as they moved south toward Rudolf's court in Prague. They arrived in Prague without much incident on October 11, and at Rudolf's expense settled into a luxurious lifestyle. Sherley quickly racked up his usual mountain of debt and had his portrait engraved alongside Ali Beg's by the court artist Aegidius Sadeler. The Venetian ambassador Piero Duodo reported, "What the mission of this Embassy may be we do not know yet," but he believed that "it is a matter of moment and that there is question of a written treaty. There are other and wilder rumors, that the Persian will become a Christian."[53]

Within weeks the two ambassadors had been granted an audience with the curious emperor Rudolf. Duodo followed events with a keen interest and on November 8 he reported to the Seignory: "Yesterday the ambassadors from the King of Persia had an audience. The Englishman spoke in Spanish, and the substance of that king's offer to his imperial majesty [Rudolf] was that he would arm against the Turk, and would also make the Arabs and the Georgians take the field with him."[54] The Venetian noted with satisfaction that the Spanish ambassador was appalled by the proposed alliance, which threatened Spain's interests by proposing to divert the spice trade overland through Russia and into the Low Countries.

Rudolf was clearly impressed by Sherley and Ali Beg. He issued a formal response to their orations almost immediately, announcing that it was "right pleasing" to receive them, and that he would propose an alliance "with other Christian Princes against the Turk," whom he had "been struggling against without intermission." He pointed out that he had "already attempted to form a league with other Sovereigns. He will do his best to secure such a league; and meantime he promises that he will continue the war with all his might, and will omit nothing which may be needed to break the power of the Turk. He will summon a Diet of the Empire, will raise funds, and will urge all Christian nations to join him; he will send embassies, and will endeavor to prohibit the commerce of Christians with Turks." If the Persians "should do much the same on his side with the Georgians and Muscovites," they could anticipate an irresistible military alliance and "the following spring should see a joint attack."[55]

Rudolf's bellicose rhetoric was in fact not much more than a minor variation on ineffectual Christian calls for crusade stretching back hundreds of years. The proposal began to unravel almost immediately. Rudolf's advisers suggested that Sherley and Ali Beg report back to the shah, to whom the emperor would send his own messengers with a formal offer of a military and political alliance. Their refusal aroused suspicions: did this vain and profligate Englishman have the authority to propose a pan-European alliance with Persia when everyone knew that Elizabeth was in league with the Turks? Even if it were politically feasible, the Venetian diplomat Duodo noted that the coordination of a war against the Ottomans was logistically impossible. During the winter of 1600–1601, the astute Venetian was busy discovering Sherley's plans, writing triumphantly to the doge, "I suspected some secret negotiation, and my suspicions were just." He provided a devastating assessment of Sherley's threadbare scheme and increasingly straitened circumstances. "His object is to divert the India trade altogether from Egypt, and send it through Muscovy. Grand schemes, impossible to accomplish. I have seen his credentials; they do not give him the title of ambassador, which the Persian who is with him has. He has spent much and made presents. Although living at his majesty's charges, he has contracted 46,000 thalers of debt; and his creditors are after him."[56]

It was time for Sherley to move on once more, and in February 1601 he left Prague and his debts behind and headed for Italy. He went with Rudolf's blessing and more than two thousand of his florins. With the proposals for an alliance quietly dropped, it must have felt more like a payoff, the relieved Rudolf happy to see the back of the troublesome Englishman and his sullen Persians. Slowly but surely, doors started shutting on Sherley. He planned to travel to Venice, but when he sent emissaries ahead to announce his imminent arrival, they returned with news that a Turkish delegation had arrived, and considering Sherley's anti-Ottoman credentials it would be "inconvenient" for him to enter the city. They headed instead for Rome via Florence, where a Medici representative gave a damning assessment: "This Englishman does not appear bodily hale and sound to me. I know nothing about his soul. His face does not strike my fancy. I feel that if we were to go to an inn together for dinner, I would end up with the bill."[57]

Events seemed to be taking their toll on Sherley, who spent the whole journey to Rome fighting with Ali Beg over their formal titles and the lost presents. "They arrived in such a state of hostility over precedence," remarked the Spanish ambassador in early April 1601, "that they came to blows" and had to be separated.[58] Oblivious to their behavior, Pope Clement VIII received them with great public fanfare. Like Rudolf II, he hoped—somewhat optimistically—that the Persians offered a chance to challenge the Ottomans' military supremacy. The French cardinal Arnaud d'Ossat was not so sure; he reported that "the Pope has given them lodging in the Borgo, near St. Peter's," over which they fought for the best apartment, and that no audience had been arranged because "each claims the right to precede his companion." Sherley claimed priority as a Christian, but Ali Beg accused him of lacking formal diplomatic credentials and reiterated the charge of stealing presents that the Persian might have presented to Pope Clement. Having fought on their arrival, they even returned to their lodgings and "fell on each other on the staircase." It was another farcical scene, but also tragic for a proud and haughty man like Sherley that a statesman like d'Ossat should regard him as absurd and his mission as faintly comical. "Perhaps someone may be found," wrote d'Ossat drily, "who shall tell them that since they, being but two and sent by the same prince on the same mission, cannot agree between themselves, they will find it difficult to bring about a union of so many Christian princes and others in order to ruin the Empire of the Turk."[59]

It seemed nothing could be done to resolve their difficulties, until finally a compromise was reached. Both men were named "orators" and given separate audiences with the pope. On April 25, Sherley went first, sitting cross-legged in the Persian fashion before Clement, assuring him that "God had so touched the heart of his master [Shah Abbas] that he and all his kingdom might be converted." The pope's obvious delight at this news evaporated at the following day's audience when Ali Beg accused Sherley of all kinds of "fraud and craft," from embracing Islam to stealing the pope's gifts. The diplomatic consensus was that Clement took the Persian's side "because he has always spoken consistently. The Englishman is doubtless a liar and unreliable though a great talker and well informed."[60]

It was at this time that news from London reached Rome about Sherley's patron the Earl of Essex. On Sunday, February 8, 1601, the disaffected Essex had left his house on the Strand and marched into the City with three hundred armed supporters. Londoners refused to support him, and by Sunday evening he was under arrest for treason. On February 25, he was beheaded at the Tower of London.[61] The devastated Sherley had lost his biggest patron. It didn't take him long to cast around for another. In April the Spanish ambassador wrote to King Philip III about Sherley's situation. "The Englishman was very much bound to the Count of Essex," he declared, "and since the latter's imprisonment and death, he is completely without hope of ever again being admitted to the presence of the queen. . . . [As a result] he is determined to serve your majesty if your majesty should so desire."

Sherley was playing all angles. D'Ossat told the French court that Sherley had visited him and "wished to be my servant," offering his services to Henry IV. The wily cardinal advised caution, revealing that the Spanish "have exploited and interrogated" Sherley already, "and have made him fine offers in order to win him over to their side, as much by reason of their ancient designs against England as for these affairs of Persia and the Turk. And it may be that he, being far from his own country and in need of money, will accept a post from the Spaniards, who pay more willingly for wrong-doing than for any other thing."[62]

Another event seems to have propelled Sherley into the arms of the Spanish. On April 30, the Jesuit Robert Parsons, rector of the English College in Rome, wrote a letter to a fellow Jesuit in England that made extraordinary claims about Sherley. In it Parsons insisted that he "denieth himself to have been a Protestant ever since his first being at Venice [in 1598] for that there he was reconciled [to Catholicism]. . . . And since his being at Prague, and here also, he hath used to frequent confession every seven or eight days." Parsons also reported that over Easter Sherley had dined at the English College, where he discussed the "likelihood of casting religion [missionary work] in Persia." Parsons added that Sherley "hath no great minds to return any more into England as well for that the Earl of Essex and most of his special friends are gone," and that "the queen resteth £22,000 in his debt."[63] Honesty and modesty had never been Sherley's strongest qualities, but even by his standards these revelations of conversion and treachery were shocking. He never confessed to the exact time or place of his conversion. Maybe it was genuine, but given the circumstances it smacks of desperation. Perhaps it was another example of his claim that religion was a pragmatic "uniter of men's minds," no more than a "toy." Perhaps he was now lost in such a tangled web of deceit that he could no longer tell the difference between belief and disbelief.

On May 10, 1601, Pope Clement officially dismissed the ambassadors, giving them both a thousand crowns in an effort to get rid of them as quickly as possible. Their destination was ostensibly Spain, to deliver the shah's letters to King Philip III, but to all intents and purposes the embassy was over, destroyed by factionalism, rivalries and apostasy. The Persian cook, barber and undersecretary all converted to Catholicism and vowed to stay in Rome, while the mortified Ali Beg left immediately for Spain. En route, another three members of his surviving retinue converted, including his nephew Uruch Beg, who was baptized Don Juan, settled in Spain and wrote a colorful memoir of his escapades. For some reason Sherley did not travel with them but stayed in Rome. At this stage his activities become more opaque than ever. He wrote offering his services to the Stuart king James VI of Scotland, perhaps aware that James was the most likely candidate to succeed the aged Elizabeth. James appears to have been taken in by Sherley, and he would prove to be a remarkably forgiving ally over subsequent years. Sherley wrote darkly that he was about to leave Rome "and am gone in that sort that, except the Pope himself, no man knoweth whither." The intimation was clear: despite the dismissal of his embassy, his conversion had led him to offer to spy for Clement. Whether he had actually made such an offer, and if so whether it had been accepted, is unknown. By the end of May 1601, Sherley had claimed at one point or another to be working for England, Scotland, Spain, France, Persia and the pope, representing Muslim, Protestant and Catholic interests. The only significant power missing was the Ottomans, but his path to them was closed, because a servant had stolen his Persian letters and sent them to Constantinople.

By the time he left Rome Sherley was a renegade, working (perhaps) for everyone but wanted by nobody. The Persian embassy was over and he needed a new patron and new adventures. His only option was to head for Venice, where he arrived in the late summer. He had been there three years earlier as a Protestant Englishman proposing to break the Spanish control over the Persian trade. Now he was working for at least two Catholic powers and was notoriously trying to build a

Euro-Persian alliance against the Ottomans. The Venetians were attempting to negotiate yet another entente with Sultan Mehmed III, so they treated Sherley's appearance with the utmost suspicion, as did everyone else. Sherley arrived claiming to represent the Scottish king James's interests as well as those of the Spanish (and probably the papacy), which earned him the attentions of two of Cecil's agents, who followed his every move.

As usual, trouble soon found him. A bullet was fired into his house, he dabbled in alchemy, and there were the inevitable accusations of plots, thefts and debts. In June 1602 one of Cecil's spies wrote with wry skepticism that Sherley "hath been lately assaulted in this city, or at least maketh it to be given out so, and that one of his company was sorely hurt; himself happily escaping the blow, was borne over a bridge into the water." Sherley's household muttered darkly that the culprit was probably a Jew in the pay of the Turks, although one of Cecil's spies reported that it was more likely a creditor seeking settlement of a wine bill. Dozens of merchants cheated by Sherley over the years must have wished they had pushed him off the bridge; the only surprise is that it took so long for someone to try.

By the spring of 1603, Sherley's behavior was becoming ever more capricious. He proposed increasingly fantastical schemes to the Spanish, demanded that he be allowed back to England, and even ingratiated himself with a newly arrived Persian merchant. It was all too much for the Venetians, who arrested and imprisoned him that March. His situation was made all the more precarious when news of his feckless elder brother, Sir Thomas, reached Venice that spring. In February, after attacking Venetian shipping in the Cyclades Islands, Thomas had been captured by the Ottomans and was now languishing in prison in Constantinople. With Sir Robert still a hostage in Persia, the three brothers were now all being held in captivity, by three different foreign powers. Sir Thomas's privateering was seen as yet another example of the Sherleys' anti-Venetian activities, and can have done Anthony little favor.

During the final years of Elizabeth's reign, nobody was better known for his oriental adventures than Sir Anthony Sherley. His exploits were so outlandish that Shakespeare had no need to write a play about them:

the passing reference in *Twelfth Night* was all that his audience needed to imagine a bombastic, swaggering, slightly ridiculous nobleman. His was the tragicomic story of a man who aspired to the international grandeur of advising sultans, shahs and emperors, but who was reduced to exile and obloquy. Ultimately Sherley resembled not the comical, aristocratic rogue Sir Toby Belch but the tragic Malvolio: an avid social climber, humiliated in his schemes of preferment, raging against his enemies—the Persian, Turkish, Russian, even English dogs who conspired against him—still planning to be avenged on the whole pack of them. A recusant Catholic who ended up allying himself with Shi'a Muslims in opposition to a Protestant-Sunni alliance between Elizabethan England and the Ottoman sultans, Sherley exemplified just how complex these relationships had become. But such relationships were also fraught with danger and disenchantment. Like so many Elizabethans before him, he had gone eastward in the hope of riches and preferment, but ended up disillusioned and displaced, a stranger in a strange land, with little sense of where home was anymore.

In 1888 the Reverend Scott Surtees of Dinsdale-on-Tees joined in the fashionable debates over the authorship of Shakespeare's plays with the publication of a short pamphlet called *William Shakespeare, of Stratford-on-Avon, His Epitaph Unearthed, and the Author of the Plays run to Ground.* Instead of endorsing more obvious candidates like Sir Francis Bacon or the Earl of Oxford, Surtees was drawn to a more cosmopolitan individual, someone with naval and battlefield experience, a background in law, trade, diplomacy and "the habits and the ways, the customs, dresses, manners, laws of almost every known nation," including Aleppo, Algiers, Bermuda, Cyprus, Greece, India, Mauretania, Mexico, Persia, Rome, Russia, Tunis, Venice, Verona and Vienna, and someone obsessed with naming his characters "Antonio." So, Surtees asked triumphantly, "What is Antonio everywhere but Anthony 'writ new'?" As far as Surtees was concerned, the answer to the authorship controversy was obvious: "Anthony Sherley and no other was he who wrote these plays."[64]

11

More Than a Moor

In June 1599, just weeks after Sir Anthony Sherley had left Isfahan for Moscow, the English merchant and spy Jasper Thomson wrote a letter from Marrakesh to his relative Richard Thomson in London. Jasper's letter described a recent meeting with al-Mansur's principal secretary, al-Caid Azouz, at which he recounted that Azouz had discovered that "I had been employed some years in Turkey and that, in this last journey into Hungary which the Grand Signor [Mehmed III] made in person, I was present." Al-Mansur ordered Azouz to spend "the whole night" questioning Thomson "upon the many particularities concerning the Grand Signor and his proceedings (for I see nothing is more pleasing to the king than to hear that the Turks' affairs succeeded not well)." As Thomson related news of recent Austrian victories over the Turks in Hungary, Azouz turned the conversation to England's relations with the Ottomans. He "was desirous to know what reason or wherefore the queen had required aid of the Turk against the Spaniard." Thomson protested rather weakly that "never any such thing was demanded," but after "much talk" about Elizabeth's policy toward Spain and the Ottomans, as well as about the size of her army in France, Azouz asked the Englishman

> whether I thought the queen would be content to make such another army to land in some port in Spain with twenty thousand footmen, and with vessels to transport twenty thousand horses and men from Barbary, and so to join together in conquest of the

country; whereof, said he, there is no doubt but it may be performed, if her majesty and his king should join together in the
action.[1]

He wanted to know if Thomson had "friends that could procure by
word of mouth to move the queen therein." The Englishman responded
with understandable caution. The Thomson clan were servants of Sir
Robert Cecil's and always on the lookout for intelligence they could
relay to their London paymaster. Nevertheless, Jasper could not afford
to be presumptuous. He told the Moroccan that he was unaware of the
queen's latest policy toward Spain, especially in the wake of Philip II's
recent death in September 1598, but advised him that, if al-Mansur was
serious, "it were good he sent an ambassador to her majesty, about the
negotiation of whom I was assured he should have a princely answer."
He concluded his letter with news of the return of al-Mansur's military
commander responsible for the conquest of Songhai, the vast west
Afrian empire that included parts of Nigeria, back in 1591. "He brought
with him thirty camels laden with tyber, which is unrefined gold," he
wrote, estimating the gold's value at over £600,000, equivalent to
Elizabeth's entire annual revenue, and twice the national debt. He also
noted the arrival of a "great store of pepper, unicorns' horns and a
certain kind of wood for dyers . . . all which he presented unto the
king, with fifty horse, and great quantity of eunuchs, dwarfs and
women and men slaves, besides fifteen virgins, the king's daughters of
Gago [Songhai], which he sendeth to be the king's concubines. You
must note all these be of the coal black hair, for that country yieldeth
no other."[2] Like many of his contemporaries working in the Muslim
world, Thomson switched effortlessly between cool political calcula-
tion and lurid exoticism.

Judging by the flurry of correspondence between the English and
Moroccan rulers over the next few months, Azouz's proposal was
clearly taken seriously in London. In March 1600, Elizabeth wrote to
request the release of nine Dutch captives held by the Moroccans, and
by June al-Mansur told her he was sending a diplomatic embassy disguised as a trade delegation traveling via Aleppo, a somewhat unlikely

route to London. The delegation was led by Abd al-Wahid bin Masoud bin Muhammad al-Annuri, al-Mansur's adviser, who was given powers to discuss a proposed Anglo-Moroccan attack on Spain "verbally and in secret."[3] News of the plan leaked, and speculation soon mounted among the English merchants in Marrakesh. One of them, John Waring, wrote to Robert Cecil about the imminent departure of al-Annuri's embassy, along with the "nine Dutchmen taken long since captives by the barbarians and became slaves to Mully Hamett, King of Barbary." He observed that "it is thought most meet that the said captives do accompany the Moors, until they come one with the other unto her majesty or your honor's presence, to acknowledge her majesty's great bounty and liberality."[4] The real motives behind the embassy could be hidden under the pretense of trade and the routine repatriation of Christian captives, which made Elizabeth look good in the eyes of the Dutch Calvinists.

A few weeks later Jasper Thomson's cousin George sent Cecil a detailed report of what to expect from al-Annuri and his entourage. Although he confessed that the mission was "so secret that none knoweth the ground of their going," his personal contacts with most of the Moroccans meant he could provide his master with a fulsome report concerning the whole crew. The delegation included two prominent merchants, "Side al-Hage Messa [Hajj Musa]," who lost the opportunity to lead it when allegations surfaced that he had withheld precious stones from al-Mansur, and "Al-Hage Bahanet," both delegated to represent commercial interests. They were accompanied by a friend of Thomson's called "Side Abdala Dodar [Abdullah Dudar], an Andalusian who goeth for trudgman or interpreter, who telleth me he will speak Italian to her majesty; but I take it he will use the Spanish tongue, being his natural language." Thomson also provided a detailed description of al-Annuri, who he believed was "a natural Moor born, but of the race of Fessians, which the natural Moor holdeth baseness," as Fez was incorporated into the Sa'adian dynasty only in 1548. Thomson warned Cecil that, although al-Annuri possessed a "sharpness of wit and gift of pen," he was a proud and boastful man, with a "baseness of mind" who lacked "gentility." This condemnation should be treated with some caution, as Thomson also told Cecil that al-Annuri "much relieth on Waring's friends and no doubt but the merchants which trade to this place will be liberal unto him."[5] As he wrote, three of his cousins were embroiled in an interminable legal dispute with John Waring over goods and money, which became so intractable that Elizabeth wrote to al-Mansur asking him to intervene.[6] Whether he did so or not is unclear, but if al-Annuri should be treated with suspicion, then so should George Thomson.

The Moroccan ambassador's arrival was anticipated throughout the spring of 1600, as diplomats from both sides negotiated the terms of his mission. In late June a sixteen-man delegation left Morocco on board the *Eagle*. As they sailed north, English spies were writing to Robert Cecil, telling him that a Spanish warship had tried to intercept the *Eagle* and adding, "the Spaniards here reported that our queen (whom the Lord long preserve!) was dead."[7]

On August 8, the *Eagle* docked in Dover, where representatives of the Barbary Company trading in Morocco met al-Annuri and brought his party to London. Cecil entrusted their care to Thomas Gerard, a prominent Staffordshire landowner and member of Parliament. It was a shrewd move. Gerard had been a close friend and supporter of Essex, but following the earl's return from Ireland he had seen that Essex's star was on the wane and had switched his political allegiance. Cecil was eager to secure Gerard's loyalty going forward.

On August 11, Gerard wrote Cecil to confirm that he had met al-Annuri and had arranged for the ambassador and his entourage to stay in Anthony Radcliffe's house on the Strand, near the Royal Exchange. A former London sheriff and master of the Guild of Merchant Taylors, Radcliffe was a good choice to host the Moroccan delegation, as he could put them in touch with London's merchant community. On August 15 the Moroccans landed at Tower Wharf and were taken in four coaches to Radcliffe's home. Gerard reported that not everyone in the neighborhood seemed pleased with the embassy's arrival. Some observers worried that "they are very strangely attired and behavioured."[8] Gerard had approached London's Barbary merchants to pay "for the ambassador's diet, but they all plead poverty, and except her majesty discharge it, it will rest upon himself." The delegation was to be accommodated "without scandal, and for that purpose they are lodged in a house apart, where they feed alone."[9] Five days later they rode through Cheapside to Westminster, crossed over to Lambeth by boat and then took the ten-mile coach ride to Nonsuch Palace in Surrey for an audience with the queen.

One eyewitness described at some length the elaborate royal preparations for the Moroccan ambassador's visit: "Rich hangings and furniture sent for from Hampton Court; the guard very strong, in their rich coats; the pensioners [royal bodyguards] with their axes; the lords of the Order [of the Garter] with their collars; a full court of lords and ladies." Al-Annuri "passed through a guard of halberds to the council chamber, where he rested; he was brought to the presence, so to the privy chamber, and so to the gallery; where her Majesty sat at the further end in very great state, and gave them audience."[10] The formalities dispensed with, the Moroccan and English delegations began discussing the business at hand.

Their conversation, held in Spanish, translated for the queen by the diplomat and courtier Sir Lewis Lewkenor, touched primarily on the commercial relations between the two crowns, but one of the English courtiers reported, "Ere they departed, the interpreter of the embassy spoke Italian, and desired to deliver some thing in private, which her majesty granted."[11] No reliable record remains of what they discussed, but one of the English diplomats wrote that at the end of al-Annuri's reception Elizabeth called in the Dutch ambassador and made a great show of handing over the nine Dutch prisoners whose release she had secured as a condition for al-Annuri's visit.[12] By this account she appeared to be using the captives' release to show off to the watching Dutch her power over Morocco. Another observer, a merchant named Rowland Whyte, offered a different interpretation of why the Dutch were called in. Whyte noted, "It is given out that they come for her majesty's letters to the Turk, to whom a brother of this king of Barbary is fled, to complain against him."[13] One perspective stressed England's anti-Catholic alliance with the Dutch and the Moors; the other, Elizabeth's alliance with the Ottoman sultan. Whatever was actually said, many present would have understood this as a meeting of three of Catholic Spain's greatest political and theological enemies whose real agenda went far beyond trade agreements.

Following the audience with the queen, the Moroccan delegation returned to its central London lodgings. Over the next few months many of Elizabeth's courtiers believed that what at first appeared to be just another trade delegation—admittedly from an exotic part of the world—was actually a secret attempt to initiate a new military alliance with plans to invade Spain, and possibly to launch a concerted attack on al-Mansur's other great enemy, the Ottomans, notwithstanding Elizabeth's continued friendship with them. If concluded, such an alliance would set Christian against Christian, and Muslim against Muslim, in an unprecedented and unholy alliance.

A second audience was arranged three weeks later, this time at Oatlands Palace in Surrey. Rowland Whyte wrote that what al-Annuri "delivered was in private to the queen; his business hath been very secretly handled, which is not yet come to light; it is supposed that he makes good offers to her majesty, if she will be pleased to aid him with shipping, fit for his ports, to conduct in safety some treasure he hath by mines in part of the Indies conquered by him."[14] There is no truth whatsoever to Whyte's claims that the Moroccans were trying to enlist Elizabeth's help in smuggling New World treasure across the Atlantic, but his garbled report did bear some relationship to what transpired.

The proposal al-Annuri had been instructed to submit to Elizabeth at Oatlands was in fact one of the most audacious in the history of Anglo-Islamic relations. In a memorandum dated September 13, 1600, al-Annuri explained that he was offering a formal military alliance that would result in the English and Moroccan fleets combining to attack Spain. Having come to London "to speak in secret to her serene majesty" about "the King of Spain's perfidious ways and dealings, and his incessant treachery," al-Annuri argued that it would "be an act of compassion and humanity for the benefit of all mankind if her serene majesty should embrace the perpetual friendship between her and the serene emperor his master and join forces against the King of Spain, their common foe and enemy." England and Morocco would invade

Spain together to realize the long-standing Moroccan dream of a Muslim reconquest of Al-Andalus (the Arab name for the Spanish mainland). "He will take the war to Spain," wrote al-Annuri,

> since our land is closer. Moreover, we have a large cavalry and infantry and all manner of munitions, as well as gunpowder and everything else needed to wage war, and plenty of wheat and other provisions. We also have forests with trees for shipbuilding, and iron to fit them, pursuant to the art of war. And should Her Serene Majesty capture any strongholds or cities in Spain that are close to us and which she wishes to supply with soldiers, munitions or money, the Emperor his master shall see to all this, because the Emperor will accede with great love to whatever Her Serene Majesty should ask of him, bound by the ancient friendship between them.[15]

An attack on Spain was not all that the Moroccan king proposed. Al-Annuri was instructed to suggest an even more audacious joint campaign against Spain's colonies in the Americas and the Far East:

> If the two Serene Majesties should forge this alliance, they could also wrest the East and West Indies from the Spanish, thus strengthening both Her Serene Majesty and the Emperor and weakening the King of Spain, because his strength as King of Spain comes solely from his control of the Indies.
>
> The Emperor would meet the needs of Her Serene Majesty's fleet in terms of wheat, munitions, gunpowder and provisions, as well as infantry and money. He would be best placed to supply the infantry because his people would be better accustomed to the heat of the Indies. Indeed, His Majesty the Emperor has conquered a very powerful kingdom on the River Niger in Guinea in which he has won land spanning ninety days' march and taken eighty-six thousand towns and cities and supplied them with all they need, as well as soldiers and munitions; and his people have borne the great heat of the hot climate there.[16]

Al-Mansur's relations with Elizabeth now led him to believe he could rid the world of Catholic Spain altogether. It seems ridiculously far-fetched, but the response of Elizabeth's advisers suggests that any proposal from a Muslim ruler that threatened to open up a new front against the Spanish was given serious consideration.

In the end the queen and her advisers demurred over the proposed alliance. Perhaps they feared fracturing their close commercial and diplomatic ties with the Ottomans. Instead they countered with their own offer. They seem to have believed that al-Annuri was not originally from Fez as Thomson believed, but was a Morisco who had "reverted" to Islam. Cecil knew that al-Mansur regarded the allegiance of the Moriscos with deep suspicion, even though they hated the Spanish as much as the Moors did. Based on this assumption, Elizabeth's advisers offered al-Annuri the opportunity to join the English forces in their ongoing campaign against Spain, which was at this point primarily waged at sea rather than on land.

At least one of the ambassador's party, the translator Abdullah Dudar, was unquestionably a Morisco (or "Andalusian") whose native tongue was Spanish, and it appears that he and Hajj Musa led some kind of revolt against al-Annuri, possibly because they were interested in accepting the English offer. On October 15, the indefatigable diarist John Chamberlain observed, "The Barbarians take their leave some time this week to go homeward; for our merchants nor mariners will not carry them into Turkey, because they think it a matter odious and scandalous to the world to be too friendly or familiar with infidels." Then, exhibiting the contradictory approach of so many Englishmen toward the Moors, Chamberlain continued, "But yet it is no small honor to us that nations so far remote, and every way different, should meet here to admire the glory and magnificence of our Queen of Sheba."[17] The Old Testament story of the oriental Queen of Sheba visiting Solomon is inverted by Chamberlain, who sees Elizabeth as an aged Sheba awaiting visitations from the other side of the world. Six days later, Chamberlain noted, "The Barbarians were yesterday at court to take their leave and will be gone shortly; but the eldest of them [Hajj Musa], which was a kind of priest or prophet, hath taken his leave of the world and is gone to prophesy *apud inferos* [in Hell] and to seek out Mahound their mediator."[18]

Chamberlain's rather poor joke was followed by subsequent reports with far darker accusations. The London chronicler John Stow wrote, "They poisoned their interpreter being born in Granada, because he commended the estate and bounty of England. The like violence was thought to be done unto their reverend aged pilgrim [Hajj Musa], lest he should manifest England's honor to their disgrace. It was generally judged, by their demeanours, that they were rather espials than honorable ambassadors, for they omitted nothing that might damnify the English merchants."[19]

Had al-Annuri murdered rebellious members of his party on the Strand and then ordered a hasty departure? Or were the rumors of murder and insurrection malicious slanders resulting from disagreements between various commercial and political factions? As speculation grew, the Privy Council was debating action against English merchants artificially inflating the price of Barbary sugar, while petitioning the Levant Company to cover the costs of transporting the Moroccan delegation to Aleppo.

Elizabeth responded to al-Annuri's overtures for a full-scale military alliance with a studiedly noncommittal letter to al-Mansur, thanking him for his "many effusive expressions of true kindness," and hoping that "these letters of ours will communicate our deepest gratitude." She reminded al-Mansur, "We have always been keenly aware of the great esteem in which Your Majesty holds our longstanding correspondence over many years regarding trade and agreements between our subjects," but then she raised the issue of "some considerable monies owed to several of our subjects, who, along with their merchants, have been treated most harshly" in Morocco. She thanked him for the release of the Dutch merchants, pointing out that it emphasized "our undertaking to safeguard the wellbeing of those who, like ourselves, recognize the name of Jesus the Redeemer and Savior of all men."

This was hardly an attempt to encourage an Anglo-Moroccan alliance against Spain. She went on to hint at the conflicts raised by the embassy, both among its members and within the wider London community. "We have," she wrote, "taken Your Majesty's request for ships to convey your ambassadors to Aleppo into great consideration and we are loath to refuse this or any other greater courtesy." However, she admitted, "we have been informed and advised that such an operation would entail many inconveniences and difficulties both to our ships and to the ambassadors themselves, out of respect to very many great concerns. We have therefore been so bold as to inform your ambassadors of these circumstances and ensure them that Your Majesty will not find any fault with them for having followed our wishes and instructions."[20] The disgruntled merchants of the Levant Company had refused to pay for al-Annuri's official onward journey to Aleppo. Regardless of what was happening behind closed doors on the Strand, the Moroccans seemed to be heading home.

And yet a month later, on November 17, 1600, al-Annuri and his remaining entourage were still in London, publicly celebrating the Accession Day festivities held in Whitehall marking the anniversary of Elizabeth's reign. Al-Annuri was instantly distinguishable from the crowd thanks to his long black robe, white linen turban and richly decorated steel scimitar. His appearance and demeanor marked him out as a traveler of obvious stature, but also as an exotic stranger.

Al-Annuri took his place beneath a canopy at one end of the yard, along with his retinue, to watch a jousting match between some of England's most famous lords and knights, who entered to the blare of trumpets, some dressed in armor, others in elaborate disguises, accompanied by attendants reciting songs and verse. Thousands of Londoners came out to see the spectacle—"so great an assembly of people," wrote John Stow, "as the like hath not been seen in that place before."[21]

Had he glanced up, al-Annuri would have glimpsed the queen and her ladies watching the entertainment from the windows of one of the palace galleries. From this distance he might not have seen her blackened teeth, "a defect," the German traveler Paul Hentzner wrote, that "the English seem subject to, from their great use of sugar."[22] Elizabeth's importation of Moroccan sugar since the beginning of her reign led to a passion for candied fruits, which had taken a terrible toll on her teeth. The French ambassador, Monsieur de Boissie, and his Russian counterpart, Grigorii Mikulin, had both been honored with seats next to Elizabeth, but al-Annuri and his followers had been relegated to standing among the queen's subjects.

Exactly forty-two years had passed since Elizabeth's accession to the throne, a date she celebrated every year with a carefully staged ceremonial entrance into London. Across the kingdom the day was marked by sermons, public feasts, bell ringing, prayers and bonfires designed to celebrate the rule of the Virgin Queen. The plans for the Tilts in 1600 were meant to show a kingdom at peace. The queen's chief adversary, King Philip II, had died two years earlier, and although England was still officially at war with Spain, the threat of invasion had receded. But behind the tiltyard's glittering façade and noisy display, the seemingly unalterable edifice of more than four decades of Elizabethan rule was starting to crumble.

At some point around this time al-Annuri sat for his portrait. Perhaps this event and the delay in the embassy's departure were not unconnected. The portrait appears to have been designed to mark a specific diplomatic event—al-Annuri's formal appearance at the Whitehall celebration, or possibly a formal treaty—with its date of "1600." Al-Annuri's Anglicized name and his age ("42") are inscribed on the left, and his title ("Legate of the King of Barbary to England") on the right. The painting appears to have been tied to Elizabeth's Accession Day triumphs in some way, as it was surely no coincidence that al-Annuri's age, marked so prominently on the painting, was the same as the length of Elizabeth's reign. The portrait could have been painted in response to Elizabeth and Cecil's attempts to commemorate some aspect of his visit, anticipating an Anglo-Morisco alliance or anti-Spanish union that stopped short of full-scale invasion. Who commissioned or painted his likeness remains a mystery, but the portrait offers a tantalizing glimpse of its subject and is remarkable as the earliest surviving portrait of a Muslim painted from life in England. Its existence is surprising, given Islam's official injunction against figurative images—all the more so because, more than many other Muslim rulers, al-Mansur observed the Islamic Hadith injunction against figurative representation, never showing his face and speaking in public from behind a veil.

On the same day that al-Annuri watched Elizabeth's anniversary festivities, the queen's printers published *A Geographical Historie of Africa, written in Arabicke and Italian by Iohn Leo a More, borne in Granada, and brought vp in Barbarie,* by John Pory. The "More," or Moroccan, of Pory's title was better known to his Christian readership as Leo Africanus, though his given name was al-Hasan ibn Muhammad ibn Ahmad al-Wazzan. A Muslim born in Granada, al-Wazzan had grown up in Fez and been captured by Christian forces while crossing the Mediterranean in 1518. He converted to Catholicism in captivity and wrote his description of Africa in Rome in the 1520s; it was subsequently published in Latin, Italian and French before Pory translated it into English. Pory dedicated the book to Robert Cecil, suggesting that it was particularly timely, "in that the Moroccan ambassador (whose king's dominions are here most amply and particularly described) hath so lately treated with your honor concerning matters of state."[23] Pory's book provided the queen's ministers with crucial information on a Muslim ally with which England was about to ratify a formal alliance.

Elizabeth would not countenance a full military alliance with the Barbary kingdom, but she would consider doing what her sailors did best and raid the Spanish fleet in the Caribbean, if al-Mansur would keep his promise to cover the costs. Agreeing to such a plan was evidently beyond al-Annuri's authority, and by January 1601 negotiations seemed to have stalled just as public hostility toward the Moroccans grew more pronounced.

One of Cecil's spies, Philip Honeyman, provided one possible explanation for this hostility, with the claim that al-Annuri's mission was "to learn here how merchandise went, and what gain we made of their sugars, that he might raise the prices accordingly. The merchants took little pleasure in his being here."[24] John Stow offered yet another perspective:

> Notwithstanding all this kindness shown them together with their diet and all other provisions for six months space wholly at the queen's charges, yet such was their inveterate hate unto our Christian religion and estate as they could not endure to give any

manner of alms, charity or relief, either in money or broken meet, unto any English poor, but reserved their fragments and sold the same unto such poor as would give most for them. They killed all their own meat within their house, as sheep, lambs, poultry and such like, and they turn their faces eastward when they kill any thing; they use beads, and pray to Saints.[25]

Having scorned the Moroccans' religious practices, Stow went on to doubt the sincerity of their commercial activity:

Whereas the chief pretense of their embassy was to require continuance of her majesty's special favor toward their king, with like entreaty of her naval aid, for sundry especial uses, chiefly to secure his treasure from the parts of Guinea, yet the English merchants held it otherwise, by reason that during their half year's abode in London they have used all subtlety and diligence to know the prices, weights, measures and all kinds of differences of such commodities, as either their country sent hither, or England transported thither.[26]

After nearly six months the diplomatic, religious and commercial tensions that arose from the Moorish embassy's presence finally brought it to an end. With no military or diplomatic agreement in sight, and London's Barbary and Levant merchants increasingly unhappy about the commercially sensitive intelligence they believed al-Annuri was gathering, it was time for them to leave.

As they began to plan their departure, events conspired to hasten it. In late January, Elizabeth issued a proclamation with a direct bearing on al-Annuri's retinue. It read:

Whereas the Queen's majesty, tendering the good and welfare of her own natural subjects, greatly distressed in these hard times of dearth, is highly discontented to understand the great number of negroes and blackamoors which (as she is informed) are carried into this realm since the troubles between her highness and the King of Spain; who are fostered and powered here, to the great annoyance of her own liege people that which covet the relief which these people consume, as also for that the most of them are infidels having no understanding of Christ or his Gospel: hath given a special commandment that the said kind of people shall be with all speed avoided and discharged out of this her majesty's realms.[27]

The proclamation was a sign of the deteriorating political situation in England. The country was in a state of famine due to poor harvests and the devastating impact of enclosures. Elizabeth's grip on power was slipping, and her immediate response was that of political leaders since time immemorial when faced with a crisis: attack economic immigrants, refugees fleeing religious persecution and "aliens," even though in this case it made little sense considering the commercial benefits of her long-standing alliance with Morocco. Nor were the proclamation's proposed deportations of blacks and Moors quite what they seemed. Elizabeth had "appointed Casper van Zenden, merchant of Lubeck, for their speedy transportation." Van Zenden was a particularly unscrupulous character who four years earlier had hit on the idea of deporting black slaves and selling them in Spain. It was none other than a bankrupt Sir Thomas Sherley the elder who, spotting a lucrative business opportunity, petitioned Cecil to grant van Zenden the license in 1601, presumably in return for a percentage of the unsavory profits.[28]

Whether or not Elizabeth's proclamation had any bearing on al-Annuri's decision to go, within weeks of its publication he and his retinue had slipped quietly away. By February 27, 1601, they were back in Morocco. Al-Mansur's subsequent letters to Elizabeth reveal that al-Annuri's loyalty to him remained unshakable and also clarified the confusion over his origins. Al-Mansur wrote in May explaining that "the Andalusian came before our high Porte and relayed to us all your intentions and plans which you had discussed with him and conveyed to him. We listened with attentive ears until we understood them all, and became alert to all you had plotted." Confirming that al-Annuri was a Morisco (or "Andalusian"), al-Mansur explained with obvious satisfaction that he knew all about Elizabeth's covert scheme to recruit the Spanish-born Muslims in the ambassadorial party for a separate

English-led attack on Spain. He would not countenance any Anglo-Morisco alliance because, as he explained to Elizabeth, he feared that the Moriscos might revert back to Christianity, or as he put it, "we fear that they may be swayed [against us] by the enemy," the Spanish.[29]

Nevertheless, al-Mansur hoped Elizabeth might still agree to a joint venture against the Spanish in the Americas. He reminded her, "You say the fleet to be employed in that action shall need treasure for the charge to the value of £100,000, and that we should assist you therewith in secret, that the Spaniard may not come to the knowledge thereof." He told her that the money "is ready and provided"; all she needed to do was send "a strong and tall ship, and some person of account" to collect it. His other concern was the Muslim colonization of the Americas. "For our intent," he wrote blithely, "is not only to enter upon the land to sack it and leave it, but to possess it and that it remain under our dominion for ever and—by the help of God—to join it to our estate and yours." He concluded grandly, "If your power and command shall be seen there with our army, all the Moors will join and confederate themselves—by the help of God—with us and you."[30] This was the first and last time that a Protestant-Muslim confederation was proposed to rule Latin America.

Elizabeth was sufficiently interested in using al-Mansur's forces to threaten Spain to praise al-Annuri for his "utmost discretion," and send her agent Henry Prannell to continue negotiations in Morocco.[31] But any real hopes for an attack on Spain had died with Essex: the political will and much of the queen's personal strength were gone. The court's interest in a Moroccan alliance for political and commercial reasons seemed to have reached an impasse.

Despite the receding enthusiasm for an Anglo-Moroccan alliance at the highest political levels, interest in the Moroccan delegation beyond Elizabeth's innermost circle was intense. Writers continued to publish histories and translations of Christianity's fraught relationship with Islam, while dramatists exploited the combustible mix of politics, religion and espionage generated by Elizabeth's Muslim alliances.

In the spring of 1600, a lawyer named Ralph Carr published *The*

Mahumetane or Turkish Historie, a translation of various French and Italian accounts of the origins and rise to power of the Ottomans. It ranged across Islamic history, beginning with the Prophet Muhammad—described as "a gentile and very idolater"—and culminating in lengthy descriptions of the recent conflict in Malta and "the war of Cyprus, held betwixt the Turk and Venetians, some thirty years ago."[32]

Carr reflected at some length on the religious schism within Islam, describing how Muhammad's cousin 'Ali ibn Abi Talib, whom he called "Haly," "changed, or rather annulled" Muhammad's religious edicts "and made new of his own invention, through which innovation of religion, or rather superstition, the Saracens became marvelously divided" between Sunni and Shi'a. He concluded that "albeit the Turks and Persians also are in effect very Mahometists, yet differ they so in ceremonies, and other contraries of opinion, that the one do account the other very heretics."[33] Carr's account was typical of the equivocal Elizabethan responses to the rise of the Ottomans. At one moment, he argued, "You shall find them in my conceit not inferior but superior far in every thing which hath given estimation to former ages"; at another, he warned his audience in terms reminiscent of Erasmus that it was a story "telling of ensuing danger, not much divided from our own doors, when daily we lamentably see our neighbors' houses not far off flaming."[34]

The excitement and danger created by English relations with the Moroccans and Ottomans continued to inspire plays that reveled in the audience's compulsive fascination with the east. Within months of the publication of Carr's book, sometime in late 1600 or early 1601, a play appeared entitled *Lust's Dominion; or The Lascivious Queen* (also known as *The Spanish Moor's Tragedy*), most likely written by Shakespeare's associate Thomas Dekker, with the collaboration at various points of several other playwrights.[35] It is a nasty, bloody drama, a throwback to the "Turk" and "Moor" plays of Peele, Greene, Kyd and Marlowe (to whom it was attributed until the early nineteenth century), yet it added a new and topical twist, showing the Moors literally in bed with the Spanish.

At the center of the dramatic action is Eleazer, a Moor and Prince of Fez and Barbary, who is married to Maria, a Spanish noblewoman. Although admired for his military prowess, Eleazer lives as a royal prisoner after his father's defeat at the Spaniards' hands left him "captive to a Spanish tyrant." Although he is described variously as a "devil," a "slave of Barbary," a "dog" and a "black fiend"[36] (the word "black" appears in the play twenty-eight times), Eleazer boasts that his blood is "as red and royal as the best / And proudest in Spain."[37] Unlike previous Moors onstage, Eleazer is a noble character accepted as part of a Christian community.

The play's opening is reminiscent of Shakespeare's *Titus Andronicus,* with Eleazer revealed as the "minion" and lover of the "lascivious queen," wife of the cuckolded and dying Spanish king Philip. The king's subsequent death splits his court into rival factions; one tries to expel Eleazer, but he sidesteps banishment and vows to avenge his humiliating captivity and his father's defeat at the hands of the Spanish. The uncontrollable passion and "lust" of both Spaniards and Moors leads to civil war as Eleazer plots the murder of his rivals and sacrifices both the queen and his wife in a spree of gleeful villainy that culminates in his usurping "the imperial chair of Spain."[38] Eleazer's brief reign of terror is ended only when the king's son Philip (modeled loosely on the Spanish king Philip III) disguises himself as a Moor by painting his face "with the oil of hell" and stabs the Moor. Like Aaron and Barabas, Eleazer dies unrepentant, shouting at the devils that come to claim him that he will "Out-act you all in perfect villainy."[39] As Philip assumes the throne, he closes the play by announcing:

> And for this Barbarous Moor, and his black train,
> Let all the Moors be banished from Spain![40]

The play was performed as Elizabeth's proclamation demanding the expulsion of "blackamoors" from England was being circulated; later, in 1609, Philip III would formally decree that all Moriscos should be expelled from Spain.[41] The play could be seen as offering a solemn comment on the Moorish policies of Elizabeth I and Philip III. Yet Dekker's drama was more ambiguous than this. It ends with a Spanish king still dressed and painted as a Moor, with his "lascivious" mother halfheartedly forgiven for her affair with Eleazer. Rather than aiming to offer solemn diplomatic advice about the dangers of England's prospective alliance with a Moorish ruler, *Lust's Dominion* revels in a dramatic fantasy where Spanish Catholics and Moorish Muslims are shown as two facets of the same apostasy. The English Protestant audience could gape and laugh at all of the ensuing violence, lascivious passion, tyranny and crime, appalled and delighted in equal measure by the play's antihero Eleazer, a Moor who could be admired when causing chaos in the Spanish court, but was probably not to be trusted by the English.

In late 1601 or early 1602, Shakespeare began work on a new play drawing on Muslim characters, close in its outlook to Dekker's play, which he may have read or seen. It was set in the Mediterranean world of Ottomans, Venetians and Moors that was so familiar to a generation of Levant and Barbary Company employees and London theatergoers. Its tragic hero would contain elements of the exotic, bombastic characters in Marlowe's and Peele's plays and the more recent black Moors associated with Spain in plays like *Lust's Dominion*. He was another ambivalent warrior with suspect allegiances required to combat a powerful enemy, pushed to his physical and emotional limits, who marries outside his community. The play begins in Venice, and invited its audience to consider what might have happened if the valiant Prince of Morocco had guessed correctly and married the noble Portia. It was called *The Tragedy of Othello*.

Othello is generally regarded as one of Shakespeare's greatest tragedies, ranking alongside *Hamlet, Macbeth* and *King Lear,* all written in a remarkable six-year burst of creativity between 1600 and 1606. While it returns to Venice, we are no longer in the company of merchants or Jews; instead we meet Othello, a Moor living in a Christian world at the center of a political, romantic and military drama of which he is both master and captive. It is a play in which nothing is quite what it seems. Black and white, race and sex, seeing and believing, good and evil, are all subject to pitiless examination in some of Shakespeare's most intense language and dramatic action. It has been called a "tragedy of probability," testing the limits of what the audience is prepared to believe is true.[42] Even its date is subject to intense speculation. The play was first performed in November 1604. Recent editors have argued that Shakespeare probably began writing it within months of the first appearances of *Lust's Dominion,* during the winter of 1601–1602, based on similarities with his earlier plays *Hamlet* (c. 1600) and *Twelfth Night* (c. 1601).

The first printed edition, entitled *The Tragedy of Othello, The Moor of Venice,* was published in 1622 in a small, pocket-sized quarto format (hence its description as "Quarto"). Just a year later a second edition was published in the celebrated First Folio collection ("Folio") in the section "Tragedies," under the same title. However, this second edition contained 3,685 lines, 160 more than the first edition. At some point more than thirty passages were added to the Folio (or, alternatively, had been cut from the Quarto and then subsequently reinstated). To add to the confusion, both editions were published after Shakespeare's death in 1616, making it almost impossible to ascertain which version is closest to Shakespeare's original intention. Editors are at a loss to provide conclusive evidence as to how and why these changes occurred. Some argue that the Quarto represents Shakespeare's first version of the play, probably intended for a shortened performance, and that the Folio represents his revised "second thoughts." Others claim that the changes are the result of the inevitable corruption that took place once the handwritten text of the play passed through the diverse hands of compositors, proofreaders and printers in the chaotic atmosphere of printing shops, and that the Quarto may have been a reduced version of the Folio.[43]

The problem of the play's two versions is compounded by the perennial question of race. For over three hundred years, most Shakespeareans in the English-speaking world fixated with horror on Othello's blackness and his seemingly "unnatural" union with the "fair" Desdemona, while the later twentieth century reacted with equal abhorrence to the play's blatant racial slurs. As early as 1693 the critic Thomas Rymer wondered why Shakespeare would write a play in which the Venetians "will set a negro to be their general, or trust a Moor to defend them," concluding with the sneering condescension of someone used to seeing black men as servants that "with us a blackamoor might rise to be a trumpeter; but Shakespeare would not have him less than a Lieutenant-General."[44] Samuel Taylor Coleridge denied Othello's ethnicity altogether, claiming he "must not be conceived of as a negro" because "it would be something monstrous to conceive this beautiful Venetian girl falling in love with a veritable negro."[45] It was only with the advent of decolonization and the rise of the African American civil rights movement that a profound reassessment of the play's racial politics began. Writing in 1997 the Nigerian-born novelist Ben Okri voiced a commonly held feeling among black writers that it "hurts to watch *Othello*." Okri argues that "if it did not begin as a play about race . . . then its history has made it one." [46]

Okri is right: *Othello* did not begin life as a play about race in our modern understanding of the term. Our conception of race—identifying people by their physical features (such as skin color) or ethnic characteristics—entered the English language only in the eighteenth century. It is derived from the Middle French *rasse,* meaning a group of people connected by common descent, and the Spanish *raza* and the Portuguese *raça,* both referring to lineage and genealogy.[47] This is how Shakespeare used the word, such as when Mark Antony speaks of the "lawful race" of Rome in *Antony and Cleopatra* (1607–1608).[48] The crux is Shakespeare's use of the term "Moor." In *Othello,* Shakespeare exploited its dual meaning of "Mahometan," or Muslim, and "Maurus," or black. The play uses both meanings but Othello's blackness has come to predominate.

Shakespeare did not invent the high-ranking Moor: like most playwrights of this period he took his stories and ideas from other writers, and drew inspiration directly from a source he had used before. The Italian Giovanni Battista Giraldi, popularly known as "Cinthio," wrote a series of short stories known as the *Hecatommithi* (1565), which, like Boccaccio's *Decameron* (1353), revolve around a morality tale. In Cinthio's story the character on which Shakespeare based Othello is called simply "a Moor, a very gallant man." His blackness is mentioned only once, there are no Turks and the tragedy is primarily domestic.

The inspiration for Shakespeare's Iago is referred to simply as "the Ensign," and only Othello's wife is given a proper name: "Disdemona." In Cinthio's version although the two men collude in questioning Disdemona's virtue, it is the Ensign who beats her to death. Both men's deaths are reported as happening much later, Othello's following his banishment for his part in the affair, and the Ensign's after being tortured. Cinthio's story was a standard example of moralized tales castigating the infidelity of husbands and wives that stretched back through Boccaccio as far as Socrates. What Shakespeare brought to the story was a generation of Elizabethan England's fascination with the figure of the Moor, not incidentally at the very time of al-Annuri's embassy.

The play's opening lines immediately set a tone of profound ambiguity. Iago appears, describing himself as "his Moorship's ancient," or standard-bearer, who has been passed over for promotion by his superior, Othello. He meets the wealthy and foolish Roderigo, who is in love with Desdemona, and persuades him to defame her for marrying Othello. He tells the bemused Roderigo, "Were I the Moor, I would not be Iago. / In following him I follow but myself," concluding, "I am not what I am."[49] Iago's elliptical reference to both himself and Othello begins one of Shakespeare's most troubling presentations of psychological manipulation. Iago is going to penetrate Othello's psyche in order to destroy him. "I am not what I am," he states defiantly, and by the end of the play he leaves hardly any characters with an unequivocal sense of who they are. Iago's line has a powerful religious dimension that none of its contemporary audience could have missed. He is the opposite of the Old Testament God, who says "I am that I am" (Exodus 3:14). At this stage, although the Moor has yet to appear, the audience has already met a version of him in Iago, who is behaving rather like the "irreligious" blackamoor, Aaron. When Shakespeare had written *Titus Andronicus* ten years earlier, he followed fashion by showing the Moor as a villainous outsider who destroys the virtuous warrior Titus. His first disturbing innovation in *Othello* was to invert these roles, giving the part of the villain to the Italian lieutenant and making the virtuous warrior a Moor.

Within twenty lines Iago is standing in the shadows outside the house of Brabantio, Desdemona's father, taunting him:

> Zounds, sir, you are robbed, for shame put on your gown!
> Your heart is burst, you have lost half your soul,
> Even now, now, very now, an old black ram
> Is tupping your white ewe! Arise, arise,
> Awake the snorting citizens with the bell
> Or else the devil will make a grandsire of you.[50]

Iago accuses the Moor—who has still not been named—of everything from stealing Desdemona from the paternal household, to bestial sexual behavior and representing the devil. When Brabantio demands that Iago and Roderigo explain themselves, Iago imagines Othello and Desdemona having sex, warning of the "monstrous" offspring that could ensue. He goads Brabantio, "you'll have your daughter covered with a Barbary horse; you'll have your nephews neigh to you, you'll have coursers for cousins and jennets for germans!"[51]

Iago uses the image of a Barbary horse to identify Othello as North African and offers up a prurient vision of miscegenation, or crossbreeding. His insults are rather opaque today—"jennets" are Spanish horses and "coursers" chargers, noted for their speed and stamina—but by drawing on the aristocratic language of horse breeding, Iago attempts to appeal to Brabantio's sense of propriety. His insinuation is that Othello's marriage to Desdemona disrupts the natural order of decorum and lineage. It is precisely this kind of insidious racism that makes Shakespeare's play so uncomfortable to watch: today this is the language of white Christian superiority that delights in mocking the black man. Driving home his point with voyeuristic pleasure, Iago says, "your daughter and the Moor are now making the beast with two backs."[52]

Roderigo's speech (only in the 1623 Folio text and not the 1622 Quarto edition) reiterates Iago's slander and claims that Desdemona is in "the gross clasps of a lascivious Moor."[53] She has

> made a gross revolt,
> Tying her duty, beauty, wit and fortunes

In an extravagant and wheeling stranger
Of here and everywhere.[54]

This accusation finally stirs Brabantio to action. Without Roderigo's intercession the audience sees Iago as a spiteful lone voice; with it, a group voice begins to emerge.

When Othello finally enters, in the following scene, Iago, who intimates that Brabantio will seek to discredit him in front of the Venetian Senate, follows him. In only his second speech in the play, Othello responds grandly:

Let him do his spite;
My services, which I have done the signiory,
Shall out-tongue his complaints. 'Tis yet to know—
Which, when I know that boasting is an honor,
I shall promulgate—I fetch my life and being
From men of royal siege.[55]

His confident response proves him to be anything but a "Barbary horse," quite ready to "out-tongue" any charges made against him.

Shakespeare had probably seen al-Annuri at one of his many widely reported London appearances or during the performances of his theatrical company, the Lord Chamberlain's Men, at Elizabeth's court in the winter of 1600–1601, when the Moroccan was locked in negotiations with Elizabeth and her advisers. When Othello is called before the Venetian Senate in the play's third scene, the setting resembles a royal audience. Just as Elizabeth's counselors were considering Turkish affairs, so the duke and senators gather to respond to a serious threat to Venice's security: "A Turkish fleet, and bearing up to Cyprus."[56] Cinthio mentions Cyprus—the *Hecatommithi* was written before the island fell to Sultan Selim II in 1573—but not Turks. Shakespeare introduces them here as a shadowy, emblematic menace to Venetian interests. As the Venetians discuss how to combat the Turkish threat, Brabantio and Othello enter. The Venetian duke then addresses Othello using his proper name for the first time in the entire play:

Valiant Othello, we must straight employ you
Against the general enemy Ottoman.

[*to Brabantio*]
I did not see you; welcome, gentle signior;
We lack'd your counsel and your help tonight.[57]

While Othello is welcomed as "valiant," Brabantio is initially over-looked, then reproached for his absence from important decisions of state. All talk of Othello's skin color recedes: he is a "valiant" and "brave" military leader whom the Venetians need to defend themselves against the Turks. At this moment Othello looks and sounds like the Prince of Morocco, a noble Moor who has successfully wooed and married his Portia and is waving his scimitar and promising to go into battle once more against the Turks. Shakespeare now had both kinds of Moor onstage: the diabolical blackamoor Aaron reborn in the guise of Iago, and the chivalric Moroccan prince recast as the exotic mercenary Othello, whose name sounds uncomfortably close to the Ottomans he must confront in defense of his adopted homeland.

The anxieties aroused by Othello are hard to dispel. Brabantio accuses him of using witchcraft to entrap Desdemona, and when asked to explain himself, Othello delivers an oratorical tour de force designed to "out-tongue" Brabantio:

Her father loved me, oft invited me,
Still questioned me the story of my life
From year to year, the battles, sieges, fortunes
That I have passed.
I ran it through, even from my boyish days
To the very moment that he bade me tell it,
Wherein I spake of most disastrous chances,
Of moving accidents by flood and field,
Of hair-breadth scapes i' th' imminent deadly breach,
Of being taken by the insolent foe
And sold to slavery, of my redemption thence,
And portance in my traveler's history,
Wherein of antres vast and deserts idle,
Rough quarries, rocks and hills whose heads touch heaven,
It was my hint to speak. Such was my process,

And of the cannibals that each other eat,
The Anthropophagi, and men whose heads
Do grow beneath their shoulders. This to hear
Would Desdemona seriously incline.[58]

The speech has shades of Tamburlaine in its high-flown rhetoric—
the young Othello sounds as if he could have fought for the Scythian
emperor—but the point is not so much his warriorlike feats as the seductive quality of his storytelling. Othello describes how he was invited
by Brabantio to tell the story of his life as a boy soldier (from the age of
seven, as he tells the senators). His exotic tales of his travels, including
epic battles and encounters with the monstrous races of Anthropophagi
(cannibals) and headless monsters enthralled Desdemona.[59] If Shakespeare had read Pliny's fantastical tales of Africa, then he could
also have come across reports of slavery, warfare and vast wealth
gathered by English travelers like Jasper and George Thomson, who
regaled readers back home with stories of gold, unicorns, dwarfs and
concubines.

What is particularly striking about Othello's speech is his description
of how he ended up in Venice. We assume that as a Moor he grew up
in Morocco (or what Shakespeare calls "Mauretania" later in the play),
but his childhood is a blank. He claims to have been captured "by the
insolent foe," to have been sold into slavery and then to have experienced
some form of "redemption." Intriguingly, for the Elizabethans, "redemption" meant both "delivered from sin" and "freed from slavery":
Othello is bought, set free and offered salvation through the sacrament
of baptism to become the first Christian Moor on the Elizabethan stage.
This would suggest that the "insolent foe" is the Turk who captured and
sold Othello as a galley slave before Christians rescued and converted
him. What he does not say is if he was born a Muslim, or a pagan, like
many other Berbers in sixteenth-century Mauretania. Whatever the
case, the audience is presented with a character who moves with suspicious ease from one religion to another. Having turned away from one
religion, might he not just as easily embrace another?

There were various examples of conversion from which Shakespeare could have drawn inspiration, notably that of Chinano the Turk, baptized at St. Katharine's Church in 1586 (see chapter 6). There was also the case of al-Wazzan, or Leo Africanus, as described in his book *A Geographical Historie of Africa*. If, as many believe, Shakespeare read al-Wazzan, he would have discovered that many inhabitants of Mauretania were categorized as "pagans." Like Othello, al-Wazzan had converted to Christianity after being captured by Christian pirates while returning to Fez from Cairo in 1518. Like Othello his birth name was discarded in favor of a Christian name—and only he knew how far his baptism was genuine. Just seven years later, he returned to North Africa and seems to have reverted to Islam.[60] Then there was al-Annuri, another Moor around whose identity contradictory suppositions revolved, someone who spoke well and thought much of himself, but who some claimed was from Fez, and therefore not a "true" Sa'adian Moroccan; indeed, according to al-Mansur, his ambassador was a Muslim-born Morisco, forcibly converted to Christianity, who at some point had reverted to Islam. Whatever his exact origins, al-Annuri offered another example of how religious conversion was accepted as part of the fabric of imperial and diplomatic business.

Listening to Othello's enigmatic yet captivating tales of romance, monsters and warfare, the duke is forced to admit, "I think this tale would win my daughter too." Shakespeare gives his "extravagant" stranger a history so that he stands before us, unlike Iago, as he is and declares: "This only is the witchcraft I have used."[61]

With Brabantio defeated, Othello agrees to travel to Cyprus to lead the "war against the Ottomites." Having just clandestinely married Othello, Desdemona then pleads successfully to travel with her husband. Brabantio walks out, delivering the valedictory lines:

> Look to her, Moor, if thou hast eyes to see:
> She has deceived her father, and may thee.[62]

By the close of the first act, with Othello bound for Cyprus, the play looks as though it may end as a comedy. Like so many of Shakespeare's early comedies, this play has two apparently mismatched lovers facing the wrath of a father and the machinations of a malcontent intent on ruining the relationship. By retreating to another world, like a forest or an island, the ensuing conflict and chaos are resolved and everyone is reconciled. But in *Othello,* as soon as the action moves to Cyprus, the play swerves away from comedy and irrevocably toward tragedy.

Upon landing in Cyprus, an advance party of Venetians discover that a "desperate tempest hath so banged the Turks / That their design-ment halts" and their fleet is scattered. Othello arrives and announces with grandiloquent complacency "our wars are done, the Turks are drowned."[63] It seems as though the Turkish threat was just an awkward plot device to get the protagonists to Cyprus, but Shakespeare trans-forms the Turk gradually from a military into a more insidious threat. When Iago engineers a drunken brawl between Roderigo and the lieu-tenant Michael Cassio, Othello intervenes, horrified at their divisions in contrast to the famed Turkish military discipline:

> Are we turned Turks, and to ourselves do that
> Which heaven hath forbid the Ottomites?
> For Christian shame, put by this barbarous brawl.[64]

The idea was familiar to many who knew Erasmus's warning in his essay "On the War Against the Turks": that if Christians wanted to eradicate the Turk they must first expel from their hearts the "Turkish" traits of ambition, anger, hatred and envy. Yet these are precisely the vices that Iago has unleashed in Cyprus and which he cultivates in Othello as he tries to persuade him that Desdemona has been unfaithful with Cassio.

As Othello begins to accept this "monstrous" deception, he and Iago take on Turkish traits and become increasingly as cruel and deceitful. The audience know from early on in the play that Iago will destroy Othello in part because the former's name is the Spanish for James. St. James, or Santiago, is the patron saint of Spain, popularly known as Matamoros—the "Moor-killer."[65] Iago has flirted with the idea that he too might turn Turk, joking with his wife, Emilia, and Desdemona that women are sexually duplicitous "or else I am a Turk."[66] Othello also invites the comparison. Once Iago has convinced him of Desdemona's adultery, they make a pact to kill her, which Iago fears Othello will renounce. The geographical grandeur of Othello's response is reminiscent of Tamburlaine:

> Never, Iago. Like to the Pontic sea
> Whose icy current and compulsive course
> Ne'er feels retiring ebb, but keeps due on
> To the Propontic and the Hellespont,
> Even so my bloody thoughts with violent pace
> Shall ne'er look back, ne'er ebb to humble love
> Till that a capable and wide revenge
> Swallow them up.[67]

Othello's vengeance is as irreversible as the sea flowing into the ocean. The one he chooses is not accidental. The Pontus, or Black Sea, flows past Constantinople into the Propontis, or Sea of Marmara, before debouching into the Aegean via the Hellespont or Dardanelles. By associating him with the iconic topography of the Ottoman Empire, Shakespeare adds another layer to Othello's already complex identity: Moor, convert, pagan, revert and finally murderous raging Turk.

Even as Othello starts to behave like an Ottoman Turk, Desdemona travels in the opposite direction, until she makes a final extraordinary identification with Barbary. In the fourth act, Othello accuses Desdemona publicly of infidelity and hits her before sending her to her bedchamber with her serving woman Emilia, Iago's wife. In one of the most poignant and intimate scenes in the whole play, known as the "Willow Song" scene, Desdemona is undressed for bed by Emilia, and they discuss marriage and infidelity. Emilia attacks Othello for slandering Desdemona, but Desdemona defends him, saying "my love doth so approve him"[68] that she forgives his anger. Suddenly she remembers a song from her childhood, the "Willow Song," an old Tudor refrain about a spurned, doomed lover:

> My mother had a maid called Barbary:
> She was in love, and he she loved proved mad
> And did forsake her. She had a song of "willow,"
> An old thing 'twas, but it expressed her fortune

And she died singing it. That song tonight
Will not go from my mind. I have much to do,
But to go hang my head all at one side,
And sing it like poor Barbary.[69]

She starts to sing the song of Barbary's abandonment by her lover but as she comes to the end of the first verse she misremembers its last line: "Let nobody blame him, his scorn I approve— / Nay, that's not next."[70] It is one of the play's most devastating moments: Desdemona admits she loves Othello so much she even approves of his public humiliation of her reputation, even though she has done nothing wrong. She alters the song to fit her own circumstances, not only mistaking the last line but also changing the gender of the spurned lover from male to female.[71]

For just a moment she becomes her mother's Barbary maid. "Barbary" suggests the woman came from Barbary, a loyal servant (or possibly slave) of the Venetian state without her birth name—not unlike Othello, the Moor of Venice, and the Barbary horse of Iago's insults. Desdemona identifies herself as a Barbary maid while Othello has been tempted to turn Turk. They have both undergone a "monstrous" and irrevocable metamorphosis, and within hours both will be dead.

Once he murders Desdemona and discovers his terrible mistake, Othello turns on the "demi-devil" Iago, to ask why he "ensnared my soul and body."[72] In one of the most chilling couplets uttered by any of Shakespeare's villains, Iago describes himself as a mute slave, which evokes immediate associations with the Ottomans:

Demand me nothing. What you know, you know.
From this time forth I never will speak word.[73]

He never speaks again and is led off to be tortured; like another "demi-devil," his predecessor Aaron, death is too good for him.

Having realized the tragedy of his situation, Othello prepares to take his own life, but not before he undergoes one final shocking transformation. As the Venetians try to arrest him, he ends where he began, telling a story:

> Soft you; a word or two before you go.
> I have done the state some service, and they know't.
> No more of that. I pray you, in your letters,
> When you shall these unlucky deeds relate,
> Speak of me as I am; nothing extenuate,
> Nor set down aught in malice. Then must you speak
> Of one that loved not wisely but too well;
> Of one not easily jealous, but being wrought,
> Perplexed in the extreme; of one whose hand,
> Like the base Indian, threw a pearl away
> Richer than all his tribe; of one whose subdued eyes,
> Albeit unused to the melting mood,
> Drop tears as fast as the Arabian trees
> Their medicinal gum. Set you down this,
> And say besides that in Aleppo once,
> Where a malignant and a turbaned Turk
> Beat a Venetian and traduced the state,
> I took by th' throat the circumcised dog
> And smote him—thus!
> *[He stabs himself.]*[74]

Ever the fabulist, Othello asks that the Venetian authorities be told one last story of his exploits as a loyal servant of the state. It includes his naive deception at the hands of Iago, and how he lost the precious "pearl" Desdemona.

Nowhere in this speech does Othello mention his own ethnic identity. He compares himself first to an Indian, and then to a Turk. Both comparisons are riddled with contradictions. His behavior toward Desdemona is like that of an Indian who threw away a pearl richer than all his tribe. "Indian" is the word used in the 1622 Quarto version of the play, but the 1623 Folio version has "Iudean." It is a crux that goes to the heart of who Othello is. Pliny spoke of the wealth of India and the supposed ignorance of its inhabitants who discarded pearls, though Shakespeare could also have been referring to Native American Indians.

Most modern editors choose the Quarto's "Indian," even though when confronted with cruxes elsewhere their default position is to choose the Folio's version, as it is seen as the "better," later text. Racially it seems obvious to align the Moor with an Indian rather than a "Iudean," or Jew. But, as we have seen, the Elizabethans were convinced that Jews and Muslims were as one in refusing to accept Jesus as the Son of God. The "Iudean" of the Folio could refer to either Judas Iscariot's betrayal of Christ or Herod's execution of his wife, Mariamne, both of which make absolute sense as metaphors for Othello's behavior.[75] Which was correct? Did Shakespeare change his mind in revising his text, or did someone else quietly amend it? We will probably never know, but it is striking that this irresolvable crux captures Othello's overdetermined character, part Muslim, Christian, Jew and even pagan.

It is a conflation that finds its most extraordinary conclusion in the final lines. Othello takes us to Aleppo, the Syrian city where Anthony Jenkinson first met Süleyman the Magnificent fifty years before, where al-Annuri had claimed he was heading, and which today has a very different tragic resonance. Othello has traveled a long way east from his homeland in Barbary, via Venice and Cyprus deep into the Ottoman Empire, into Arabia with its "medicinal" trees, and finally to Syria. The Turk he kills is "turbaned" and "circumcised," a sign that these are not attributes he shares. If he is not circumcised, then surely he cannot have been born a Muslim. Nor does he share sartorial affinities with the ostentatiously turbaned al-Annuri. But in acting out his stabbing of the Turk, Othello enacts the most remarkable moment of tragic self-division in all of Shakespeare. He has been interpreted as a loyal Christian soldier, atoning for his sins by defending Venice against the Turk and killing the heresy within himself, or as finally embracing his true barbarism as a demonic, murderous apostate, who becomes the raging, violent Turk, the culmination of a generation of plays depicting the Ottomans. He is of course both simultaneously: a profoundly ambivalent figure who embodies so much of Elizabethan England's contradictory relations with the Islamic world. Here, in the split second of saying "thus," Othello briefly becomes a Turk.

Othello was the culmination of more than a decade of the Elizabethan theater's fascination with Turks and Moors. Just two years earlier

Shakespeare had written *Hamlet,* a revenge tragedy that eclipsed all previous examples and redefined the genre. *Othello* did something similar in combining every facet of the Muslim characters that had appeared on the stage up to that point. It drew on the bombast of Tamburlaine, the evil of Aaron, the melancholic grandeur of the Prince of Morocco and the raging Turk buried deep within *Henry V.* The audience, then as now, are not asked to sympathize with Othello, but to delight guiltily in the dreadful prejudices and violent fantasies unleashed by this most ambivalent of characters and by his nemesis Iago, safe in the knowledge that it was, after all, just a performance.

Although he could not have known it, Shakespeare wrote *Othello* at the zenith of Elizabethan England's relationship with the Muslim world, which was about to come to an abrupt end. Queen Elizabeth never saw the play. She died on March 24, 1603, at the age of sixty-nine. She had ruled her kingdom for forty-five years, during which time she had repelled foreign Catholic invasion, firmly established Protestantism as the state religion, established a stable if unwieldy government and expanded her commercial and political interests abroad, nowhere more successfully than in the Islamic world. She was succeeded by her cousin the Scottish Stuart king James VI, who would rule as James I. He was under no illusions that Elizabeth would be a hard act to follow, and that the country he inherited required immediate links to the rest of Europe if it was to have any hope of future prosperity.

James, guided by Robert Cecil, opened negotiations for peace with Catholic Spain almost immediately. He was eager to bring England back into the economic and political life of Europe after half a century of self-imposed exile. In the summer of 1604, another embassy arrived from the south, but this time the ambassador was Spanish and Catholic. All thought of a Moroccan-English alliance against Spain had passed, as James had no more appetite for waging war overseas. That August, Spanish and English diplomats signed the Treaty of London, ending nineteen years of war between the two kingdoms. It was a tacit acknowledgment—albeit with grave circumspection—of Protestant England's right to exist within Christian Europe. King James had ended England's diplomatic isolation from the rest of Europe.

In that same month Ahmad al-Mansur died of the plague. His three sons fought for the right to succeed him, and the kingdom of Morocco descended into a bloody civil war that temporarily put an end to all diplomatic and commercial relations with England. Elizabeth's other great Muslim ally, Sultan Mehmed III, had died of a sudden heart attack in December 1603, nine months after her. Mehmed had spent most of his eight-year reign battling unrest abroad and within his troublesome court, with little time to cultivate his father's alliance with Elizabeth. As the Spanish and English sat down at Somerset House to agree to the Treaty of London, the only visible sign that remained of the Anglo-Ottoman alliance was the large carpet atop the table between them.

On November 1, 1604, James and his new royal court watched the first recorded production of *Othello* at the Banqueting House in White-hall. It is one of the play's many paradoxes that a king called James saw his villainous namesake destroying a Moor, but perhaps James took comfort from watching Othello kill the specter of the circumcised and turbaned Turk. Nine years earlier, while king of Scotland, James had written a rather indifferent poem called "Lepanto." It celebrated the victory of the Holy League in 1571:

> Which fought was in Lepanto's gulf,
> Betwixt the baptized race
> And circumcised turban'd Turks.[76]

The new king had no interest in pursuing alliances with the Moors or what he elsewhere called the "faithless Turks." The Elizabethan age was over, and with it England's alliance with the Islamic world.

Epilogue

By the time Shakespeare prepared to say farewell to the London stage and retire to Stratford in 1611, the English were leading figures in the eastern Mediterranean trade. The Levant Company was exporting English goods worth £250,000 per annum to Turkey, prompting one of its merchants, Sir Lewis Roberts, to write that the company had "grown to that height that (without comparison) it is the most flourishing and beneficial company to the commonwealth of any in England."[1] The company was beginning to face competition from a newer joint-stock initiative, the East India Company, which had been awarded its royal charter in December 1600—during al-Annuri's time in London—with the aim of trading throughout the vast emporium of the Indian and Pacific oceans, stretching eastward from the Cape of Good Hope to the Strait of Magellan. By the 1630s the East India Company was exporting more than £100,000 of bullion and importing more than £1 million worth of pepper and spices with a variety of trading communities of different religions throughout India and the Indonesian archipelago.

Like the Levant Company, the East India Company did not involve itself in its early years in the kind of diplomatic or military state policy that had led the Elizabethans into such close alliances with Muslim rulers. James's rapprochement with Spain brought him into closer alignment with the rest of Europe. He opposed Ottoman expansion just at the time when the Turks disengaged from Europe to focus on the Persian threats on their eastern borders. The new Stuart king's delusions of grandeur led him to believe that his destiny was to unify Christendom, which resulted in peace with Spain and correspondence with leading figures in the Greek Orthodox Church, to whom he proposed a Christian union with the Church of England. It can have done little to ingratiate him with the new Ottoman sultan, Ahmed I.[2]

James had no interest in appealing to the Ottoman sultan for military assistance during the central European conflict that dogged the later years of his reign, the Thirty Years' War (1618–1648). He was no doubt influenced in this by his decision to marry his eldest daughter, Elizabeth, to Frederick V, Elector Palatine and a claimant to the Bohemian crown. Besides, where Elizabeth had turned her sights on the east, James's interests were drawn west, to the New World. In 1606 he sanctioned the creation of the Virginia Company, a new joint-stock initiative aimed at settling English colonies on the northeast coast of America. The company could hardly compete with the Spanish domination of the Americas, but it represented the beginnings of a global dimension to English foreign and commercial policy, which was from that point forward no longer centered on the Mediterranean and Muslim world.

While most of England lamented Queen Elizabeth's death, back in Venice, Anthony Sherley must have celebrated, as it brought one of his greatest supporters to the English throne. Never renowned as a shrewd judge of character, James had been flattered by Sherley's prolix correspondence, and in May 1603 he wrote to the Venetian authorities insisting that Sir Anthony "is not the bad subject he is represented to be." He asked the Venetians to hand over one brother and intercede with the Ottomans on behalf of the other.[3] It took another two years to secure Sir Thomas's release, but Sir Anthony was free again the very next month. James seems to have realized his mistake, because by February 1604 he issued a license permitting Sherley "to remain beyond the seas some longer time, and recommended to the princes [and] strangers by whom he may pass."[4] This gave Sherley some formal status as an Englishman abroad, but it was hardly a ringing endorsement, and talk of a return to England was quietly dropped. Sherley reverted to his old ways, passing intelligence about Turkish troop movements to Rudolf II in Prague, promising "I work still for your majesty and am ready for any sacrifice for your cause."[5] On December 1, the Venetian authorities voted unanimously to banish Sir Anthony from the city forever. He was given four days to leave, on pain of death. Nothing he or James could say would change their minds, and so within days he departed Venice for the last time.

With his final exile from Venice, his Persian embassy was definitively over. James had no interest in pursuing alliances with either Persians or Ottomans; his primary aim was peace with Spain, which left Sherley with little diplomatic leverage (not that his increasingly erratic behavior left him much of that anyway). And yet this was still not the end of his picaresque story. He returned to Prague, from where he went to Morocco in 1605 to propose a Moorish campaign against the Turks in Algiers. Perhaps predictably it came to nothing. By the following year, he was working for the Spanish court in Madrid, persuading a gullible Philip III to fund a privateering fleet, with disastrous results.

In 1607 the Sherley brothers' stories became so famous that a group of journeymen playwrights wrote a play about their exploits, entitled *The Travailes of the Three English Brothers,* although it came nowhere near capturing the sheer strangeness of their adventures. By this time, Shah Abbas had grown so frustrated by the lack of news from Sir Anthony that in 1608 he dispatched Sir Robert on a similar mission. Sir Robert had not been idle in his brother's absence, converting to Catholicism and marrying the daughter of a Circassian chieftain, the nineteen-year-old Sampsonia, baptized by Carmelites as Teresa. He traveled across Europe, was made a count by the pope and then traveled to Madrid, where in April 1611 he was finally reunited with his brother Anthony after twelve years. The elder brother's immediate response to their reunion was to denounce Robert as an English spy to the Spanish authorities. The youngest had finally eclipsed the elders: Sir Robert went on to serve King James and his son King Charles I until his death in 1628. Sir Thomas was released from prison and returned to England, depressed and destitute, dying on the Isle of Wight in 1633.

Sir Anthony stayed in Spain, an increasingly marginal and pathetic figure, living off a meager Spanish pension. He remained full of impossible dreams of power and influence yet was racked with debt, with "scarce money to buy him bread," living "in a *bodegon,* which is little worse than an English ale house." Somehow he persuaded Robert to take his account of the Persian embassy back to London and publish it as his *Relation* in 1613, but nobody paid much attention. In the 1620s he wrote two similarly sententious treatises addressed to the ministers of Philip IV, who had succeeded his father in 1621, proposing ever more deluded plans for his and Spain's greater glory. The final damning picture of Sherley was given by Francis Cottington, England's ambassador to Spain, who wrote, "The poor man comes sometimes to my house, and is as full of vanity as ever he was, making himself believe that he shall one day be a great prince, when for the present he wants shoes to wear."[6] His fall from grace was so profound that he died in Spain in complete obscurity at an unknown date in the 1630s.

Shakespeare never again portrayed Moors or Turks with the detail or intensity of the plays he wrote between *Henry VI* and *Othello*. But he still had something to say about the growing scale and plight of migrants and refugees in early seventeenth-century London. Sometime around 1603–1604, he was involved in drafting revisions to a play written by several other playwrights (including Thomas Dekker) called *Sir Thomas More,* which dramatized the life and times of Henry VIII's famous counselor.[7] Scene 6 is now believed to have been drafted by Shakespeare, and a manuscript survives that is the only example of a section of a play written in the author's hand. It was written in response to the infamous May Day riots of 1517, when English artisans attacked foreign residents—or, in the language of the time, "strangers" or "aliens"— whom they blamed for monopolizing trade and taking "local" jobs. Such riots had taken place throughout London in the sixteenth century, some as recently as the early 1590s, so it was a highly sensitive and topical subject (as it is today). In scene 6, Shakespeare re-creates the moment More tries to calm the rioters, who demand "the removing of the strangers," to which he responds:

> Grant them removed, and grant that this your noise
> Hath chid down all the majesty of England.
> Imagine that you see the wretched strangers,

Their babies at their backs, with their poor luggage,
Plodding to th' ports and coasts for transportation,
And that you sit as kings in your desires,
Authority quite silenced by your brawl,
And you in ruff of your opinions clothed;
What had you got? I'll tell you: you had taught
How insolence and strong hand should prevail,
How order should be quelled. And by this pattern
Not one of you should live an aged man;
For other ruffians, as their fancies wrought,
With self same hand, self reasons, and self right,
Would shark on you, and men like ravenous fishes,
Would feed on one another.[8]

It is a powerful and emotive rejection of xenophobia, arguing that if mob rule triumphs over the dispossessed and the rule of law, it will unleash a vicious and anarchic individualism where everyone will "feed on one another." To clinch his point, Thomas More asks the rioters what might happen if their roles were reversed with those of the aliens and they found themselves seeking asylum:

Say now the king,
As he is clement if th' offender mourn,
Should so much come too short of your great trespass
As but to banish you: whither would you go?
What country, by the nature of your error,
Should give you harbor? Go you to France or Flanders,
To any German province, Spain or Portugal,
Nay, anywhere that not adheres to England:
Why, you must needs be strangers. Would you be pleased
To find a nation of such barbarous temper
That, breaking out in hideous violence,
Would not afford you an abode on earth,
Whet their detested knives against your throats,
Spurn you like dogs, and like as if that God
Owed not nor made not you, nor that the elements

Were not all appropriate to your comforts
But chartered unto them? What would you think
To be thus used? This is the strangers' case,
And this your mountainish inhumanity.[9]

More's speech works and the rioters disperse. His compassionate plea for toleration of aliens and strangers might seem inconsistent coming from a playwright who seemed to relish expelling aliens and outsiders from his plays, from Aaron and the Prince of Morocco to Shylock and Othello. But perhaps, buried within these tortuous dramas is an abiding sympathy, an instinct for toleration and reconciliation that finds its clearest expression in this fragment from another play.[10] It is surely one of the reasons Shakespeare's plays continue to hold our attention four hundred years later.

This desire for reconciliation can be found in another play Shakespeare wrote at the end of his career. Around 1611 he returned to the Mediterranean a final time for the setting of one of his plays: *The Tempest*. Act I opens on board a storm-tossed ship carrying Alonso, King of Naples, and Antonio, Duke of Milan, with other members of a wedding party. They are returning to Italy after marrying Alonso's daughter Claribel to the King of Tunis and are shipwrecked on an island somewhere between Tunis and Naples—the same island where Antonio's deposed brother, Prospero, had been exiled with his daughter, Miranda. Prospero was washed up on the island with his young daughter and all the books he could salvage from his library. Tutored in the arts of magic, Prospero established a way of life on the island with his "spirit" Ariel[11] and his onetime companion, now slave, Caliban. But the island has a longer history: Ariel had been imprisoned in a cloven pine by the island's previous resident, the "damn'd witch Sycorax,"[12] Caliban's mother. With the witch gone and Ariel released, the "bare isle" is governed by Prospero and inhabited by his daughter, his slave and his ethereal assistant.

For centuries, critics have debated the location of Prospero's island, some placing it in what Ariel calls "the Mediterranean float [sea]," others noting that in the same speech he speaks of "the still vexed Bermudas."[13]

This, alongside Caliban's apparent similarity to Native Americans, has led many scholars (mostly Americans) to assume that the play is set in the "brave new world"[14] of the Americas. Such interpretations point to reports from the recently established colony of Jamestown, in Virginia, to which a fleet of English ships had been sent in 1609 to reinforce the beleaguered English settlement. The fleet was struck by storms and was shipwrecked in the Bermudas, but miraculously everyone survived and managed to reach Jamestown.

Yet Shakespeare's play was rooted in the myths and histories of the Mediterranean world. He reminds his audience that Caliban's mother was born "in Algiers,"[15] an Ottoman stronghold throughout the late sixteenth and seventeenth centuries. One of Shakespeare's sources for the story was the Roman poet Virgil's classical epic of the foundation of Rome, the *Aeneid,* in which its hero, Aeneas, travels from Troy to Rome via Carthage, where he meets its queen, Dido. The play's courtiers even quibble over Dido's and classical Carthage's location in relation to sixteenth-century Tunis. One of them insists, "This Tunis, sir, was Carthage,"[16] a dispute that serves to remind the audience of the transitory nature of empire.

As in Virgil's poem, Shakespeare imagines the gulf between North Africa and Europe as vast. The seaborne crossing between Tunis and Naples is less than 370 miles, but Claribel, the "Queen of Tunis," is described as "she that dwells / Ten leagues beyond man's life,"[17] in Muslim North Africa. One of Alonso's courtiers accuses him of failing to marry his daughter off to a European prince, "But rather lose her to an African."[18] Once again, Shakespeare returns to a story of a Christian woman—first Portia, then Desdemona, finally Claribel—being offered in marriage to a North African man—the Prince of Morocco, Othello, now the King of Tunis. In *The Tempest,* the far away becomes near at hand as the various dreams of colonization, interracial marriage, republicanism and revolution are rehearsed through the characters as they arrive or reflect on this "desolate isle."

In this play Claribel, the King of Tunis and the Algerian witch Sycorax remain far away, and never appear onstage. The rich potential of the island's location and history remains buried in its many layers of meaning. The stories of trade, and the threats of privateering, piracy, enslavement and conversion that affected thousands of English men, women and children throughout the Mediterranean as it was being performed in London, are almost completely silenced. Only a whisper can be heard in the implied histories of Ariel, Caliban, Tunis, Algiers, Naples and Bermuda. The geography of *The Tempest* is relevant only insofar as it is labeled self-consciously as irrelevant: the island is nowhere and anywhere, a utopia in the Greek sense of the term *ou-topos,* meaning both "good place" and "nowhere." Shakespeare understood that by 1611 King James's foreign and economic policies left Jacobean England looking east *and* west, gazing backward to the Mediterranean "Old World" of Greece, Rome, Spain and the Ottoman Empire, and forward to the Atlantic "New World" of the Americas. His play uses this new global awareness to tell a story of uncertain habitation and conflicted identity, filtered through the layered history of the Mediterranean.

The Tempest provides a fitting conclusion to the history of Elizabethan England's relations with the Islamic world. Shakespeare grew up under a regime whose isolation from much of Catholic Europe propelled it into alliances with Muslim rulers from Marrakesh, Algiers, Tunis, Constantinople, Qazvin and Isfahan. With the accession of King James, this policy came to an abrupt end, and with it a tradition of representing formidable, eloquent and savage Turks, Moors and Persians on the Elizabethan stage. They would be reinvented in a different key by a new generation of Jacobean playwrights.

As we have seen, the Sherleys had already been given their own play, *The Travailes of the Three English Brothers,* first performed at the Curtain Theater in 1607. Robert Daborne was at work on *A Christian Turned Turk* (1612), the story of the English pirate and Muslim convert John Ward, who took the name Yusuf Reis and lived out his life in Tunis in opulent luxury. In 1624 Philip Massinger premiered his tragicomedy *The Renegado,* also set in the privateering capital of Tunis, where Christian and renegade Italians flee the temptations of the Muslim court to return to Italy. In contrast to *The Tempest,* plays like Massinger's responded to reports of English men and women living and working in the Mediterranean, some captives, others converts (willing or forced) to Islam. But the preoccupations of their authors were not those of Marlowe, Peele and Shakespeare; their interests were primarily historical, their tone comical, their aim pure entertainment, lacking the urgent topicality of the 1590s, when many feared that Protestant England could at any moment be invaded. The Islamic world was just one of many within the emerging global economy with which the Jacobeans found themselves entangled. The threat—or hope—of a rapprochement between Protestants and Muslims was now a thing of the past.

As if to emphasize this shift, in 1632 the London draper Thomas Adams endowed the first English professorship in Arabic at Cambridge University for "the good service of the King and State in our commerce with those Eastern nations, and in God's good time to the enlarging of the borders of the Church, and propagation of Christian religion to them who now sit in darkness."[19] In 1636 Oxford followed suit when Archbishop William Laud, then chancellor of the university, appointed Edward Pococke, an English chaplain working in Aleppo, as the first Laudian Professor of Arabic (the post still exists, and it was recently filled by a woman for the first time in its history).[20] In 1649 the first English translation of the Qur'an was published; entitled *The Alcoran of Mahomet,* it was based on André Du Ryer's French edition, *L'Alcoran de Mahomet translaté d'arabe en françois.*[21] The Arabic-speaking Islamic world became the subject of scholarly study that promised (though did not always manage) to dispel the fantasies, misconceptions and prejudices that had driven English perceptions of the subject for centuries and that were so rich a resource for Shakespeare and his contemporaries. England would now try to contain the Islamic world through orientalist scholarship and the painstaking study of philology, archaeology and comparative religion.

Scholarly endeavor was aided by political disengagement. The long, slow decline of the Ottoman Empire and its withdrawal from western Europe's borders from the end of the seventeenth century enabled European scholars to re-create the "Orient" anew. It became an exotic, sensuous world that was regarded as despotic and backward, where Europeans needed to impose order, rationality and enlightenment (though only on their own terms). The orient isle of Elizabethan England, for so long almost a confederate of the Islamic world, became an island of orientalism, as one set of myths and misconceptions of Islam gave way to another. Over time, England's early relations with Islam were quietly forgotten as the grander, more memorable fables of imperialism and orientalism prevailed. But that is part of another era's history.

The story told in this book is one of a largely unknown connection between England and the Islamic world, one that emerged out of a very specific set of circumstances during the European Reformation. English history still tends to view the Elizabethan period as defined by the timeless rhythms of agrarian Anglo-Saxon traditions, ethnically pure and exclusively white. But, as I hope this book has shown, there are other aspects to this island's national story that involve other cultures, and in the Elizabethan period one of them was Islam. To occlude the role Islam played in this past only diminishes its history. Now, when much is made of the "clash of civilizations" between Islam and Christianity, seems to me a good time to remember that the connections between the two faiths are much deeper and more entangled than many contemporary commentators seem to appreciate, and that in the sixteenth century Islamic empires like those of the Ottomans far surpassed the power and influence of a small and relatively insignificant state like Elizabethan England in their military power, political organization and commercial reach. It turns out that Islam in all its manifestations—imperial, military and commercial—is part of the British national story.

One way of encouraging tolerance and inclusiveness at a time when both are in short supply is to show both Muslim and Christian communities how, more than four centuries ago, absolute theological belief often yielded to strategic considerations, political pressures and mercantile interests. In a period of volatile and shifting political and religious allegiances, Muslims and Christians were forced to find a common language of messy and uneasy coexistence. Despite the sometimes intemperate religious rhetoric, the conflict between Christian Europe and the Islamic world was then, as now, defined as much by the struggle for power and precedence as by theology.

Today Britain is a multicultural society, with a significant community of Muslim believers, as is the United States, a country whose mores and institutions would come to be formed in its image. Developments over the past half century, intensified by recent events, have forced us to confront once more the question of Britain's relation with Islam, although they are very different from those experienced by the Elizabethans, when mass migration was almost nonexistent.

The impetus toward cultural integration that (mostly) followed the mass immigration of various communities into Britain as its empire collapsed in the mid-twentieth century, including Muslim communities from South Asia, is now being questioned as politicians and the media of various persuasions accuse British Muslims of failure to assimilate into the national culture. Born in Bradford in the north of England in the late 1960s, I went to school in nearby Leeds with Muslims, Hindus and Sikhs and we hardly ever spoke about religious belief and sectarian divisions as we played and learned together. It was not a multicultural idyll, but neither was our world defined by theological absolutes. This was my experience of Englishness, and I realize now that it partly explains why I wrote this book. If what I have written makes a small contribution to understanding the long and often difficult history of connections between Islam and the West, then it will have been worth the while.

Acknowledgments

Writing acknowledgments brings with it the realization that the origins of a book often go back much further than its author has appreciated. In my case they reach all the way to my inspirational English teacher in secondary school, Maggie Sheen, who first interested me in Shakespeare. She started me on a path that eventually led to this book, and to another important figure in my life, my great mentor, collaborator and friend Lisa Jardine. In the 1990s Lisa and I worked together on exchanges between western and eastern cultures in the Renaissance. Lisa's untimely death in the autumn of 2015 robbed Britain of one of its great public intellectuals, and it left me bereft of a dear friend and confidante who made me believe anything was possible. I wish she were still with us for many reasons, not least to see the publication of a book that, like its subject, is haunted by her absent presence.

Family and friends provided practical support, shrewd guidance and less tangible but equally crucial care and encouragement as I tussled with this book. For that I would like to thank Peter Barber, Jonathan Burton, Miles and Ranj Carter, Rebecca Chamberlain, Nick Crane, Kath Diamond, Simon Curtis, Dave and Sarah Griffiths, Lucy Hannington and Bence Hegedus, Helen Leblique, Ita MacCarthy, Nabil Matar, Nick Millea, Patricia Parker, Richard Scholar, Vik Sivalingam, Guy Richards Smit, Tim Supple, Ben and Katherine Turney, Dave and Emily Vest and Dan Vitkus. Emma and James Lambe provided their characteristically unwavering calm and unhesitating domestic help. Alexander Samson kindly shared unpublished research with me, Mia

Hewitt and Alice Agossini helped translate documents from the Spanish, Ton Hoenselaars read related articles and encouraged me to continue writing when I thought the project had defeated me, as did my dear old friend Maurizio Calbi. I am grateful to Patrick Spottiswoode, director of education at the Globe Theatre, for inviting me to hold the International Shakespeare Globe Fellowship in 2004 on the topic "Shakespeare and Islam," which allowed me to develop some of this book's ideas; to William Dalrymple, for allowing me a memorable opportunity to present the work in Jaipur; and to Peter Florence, who generously allows me to say and do marvelous things at his remarkable festivals in Hay and beyond. My agent, Peter Straus, has supported me tirelessly for a decade now, and I'm glad to have him by my side. At Viking, I wish to thank Joy De Menil for her tireless and exacting editorial work, as well as the rest of her team, especially Benjamin Sandman, Haley Swanson and Bruce Giffords. Once again Cecilia Mackay proved herself to be the best picture researcher in the business.

Every book I have ever written has celebrated the unique environment provided by Queen Mary University of London, where I have studied and worked for over twenty years. A dedicated team of people within the School of English and Drama make my working environment a real pleasure, and for that I want to thank Faisal Abul, Jonathan Boffey, Richard Coulton, Rob Ellis, Jenny Gault, Patricia Hamilton, Suzi Lewis, Huw Marsh, Matthew Mauger, Kate Russell and Bev Stewart. I am also proud to be an associate of the People's Palace Projects at Queen Mary, led by the inspirational Paul Heritage, and thank him and his team, especially Rosie Hunter and Thiago Jesus, for allowing me to work with them in Brazil on Shakespeare and many other exciting initiatives. Among my departmental colleagues I am lucky enough to have the support and friendship of Ruth Ahnert, John Barrell (who goes back even further), Michèle Barrett, Julia Boffey, Mark Currie, Markman Ellis, Katie Fleming, Paul Hamilton, Alfred Hiatt, Pete Mitchell, Claire Preston, Kirsty Rolfe, Morag Shiach, Bill Schwarz and Andrew van der Vlies. Acting as associate director on my old friend David Schalkwyk's Global Shakespeare project has also given me fantastic opportunities to explore Shakespeare beyond this sceptered isle. It would embarrass David Colclough

Acknowledgments

were I to tell him how much I cherish our enduring friendship, so I will stop here. I seem to have a weakness for Miltonists, because Joad Raymond has become a great friend since his arrival at Queen Mary, and I hope our alliance will generate more than one Penguin.

Several people were kind enough to read the whole manuscript and pointed out various omissions and infelicities. Matthew Dimmock and Gerald "Mac" MacLean gave me the benefit of their unrivaled expertise in the field, while the masterly Timothy Brook and his wife, Fay, offered sage advice on tone and structure. I am extremely grateful to them for taking time out of their busy schedules: friends indeed. Adam Lowe watched it all unfold from far away but is always near at hand, and I am very lucky to have him. My father, Alan Brotton, has not read the book, nor should he: all he needs to know is the love and admiration I feel for him sticking by me long enough for us to understand how much we care for each other.

The book is dedicated to my wife, Charlotte, not to settle a debt, but to honor a meeting of minds. A distinguished Shakespeare scholar in her own right, she read and commented on every line of this book, improving it immeasurably while also writing her own, bringing our daughter, Honey, into the world, and holding everyone in our family together with an effortlessness born of supreme endeavor. She will understand if I leave it to Shakespeare to tell her that my bounty is as boundless as the sea, my love as deep; the more I give to her, the more I have, for both are infinite.

Notes

ABBREVIATIONS

APC *Acts of the Privy Council*

Castries Henri de Castries et al., eds., *Sources inédites pour l'histoire du Maroc*, 26 vols. (Leiden: Martinus Nijhoff, 1905–1965)

CP Cecil Papers at Hatfield House, Hertfordshire, UK

CSPD *Calendar of State Papers, Domestic*

CSPF *Calendar of State Papers, Foreign*

CSPS *Calendar of State Papers, Spain*

CSPV *Calendar of State Paper, Venice*

Hakluyt Richard Hakluyt, *The Principal Navigations, Voyages, Traffiques and Discoveries of the English Nation*, 7 vols. (London: Everyman's Library/J. M. Dent, 1907)

LP *Letters and Papers, Foreign and Domestic, Henry VIII*

ODNB *Oxford Dictionary of National Biography*

OED *Oxford English Dictionary* Online

TNA The National Archives of the United Kingdom

All the official government records and reference books listed above are available online. All references to Shakespeare's plays (with the exception of *Othello*) are taken from Stephen Greenblatt et al., eds., *The Norton Shakespeare* (New York: W. W. Norton, 1997).

Introduction

1. Quoted in Susan A. Skilliter, *William Harborne and the Trade with Turkey, 1578– 1582: A Documentary Study of the First Anglo-Ottoman Relations* (Oxford: Oxford University Press, 1977), p. 69.
2. Quoted in ibid., pp. 69–70.

Notes

3. Caroline Finkel, *Osman's Dream: The Story of the Ottoman Empire, 1300–1923* (London: John Murray, 2005), pp. 164–78.
4. Leslie Peirce, *The Imperial Harem: Women and Sovereignty in the Ottoman Empire* (Oxford: Oxford University Press, 1993).
5. Skilliter, *William Harborne*, p. 37.
6. Edward Hall, *Hall's Chronicle: Containing the History of England during the reign of Henry the Fourth, and the succeeding Monarchs, to the end of the reign of Henry the Eighth* (London: British Museum, 1809), p. 513.
7. Miriam Jacobson, *Barbarous Antiquity: Reorienting the Past in the Poetry of Early Modern England* (Philadelphia: University of Pennsylvania Press, 2014), pp. 2–4.
8. See "Muslim, n. and adj." OED.
9. See "Islam, n." OED.
10. Richard Knolles, *The General Historie of the Turkes, from the first beginning of that Nation to the rising of the Othoman Familie* (London, 1603), sig. B47.
11. *Othello*, 1.1.135. This and all subsequent references to the play are taken from E. A. J. Honigmann, ed., *Othello* (Walton-on-Thames: Arden/Thomas Nelson, 1997).
12. Ibid., 1.3.140.
13. Ibid., 1.3.133–34.
14. John Ayre, ed., *The Early Works of Thomas Becon* (Cambridge: Cambridge University Press, 1843), p. 239.
15. Quoted in Noel Malcolm, "Positive Views of Islam and of Ottoman Rule in the Sixteenth Century: The Case of Jean Bodin," in *The Renaissance and the Ottoman World,* ed. Anna Contadini and Claire Norton (Farnham: Ashgate, 2013), pp. 197–220; at p. 212.

Chapter 1: Conquering Tunis

1. CSPS, vol. 13, *1554–1558,* no. 60, p. 49.
2. John Elder, "The Copy of a Letter Sent into Scotland, of the Arrival and Landing, and Most Notable Marriage of the Most Illustrious Prince, Philip of Spain," in *The Chronicle of Queen Jane,* ed. J. G. Nichols (London: Camden Society, 1850), appendix x, pp. 139–40.
3. Ibid.
4. Ibid.
5. Quoted in Henry Kamen, *Philip II* (New Haven: Yale University Press, 1997), p. 59.
6. Elder, "Copy of a Letter," pp. 139–40.
7. Quoted in Alexander Samson, "Changing Places: The Marriage and Royal Entry of Philip, Prince of Austria, and Mary Tudor, July–August 1554," *Sixteenth Century Journal* 36, no. 3 (2005), pp. 761–84; at p. 767.
8. CSPV, vol. 5, *1534–1554,* no. 898, p. 511. I am grateful to Alexander Samson for drawing this reference to my attention and allowing me to read his forthcoming work on the subject.
9. Quoted in James D. Tracy, *Emperor Charles V, Impresario of War: Campaign Strategy, International Finance, and Domestic Politics* (Cambridge: Cambridge University Press, 2002), pp. 155–56.
10. On the campaign, see Hendrick J. Horn, *Jan Cornelisz Vermeyen, Painter of Charles V and His Conquest of Tunis: Paintings, Etchings, Drawings, Cartoons and Tapestries,* 2 vols. (The Hague: Davaco, 1989).
11. CSPS, vol. 13, *1554–1558,* no. 227, p. 236.
12. LP, vol. 9, *August–December 1535,* no. 596, p. 200.
13. Thomas Burman, *Reading the Qur'ân in Latin Christendom, 1140–1560* (Philadelphia: University of Pennsylvania Press, 2009).

14. For the classic account of these prejudices, see Norman Daniel, *Islam and the West: The Making of an Image* (Edinburgh: Edinburgh University Press, 1960).
15. Margaret Meserve, *Empires of Islam in Renaissance Historical Thought* (Cambridge, Mass.: Harvard University Press, 2008); Nancy Bisaha, *Creating East and West: Renaissance Humanists and the Ottoman Turks* (Philadelphia: University of Pennsylvania Press, 2004).
16. Dorothee Metlitziki, *The Matter of Araby in Medieval England* (New Haven: Yale University Press, 1977).
17. See Suzanne Conklin Akbari, "The Non-Christians of *Piers Plowman*," in *The Cambridge Companion to Piers Plowman*, ed. Andrew Cole and Andrew Galloway (Cambridge: Cambridge University Press, 2014), pp. 160–78; at p. 170.
18. Quoted in Michael J. Heath, *Crusading Commonplaces: La Noue, Lucinge and Rhetoric Against the Turks* (Geneva: Droz, 1986), p. 15.
19. Burman, *Reading the Qur'ân*, pp. 110–16.
20. Quoted in Ina Baghdiantz McCabe, *Orientalism in Early Modern France: Eurasian Trade, Exoticism and the Ancien Regime* (Oxford: Berg, 2008), pp. 33–34.
21. Adam S. Francisco, *Martin Luther: A Study in Sixteenth-Century Polemics and Apologetics* (Leiden: Brill, 2007), pp. 69–70.
22. Martin Luther, "On the War Against the Turk," in *Luther's Works,* vol. 46, trans. Robert C. Schultz (Philadelphia: Concordia Press, 1962–1971), pp. 157–205.
23. CSPV, vol. 3, *1520–1526,* no. 616, p. 297.
24. Sir Thomas More, "A Dialog Concerning Heresies," in *The Yale Edition of the Complete Works of St. Thomas More,* ed. Thomas Lawler et al., vol. 6, Parts I and II, *A Dialog Concerning Heresies* (New Haven: Yale University Press, 1981), pp. 1–435; at p. 236.
25. "Instruction Given to the Emperor by the Most Reverend Cardinal Campeggio at the Diet of Augsburg, 1530," in Leopold von Ranke, *The History of the Popes During the Last Four Centuries,* 3 vols. (London: Bell & Sons, 1913), vol. 3, p. 40.
26. Gülru Necipoğlu, "Süleyman the Magnificent and the Representation of Power in the Context of Ottoman-Hapsburg-Papal Rivalry," *Art Bulletin* 71, no. 3 (September 1989), pp. 401–27.
27. Dorothy Vaughan, *Europe and the Turk: A Pattern of Alliances* (Liverpool: Liverpool University Press, 1954).
28. Desiderius Erasmus, "A Most Useful Discussion Concerning Proposals for War Against the Turks, Including an Exposition of Psalm 28," trans. Michael J. Heath, in *The Collected Works of Erasmus*, ed. Dominic Baker-Smith, vol. 64, *Expositions of the Psalms* (Toronto: Toronto University Press, 2005), pp. 201–66; at pp. 218, 231, 258–59.
29. Ibid., p. 242.
30. J. R. Tanner, ed., *Tudor Constitutional Documents, 1485–1603* (Cambridge: Cambridge University Press, 1922), p. 124.
31. John Foxe, *The Unabridged Acts and Monuments Online* (Sheffield: HRI Online Publications, 2011); available at www.johnfoxe.org, 1563 ed., book 5, p. 957.
32. Eamon Duffy, *Fires of Faith: Catholic England Under Mary Tudor* (New Haven: Yale University Press, 2009).
33. Samson, "Changing Places."
34. Ian Lancashire, *Dramatic Texts and Records of Britain: A Chronological Topography to 1558* (Cambridge: Cambridge University Press, 1984), p. 213.
35. Hakluyt, vol. 2, pp. 227–28.
36. Ibid., p. 267.
37. Ibid., p. 253.
38. Ibid., pp. 318–29.
39. Robert Batchelor, *London: The Selden Map and the Making of a Global City, 1549–1689* (Chicago: University of Chicago Press, 2014), p. 40.
40. Peter Barber, *The Queen Mary Atlas* (London: Folio Society, 2005), pp. 3–81.

Chapter 2: The Sultan, the Tsar and the Shah

1. David Loades, *Elizabeth I: A Life* (London: Hambledon Press, 2003), p. 138.

2. E. Delmar Morgan and C. H. Coote, eds., *Early Voyages and Travels to Russia and Persia by Anthony Jenkinson and Other Englishmen,* 2 vols. (London: Hakluyt Society, 1886), vol. 2, p. 341.

3. Anthony Jenkinson, "The Manner of the Entering of Süleyman the Great Turk with his Army into Aleppo," in ibid., vol. 1, pp. 1–5.

4. Quoted in Palmira Brummett, "The Myth of Shah Ismail Safavi: Political Rhetoric and 'Divine' Kingship," in *Medieval Christian Perceptions of Islam,* ed. John Tolan (New York: Routledge, 2000), pp. 331–59; at p. 343.

5. Quoted in Max Scherberger, "The Confrontation Between Sunni and Shi'i Empires: Ottoman-Safavid Relations Between the Fifteenth and the Seventeenth Century," in *The Sunna and Shi'a in History,* ed. Ofra Bengio and Meir Litvak (New York: Palgrave, 2011), pp. 51–68; at p. 55.

6. Quoted in Palmira Brummett, *Ottoman Seapower and Levantine Diplomacy* (Albany: State University of New York Press, 1994), p. 36.

7. Quoted in ibid., p. 29.

8. Ibid.

9. Morgan and Coote, *Early Voyages and Travels to Russia,* vol. 1, pp. 5–6.

10. Hakluyt, vol. 1, p. 390.

11. Morgan and Coote, *Early Voyages and Travels to Russia,* vol. 1, p. 30.

12. Ibid., pp. 58, 97.

13. Ibid., pp. 84–85.

14. Ibid., pp. 87–88.

15. Ibid., p. 93.

16. Ibid., p. 97.

17. Ibid., pp. 108–9.

18. Ibid., p. 58.

19. Daryl Palmer, *Writing Russia in the Age of Shakespeare* (Aldershot: Ashgate, 2004), p. 54.

20. Morgan and Coote, *Early Voyages and Travels to Russia,* vol. 1, pp. 112–13.

21. Ibid., pp. 113–14.

22. Ibid., p. 125.

23. Ibid., p. 126.

24. Ibid., pp. 143, 133.

25. Ibid., p. 140.

26. Kathryn Babayan, *Mystics, Monarchs, and Messiahs: Cultural Landscapes of Early Modern Iran* (Cambridge, Mass.: Harvard University Press, 2002), pp. 295–348.

27. Jean-Do Brignoli, "Princely Safavid Gardens: Stage for Rituals and of Imperial Display and Political Legitimacy," in *Middle East Garden Traditions: Unity and Diversity,* ed. Michael Conan (Washington, D.C.: Dumbarton Oaks, 2007), pp. 113–39.

28. Morgan and Coote, *Early Voyages and Travels to Russia,* vol. 1, pp. 153–54.

29. Ibid., pp. 145–47.

30. Colin P. Mitchell, "Am I My Brother's Keeper? Negotiating Corporate Sovereignty and Divine Absolutism in Sixteenth-Century Turco-Iranian Politics," in *New Perspectives on Safavid Iran,* ed. Colin P. Mitchell (London: Routledge, 2011), pp. 33–58.

31. Morgan and Coote, *Early Voyages and Travels to Russia,* vol. 1, pp. 144, 148.

32. Ibid., pp. 149–50.

33. Ibid., pp. 155–56.

34. Kenneth Andrews, *Trade, Plunder and Settlement: Maritime Enterprise and the Genesis of the British Empire, 1480–1630* (Cambridge: Cambridge University

Press, 1984), pp. 76–86; Jane Grogan, *The Persian Empire in English Renaissance Writing, 1549–1622* (Basingstoke: Palgrave, 2014), pp. 20–21.

35. Andrea Bernadette, "Elizabeth I and Persian Exchanges," in *The Foreign Relations of Elizabeth I*, ed. Charles Beem (Basingstoke: Palgrave, 2011), pp. 169–99; at pp. 184–85. Ippolyta appears to have had an important influence upon female portraiture of the time, including Marcus Gheeraerts's mysterious painting known as *The Persian Lady*, c. 1590.

36. Quoted in Morgan and Coote, *Early Voyages and Travels to Russia,* vol. 1, p. cxlix.

Chapter 3: The Battle for Barbary

1. Hakluyt, vol. 4, p. 32.
2. Ibid., p. 34.
3. T. S. Willan, *Studies in Elizabethan Foreign Trade* (Manchester: Manchester University Press, 1959), pp. 98–99.
4. Ibid., pp. 113, 314.
5. CSPF, vol. 5, *1562*, no. 103, p. 54.
6. "Garrard, Sir William (c. 1510–1571)," ODNB.
7. Quoted in Gustav Ungerer, "Portia and the Prince of Morocco," *Shakespeare Studies* 31 (2003), pp. 89–126; at p. 100.
8. Quoted in Willan, *Studies in Elizabethan Foreign Trade,* p. 127.
9. "Felton, John (d. 1570), Roman Catholic Martyr," ODNB.
10. "The Bull of Excommunication, 1570," in *Tudor Constitutional Documents, 1485–1603,* ed. J. R. Tanner (Cambridge: Cambridge University Press, 1922), pp. 143–46.
11. "Felton, John," ODNB.
12. Robert Horne, Bishop of Winchester, *An Answeare Made by Rob. Bishoppe of Wynchester, to a Booke entituled, The Declaration of svche Scruples, and staies of Conscience, touchinge the Othe of the Supremacy, as M. Iohn Fekenham, by wrytinge did deliuer vnto the L. Bishop of Winchester, with his Resolutions made thereunto . . .* (London, 1566), p. 102v.
13. Nate Probasco, "Queen Elizabeth's Reaction to the St. Bartholomew's Day Massacre," in *The Foreign Relations of Elizabeth I*, ed. Charles Beem (Basingstoke: Palgrave, 2011), pp. 77–100.
14. Quoted in Sophia Menache, *Clement V* (Cambridge: Cambridge University Press, 1998), p. 106.
15. Jerry Brotton and Lisa Jardine, *Global Interests: Renaissance Art Between East and West* (London: Reaktion, 2000); Christine Isom-Verhaaren, *Allies with the Infidel: The Ottoman and French Alliance in the Sixteenth Century* (London: I. B. Tauris, 2011).
16. Andrew C. Hess, "The Moriscos: An Ottoman Fifth Column in Sixteenth-Century Spain," *American Historical Journal* 74, no. 1 (1968), pp. 1–25.
17. Andrew C. Hess, *The Forgotten Frontier: A History of the Ibero-African Frontier* (Chicago: University of Chicago Press, 1978), pp. 85–90.
18. For the best recent account of the battle placed in the context of Christian-Islamic exchanges, see Noel Malcolm, *Agents of Empire: Knights, Corsairs, Jesuits and Spies in the Sixteenth-Century Mediterranean World* (London: Allen Lane, 2015), pp. 151–74.
19. Quoted in Benjamin Paul, "'And the moon has started to bleed': Apocalyptism and Religious Reform in Venetian Art at the Time of the Battle of Lepanto," in *The Turk and Islam in the Western Eye, 1450–1750,* ed. James G. Harper (Aldershot: Ashgate, 2011), pp. 67–94; at p. 69.
20. Raphael Holinshed, *The Third Volume of Chronicles* (London, 1587), pp. 1226–27.
21. Kervyn de Lettenhove, *Relations politiques des Pays Bas et de l'Angleterre sous le règne de Philippe II,* 11 vols. (Louvain, 1882–1900), vol. 6, p. 225.
22. Letters of William Herle Project, Center for Editing Lives and Letters, www.livesandletters.ac.uk; transcript ID: HRL/002/HTML/022.

23. Kenneth Andrews, *Trade, Plunder and Settlement: Maritime Enterprise and the Genesis of the British Empire, 1480–1630* (Cambridge: Cambridge University Press, 1984), p. 111.
24. Castries, vol. 1, p. 201.
25. Ibid.
26. Ibid., p. 202.
27. Ibid., pp. 204–5.
28. Ibid., pp. 212–13.
29. Ibid., pp. 226–27.
30. CSPF, vol. 12, *1577–1578*, August 9, 1577, no. 94, p. 68.
31. Quoted in Andrew C. Hess, "The Battle of Lepanto and Its Place in Mediterranean History," *Past and Present* 57 (1972), pp. 53–73; at p. 54.
32. Quoted in Susan A. Skilliter, *William Harborne and the Trade with Turkey, 1578–1582: A Documentary Study of the First Anglo-Ottoman Relations* (Oxford: Oxford University Press, 1977), p. 37.
33. Hakluyt, vol. 3, p. 51.
34. Skilliter, *William Harborne,* pp. 1–2.
35. "Stucley, Thomas (c. 1520–1578)," ODNB.
36. Charles Edelman, ed., *Three Stukeley Plays* (Manchester: Manchester University Press, 2005), p. 7.
37. Quoted in Susan Iwanisziw, "England, Morocco, and Global Geopolitical Upheaval," in *Envisioning an English Empire,* ed. Robert Applebaum and John Sweet (Philadelphia: University of Pennsylvania Press, 2005), pp. 152–71; at p. 163.
38. John Polemon, *The Second Part of the Booke of Battailes, Fought in Our Age Taken out of the Best Authors and Writers in Sundrie Languages* (London, 1587), p. 79.
39. E. W. Bovill, *The Battle of Alcazar: An Account of the Defeat of Don Sebastian of Portugal at El-Ksar El-Kebir* (London: Batchworth, 1952), p. 97.
40. Edelman, *Stukeley Plays,* p. 15.
41. Polemon, *Booke of Battailes,* p. 86.
42. Bovill, *Battle of Alcazar,* p. 145.

Chapter 4: An Apt Man in Constantinople

1. Quoted in Susan A. Skilliter, *William Harborne and the Trade with Turkey, 1578–1582: A Documentary Study of the First Anglo-Ottoman Relations* (Oxford: Oxford University Press, 1977), pp. 28–30.
2. On Harborne's life see "Harborne, William (c. 1542–1617)," ODNB.
3. Zeynep Çelik, *The Remaking of Istanbul: Portrait of an Ottoman City in the Nineteenth Century* (Berkeley: University of California Press, 1993), pp. 22–29.
4. Emine Fetvaci, *Picturing History at the Ottoman Court* (Bloomington: Indiana University Press, 2013), pp. 43–46.
5. Skilliter, *William Harborne,* p. 45.
6. Hakluyt, vol. 3, p. 51.
7. Skilliter, *William Harborne,* pp. 62–64.
8. Ibid., p. 63.
9. Ibid., p. 49.
10. Hakluyt, vol. 3, p. 52.
11. Ibid., pp. 52–53.
12. Skilliter, *William Harborne,* p. 54.
13. Ibid., p. 59.
14. CSPF, vol. 14, *1579–1580,* no. 71, p. 77.
15. Rayne Allinson, *A Monarchy of Letters: Royal Correspondence and English Diplomacy in the Reign of Elizabeth I* (Basingstoke: Palgrave, 2012), pp. 131–50.
16. Skilliter, *William Harborne,* p. 51.

17. CSPS, vol. 2, *1568–1579,* no. 609, pp. 705–6.
18. Ibid., p. 706.
19. Ibid., p. 710.
20. Hakluyt, vol. 3, p. 54.
21. Cornell H. Fleischer, *Bureaucrat and Intellectual in the Ottoman Empire: The Historian Mustafa Ali (1541–1600)* (Princeton, N.J.: Princeton University Press, 1986), pp. 72–73.
22. Skilliter, *William Harborne,* pp. 79–80.
23. Hakluyt, vol. 3, p. 58.
24. Ibid., p. 61.
25. Skilliter, *William Harborne,* p. 120.
26. Ibid., p. 151.
27. Quoted in Andrew P. Vella, *An Elizabethan-Ottoman Conspiracy* (Valletta: Royal University of Malta Press, 1972), pp. 41–42.
28. Skilliter, *William Harborne,* p. 159.
29. Vella, *Elizabethan-Ottoman Conspiracy,* p. 46.
30. Ibid., pp. 46–47.
31. Skilliter, *William Harborne,* pp. 155–57.
32. De Lamar Jensen, "The Ottoman Turks in Sixteenth-Century French Diplomacy," *Sixteenth Century Journal* 16, no. 4 (1985), pp. 451–70.
33. Vella, *Elizabethan-Ottoman Conspiracy,* pp. 64–65.
34. Skilliter, *William Harborne,* p. 166.

Chapter 5: Unholy Alliances

1. Quoted in T. S. Willan, *Studies in Elizabethan Foreign Trade* (Manchester: Manchester University Press, 1959), p. 155.
2. John Wheeler, *A Treatise of Commerce* (London, 1601), p. 13.
3. Hakluyt, vol. 3, p. 65.
4. Stephen Gosson, *The School of Abuse* (London, 1579), sig. D3r.
5. Stephen Gosson, *Plays Confuted in Five Actions* (London, 1582), sig. G8r.
6. Peter Thomson, *Shakespeare's Professional Career* (Cambridge: Cambridge University Press, 1992), p. 69.
7. Andreas Höfele, *Stage, Stake and Scaffold: Humans and Animals in Shakespeare's Theater* (Oxford: Oxford University Press, 2011).
8. Robert Wilson, *The Three Ladies of London,* 1.11–17. This and all subsequent references to the play are taken from Lloyd Edward Kermode, ed., *Three Renaissance Usury Plays* (Manchester: Manchester University Press, 2009), pp. 79–163.
9. Ibid., 2.222.
10. Ibid., 2.228, 241.
11. Ibid., 3.32.
12. Ibid., 3.42–46.
13. Ibid., 3.53–57.
14. Jonathan Gil Harris, *Sick Economies: Drama, Mercantilism and Disease in Shakespeare's England* (Philadelphia: University of Pennsylvania Press, 2003).
15. Lloyd Edward Kermode, "Money, Gender and Conscience in Robert Wilson's *The Three Ladies of London*," *Studies in English Literature 1500–1900* 52, no. 2 (2012), pp. 265–91.
16. Wilson, *Three Ladies,* 9.3–9.
17. Ibid., 9.26–27.
18. Ibid., 9.34.
19. Ibid., 14.13.
20. Ibid., 14.15–16.
21. Ibid., 14.20.
22. Ibid., 14.49.

23. Ibid., 14.58–59.
24. Alan Stewart, "'Come from Turkey': Mediterranean Trade in Late Elizabethan London," in *Remapping the Mediterranean World in Early Modern English Writings,* ed. Goran Stanivukovic (Basingstoke: Palgrave, 2007), pp. 157–78.
25. Wilson, *Three Ladies,* 17.103.
26. Norman Jones, *God and the Moneylenders: Usury and the Law in Early Modern England* (Oxford: Blackwell, 1989); Craig Muldrew, *The Economy of Obligation: The Culture of Credit and Social Relations in Early Modern England* (Basingstoke: Palgrave, 1998).
27. John Aylmer to Lord Mayor of London, September 23, 1582, London Metropolitan Archive (LMA) COL/RMD/PA/01 f. 199r. For a discussion of the letter's significance, see Matthew Dimmock, "Early Modern Travel, Conversion, and Languages of 'Difference,'" *Journeys* 14, no. 2 (2013), pp. 10–26. I am grateful to Professor Dimmock for bringing this letter to my attention.
28. CSPS, vol. 3, *1580–1586,* no. 265, pp. 366–67.
29. Alfred C. Wood, *A History of the Levant Company* (London: Oxford University Press, 1935), pp. 12–13.
30. Susan A. Skilliter, *William Harborne and the Trade with Turkey, 1578–1582: A Documentary Study of the First Anglo-Ottoman Relations* (Oxford: Oxford University Press, 1977), p. 183.
31. Hakluyt, vol. 3, pp. 85–88.
32. Quoted in Nabil Matar, "Elizabeth Through Moroccan Eyes," in *The Foreign Relations of Elizabeth I,* ed. Charles Beem (Basingstoke: Palgrave, 2011), pp. 145–67; at p. 147.
33. Castries, vol. 1, p. 391.
34. CSPS, vol. 3, *1580–1586,* no. 150, p. 199.
35. Quoted in Willan, *Studies in Elizabethan Foreign Trade,* p. 167.
36. Castries, vol. 1, pp. 413–16.
37. Ibid., pp. 418–19.
38. Ibid., p. 419.
39. "Barton, Edward (1562/3–1598)," ODNB.
40. Hakluyt, vol. 3, p. 109.
41. CSPV, vol. 8, *1581–1591,* no. 131, pp. 55–56.
42. Bodleian Library MS. Landsdowne 57, f. 66r, Oxford.
43. Hakluyt, vol. 3, p. 114.
44. Quoted in H. G. Rawlinson, "The Embassy of William Harborne to Constantinople, 1583–88," *Transactions of the Royal Historical Society,* 4th series, vol. 5 (1922), pp. 1–27; at p. 8.
45. CSPV, vol. 8, *1581–1591,* nos. 126, 130, pp. 50–53.
46. Ibid., no. 131, p. 56.
47. CSPF, vol. 17, *January–June 1583,* addenda, May 12 and 23, 1583, no. 738.
48. J. Horton Ryley, *Ralph Fitch: England's Pioneer to India and Burma* (London: Unwin, 1899).
49. *Macbeth,* 1.3.6.
50. Castries, vol. 1, p. 459.
51. Ibid., p. 460.
52. Hakluyt, vol. 4, pp. 268–73.
53. Ibid., vol. 3, pp. 146–47, 150.
54. Ibid., p. 159.
55. Colin Martin and Geoffrey Parker, *The Spanish Armada* (London: Hamish Hamilton, 1989), pp. 89–90.
56. Letters of William Herle Project, Center for Editing Lives and Letters, www.livesandletters.ac.uk; transcript ID: HRL/002/PDF/325.
57. Conyers Read, *Mr. Secretary Walsingham and the Policy of Queen Elizabeth,* 3 vols. (Oxford: Clarendon Press, 1925), vol. 3, p. 226.

58. Ibid., p. 228.
59. Quoted in Arthur Leon Horniker, "William Harborne and the Beginning of Anglo-Turkish Diplomatic and Commercial Relations," *Journal of Modern History* 14, no. 3 (1942), pp. 289–316; at p. 315.
60. Castries, vol. 1, p. 545.
61. Hakluyt, vol. 4, p. 274.
62. Quoted in Mercedes García-Arenal, *Ahmad al-Mansur: The Beginnings of Modern Morocco* (Oxford: Oneworld, 2009), p. 115.
63. Hakluyt, vol. 4, p. 274.
64. Emily Gottreich, *The Mellah of Marrakesh: Jewish and Muslim Space in Morocco's Red City* (Bloomington: Indiana University Press, 2007).
65. Nabil Matar, *Islam in Britain, 1558–1685* (Cambridge: Cambridge University Press, 1998), pp. 22–23.
66. Carsten L. Wilke, *The Marrakesh Dialogs: A Gospel Critique and Jewish Apology from the Spanish Renaissance* (Leiden: Brill, 2014).
67. Hakluyt, vol. 4, p. 274.
68. Castries, vol. 1, pp. 480–83.
69. Willan, *Studies in Elizabethan Foreign Trade,* pp. 253–55.
70. Wood, *Levant Company,* p. 17.
71. CSPV, vol. 8, *1581–1591,* no. 336, p. 154.

Chapter 6: Sultana Isabel

1. Meredith Hanmer, D. of Diuinitie, *The Baptizing of a Turke: a sermon preached at the Hospitall of Saint Katherin, adioyning vnto her Maiesties Towre the 2. of October 1586. at the baptizing of one Chinano a Turke, borne at Nigropontus* (London: Robert Waldegrave, 1586).
2. D. B. Quinn, *Explorers and Colonies: America, 1500–1625* (London: Hambledon Press, 1990), pp. 198–204.
3. APC, England, vol. 14, *1586–1587,* p. 205.
4. Bodleian Library MS. Tanner 77, f. 3v, Oxford.
5. Hakluyt, vol. 3, p. 150.
6. Nabil Matar, *British Captives from the Mediterranean to the Atlantic, 1563–1760* (Leiden: Brill, 2014), pp. 71–75; Daniel Vitkus, ed., *Piracy, Slavery, and Redemption: Barbary Captivity Narratives from Early Modern England* (New York: Columbia University Press, 2001).
7. C. E. Bosworth, *An Intrepid Scot: William Lithgow of Lanark's Travels in the Ottoman Lands, North Africa and Central Europe, 1609–21* (Aldershot: Ashgate, 2006), p. 115.
8. Quoted in Gerald MacLean, *Looking East: English Writing and the Ottoman Empire Before 1800* (Basingstoke: Palgrave, 2007), ch. 3, n15.
9. Hakluyt, vol. 3, p. 131.
10. Edward Webbe, *The Rare and Most Wonderfull Things Which Edward Webbe an Englishman Borne, Hath Seene and Passed in His Troublesome Travailes, in the Cities of Jerusalem, Damasko, Bethlehem and Galely: and in the Landes of Jewrie, Egypt, Grecia, Russia, and Prester John* (London: William Wright, 1590).
11. "Webbe, Edward (b. 1553/4)," ODNB.
12. Bodleian Library MS. Tanner 77, f. 4r.
13. Ibid.
14. Quoted in Susan A. Skilliter, *William Harborne and the Trade with Turkey, 1578–1582: A Documentary Study of the First Anglo-Ottoman Relations* (Oxford: Oxford University Press, 1977), p. 36.
15. Bodleian Library MS. Tanner 77, f. 4r.
16. Roger M. Savory, *Iran Under the Safavids* (Cambridge: Cambridge University Press, 1980), pp. 72–75.

17. Conyers Read, *Mr. Secretary Walsingham and the Policy of Queen Elizabeth,* 3 vols. (Oxford: Clarendon Press, 1925), vol. 3, pp. 329–30.
18. Ibid., p. 330.
19. Quoted in Arthur Leon Horniker, "William Harborne and the Beginning of Anglo-Turkish Diplomatic and Commercial Relations," *Journal of Modern History* 14, no. 3 (1942), pp. 289–316; at pp. 309–10.
20. Bodleian Library MS. Tanner 77, ff. 4r–5r.
21. Ibid., f. 4r.
22. Quoted in H. G. Rawlinson, "The Embassy of William Harborne to Constantinople, 1583–88," *Transactions of the Royal Historical Society,* 4th series, vol. 5 (1922), pp. 1–27; at p. 15.
23. CSPF, vol. 22, *July–December 1588,* pp. 97–110.
24. Hakluyt, vol. 3, p. 368.
25. Castries, vol. 1, p. 502.
26. The description of these events is based on Gustav Ungerer, "Portia and the Prince of Morocco," *Shakespeare Studies* 31 (2003), pp. 89–126; at pp. 97–98.
27. Quoted in Nabil Matar, "Elizabeth Through Moroccan Eyes," in *The Foreign Relations of Elizabeth I,* ed. Charles Beem (Basingstoke: Palgrave, 2011), pp. 145–67; at p. 150.
28. Ibid., pp. 150–51.
29. David Loades, *Elizabeth I: A Life* (London: Hambledon Press, 2003), p. 253.
30. Matar, "Elizabeth Through Moroccan Eyes," p. 150.
31. Hakluyt, vol. 4, p. 275.
32. Ibid.
33. Quoted in Matar, "Elizabeth Through Moroccan Eyes," p. 152.
34. Hakluyt, vol. 4, p. 275.

Chapter 7: London Turns Turk

1. Castries, vol. 1, pp. 513–14.
2. R. B. Wernham, "Elizabeth and the Portugal Expedition of 1589," *English Historical Review* 66, no. 258 (1951), pp. 1–26.
3. Castries, vol. 1, pp. 516–17.
4. T. S. Willan, *Studies in Elizabethan Foreign Trade* (Manchester: Manchester University Press, 1959), pp. 229–32.
5. Robert Wilson, *The Three Ladies of London,* Prolog, 1–2.
6. Christoper Marlowe, *Tamburlaine the Great, Part 1,* Prolog, 1–8. All references to both parts of *Tamburlaine the Great* are taken from *Christopher Marlowe: Doctor Faustus and Other Plays,* ed. David Bevington and Eric Rasmussen (Oxford: Oxford University Press, 1995), pp. 1–68.
7. C. H. Herford, Percy Simpson, and Evelyn Simpson, eds., *Ben Jonson: The Complete Works,* 11 vols. (Oxford: Clarendon Press, 1925–1963), vol. 8, p. 587.
8. Thomas Nashe, "To the Gentlemen Students of Both Universities," in Robert Greene, *Greene's Arcadia or Menaphon* (London, 1589), sig. A2.
9. Robert Greene, *Perimedes the Black-Smith* (London, 1588), sig. A3r. Buskins are boots often worn by actors.
10. Marlowe, *Tamburlaine, Part 1,* 3.3.40–47.
11. Ibid., 4.2.2.
12. Ibid., 4.2.31–32.
13. John Michael Archer, "Islam and Tamburlaine's World Picture," in *A Companion to the Global Renaissance: English Literature and Culture in the Era of Expansion,* ed. Jyotsna Singh (Oxford: Blackwell, 2009), pp. 67–81; at pp. 76–77.
14. Marlowe, *Tamburlaine, Part 2,* 1.1.137–42.
15. Ibid., 5.1.171–74.
16. Ibid., 5.1.185–89.

17. Ibid., 5.1.190–95.
18. Ibid., 5.1.196, 198.
19. Ibid., 5.3.42–53.
20. David Riggs, "Marlowe's Life," in *The Cambridge Companion to Christopher Marlowe*, ed. Patrick Cheney (Cambridge: Cambridge University Press, 2004), pp. 24–40.
21. Title page of the first edition of the two parts of Christopher Marlowe, *Tamburlaine the Great* (London, 1590).
22. George Peele, *The Battle of Alcazar*, 1. Prolog, 6–7, 16. All references to Peele's play are taken from Charles Edelman, ed., *Three Stukeley Plays* (Manchester: Manchester University Press, 2005), pp. 59–128.
23. See "Moor, n.2." OED.
24. Leo Africanus, quoted in Jerry Brotton, "Moors," in *The Oxford Companion to Shakespeare*, ed. Michael Dobson and Stanley Wells (Oxford: Oxford University Press, 2011), p. 304.
25. Peele, *Battle of Alcazar*, 1.1.64–65.
26. Ibid., 1.1.10–11.
27. Ibid., 2.2.15–16.
28. Ibid., 2.2.69–82.
29. Emily C. Bartels, *Speaking of the Moor: From Alcazar to Othello* (Philadelphia: University of Pennsylvania Press, 2008), pp. 21–44.
30. George Peele, "A Farewell Entitled to the Famous and Fortunate Generals of Our English Forces," in *The Works of George Peele*, ed. Alexander Dyce, 2 vols. (London: William Pickering, 1829), vol. 2, pp. 169–72: at p. 170. "Poo" is an archaic word for poll, or head.
31. Wernham, "Elizabeth and the Portugal Expedition," first part, pp. 19–23.
32. Quoted in R. B. Wernham, "Elizabeth and the Portugal Expedition of 1589 (Continued)," *English Historical Review* 66, no. 259 (1951), pp. 194–218; at p. 207.
33. Nabil Matar, *Britain and Barbary, 1589–1689* (Gainesville: University Press of Florida, 2005), pp. 18–19; Mercedes García-Arenal, *Ahmad al-Mansur: The Beginnings of Modern Morocco* (Oxford: Oneworld, 2009), pp. 84–85.
34. Castries, vol. 1, pp. 532–34.
35. Ibid., pp. 537–38.
36. Ibid., pp. 536–37.
37. Matar, *Britain and Barbary*, p. 19.
38. Quoted in Nabil Matar, "Elizabeth Through Moroccan Eyes," in *The Foreign Relations of Elizabeth I*, ed. Charles Beem (Basingstoke: Palgrave, 2011), pp. 145–67; at p. 152.
39. *The Fugger Newsletter, Second Series: Being a Further Selection from the Fugger Papers Specially Referring to Queen Elizabeth and Matters Relating to England During the Years 1568–1605* (London: John Lane, 1926), p. 217.
40. Quoted in García-Arenal, *Ahmad al-Mansur*, p. 105.
41. Matar, "Elizabeth Through Moroccan Eyes," p. 154.
42. Peter Berek, "Tamburlaine's Weak Sons: Imitation as Interpretation Before 1593," *Renaissance Drama* 13 (1982), pp. 55–82; at p. 58.
43. All references to Greene's play are taken from Daniel Vitkus, ed., *Three Turk Plays from Early Modern England* (New York: Columbia University Press, 2000), pp. 55–148.
44. Greene, *Selimus*, 10.16, 12.20, 2.98, 2.102, 2.105.
45. Ibid., Conclusion, 5–6.
46. Robert Greene, *Alphonsus, King of Aragon*, 3.3.1248, s.d. All references to this play are taken from W. W. Greg, ed., *Alphonsus, King of Aragon, 1599* (Oxford: Malone Society, 1926).
47. Ibid., 5.1.2077.

48. Jonathan Gil Harris, *Untimely Matter in the Time of Shakespeare* (Philadelphia: University of Pennsylvania Press, 2009), pp. 77–81.
49. Christopher Marlowe, *The Jew of Malta*, 1.1.37, 127. This and all subsequent references to the play are from Bevington and Rasmussen, *Christopher Marlowe*, pp. 247–322.
50. Ibid., 2.3.216.
51. Ibid., 5.5.83–85.
52. Ibid., 2.3.175–81, 192–99.
53. James Shapiro, *Shakespeare and the Jews* (New York: Columbia University Press, 1996).
54. Marlowe, *The Jew of Malta*, 1.1.19–24.
55. Ibid., 1.1.37.
56. Charles Nicholl, *The Reckoning: The Murder of Christopher Marlowe* (London: Jonathan Cape, 1992).

Chapter 8: Mahomet's Dove

1. R. A. Foakes, ed., *Henslowe's Diary*, 2d ed. (Cambridge: Cambridge University Press, 2002), pp. 16–18. On the exact sequence in which the three parts of *Henry VI* were written and with whom, see Gary Taylor, "Shakespeare and Others: The Authorship of *Henry the Sixth, Part One*," *Medieval and Renaissance Drama* 7 (1995), pp. 145–205.
2. James Bednarz, "Marlowe and the English Literary Scene," in *The Cambridge Companion to Christopher Marlowe*, ed. Patrick Cheney (Cambridge: Cambridge University Press, 2004), pp. 90–105; Jonathan Bate, *The Genius of Shakespeare* (London: Picador, 1997), p. 108.
3. Quoted in the introduction to *Henry VI, Part 1*, in *The Oxford Shakespeare*, ed. Michael Taylor (Oxford: Oxford University Press, 2003), p. 2.
4. *Henry VI, Part I*, 1.2.52–54.
5. Ibid., 1.2.72, 84.
6. Ibid., 1.2.140–45.
7. Meredith Hanmer, D. of Diuinitie, *The Baptizing of a Turke: a sermon preached at the Hospitall of Saint Katherin, adioyning vnto her Maiesties Towre the 2. of October 1586. at the baptizing of one Chinano a Turke, borne at Nigropontus* (London: Robert Waldegrave, 1586), p. 9.
8. Sir Walter Raleigh, *The History of the World*, 6 vols. (Edinburgh, 1820), vol. 2, p. 170.
9. Thomas Nashe, "The Terrors of the Night, or a Discourse of Apparitions," in *The Unfortunate Traveler and Other Works*, ed. J. B. Steane (London: Penguin, 1972), p. 214.
10. Wallace T. MacCaffery, *Elizabeth I: War and Politics 1558–1603* (Princeton, N.J.: Princeton University Press, 1992), pp. 137–83; Chris Fitter, "Emergent Shakespeare and the Politics of Protest: 2 *Henry VI* in Historical Contexts," *English Literary History* 72, no. 1 (2005), pp. 129–58.
11. Quoted in Matthew Dimmock, *New Turkes: Dramatizing Islam and the Ottoman Empire in Early Modern England* (Aldershot: Ashgate, 2005), p. 163.
12. "Barton, Edward (1562/3–1598)," ODNB; De Lamar Jensen, "The Ottoman Turks in Sixteenth Century French Diplomacy," *Sixteenth Century Journal* 16, no. 4 (1985), pp. 451–70; at p. 468.
13. Quoted in Nancy Lyman Roelker, *One King, One Faith: The Parlement of Paris and the Religious Reformations of the Sixteenth Century* (Berkeley: University of California Press, 1996), p. 412.
14. Quoted in MacCaffery, *Elizabeth I*, p. 178.
15. Richard Verstegen, *A Declaration of the True Causes of the Great Troubles, Presupposed to be Intended against the Realm of England* (Antwerp, 1592), p. 48.

16. Ibid., pp. 48–49.
17. Francis Bacon, "Certain Observations made upon a Libel Published this Present Year, 1592," in *The Letters and the Life of Francis Bacon,* ed. James Spedding, 7 vols. (London, 1861–1874), vol. 1, pp. 146–208; at p. 204.
18. CSPD, vol. 3, *1591–1594,* no. 79, April 27, 1594.
19. Hakluyt, vol. 4, p. 8.
20. Leslie P. Peirce, *The Imperial Harem: Women and Sovereignty in the Ottoman Empire* (Oxford: Oxford University Press, 1993), pp. 224–28; Susan Skilliter, "Three Letters from the Ottoman 'Sultana' Safiye to Queen Elizabeth I," in *Documents from Islamic Chanceries,* ed. S. M. Stern (Cambridge, Mass.: Harvard University Press, 1965), pp. 119–57.
21. Quoted in Skilliter, "Three Letters," pp. 131–32.
22. Arthur Golding, trans., *The xv bookes of P. Ovidius Naso, entytuled Metamorphosis* (London, 1567), sig. B1.
23. *Titus Andronicus,* 3.1. s.d.
24. Ibid., 2.4.12.
25. Ibid., 3.1.184.
26. T. S. Eliot, "Seneca in Elizabethan Translation," in *Selected Essays, 1917–1932* (London: Faber & Faber, 1932), pp. 65–105.
27. Quoted in Dominic Shellard, *Kenneth Tynan: A Life* (New Haven: Yale University Press, 2003), p. 137.
28. www.theguardian.com/commentisfree/2014/may/12/theater-blood-gore-titus-andronicus.
29. *Titus Andronicus,* 4.2.65.
30. Ibid., 5.1.63–64.
31. Ibid., 4.2.91.
32. Ibid., 5.3.178.
33. For the case that Peele wrote much of the play's first act and three other scenes, see Brian Vickers, *Shakespeare, Co-Author: A Historical Study of Five Collaborative Plays* (Oxford: Oxford University Press, 2002), pp. 148–243. Vickers argues that the preponderance of alliteration and polysyllabic words suggests Peele had a hand in writing the first act and some of the later scenes.
34. *Titus Andronicus,* 5.3.120.
35. Ibid., 2.3.34–36.
36. Ibid., 3.1.203–4.
37. Ibid., 5.1.124–44.
38. Ibid., 5.3.184–89.
39. Ibid., 5.1.21.
40. Ibid., 5.1.68, 71.
41. Ibid., 5.1.73–83.
42. Castries, vol. 2, pp. 89–90.
43. R. B. Wernham, *The Return of the Armadas: The Last Years of the Elizabethan War Against Spain, 1595–1603* (Oxford: Oxford University Press, 1994), pp. 91–113; Edward Tenace, "A Strategy of Reaction: The Armadas of 1596 and 1597 and the Spanish Struggle for European Hegemony," *English Historical Review* 118, no. 478 (2003), pp. 855–82; Paul E. J. Hammer, "Myth-making: Politics, Propaganda and the Capture of Cadiz in 1596," *Historical Journal* 40, no. 3 (1997), pp. 621–42.
44. Castries, vol. 2, pp. 93–94.
45. Quoted in Wernham, *Return of the Armadas,* p. 107.
46. Quoted in Nabil Matar, "Elizabeth Through Moroccan Eyes," in *The Foreign Relations of Elizabeth I,* ed. Charles Beem (Basingstoke: Palgrave, 2011), pp. 145–67; at p. 156.
47. See Nabil Matar, *Britain and Barbary, 1589–1689* (Gainesville: University Press of Florida, 2005), p. 21; he characterizes this moment as a "jihad."

48. Wernham, *Return of the Armadas,* pp. 130–69.
49. *The Merchant of Venice,* 4.1.304–5.
50. Ibid., 4.1.382.
51. Quoted in James Shapiro, *Shakespeare and the Jews* (New York: Columbia University Press, 1996), p. 73.
52. *The Merchant of Venice,* 3.1.49–54.
53. Ibid., 3.1.54–61.
54. Ibid., 4.1.169.
55. Ibid., 1.2.109–10.
56. Ibid., 2.1.1–7.
57. Ibid., 2.1.8–12.
58. Ibid., 2.1.24–26.
59. Ibid., 2.7.78–79.
60. Castries, vol. 2, p. 64.
61. T. S. Willan, *Studies in Elizabethan Foreign Trade* (Manchester: Manchester University Press, 1959), p. 296.

Chapter 9: Escape from the Seraglio

1. Quoted in H. E. Rosedale, *Queen Elizabeth and the Levant Company* (London, 1904), p. 18.
2. Quoted in ibid., p. 27.
3. Quoted in ibid., pp. 27–28, 39.
4. Quoted in Gerald MacLean, *The Rise of Oriental Travel: English Visitors to the Ottoman Empire, 1580–1720* (Basingstoke: Palgrave, 2004), p. 40.
5. "Barton, Edward (1562/3–1598)," ODNB.
6. Quoted in Franklin L. Baumer, "England, the Turk and the Common Corps of Christendom," *American Historical Review* 50, no. 1 (1944), pp. 26–48; at p. 35.
7. Alfred C. Wood, *A History of the Levant Company* (London: Oxford University Press, 1935), pp. 22–24.
8. Anders Ingram, "English Literature on the Ottoman Turks in the Sixteenth and Seventeenth Centuries," PhD thesis, University of Durham, 2009, pp. 388–95; available at Durham E-Theses Online: http://etheses.dur.ac.uk/86/. See also his book *Writing the Ottomans: Turkish History in Early Modern England* (Basingstoke: Macmillan, 2015).
9. On carpets, rugs and other material imports through the Ottoman territories, see Gerald MacLean, *Looking East: English Writing and the Ottoman Empire Before 1800* (Basingstoke: Palgrave, 2007), pp. 27–62.
10. Karen Hearn, *Dynasties: Painting in Tudor and Jacobean England, 1530–1630* (London: Tate Publishing, 1996), p. 64.
11. Jean Lobbet to Philip Sidney, Strasburg, July 5, 1575, in *The Correspondence of Sir Philip Sidney,* ed. Roger Kuin, 2 vols. (Oxford: Oxford University Press, 2012), vol. 1, p. 483.
12. R. W. Maslen, ed., *An Apology for Poetry (or The Defense of Poesy): Philip Sidney* (Manchester: Manchester University Press, 2002), p. 105.
13. Charles Lethbridge Kingsford, "Essex House, Formerly Leicester House and Exeter Inn," *Archaeologia, or Miscellaneous Tracts Relating to Antiquity* 73 (1923), pp. 1–51.
14. Lionel Cust, "The Lumley Inventories," *Walpole Society* 6 (1918), pp. 15–35.
15. Robert Brenner, *Merchants and Revolution: Commercial Change, Political Conflict, and London's Overseas Traders, 1550–1653* (Cambridge: Cambridge University Press, 1993), pp. 25, 42.
16. *The Taming of the Shrew,* 2.1.345.
17. *The Comedy of Errors,* 4.1.104.

18. Santina M. Levey, *The Embroideries at Hardwick Hall: A Catalog* (London: National Trust Books, 2007), pp. 380–85; Hakluyt, vol. 2, pp. 201–3.
19. Wood, *Levant Company,* p. 24; T. S. Willan, "Some Aspects of English Trade with the Levant in the Sixteenth Century," *English Historical Review* 70, no. 276 (1955), pp. 399–410.
20. Sir William Foster, ed., *The Travels of John Sanderson in the Levant, 1584–1602* (London: Hakluyt Society, 1931), pp. 32, 33.
21. Gillian White, "'That whyche ys nedefoulle and nesesary': The Nature and Purpose of the Original Furnishings and Decoration of Hardwick Hall, Derbyshire," PhD thesis, University of Warwick, 2 vols., 2005, vol. 1, p. 99.
22. Levey, *The Embroideries at Hardwick Hall,* pp. 99–109.
23. Matthew Dimmock, *New Turkes: Dramatizing Islam and the Ottoman Empire in Early Modern England* (Aldershot: Ashgate, 2005), pp. 167–68.
24. *Richard II,* 4.1.125–32.
25. *Henry IV, Part 1,* 1.1.12–13.
26. Ibid., 1.1.19–27.
27. Ibid., 5.2.85.
28. Ibid., 2.4.94–97.
29. *Henry IV, Part 2,* 2.4.136, 141, 155.
30. Ibid., 5.2.44–49.
31. William Hazlitt, *Characters of Shakespeare's Plays* (London, 1817), p. 192.
32. Norman Rabkin, "Rabbits, Ducks and *Henry V,*" *Shakespeare Quarterly* 28, no. 3 (1977), pp. 279–96.
33. *Henry V,* 3.4.38–41.
34. Nabil Matar and Gerald MacLean, *Britain and the Islamic World, 1558–1713* (Oxford: Oxford University Press, 2011), p. 28; Jonathan Burton, *Traffic and Turning: Islam and English Drama, 1579–1624* (Newark: University of Delaware Press, 2005), p. 163; Deanne Williams, *The French Fetish from Chaucer to Shakespeare* (Cambridge: Cambridge University Press, 2004), pp. 51–52.
35. *Henry V,* 3.1.34.
36. John Calvin, *Institutes of the Christian Religion,* ed. John Allen, 2 vols. (London: Thomas Regg, 1844), vol. 2, pp. 94–95.
37. John Foxe, *The Unabridged Acts and Monuments Online;* available at www.john foxe.org, 1570 ed., Book 6, p. 893.
38. Ronald Lightbown, *Carlo Crivelli* (New Haven: Yale University Press, 2004), p. 117.
39. Edward Seymour Forster, ed., *The Turkish Letters of Ogier Ghiselin de Busbecq* (1927; repr., Oxford: Oxford University Press, 1968), pp. 54–55.
40. Ibid., pp. 56, 131.
41. Richard Johnson, *The Most Famous History of the Seven Champions of Christendom* (London, 1596), pp. 16, 21.
42. Ibid., p. 23.
43. Ibid., p. 101.
44. *Henry V,* 5.2.193–96.
45. Ibid., Epilog, 9-13.
46. Foster, *Travels of John Sanderson,* p. 242.
47. Hakluyt, vol. 1, p. 43.
48. CSPD, vol. 6, *1598–1601,* January 31, 1599, p. 156.
49. CSPV, vol. 9, *1592–1603,* no. 814, p. 375.
50. Ibid., October 2, 1599, no. 817, p. 377.
51. Thomas Dallam, "The Diary of Master Thomas Dallam, 1599–1600," in *Early Voyages and Travels in the Levant,* ed. J. Theodore Bent (London: Hakluyt Society, 1893), pp. 1–99; at pp. 67–68.
52. Ibid., pp. 74–75.
53. Ibid., p. 84.

54. Quoted in Leslie P. Peirce, *The Imperial Harem: Women and Sovereignty in the Ottoman Empire* (Oxford: Oxford University Press, 1993), p. 228. This amends the version translated in Susan Skilliter, "Three Letters from the Ottoman 'Sultana' Safiye to Queen Elizabeth I," in *Documents from Islamic Chanceries,* ed. S. M. Stern (Cambridge, Mass.: Harvard University Press, 1965), pp. 119–57; at p. 139.
55. Skilliter, "Three Letters," p. 139, n57.
56. Ibid., p. 143.
57. Alison Games, *The Web of Empire: English Cosmopolitans in an Age of Expansion, 1560–1660* (Oxford: Oxford University Press, 2008), p. 171.
58. Quoted in Skilliter, "Three Letters," p. 153.
59. "Dallam, Thomas (bap. 1575, d. in or after 1630)," ODNB.

Chapter 10: Sherley Fever

1. *Twelfth Night,* 1.2.52.
2. Ibid., 5.1.365.
3. Ibid., 3.2.67–68.
4. Patricia Parker, "*Twelfth Night:* Editing Puzzles and Eunuchs of All Kinds," in *Twelfth Night: New Critical Essays,* ed. James Schiffer (London: Routledge, 2011), pp. 45–64; at p. 47. On Wright's map, see Helen Wallis, "Edward Wright and the 1599 World Map," in *The Hakluyt Handbook,* ed. D. B. Quinn, 2 vols. (Cambridge: Hakluyt Society, 1974), vol. 1, pp. 69–73.
5. *Twelfth Night,* 2.5.156–57.
6. Ibid., 3.4.243–48.
7. See Richard Wilson, "'When Golden Time Convents': *Twelfth Night* and Shakespeare's Eastern Promise," *Shakespeare* 6, no. 2 (2010), pp. 209–26.
8. Samuel Purchas, *Hakluytus Posthumus, or Purchas His Pilgrimes,* 20 vols. (Glasgow: James MacLehose, 1905), vol. 1, p. 374.
9. Quoted in R. M. Savory, "The Sherley Myth," *Iran* 5 (1967), pp. 73–81.
10. *Gentleman's Magazine,* n.s., vol. 22 (1844), p. 474.
11. See Sir Edward Denison Ross, *Sir Anthony Sherley and His Persian Adventure* (London: Routledge, 1933); Boies Penrose, *The Sherleian Odyssey: Being a Record of the Travels and Adventures of Three Famous Brothers During the Reigns of Elizabeth, James I, and Charles I* (London: Simpkin Marshall, 1938); D. W. Davies, *Elizabethans Errant: The Strange Fortunes of Sir Thomas Sherley and His Three Sons, as Well in the Dutch Wars as in Muscovy, Morocco, Persia, Spain, and the Indies* (Ithaca, N.Y.: Cornell University Press, 1967); Kurosh Meshkat, "Sir Anthony Sherley's Journey to Persia, 1598–1599," PhD thesis, Queen Mary University of London, 2013.
12. Ross, *Sir Anthony Sherley,* pp. 86–87.
13. Penrose, *Sherleian Odyssey,* p. 245.
14. CP, Part 4, May 2, 1594, p. 522.
15. CP, Part 8, December 30, 1597, p. 526.
16. CP, Part 8, March 1598, pp. 116–17. See Sanjay Subrahmanyam, *Three Ways to Be an Alien: Travails and Encounters in the Early Modern World* (Waltham, Mass.: Brandeis University Press, 2011), pp. 91–92. A different translation appears in Davies, *Elizabethans Errant,* pp. 80–81.
17. Subrahmanyam, *Three Ways,* pp. 93–95; Davies, *Elizabethans Errant,* pp. 81–83.
18. George Mainwaring, "A True Discourse of Sir Anthony Sherley's Travel into Persia," in *The Three Brothers; or, The Travels and Adventures of Sir Anthony, Sir Robert and Sir Thomas Sherley, in Persia, Russia, Turkey, and Spain* (London: Hurst, Robinson, 1825), pp. 23–96; at p. 26.
19. CSPD, vol. 7, *1601–1603,* June 27, 1602, p. 209.
20. CSPD, vol. 6, *1598–1601,* no. 6, p. 130.
21. Mainwaring, "A True Discourse," pp. 34–35.

22. Ibid., p. 55.
23. William Parry, *A New and Large Discourse of the Travels of Sir Anthony Sherley Knight, by Sea and over Land to the Persian Empire* (London: Felix Norton, 1601), pp. 15, 18.
24. On Shah Abbas and Isfahan, see Roger M. Savory, *Iran Under the Safavids* (Cambridge: Cambridge University Press), pp. 76–103, 154–76.
25. Mainwaring, "A True Discourse," p. 60.
26. Ibid., pp. 60–61.
27. Quoted in Ross, *Sir Anthony Sherley*, p. 121.
28. Quoted in ibid., p. 154.
29. Quoted in ibid., p. 158.
30. Mainwaring, "A True Discourse," p. 68.
31. Sir Anthony Sherley, *Sir Anthony Sherley his Relation of his Travels into Persia* (London: Nathaniel Butter, 1613), p. 64.
32. *A True Report of Sir Anthony Sherley's Journey* (London, 1600), sig. A4r.
33. Mainwaring, "A True Discourse," p. 69.
34. Parry, *A New and Large Discourse*, p. 21.
35. Sherley, *His Relation*, p. 29.
36. Parry, *A New and Large Discourse*, p. 23.
37. Ibid., p. 24.
38. Quoted in Ross, *Sir Anthony Sherley*, pp. 159, 162, 163.
39. Sherley, *His Relation*, p. 29.
40. Ibid., p. 74.
41. Ibid., pp. 79–82.
42. Ibid., pp. 83–85, 96, 106.
43. Ibid., pp. 113, 115–17.
44. Mainwaring, "A True Discourse," p. 92.
45. *A True Report*, sig. B1.
46. "Two Letters from Anthony Sherley from Russia," in Ross, *Sir Anthony Sherley*, p. 239.
47. Quoted in ibid., p. 167.
48. Parry, *A New and Large Discourse*, pp. 33–34.
49. Ibid., p. 35.
50. CP, Part 10, July 8, 1600, p. 227.
51. Quoted in Ross, *Sir Anthony Sherley*, pp. 244–46.
52. Quoted in ibid., p. 37.
53. CSPV, vol. 9, *1592–1603*, no. 925, p. 431.
54. Quoted in Ross, *Sir Anthony Sherley*, p. 41.
55. CSPV, vol. 9, *1592–1603*, no. 943, p. 438.
56. Ibid., no. 940, p. 437.
57. Quoted in Davies, *Elizabethans Errant*, p. 132.
58. Quoted in ibid., p. 133.
59. Quoted in Ross, *Sir Anthony Sherley*, p. 47.
60. Quoted in Penrose, *Sherleian Odyssey*, pp. 107–8; Davies, *Elizabethans Errant*, pp. 134–35.
61. "Devereux, Robert, second earl of Essex (1565–1601)," ODNB.
62. Quoted in Ross, *Sir Anthony Sherley*, pp. 49–50.
63. Quoted in Evelyn Philip Shirley, *The Sherley Brothers: An Historical Memoir of the Lives of Sir Thomas Sherley, Sir Anthony Sherley and Sir Robert Sherley, Knights* (London, 1848), p. 33.
64. Scott Surtees, *William Shakespeare, of Stratford-on-Avon, His Epitaph Unearthed, and the Author of the Plays run to Ground* (London: Henry Gray, 1888), pp. 21–22. On Sherley and Surtees, see Subrahmanyam, *Three Ways*, pp. 79–80. See also Jonathan Sell, *Rhetoric and Wonder in English Travel Writing, 1560–1613* (Aldershot: Ashgate, 2006), pp. 105–11.

Chapter 11: More Than a Moor

1. Castries, vol. 2, pp. 143–45.
2. Ibid., p. 146.
3. Ibid., p. 160.
4. Ibid., pp. 161–62.
5. Ibid., pp. 165–67.
6. T. S. Willan, *Studies in Elizabethan Foreign Trade* (Manchester: Manchester University Press, 1959), pp. 302–3.
7. Castries, vol. 2, p. 187.
8. Sir Henry Sydney, *Letters and Memorials of State*, 2 vols. (London: Arthur Collins, 1746), vol. 2, p. 211.
9. Quoted in Bernard Harris, "A Portrait of a Moor," in *Shakespeare and Race*, ed. Catherine M. S. Alexander and Stanley Wells (Cambridge: Cambridge University Press, 2000), pp. 23–36; at p. 28.
10. Sydney, *Letters and Memorials*, vol. 2, p. 212.
11. Ibid.
12. Quoted in Harris, "A Portrait of a Moor," p. 29.
13. Sydney, *Letters and Memorials*, p. 212.
14. Ibid., p. 214.
15. Castries, vol. 2, p. 178.
16. Ibid., pp. 178–79.
17. Ibid., p. 192.
18. Ibid., p. 199.
19. John Stow, *Annales, or a Generale Chronicle of England* (London: John Windet, 1603), p. 791. See also Castries, vol. 2, p. 203.
20. Castries, vol. 2, pp. 194–95.
21. Stow, *Annales*, p. 1405.
22. Paul Hentzner, *Paul Hentzner's Travels in England, During the Reign of Queen Elizabeth*, trans. Horace Walpole (London: Edward Jeffery, 1797), p. 34.
23. *A Geographical Historie of Africa, written in Arabicke and Italian by Iohn Leo a More, borne in Granada, and brought vp in Barbarie* (London, 1600), sig. A2.
24. Ibid., p. 200.
25. Stow, *Annales*, p. 791.
26. Ibid.
27. P. L. Hughes and J. F. Larkin, eds., *Tudor Royal Proclamations*, 3 vols. (New Haven: Yale University Press, 1964), vol. 3, pp. 221–22.
28. CP, Part 10, p. 399; D. W. Davies, *Elizabethans Errant: The Strange Fortunes of Sir Thomas Sherley and His Three Sons, as Well in the Dutch Wars as in Muscovy, Morocco, Persia, Spain, and the Indies* (Ithaca, N.Y.: Cornell University Press, 1967), pp. 187–88.
29. Quoted in Nabil Matar, *Britain and Barbary, 1589–1689* (Gainesville: University Press of Florida, 2005), p. 27.
30. Castries, vol. 2, pp. 208–9.
31. Ibid., p. 196.
32. Ralph Carr, *The Mahumetane or Turkish Historie Containing Three Books* (London: Thomas Este, 1600), unpaginated "Preface," and p. 103.
33. Ibid., p. 5.
34. Ibid., p. 1.
35. All references to *Lust's Dominion* are from Fredson Bowers, ed., *The Dramatic Works of Thomas Dekker*, 4 vols. (Cambridge: Cambridge University Press, 1961), vol. 4, pp. 115–230. On the question of the play's complicated authorship and date, see Charles Cathcart, "*Lust's Dominion; or, The Lascivious Queen*: Authorship, Date, and Revision," *Review of English Studies* 52, no. 207 (2001), pp. 360–75.
36. Dekker, *Lust's Dominion*, 1.1.151–52.

37. Ibid., 1.2.158.
38. Ibid., 1.2.156.
39. Ibid., 5.3.166.
40. Ibid., 5.3.182–83.
41. Emily C. Bartels, *Speaking of the Moor: From Alcazar to Othello* (Philadelphia: University of Pennsylvania Press, 2008), pp. 118–37.
42. Joel B. Altman, *The Improbability of Othello: Rhetorical Anthropology and Shakespearean Selfhood* (Chicago: University of Chicago Press, 2010).
43. For the most comprehensive and up-to-date account of the play's dating and textual history, see E. A. J. Honigmann, *The Texts of "Othello" and Shakespearian Revision* (London: Arden, 1996) and his Arden Shakespeare edition of *Othello,* pp. 344–67.
44. Thomas Rymer, "A Short View of Tragedy" [1693], in *The Critical Works of Thomas Rymer,* ed. Curt Zimansky (New Haven: Yale University Press, 1956), pp. 132–64; at p. 133.
45. Thomas Middleton Raysor, ed., *Coleridge's Shakespeare Criticism,* 2 vols. (Cambridge, Mass.: Harvard University Press, 1930), vol. 1, p. 47.
46. Ben Okri, "Leaping Out of Shakespeare's Terror: Five Meditations on *Othello,*" in *A Way of Being Free* (London: Phoenix, 1997), pp. 71–87; at pp. 72, 80.
47. "Race," OED.
48. *Antony and Cleopatra,* 3.13.107.
49. *Othello,* 1.1.33, 56–57, 64.
50. Ibid., 1.1.85–90.
51. Ibid., 1.1.109–12.
52. Ibid., 1.1.114–15.
53. Ibid., 1.1.127.
54. Ibid., 1.1.124, 132–35.
55. Ibid., 1.2.17–22.
56. Ibid., 1.3.8.
57. Ibid., 1.3.49–52.
58. Ibid., 1.3.127–45.
59. Editors use these references to date the play to sometime just after 1601, when Philemon Holland published his English translation of Pliny's *Historie of the World,* with its stories of Ethiopian cannibals and "Blemmyes," with their mouth and eyes in chest.
60. Natalie Zemon Davis, *Trickster Travels: In Search of Leo Africanus, a Sixteenth-Century Muslim Between Worlds* (New York: Hill & Wang, 2006).
61. *Othello,* 1.3.172, 170.
62. Ibid., 1.3.293–94.
63. Ibid., 2.1.21–22, 201.
64. Ibid., 2.3.166–68.
65. Barbara Everett, "'Spanish' *Othello:* The Making of Shakespeare's Moor," *Shakespeare Survey* 35 (1982), pp. 101–12; Eric Griffin, "Unsainting James: or, *Othello* and the "Spanish Spirits' of Shakespeare's Globe," *Representations* 62 (1998), pp. 58–99.
66. *Othello,* 2.1.114.
67. Ibid., 3.3.456–63.
68. Ibid., 4.3.17.
69. Ibid., 4.3.24–31.
70. Ibid., 4.3.51–52.
71. Ernest Brennecke, "'Nay, That's Not Next!': The Significance of Desdemona's 'Willow Song,'" *Shakespeare Quarterly* 4, no. 1 (1953), pp. 35–38.
72. *Othello,* 5.2.298–99.
73. Ibid., 5.2.300–301.

74. Ibid., 5.2.336–54.
75. Honigmann, ed., *Othello,* pp. 342–43; Richard Levin, "The Indian/Iudean Crux in *Othello,*" *Shakespeare Quarterly* 33, no. 1 (1982), pp. 60–67.
76. Quoted in James Craigie, ed., *The Poems of James VI of Scotland* (Edinburgh: Blackwood, 1955), p. 202.

Epilogue

1. Bruce McGowan, *Economic Life in Ottoman Europe: Taxation, Trade and the Struggle for Land, 1600–1800* (Cambridge: Cambridge University Press, 1981), p. 21; Alfred C. Wood, *A History of the Levant Company* (London: Oxford University Press, 1935), p. 42; Lewis Roberts, *A Merchant's Mappe of Commerce* (London, 1638), pp. 79–80.
2. W. B. Patterson, *King James VI and I and the Reunion of Christendom* (Cambridge: Cambridge University Press, 1997), pp. 196–219.
3. Quoted in Boies Penrose, *The Sherleian Odyssey: Being a Record of the Travels and Adventures of Three Famous Brothers During the Reigns of Elizabeth, James I, and Charles I* (London: Simpkin Marshall, 1938), p. 125.
4. Quoted in ibid., pp. 127–28.
5. Quoted in ibid., p. 256.
6. Francis Cottington to Naunton, December 12, 1619, SP 94/23/258, TNA.
7. John Jowett, ed., *Sir Thomas More: Original Text by Anthony Munday and George Chettle* (London: Arden, 2011). All references to the play are to this edition. Jowett dates the original text to c. 1600, in contrast to earlier critics who dated it to c. 1593–1595, during the period of anti-alien insurrections. Jowett dates Shakespeare's revised additions to c. 1603–1604.
8. Ibid., 6.83–98.
9. Ibid., 6.138–56. In his essay "On 'Montanish Inhumanyty' in *Sir Thomas More,*" *Studies in Philology* 103, no. 2 (2006), pp. 178–85, Karl P. Wentersdorf argues that "mountainish" should be read as "Mohammetanish," an intriguing possibility that would make it Shakespeare's second direct reference to the Prophet Muhammad, after the example discussed above in *Henry VI*.
10. The point is made in Charles Nicholl, *The Lodger: Shakespeare on Silver Street* (London: Penguin, 2007), pp. 175–88.
11. *The Tempest,* 1.2.194.
12. Ibid., 1.2.259.
13. Ibid., 2.1. 235, 230.
14. Ibid., 5.1.186.
15. Ibid., 1.2.263.
16. Ibid., 2.1.82.
17. Ibid., 2.1.242–43.
18. Ibid., 2.1.125.
19. Quoted in Christopher Brook, Roger Highfield, and Wim Swaan, *Oxford and Cambridge* (Cambridge: Cambridge University Press, 1988), p. 180.
20. G. J. Toomer, *Eastern Wisedome and Learning: The Study of Arabic in Seventeenth-Century England* (Oxford: Oxford University Press, 1996), pp. 111–26.
21. Authorship of the 1649 translation remains contested, with arguments for and against a variety of candidates: Alexander Ross, Thomas Ross or Hugh Ross. See Noel Malcolm, "The 1649 English Translation of the Koran: Its Origins and Significance," *Journal of the Warburg and Courtauld Institutes* 75 (2012), pp. 261–95; Mordechai Feingold, "'The Turkish Alcoran': New Light on the 1649 English Translation of the Koran," *Huntington Library Quarterly* 75, no. 4 (2012), pp. 475–501.

Illustration Credits

Illustrations in the Text

Page 23: Caricature of Luther with seven heads, title page of Johann Cochlaeus, *Septiceps Lutherus*, 1529. Photograph: Lebrecht Collection/Alamy

155: A silver Geuzen coined during the Dutch Revolt, 1574. Photograph: Kees38

160: Henry VIII using Pope Clement VII as a footstool, illustration from John Foxe, *Acts and Monuments*, 1583. Photograph: Pictorial Press/Alamy

Insert

Page 1: Anon., portrait of Abd al-Wahid bin Muhammad al-Annuri, c. 1600. The University of Birmingham Research and Cultural Collections. Photograph: copyright © University of Birmingham

2–3: Workshop of Willem de Pannemaker, tapestry 10 from the series *The Conquest of Tunis*, 1548–1554, Patrimonio Nacional, Madrid. Photograph: akg-images

4: Follower of Antonis Mor, portrait of Philip II of Spain and Mary Tudor, 1558. Trustees of the Bedford Estate, Woburn Abbey. Photograph: Bridgeman Images

5: Isaac Oliver, portrait of Elizabeth I (the "Rainbow Portrait"), c. 1600. Hatfield House, Hertfordshire. Photograph: Bridgeman Images

6–7: Diogo Homem, map of the Mediterranean, from the Queen Mary Atlas, 1558. British Library, London (Add. Ms. 5415A, ff. 11v–12). Photograph: Bridgeman Images

8 (top): Cristóvão de Morais (attrib.), portrait of Sebastian I of Portugal. Royal Collection Trust, copyright © Her Majesty Queen Elizabeth II, 2015. Photograph: Bridgeman Images

8 (bottom): Detail of a view of the El Badi Palace in Marrakesh, engraving by Adriaen Matham from *Palatium magni. Regis Maroci in Barbaria*, 1641. Copyright © Bibliothèque Nationale, Paris

9: Hans Eworth, *Süleyman the Magnificent on Horseback*, 1549. Private Collection

Index

Page numbers in *italics* refer to images.

327

Index

Gómez, Ruy, 14
Gore, William, 130
Gosson, Stephen, 105, 107
Granada, Moriscos in, 63
Greene, Robert, 158, 160, 272
  Alphonsus, King of Aragon, 173
  Tragicall Reign of Selimus, 172–73, 188
Gregory XIII, Pope, 76, 101
Gresham, Sir Thomas, 68, 71
Greville, Fulke, 174
Grey, Lady Jane, 15
Grocers' Company, 193

Habsburg Empire, 17, 18, 26, 27, 31, 32,
  33, 62, 63, 72, 93, 186–87, 204
"Hagarene," use of term, 20
Hakluyt, Richard, *Principal*
  Navigations, 44, 56, 74, 83–84, 88,
  206, 217–18, 226
Hamett, Mully, King of Barbary, 259
Hanmer, Meredith, 133–38, 141, 144, 180
Harborne, William, 74, 97–102, 175
  achievements of, 117–19, 146–47,
    151, 225
  and Anglo-Ottoman alliance, 89–93,
    95, 96, 97–98, 102, 107, 117–19, 183
  and *Bark Roe,* 98–101, 103, 105
  in Constantinople, 84–89, 90–93, 100,
    102, 110
  death of, 147
  and English captives, 92, 100, 134,
    138–42, 146
  as first Turkish ambassador, 10,
    113–14, 117–19, 121–24, 129,
    131–32, 140–45
  memoirs of, 141, 145
  recall requested by, 145–47
  as spy, 84, 118–19
Hardwick embroidery, 206–8
Hassan, Mulay, 17
Hassan, Seadeddin Muhammad Ben, 142
"Hassan Aga," 10, 138–39
Haughton, William, 174
Hawkins, John, 146
Hawkins, William, 135–36, 137
Hazlitt, William, 212
Hector, 219, 221–22, 223
Henry, Cardinal, 80
Henry II, King of France, 34
Henry III, King of France, 95, 97,
  101, 181
Henry IV, King of France (Henry of
  Navarre), 181–82, 230, 253

Henry VIII, King of England, 4, 25, 159,
  160, 293
  children of, 13, 19, 76
  dissolution of monasteries, 192
  separation from Roman Catholic
    Church, 13, 18
  and trade, 28–29
  wars with France, 45
Henslowe, Philip, 6, 106, 156, 178
Hentzner, Paul, 266
Herbst, Johann, 22, 24
Heredia, Juan de, 148
Herle, William, 65, 124
Hilliard, Nicholas, 185
Hobson, Harold, 188
Hogan, Edmund, 66, 67–72, 73, 83, 107,
  110–11, 175, 225, 240
Holinshed, Raphael, 65, 76
Holmden, Edward, 193
Holy League, 64, 65, 70, 72, 289
Homem, Diogo, 31
Honeyman, Philip, 268
Hope Theatre, 106
Horne, Robert, 61
Hotspur (fict.), 210
Howard, Charles, 130, 146, 155, 194
Hubblethorne, Morgan, 206
Huguenots, 61–62, 101, 181–83
Hungary, Ottoman invasion of, 186,
  203–4, 217

India, trade possibilities with, 119
"infidel," origins of term, 21
Isabella I of Castile, 25
"Ishmaelite," use of term, 20
Islam:
  Anglo-Islamic relations, 5, 8, 10–11,
    31, 36, 54, 112–13, 122, 123–25,
    145, 152–54, 162, 205, 262
  anti-Islamic views in England, 134–35
  and Catholicism, 180
  Christianity vs., 8, 25–26, 271, 298
  and clash of civilizations, 299
  converts to ("turning Turk"), 8, 20,
    138–39, 282
  first conversion to English
    Protestantism, 133–38
  five pillars of faith, 19
  and forced conversions, 63, 137–38
  history of, 271–72
  myths and misconceptions about, 5, 9,
    20, 21, 22, 299
  origins of, 19

Index

Index

Malta, 272
  Baker's trial in, 101–2
  and Holy League, 64
Maltese Knights of St. John, 98, 101
Mamluks:
  Ottoman victory over, 35
  Shi'a opposition to, 37
Mansur, Ahmad al-, Sultan, 63, 79, 80,
  126–31, 199, 282
  and anti-Spanish alliance, 6, 114, 129,
    131, 147, 148–50, 152–54, 168–72,
    193, 195, 259, 270–71
  communication with Elizabeth, 114,
    120, 147, 193, 258, 265, 270–71
  death of, 289
  and Don António, 125, 129, 147, 149,
    150, 153–54, 169
  and English trade, 103, 115, 120, 126
  and Marrakesh, 126–27, 148
  negotiations with, 257–60
  Ottoman opponents of, 7
  and Roberts, 125, 126, 128–30, 147,
    149–50
Manuel I, King of Portugal, 80
Marbeck, Roger, 194
Marín, Diego, 148
Marlowe, Christopher, 111, 216, 298
  death of, 176–77, 200
  influence of, 179, 272, 281, 284, 288
  The Jew of Malta, 174–76, 178, 188,
    190, 196, 200
  Tamburlaine, 6, 155–59, 160–63,
    165, 172–74, 178, 210, 212, 281,
    284, 288
Marrakesh:
  English ambassador (Roberts) in,
    126–30, 145, 147–50
  English merchants attacked in, 148
  redesign of, 237
Mary Stuart, Queen of Scotland, 33, 61
Mary Tudor, 44, 59
  as "Bloody Mary," 27
  coronation of, 33
  death of, 32, 33, 42
  marriage to Philip, 13–16, 18, 28, 57
  plenum dominium of, 28
  and trade, 31, 41
Massinger, Philip, *The Renegado,* 297
Mastidge, Edmond, 128
Maximilian, Archduke, 203
Mecca (holy city), 38, 86
Medina (holy city), 38, 86
Mehmed II, Sultan, 9, 84–85

Mehmed III, Sultan, 202–3, 217, 219–22,
  223, 243, 244, 255, 257, 289
Mehmed Pasha, Sokollu, 72, 87, 88, 95–96
Mello, Nicolò de, 245–47
Mendès, Alvaro, 202
Mendoza, Bernardino de, 92–93,
  112–13, 115
Mercers' Company, 40, 66, 74
Merchant Adventurers Company, 29,
  30–31, 104, 114
Middle Kingdom, 43
Mikulin, Grigorii, 267
Millers, Harvie, 118
Monson, William, 194
Moors:
  of Barbary, 55, 56
  depicted in theater, 189–92, 195–201,
    216, 276–77, 287–88, 297
  of Morocco, 7
  trade with, 218
  use of term, 5, 20, 164, 170, 276
More, Thomas:
  Dialog Concerning Heresies, 25
  drama about, 293–95
  Utopia, 25
Moriscos, 63, 264, 270, 273, 282
Morocco:
  Anglo-Moroccan alliance, 6–7, 8–9,
    68–71, 82, 129, 131, 149–50,
    152, 168, 170, 193, 195, 261–64,
    265–66, 268–71
  Barbary kingdom of, 56
  civil war in, 289
  Dar al-Makhzen palace in, 126
  first English ambassador (Roberts) to,
    125–30, 149–50
  invasion of Songhai by, 171–72
  Jewish intermediaries in, 58, 127, 200
  Ottoman Empire vs., 7, 63
  regulated commerce with, 120–21,
    122–23, 201
  sugar farms in, 58, 69, 116, 120, 126,
    131, 265, 266
  trade with, 4, 57–59, 62, 66–72, 103–5,
    112, 113, 114–16, 120, 121, 125,
    131–32, 152, 201, 216, 260, 266
  and trans-Saharan trade route, 171
Morosini, Gianfrancesco, 118,
  124–25, 141
Mu'awiyah, governor of Damascus, 37
Muhammad, Prophet:
  death of, 19, 36
  depictions of, 6, 160, 173, 180, 207, 272

Index

Muhammad, Prophet (*cont.*)
 direct line of descent, 36–37, 171
 myths of, 21–22, 180
 opponents of, 20, 134–35
 prophecies of, 19, 37
 and Qur'an, 19, 20, 24
Murad III, Sultan, 72–73, 85–87
 and anti-Spanish alliance, 124–25,
  129, 132, 142, 143–45, 182
 and Barton, 185
 commercial profits of, 132
 correspondence with Elizabeth, 1–3, 4,
  7, 89–95, 101–2, 113–14, 118, 136,
  171, 186
 death of, 202–3
 and French Capitulations, 101
 gift exchange with, 185–86
 and Harborne, 84, 117–19, 123–24,
  141, 142–45
 and Philip II, 96
 war with Persia, 73–74
Murza, Shah Ali, 52
Musa, Hajj (Messa, Side al-Hage), 259,
 264–65
Muscovy Company, 131
 charter members of, 57, 58, 114
 and Jenkinson, 34, 40, 44, 46
 as joint-stock company, 3, 31, 34, 104
 and Persian trade, 44, 45, 68, 73
 and Russian trade, 31, 45, 46, 104
 and Sherley, 248, 249, 251
 as unprofitable, 53–54, 73, 104
"Muslim":
 use of term, 5, 20, 164, 276
 see also Islam
Mustafa, Prince, 39, 51

Nashe, Thomas, 158
 The Terrors of the Night, 180
Nasr, Mulay al-, 168
Nelson, John, 138
Newberry, John, 119
New World, 291, 297
Norris, Sir John, 153–54, 166–67, 168,
 181, 230
northwest passage, 29
Nurbanu Sultan, 4, 72, 95

Okri, Ben, 276
Order of the Garter, 13, 16
Orthodox Church, 19
Osborne, Sir Edward, 74, 84, 97, 104,
 113, 119

Ottoman Empire:
 alliance of England and, 8, 9, 53,
  65–66, 93, 183, 185–86
 alliance of France and, 9, 93
 and Battle of Lepanto, 64–65, 146
 and Battle of Rabat-i-Pariyan, 238
 and Capitulations, *see*
  Capitulations
 collapse of, 96
 conflict with Persian Empire, 36, 39,
  47, 48, 73, 142, 146, 171
 decline of, 298–99
 English captives in, 92, 94–95, 100,
  118, 122–23, 134
 extent of, 3, 5–6, 9, 20, 226
 gift exchange with, 185–86, 218–19,
  221–22
 history of, 271–72
 invasion of Hungary, 186, 203–4, 217
 and "Memorandum on the Turkey
  Trade," 82–83, 96
 Morocco vs., 7, 63
 Murad as sultan of, 3–4
 peace treaty with Spain, 96–97
 Persian treaties with, 237
 rise of, 21, 25–26, 72
 Shi'a opposition to, 37, 38
 spies in, 118–19
 trade with England, 3, 4–5, 40, 41,
  53, 73–75, 88–92, 96–97, 101,
  103, 112–14, 117–19, 186, 203,
  204–5
 trade with Europe, 25–26
 trade with Venice, 9, 25, 47, 62, 72
 war with Habsburgs, 186–87, 204
 writing (script) in, 89
Ottoman Turks, 46
Ovid, *Metamorphoses,* 187

Pageant of the Shearmen and Taylors,
 The (mystery play), 212–13
Pannemaker, William de, 17–18
Parry, William, 234, 237, 239,
 240–41, 245
Parsons, Robert, 253
Pasha, Ahmad, 117
Peace of Amasya, 48, 51
Peele, George, 272, 298
 Battle of Alcazar, 163–65, 166, 189,
  210–11
 and Portugal Expedition, 166–67
 The Turkish Mahamet and Hiren the
  Fair Greek, 210

Index

Venice:
  and anti-Ottoman alliance, 38, 39,
    64, 119
  Sherley's travels to, 232–33, 234, 254–55
  trade with Ottoman Empire, 9, 25, 47,
    62, 72
Venice Company, 204
Vermeyen, Jan, 17
Verstegen, Richard, *A Declaration of the
  True Causes of the Great Troubles,*
  182–84, 186
Virgil, *Aeneid,* 229, 296
Virginia Company, 291

Walsingham, Francis:
  aging of, 181
  and Anglo-Ottoman trade, 65, 72,
    82, 124
  and anti-Spanish alliance, 123–25, 129
  and Capitulations, 183
  death of, 141
  and Hakluyt, 217
  and Harborne, 96, 102, 118, 123–24,
    141, 142–46
  intelligence networks of, 84, 118, 124,
    125, 162, 168
  and Leicester, 117, 120
  "Memorandum on the Turkey trade"
    (1578), 82–83, 96
  and Moroccan trade, 68, 71, 72, 73,
    82–83, 115–17, 119–20

and Portugal, 65, 83
and unregulated trade, 103–4,
  115–17, 120
Ward, John, 297
Waring, John, 259, 260
Warner, William, *Albion's England,*
  54–55
Warren, Sir Ralph, 205
Warwick, Robert Rich, 1st Earl of, 121
Wattasid dynasty, 56
Wazzan, al-Hasan ibn Muhammad ibn
  Ahmad al- (Leo Africanus),
  268, 282
Webbe, Edward, 140–41
West, John, 205
Wheeler, John, *Treatise of
  Commerce,* 104
White Sea, trade route via, 41, 43
Whyte, Rowland, 261, 262
Williams, John, 66–67
Willoughby, Sir Hugh, 30, 34, 40
Wilson, Robert, *The Three Ladies of
  London,* 106–10, 113, 114, 156,
  157, 196, 200
World War II, 188
Wright, Edward, 226
Wright, John, 74, 84
Wyatt, Sir Thomas, 15, 16
Wyndham, Thomas, 56–57

Zenden, Casper van, 270